The New Historicism: Studies in Cultural Poetics
Stephen Greenblatt, General Editor

AN EMPIRE NOWHERE

AN EMPIRE NOWHERE

ENGLAND, AMERICA, AND LITERATURE FROM *UTOPIA* TO *THE TEMPEST*

J E F F R E Y K N A P P

University of California Press
Berkeley · Los Angeles · Oxford

University of California Press
Berkeley and Los Angeles, California

University of California Press, Ltd.
Oxford, England

© 1992 by
The Regents of the University of California

Library of Congress Cataloging-in-Publication Data

Knapp, Jeffrey.
    An empire nowhere : England, America, and literature
from Utopia to The Tempest / Jeffrey Knapp.
        p. cm.—(The New historicism ; 16)
    Includes bibliographical references and index.
    ISBN 0-520-07361-4 (cloth : alk. paper)
    1. English literature—Early modern, 1500–1700—History
and criticism. 2. Literature and history—England—
History—16th century. 3. Literature and history—
England—History—17th century. 4. America—Discovery
and exploration—English. 5. English literature—American
influences. 6. Imperialism in literature. 7. Colonies in
literature. 8. Utopias in literature. 9. America in literature.
I. Title. II. Series.
PR129.A4K58   1992
820.9′003—dc20   91-28690
                                                         CIP

Printed in the United States of America

9 8 7 6 5 4 3 2 1

The paper used in this publication meets the minimum
requirements of American National Standard for
Information Sciences—Permanence of Paper for Printed
Library Materials, ANSI Z39.48-1984. ∞

For Dori

But by the way you may first note, that the Pycnemian or Pygnean (the Infidel) which this last year was brought from the north-west discovery, being asked (while he was yet with our countrymen in those quarters), if they in their country had any Gold or Silver or Cloth, or sundry other things: he would make evident sign that no such things were to be had in that kingdom of Pycknemay or Pycknea (which some of our men said he termed Pygmenai and other Pyckenay and other Pycknea) but all that was demanded by sign (of the like thing showed) to be at Mania: and pointed westerly towards it, and would have guided our men toward it (if they would) and added that it was but one moon sailing thither. Whereby it would appear that the city or province of Mania is rich, famous and great.

—John Dee, "Great Volume of Famous
and Rich Discoveries" (1577)

Contents

Illustrations

Acknowledgments

Portions of this book have been presented as talks at the University of California, Berkeley and Los Angeles; at Northwestern, Indiana, Wesleyan, and Harvard Universities; and at meetings of the Modern Language Association. I thank my audiences for their response. A version of chapter 3 appeared in ELH 54 (1987): 801–34, and is reprinted by permission of the Johns Hopkins University Press; a version of chapter 4 appeared in *Representations* 21 (1988): 26–66.

I am grateful to the University of California, Berkeley, the John Carter Brown Library at Brown University, the Mabelle McLeod Lewis Memorial Fund, Harvard University, the Hyder Rollins Book Fund of Harvard University, and the National Endowment for the Humanities for their generous financial assistance while I worked on this book. Many friends and colleagues have contributed their time, wisdom, and encouragement: I want particularly to thank Oliver Arnold, Deirdre D'Albertis, Kevin Dunn, Paul Danby, the late Joel Fineman, Marjorie Garber, Thomas Laqueur, Mark Maslan, Walter Michaels, Nancy Ruttenburg, James Schamus, Lynn Wardley, and Barrett Watten. I also would like to thank Barbara Lewalski, David Quint, and an anonymous reader for their exceptionally thorough and illuminating critiques of my entire manuscript; Bradley Berens for his technical assistance; and my editors Doris Kretschmer, Erika Büky, and Tony Hicks for their patience and skill.

Stephen Greenblatt inspired this book, and, along with Paul Alpers and Steven Knapp, has guided me throughout its writing. Dorothy J. Hale helped me, and helps me, with everything.

Chronology

Introduction

> I was minded also to have sent you some English verses:
> or Rhymes, for a farewell: but by my Troth, I have no spare
> time in the world, to think on such Toys.
> —Spenser, *Two Other, Very*
> *Commendable Letters* (1580)

Of the traditional explanations for England's literary Renaissance—the Reformation, the rediscovery of the classics, the rise of nationalism and of individualism, the discovery of America—the causal account most implausible on the face of it, and perhaps for that reason least often cited in this century, is the notion that the discovery of America somehow spurred the English to write. The nineteenth-century British historian and chauvinist James Froude considered Renaissance exploration and Renaissance literature such correlative triumphs that he could describe the major Elizabethan collection of travel narratives, Richard Hakluyt's *Principal Navigations* (1589; 1598–1600), as "the Prose Epic of the modern English nation."[1] But with the demise of the modern English empire that helped excite Froude's enthusiasm, his grand view of epic-making Elizabethan explorers has managed to survive in large part only on the strength of prestige now borrowed from the literature that the explorers supposedly helped to inspire. No contemporary historian, that is, would be led to claim, as the literary critics Cleanth Brooks, R. W. B. Lewis, and Robert Penn Warren have done, that "it was the English who were first seized by the epochal idea of colonization, and . . . they were the first successful colonizers" (*American Literature* 1:3). For the English were in fact remarkably slow to colonize America, and their first attempts were dismal failures. As Howard Mumford Jones points out, comparing English to Spanish colonial efforts, "When in 1585 a forlorn little band of Englishmen were trying to stick it out on Roanoke Island,

1

three hundred poets were competing for a prize in Mexico City"
(*O Strange New World*, 85).

Only after the death of Elizabeth did an English colony in
America succeed—Jamestown—but then for many years it too
seemed on shaky ground. The ineptitude of even Jacobean colonialism appeared to many Jacobean colonialists themselves strikingly exemplified by the Virginia Company's decision early in the
history of Jamestown to apply there something like the feudalist
"surrender and regrant" policy instituted in Ireland during the
1540s: as Nicholas Canny explains, "The essence of the scheme
was that the ruling [Irish] chieftains should surrender the lands of
their lordships to the king and receive them back as a fief from the
crown."[2] Accordingly, the company's agent Captain Christopher
Newport arrived in Virginia with the ceremonial appurtenances
necessary both to "crown" the Indian cacique Powhatan and to
astound him with English sophistication.[3] Yet, as Captain John
Smith (1612) reports the ceremony, the coronation so little impressed Powhatan that the English were forced in the end to apply
a comically literal form of pressure simply in order to get the
crown on his head:

> All things being fit for the day of his coronation, the presents were
> brought up, his bason, ewer, bed and furniture set up, his scarlet
> cloak and apparel (with much ado) put on him (being persuaded by
> Namontack they would do him no hurt). But a foul trouble there
> was to make him kneel to receive his crown, he neither knowing
> the majesty, nor meaning of a Crown, nor bending of the knee, en-
> dured so many persuasions, examples, and instructions, as tired
> them all. At last by leaning hard on his shoulders, he a little
> stooped, and Newport put the Crown on his head. (*Works* 1:237)

Though he finds it ludicrous, Smith also thinks the coronation
worse than a waste of time and effort, and his influential editor
Samuel Purchas (1625) agrees: "Smith and Newport," he writes,

> may by their examples teach the just course to be taken with such
> [the Indians]: the one breeding awe and dread, without Spanish or
> Panic terror, the other disgraced in seeking to grace with offices of
> humanity, those which are graceless. Neither doth it become us to
> use Savages with savageness, nor yet with too humane usage, but
> in a middle path (*medio tutissimus ibis*) to go and do so that they
> may admire and fear us, as those whom God, Religion, Civility, and
> Art, have made so far superior.[4]

When, in an earlier complaint about the coronation, Smith suggests what this via media might be, he still sounds far from the heroic exertions that Froude leads us to expect: Smith says of Powhatan that "we had his favor much better, only for a poor piece of Copper, till this stately kind of soliciting made him so much overvalue himself" (*Works* 1:234). Purchas again comments, "Children are pleased with toys and awed with rods; and this course of toys & fears hath always best prospered with wild Indians either to do them, or to make them good to us or themselves."[5] "Toys & fears": Smith's histories often present the second incentive as less an alternative to the first than a way to continue the trade in trifles even after the Indians grow unwilling; but ideally toys were supposed to help the enlightened English put all fears aside. As Smith reports at the beginning of his first narrative, *A True Relation* (1608), the original encounter between Indians and the Jamestown settlers ends in battle, but the second results in the Indians "kindly entreating us, dancing and feasting us with strawberries, Mulberries, Bread, Fish, and other their Country provisions whereof we had plenty: for which Captain Newport kindly requited their least favors with Bells, Pins, Needles, beads or Glasses, which so contented them that his liberality made them follow us from place to place, and ever kindly to respect us" (*Works* 1:27–29).

The Spanish—successful settlers in America more than a century before the English—had of course practiced trifling with the Indians from the time of Columbus's first voyage. Yet, as Purchas's reference to "Spanish or Panic terror" shows, the English generally considered Spanish colonialism far better characterized by its "more than barbarous and savage endless cruelties";[6] while at least until the massacre of Jamestown settlers in 1622, English colonialism argued itself specially inclined to benignity and thus specially dedicated to trifling.[7] Theoretically, the avoidance of war was only the first benefit that trifling was supposed to bring. If the English colonist required Indian land, trifles were seen as the way both to smooth and to justify possession: "Every soul which god hath sealed for himself he hath done it with the print of charity and Compassion, and therefore even every foot of Land which we shall take unto our use, we will bargain and buy of them for copper, hatchets, and such like commodities, for which they will even sell them-selves."[8] If Indians themselves were needed, then, as this passage suggests, trifling and not torture would best obtain their labor: listing the expenses that the English should expect in running a Guianan gold mine—reputedly the sort of enterprise that, in Spanish hands, always began with enslavement and ended with genocide—Raleigh (c. 1613) is careful to specify the price of "Hatchets knives hats shirts and other trifles for the Indians whom we must wage, to carry baskets from the Mine to the River side."[9] The repeated failures of England and the continuing success of Spain in America, however, suggest a less optimistic view of this colonial theory and practice: that, whether by necessity or choice, England's relation to the New World was essentially a frivolous one.

Yet if England's colonial trifling makes the discovery of America seem an unlikely source of inspiration for a burgeoning English literature, neither on closer inspection do the other traditional sources for England's literary Renaissance look especially capable of having taught English literature an expansive lesson.[10] After all, the Reformation meant a break with Catholic Europe, and England became a "nation" only as it also lost its possessions on the continent. England's troubled colonialism, in other words, seems only to complete a larger picture of national isolation, in the light of which even the classics might have appeared chastening: for their rediscovery gave new life to an old image of England that uncannily reflected its modern plight—an island whose inhabitants were *penitus toto divisos orbe* (Virgil, *Eclogues* 1), wholly divided from all the world.

The strange truth about this apparently depressing picture of an England as other-worldly as the New World, however, is that the English themselves loved to highlight it. Particularly after the advent of a virgin queen able to keep the English as true believers "not walking any more according to this world, but in the fruits of the Spirit,"[11] the English could see their island as much excluding the world as being excluded by it. What would otherwise have appeared dispiriting tokens of England's weakness—its littleness, its circumscription by enemies, its female monarch—could signify instead England's abjuration of material or worldly means to power and its extraordinary reliance on God: "Whosoever will humble himself shall be exalted" (Matthew 23.12). The exceptional confidence of English colonialists in both the practical and ethical utility of trifling, then, could reflect a more general faith that the power of little England, other-worldly in both its origins and its aims, would be vindicated through the conquest of a New World—achieved by means of littleness. "God hath chosen the weak things of the world, to confound the mighty things" (1 Corinthians 1.27).

To no other group in England did this conception of England's powerful immateriality more appeal than to its poets. From classical times poetry as well had been relegated to the status of a trifle; and an English poetry had been considered almost a contradiction in terms. This classical animus did not fade with the dawn of some fresh literary individualism during the Renaissance, but itself seemed rediscovered: rather than extol their new good fortune, Tudor writers far more often lamented the "scorn and derision" (Puttenham, *English Poesie*, 18) into which literature had recently fallen. Indeed, the self-consuming grievance expressed by the poet Drummond of Hawthornden early in the next century (c. 1620) seems to show the Renaissance poet as having only internalized the prevailing derogatory view of his work: "Great men in this age either respect not our toys at all; or, if they do, because they *are* toys, esteem them only worthy the kiss of their hand."[12] Yet the contemporary idealization of England as itself a kind of toy located value precisely in apparent deficiency; and, as the nation increasingly celebrated its unworldliness, England's literary writers more confidently presented themselves as superior to the worldly standards that had placed literature (especially English literature) so low. In fact, by emphasizing their reputed immateriality rather than denying it, many poets came to see themselves as peculiarly equipped to recognize the value of their little nation, to epitomize by seeming contrast England's spiritual greatness, even to help direct England in its otherworldly course. It is this perceived identity of interest, I will argue—the increasingly equated paradoxicality of national sublimity on the one hand and of poetical sublimity on the other—that in large part accounts not only for the literary boom in Renaissance England but also for another otherwise curious feature of the times: around 1580, at the height of the enthusiasm generated by Frobisher's three voyages and Drake's circumnavigation, "we find no policy-maker in the Queen's circle equal in his patronage of imperialism to Sir Christopher Hatton, whose greatest influence with Elizabeth was in the areas of entertainment; no London merchant to compete with the poets, Edward Dyer, Richard Willes, George Gascoigne, and Thomas Churchyard."[13] In Tudor England, it seems, the cause of a New World empire depended on not only the colonist's trifling beads but also the poet's trifling books.

For some Tudor writers, moreover, the poet was capable of promoting empire when abroad as well as when at home. In his *Apology for Poetry* (c. 1582), Sir Philip Sidney, for instance, maintains that the only way to civilize "the most barbarous and simple Indians" will be by "the sweet delights of poetry" (9–10). His rationales are both historical and theoretical. According to Sidney, the apparent fable about the first poet Orpheus, that he was "listened to by beasts," actually represents an historical truth disguised, that Orpheus moved "stony and beastly people" (7); as George Puttenham (1589) explains, "by his discreet and wholesome lessons uttered in harmony and with melodious instruments, he brought the rude and savage people to a more civil and orderly life" (*English Poesie*, 6).[14] But what gave Orpheus such rhetorical power? Of all the arts, Sidney maintains, poetry best inspires virtue by "being the most familiar to teach it, and most princely to move towards it" (*Apology*, 41), a claim anticipated in his earlier discussion of Aesop, "whose pretty allegories, stealing under the formal tales of beasts, make many more beastly than beasts begin to hear the sound of virtue from these dumb speakers" (30); for Sidney, in other words, poetry alone can elevate its lowly, even savage auditors because poetry alone looks commensurately, and therefore invitingly, low too. Hoping to prove his point, Sidney both begins and ends the *Apology* with just such an accommodating self-debasement, first by bemoaning the fact that, "in these my not old years and idlest times," he has "(I know not by what mischance) . . . slipped into the title of a poet" (5); and finally by apologizing for the "triflingness" of his *Apology*, which he now labels an "ink-wasting toy" (87). Like Sidney, the English literary writers most prominently associated with the New World would also represent English colonialism as an extension of the poet's ideal mastery, but a mastery that could thus be realized only through the medium of toys.[15]

In order both to demonstrate this claim and to grasp its significance—to show how England's literary Renaissance arose in large

part from circumstances that fortuitously encouraged the conjunction of separate traditions about unworldly poetry and unworldly
England, and then how this conflation of "trifles" helped motivate a peculiarly otherworldly expansionism—my book will focus
precisely on the literary "New World" texts of Renaissance England. These texts—notably More's *Utopia* (1516), Spenser's *Faerie
Queene* (1590–96), and Shakespeare's *Tempest* (1611)—prove more
closely related than critics have so far allowed, revolving as they
do around three interlocking issues: the problem of an island empire; colonialism as a special solution to the problem; and poetry
as a special model of both problem and solution. The most striking
similarity among these works, however, is their setting: in each
case they combine otherworldly poetry and nation, and then direct
them both toward the New World, only by placing England, poetry, and America—or rather by *dis*placing them—Nowhere. Such
a displacement could seem ironic, a product of skepticism regarding American ventures; and I will indeed maintain that the seemingly providential separation of England from the Catholic world
during the sixteenth century helped make many of the English
more isolationist, more absorbed in their island as the trifling material index of England's spiritual power. But the purpose of Nowhere for More, Spenser, and Shakespeare, I will argue, is rather
to turn the English into imperialists by differentiating their otherworldly potentiality from their other-worldly island: each writer
imagines the more appropriate setting for England's immaterial
value to be a literary no-place that helps the English reader see the
limitations of a material investment in little England alone. Nonetheless, Nowhere represents as much a constraint on these writers
as a release. Faced with the inescapable negativity of a power sig-
nified only by material lack, along with the increasing difficulty of
arguing that England's materially small island has no essential relation to its ideally grand destiny, these writers also have little
choice but to confine their expansionism to an indirection vari-
ously conceived as unworldliness, superstition, error, incapacity,
introversion, distraction, or disgrace—modes of contrary idealization that I subsume under the larger rubric, again, of trifling. The
supreme irony of this shadowy indirection for Spenser in particular is that his contemporaries generally take his otherworldy poetry to represent a sublime defense of the insularism he deplores.
  I begin with More, the first Tudor writer to base England's

hopes in America on the otherworldliness that both places seem to share; yet he can imagine England a Nowhere only negatively, as a nation either isolated by its material distance from Christendom or internally devastated by a materialist hunger for enclosed land. More is also the first to make the representation of the literary writer central to England's conception of America, though again only negatively, as More the character in *Utopia* professes homesickness on a journey that has taken him eastward to the Old World, not westward to the New; opposes himself to the expositor of western discoveries and colonial theory, Hythloday; and, outside his fiction, mocks his own work as an unworldly trifle. What *Utopia* seems, then, barely to initiate, *The Tempest* at the other end of the American line I trace appears conclusively to reject: Shakespeare seems to dramatize the otherworldly conjunction of England, America, and poetry as both a heresy and a failure, a substitution of devilish literary "spirits" for religious ones and an exiling of nation, colony, and poet all to an island Nowhere. I will argue, however, that Shakespeare's ostensible abandonment of otherworldliness ultimately functions in the manner of the utopic imperialism it seems to replace, as itself a negative incitement to empire. The difference between More and Shakespeare is that Shakespeare must seem to eschew colonialism even more radically so as more radically to conceive America in the image of home.

Within the chronological limits set by *Utopia* and *The Tempest*, I will examine a wide range of texts, both literary and extraliterary, concerned with English otherworldliness as a national, poetical, and imperial issue; these texts will help isolate the generally held assumptions on which both More and Shakespeare draw but will also highlight by contrast the specific motives and influence of each writer. What follows is a sampling of such works in the order of my chapters.

Written shortly after England's religious separation from the Continent, Sir Thomas Wyatt's "Tagus Farewell" (chapter 1) sketches, as *Utopia* had, a largely implicit account of England's utopicality, and yet it takes More's implications in an Elizabethan direction—by contrasting England to the Spanish empire. Though vigorously proclaiming Wyatt's love for king and country, Wyatt's poem also oddly portrays his return to England from Spain as a voyage heading "gainward the sun." Given the immediate yet unmentioned circumstances surrounding the poem's writing—the failure of Wyatt's diplomatic mission, which was supposed to reconcile Spain and England; his reputed favor with the emperor Charles V; his troubled relation with the excommunicated Henry VIII—Wyatt's insistence on the contrariness of his voyage would seem to register his anxiety about returning home, particularly when one considers that the sun whose path he has resisted shines toward a treasure far greater than even the Tagus's classically proverbial gold: that is, toward Charles's golden New World. Yet Wyatt never specifies what he has forsaken in returning to an isolated England; he only suggests that such a return seems supernaturally motivated, like Brutus's ancient westward quest for what was then the new world of England. Indeed, the more perverse Wyatt's dedication to England might seem to a knowing contemporary, the more unaccountably driven that dedication would appear; and the imperialist allusion to Brutus helps associate the mysterious compulsion behind Wyatt's return home with the American empire also negatively implied by the poem. Finally, as itself a reduction of Wyatt, a seeming bagatelle, the poem offers its own narrow limits as an exemplary image of the unexpressed potentiality that Wyatt only "gainwardly" suggests.

Fifty years later, following the defeat of Spain's invading Armada, John Lyly's *Midas* (chapter 2) shows how much more explicit and refined Wyatt's idealization of an isolated England has become. Once again Spain, empire, and gold on the one hand are opposed to England, island, and poetry on the other. The play presents Charles's son Philip II as a Midas bedeviled by his lust for gold. Having enabled him to conquer nearly all the world, Midas's gold nevertheless fails not only to bring him happiness but to buy the destruction of the one "petty" dominion that continues to resist him, the little English isle. Midas thus decides to undergo a cure, in which he renounces his world-imperial ambitions; yet he immediately demonstrates his continued worldliness by preferring the earthly music of Pan over the heavenly music of Apollo, a misvaluation that wins him ass's ears. For Lyly, it seems, the best measure of both kingly and national high-mindedness is not simply the gold one should scorn but, more important, the poetry one should prize; and England vindicates its otherworldly strength, Lyly implicitly maintains, not only by fending off Spain's far

greater material power but by recognizing how an ostensibly trifling piece of superstition like Lyly's fable can signify momentous
political and spiritual truths.

Midas also seems to imply, however, that a worldly extension of
England into empire would only debase the national spirit. Such
reverence for England's littleness can look like complacence; and
to such critics as King James the year after his accession, nothing
dramatized England's blindness to its own limitations so well as
the growing English taste for trifling imports—in particular, for
American tobacco. During the final years of Elizabeth's reign,
when England's tobacco craze began, the nation did indeed seem
strangely intent on literalizing Lyly's belief that England should
prefer spirit before gold: tobacco's enemies complained that the
English not only neglected more substantial goods in favor of
"smoke," but paid the Spanish what gold England already possessed in order to buy smoke from the Spanish who monopolized
it. John Beaumont's *Metamorphosis of Tabacco* (chapter 4) tries to
turn this seemingly insularist disaster into an imperialist gain. He
agrees with Lyly that England's trifling paradoxically promotes
high-mindedness, by freeing the English from a worldly absorption in materiality; but whereas the insularist embraces England's
material littleness as proof of its spiritual greatness, the tobacconist
finds the loved trifle to be nothing but smoke, and so must look
elsewhere than to the trifle for satisfaction. In Beaumont's account,
this elsewhere is preeminently Virginia, a potential source of more
tobacco but also, like tobacco, an American investment by which
the English seem only to lose gold, not gain it: Virginia represents
a proper imperial extension of England, in other words, because
its new-world immateriality leaves English otherworldliness vir-
ginally intact. Neither Virginia nor tobacco, however, can alone
ensure England's greatness; like Lyly, Beaumont insists that the
best means for suggesting the inadequacy of any particular matter
to the English spirit remains the trifle even less material than tobacco—poetry.

Raleigh's *Discoverie of Guiana* (chapter 5) appears to signal the
end of this immaterial colonialism: it tells the story of Raleigh's
voyage not to virginal Virginia but to a land of gold. Yet the *Discoverie* still tries to represent even Raleigh's golden colonialism as
the result of embracing a toy. Starting with his dedicatory epistle,

Raleigh in the *Discoverie* continually bemoans the fact that he has failed to honor his unconsummatable love for Elizabeth, and instead has disgraced himself by marrying a trifling material surrogate for the queen, Elizabeth Throckmorton. Although Raleigh has abandoned Virginia in search of gold, he implicitly argues that this apparent debasement of English colonial policy will nevertheless ultimately vindicate his continued devotion to Elizabeth and the immaterial satisfactions she provides: for in order to protect Elizabeth's long-term interest in Guiana, Raleigh has chastely left its golden treasures untouched. But of course, Guiana is more like Virginia than Raleigh will admit: it has no gold either, and Raleigh exploits the tradition of English otherworldliness in order to disguise his material failure. Yet Raleigh's obsession with Guiana also expresses his unbroken allegiance to Virginia's virginal colonialism in more than accidental or hypocritical ways. First, Raleigh maintains that Guiana alone will supply England all the gold it needs; the imperial potentiality of little England, Raleigh believes, will be realized in a miniature New World. Second, Raleigh's presenting his love of gold as chastity ultimately underscores a surprising insularism at the heart of both Virginian and Guianan, "fruitful" and "golden," colonialism—an English indifference in either case to actually settling America, to making the New World a new English home.

After Elizabeth's death and the confiscation by King James of Raleigh's American possessions, after the disastrous first years of Jamestown and England's continuing failure to uncover American gold mines, Captain John Smith's *Map of Virginia* (chapter 5) at last seems to herald a new, more practical interest in literally planting a colony on American soil; but ultimately Smith develops even such agricultural colonialism in otherworldly terms. The *Map*, that is, simply transforms Tudor antimaterialism into a defense of otherwise degrading manual labor: Smith, the colony's most accomplished trifler with savages, depicts himself as detached just as much from the earth he plants as from the gold for which others would dig. Like Raleigh, moreover, Smith associates the mere appearance of his materialist debasement with the mere appearance of an erotic disgrace: he shows interest in a surrogate for the now utterly unobtainable Elizabeth whom his readers would consider even more trifling than Raleigh's wife—an Indian princess, Pocahontas. Here too, however, Smith chastely forbears; the threats of his trifling physical attachment to America seem meant only to underscore his freedom from any material correlative, whether American (like Pocahontas) or English (like Elizabeth). But ultimately the very radicalness of the spiritual virginity that Smith claims for himself paradoxically helps to undermine the actual colonial labor that such virginity is meant to excuse: as a trifling proof of his strenuous but still otherworldly commitment to Virginia, Smith becomes increasingly attached to his role as colonial publicist, to his literary labor. In later years, when a colonial economy committed to trifles and not gold mines has actually become profitable, Smith may lament that the Jamestown colonists have shown themselves to be interested in planting only when they can exchange the solid ground of settlement for smoke—he reports that when Captain Samuel Argall reached Jamestown in 1617, "he found but five or six houses, the Church down, the Palisadoes broken, the Bridge in pieces, the Well of fresh water spoiled; the Store-house they used for the Church, the market-place, and streets, and all other spare places planted with Tobacco" (*Works* 2:262)—but Smith's own colonial efforts have become even more deracinated, the work of hands that no longer dig but write.

This brief overview of Wyatt, Lyly, Beaumont, Raleigh, and Smith already highlights two definitive features of the literary history that More and Shakespeare demarcate. By making the case for empire within the very terms of isolationist rhetoric, otherworldly imperialism proved especially adept at idealizing the colonial failures that kept England insular. But such idealization also had causal force: in promoting a colonialism so indistinguishable from insularism that the settlement of America had always to be seen as provisional, unsettled; and in helping to convert the trifles that suggested England's immaterial potentiality from a means of expansion to an end. To conclude this introduction, I now turn to the two figures at the heart of my study, who helped Renaissance England elaborate its insular and trifling imperialism most fully—Elizabeth and Spenser.

While one would expect her enemies to portray her as a personification of English weakness, it comes as something of a surprise that Elizabeth, like the trifling poet, herself repeatedly emphasized her apparent insufficiency. Over considerable opposition, especially during the first two decades of her reign, she also refused to ease England's embarrassment by ceding at least part of her power to a husband; and so the English were forced to accommodate a ruler who seemed to underscore not merely the weakness of the nation but its virginal isolation. By the time of the Armada, however, even other Europeans could see Elizabeth's virginity as divinely inspired, a sign and source of her island's unyielding integrity. If England, pure and insular, came increasingly to define itself in opposition to papist and imperial Spain, the articulation of this difference turned increasingly on the virgin queen who kept England a world apart.[16] Compared to Elizabeth's motto *Semper eadem* (Always the same), for instance, the impresa of the Spanish king, *Non sufficit orbis* (The world does not suffice), seemed to the Elizabethans to express an insatiability that, unlike Alexander's, had indeed found new worlds to conquer: as one Elizabethan tract claims, "even the *Spaniards* themselves do not forbear to report that by a certain celestial constitution, the monarchy of the whole world is due unto them, having as an earnest penny thereof, through their own power and might, conquered a new world to our ancestors heretofore unknown" (Marnix, *Exhortation*, 17). And yet, as I have begun to show, the English generally considered Philip's "lustful desire, and ambitious thoughts" (Keymis, *Second Voyage*, 484) too shortsighted to complete so massive an undertaking: though Philip would like the world to be "wholly *Spain*," says William Warner (1592), the merely worldly power of "*Indian* Gold" or "pope-buld [i.e., built and bulled] hopes" (*Albions England* 9:48) will ultimately fail him.[17] The true-believing English were, of course, not impervious to a little insatiability themselves: in unpublished notes, Hakluyt (1580), for instance, recommends seizing Spanish gold shipments by "taking the straights of Magellan," and like Raleigh in Guiana exaggeratedly predicts that the "Treasure and such great Spoils as shall upon this enterprise be taken upon the sudden shall be able to work wonderful effects and to carry the world etc." (Taylor, *Original Writings* 1:163–64). But Hakluyt found that his insular readers could only with the greatest difficulty be convinced to pursue more than piratical ventures in search of American gold; and their reluctance to settle even those parts of America unoccupied by

Spain, along with the apparent lack of gold there, helped keep colonial policy in line with the already compelling orthodox view that England shared the restraint, and therefore the sublimer power, of its queen. "Greater than *Alexander* she was," maintains Richard Niccols in his elegy for Elizabeth (1603), "for the world which he subdued by force, she conquered by love" (*Expicedium*, A3v). In other words, seemingly incapable of material coercion by virtue of her gender and her island nation, Elizabeth could both claim and be accorded the only means of power traditionally granted to trifling woman, which her virginity could then idealize into something "greater" than mere "force"[18]—a "love" conquering yet chaste, an immaterial expansiveness that enabled the English not only to value the strength in Elizabeth's material weakness but to picture her conquests as sacrificing neither her own nor England's purity.

In such propaganda as the entertainment at Elvetham (1591), Elizabeth's charms could in fact be imagined as enabling England to command America's riches without the English even having to travel there: the sea-god Nereus, come to pay homage to the queen, declares that

> with me came gold breasted India,
> Who, daunted at your sight, leapt to the shore,
> And sprinkling endless treasure on this Isle,
> Left me with this jewel to present your Grace.
> (Nichols, *Progresses* 3:112)

In one respect—the implicit comparison with Spain—this passage makes a familiar claim: the uncoercive imperialism that Elizabeth sponsors will in the end win more treasure in America than will Philip's barbarous tyranny there. Yet a later entertainment more fully betrays the limitations inherent in so literally ascribing England's trifling powers to the mere "sight" of Elizabeth. Alluding to an Indian prince whom Raleigh had just brought back from Guiana, the "Device Made by the Earl of Essex for the Entertainment of Her Majesty" (1595) presents another (or perhaps even the same) Guianan to Elizabeth, and tells her that, though the prince has been blind from birth, an Indian prophecy has foretold that he will ultimately "expel the Castilians" from his land. First, however, he must learn to see, and an oracle has explained where he can find his cure:

> Seated between the Old World and the New
> A land there is no other land may touch,
> Where reigns a Queen in peace and honor true;
> Stories or fables do describe no such.
> (Bacon, *Works* 3:388)

Hence the prince has traveled to virginal England and queen, where his cure, yet also his transformation, instantly begins: "Your Majesty's sacred presence hath wrought the strangest innovation that ever was in the world. You have here before you Seeing Love, a Prince indeed, but of greater territories than all the Indies" (389). Like the Elvetham entertainment, the "Device" manages, then, to celebrate the miraculously expansive strength of Elizabeth's isolated "presence"; but if the foreign territories that Elizabeth sways turn out to be far greater than even Guiana, they also end up looking like no territories in particular: the "Device" makes Elizabeth imperial only at the expense of the actual expansionism that the Guianan-turned-Cupid seemed originally intended to advance.[19]

If any of her subjects helped Elizabeth to represent herself as a conqueror more benign and therefore more powerful than the king of Spain, it was Spenser, the most "Elizabethan" poet by virtue not only of his singular attention to the queen but of the pension that the queen granted to no other writer. In fact, Spenser's own career seemed itself to demonstrate how an English "trifle" like Elizabeth could come to wield such authority: though born the son of an artisan, Spenser by the time of his death could be hailed as the English Virgil, "our principal poet."[20] In an important recent study, Richard Helgerson has argued that Spenser rose to such "laureate" rank by resisting the "pressure . . . to define himself and his work" in the self-dismissive terms of "amateur" poets (*Self-Crowned*, 67). But as I have already begun to show, both the amateur and the laureate poet in Renaissance England were able to find value in poetry precisely *as* trifling; and Spenser the laureate was only more, not less, committed than the amateur to the self-dismissive pose. Consistently presenting himself as the unworthy poet and lover of Elizabeth and England, Spenser argued that the sublimity of each was best revealed in contrast to his own "meanness," as in a sonnet addressed to yet another lesser Elizabeth, his future wife Elizabeth Boyle:

To all those happy blessings which ye have,
  with plenteous hand by heaven upon you thrown,
this one disparagement they to you gave,
  that ye your love lent to so meane a one.
Yee whose high worths surpassing paragon,
  could not on earth have found one fit for mate,
ne but in heaven matchable to none,
  why did ye stoup unto so lowly state?
But ye thereby much greater glory gate,
  then had ye sorted with a princes pere:
for now your light doth more it selfe dilate,
  and in my darknesse greater doth appeare.
Yet since your light hath once enlumind me,
  with my reflex yours shall encreased be.

                                    (*Amoretti*, sonnet 66)

As this passage first admits, however, what Spenser elsewhere calls his dark conceits (*V* 1:167) could at the same time appear to obscure the ideals he celebrates, making them not only hard to see but hard to see apart from the "meane" poetry shadowing them. And indeed, like the cult that developed around the figure of the queen, the extraordinarily high regard in which "lowly" Spenser came to be held could just as well seem to reflect England's increasing complacence about its own inconsequence. Nothing makes England's love for Spenser appear more of a "disparagement" for the nation than the contrast between Spenser and his Iberian counterparts. Where an epic like Ercilla's *Araucana* (1569–90), an account of Spain's war with the Araucanan Indians, commits itself so thoroughly to the actual events of the Conquest as to be prefaced by Ercilla's assertion that he began writing his poem in the Araucanan battlefield (1.121), Spenser's *Faerie Queene* (1590–96) derives, according to a dedicatory sonnet (*V* 3:194), from the "savadge soyle" only of Ireland, not the New World; the epic was composed by "a rustick Muse," not an heroic one; and she has chosen to represent not Indians but fairies.

I will argue, however, that Spenser welcomes such apparently invidious comparisons: he intends his fairy poem to look both trifling and epic at once, because he wants to stress that the real sinews of war consist not of worldly Spanish gold but of otherworldly English virtues. Yet, just as he deplores Spanish materialism, so Spenser also condemns England's cultish absorption in the queen's literal "presence." He wants England to recognize the real power that the "sight" of Elizabeth's weak body should contrastingly highlight—what Spenser's friend Gabriel Harvey calls "her Empiring spright" (*V* 3:187). So persistently, indeed, does Spenser attack the insularist admirers of Elizabeth that, with increasing boldness, he tries to displace the queen in England's eyes with the more errant representative trifles of both his poetry and himself. By requiring his readers to envision Elizabeth only through the conspicuously trifling mirror of a superstitious and immaterial no-place, Fairyland, Spenser hopes that his poetical *Queene* will conversely reflect a more extensive field for Elizabeth than her virginal body or virginal island; while, in his self-portrayals, he refuses to limit himself even to the excursive identity of a colonist, an identity he acknowledges, in a characteristically indirect and dismissive way, by the punning name of his pastoral, not heroic, persona, Colin.[21] Yet the polemical necessity of emphasizing first his literal distance from Elizabeth's island and second his incommensurability to any particular elsewhere he might settle increasingly forces Spenser to associate his representative otherworldliness less with the vast and uncolonized New World than with the island neighboring England that he himself helped occupy, Ireland. Spenser's allegorical trifling, in other words, ultimately proves as incapable of escaping the little, insular otherworlds that paradoxically suggest English power as is the supposedly literal-minded cult of Elizabeth—so incapable, in fact, that when later writers like Cowley and Addison reexamine the fairy empire that Elizabeth and Spenser helped create, it will appear to them truly unconnected not just to America but also to a now imperial England. For these writers, the otherworldly English potentiality that Spenser's poetry would shadow has come to seem an empire merely—yet also sublimely—poetical.

An Empire Nowhere

Some term it Stolida,
And Sordida it name:
And to be plain they do it mock,
As at a foolish game.
—Robert Seall (1563) on a
proposed expedition to Florida

Of those that make any thing, some do make much of
nothing, as God did in creating the World of naught, and
as Poets in some respects also do, whilst they feign fables
and make thereof their poesies.
—Thomas Blundeville, *The True
Order and Methode of Wryting and
Reading Hystories* (1574)

Renaissance England produced Shakespeare and colonized America. Struck by the coincidence, literary critics have generally assumed that one kind of expansiveness—the discovery and conquest of a new world—helped lead to the other—England's literary renaissance.[1] Yet modern historical scholarship has increasingly highlighted what J. H. Elliott calls "one of the most striking features of sixteenth-century intellectual history—the apparent slowness of Europe in making the mental adjustments required to incorporate America within its field of vision";[2] and of the major European nations, England was slowest of all. Columbus's first letter describing his discoveries sold throughout the Continent by 1494, but never found an English publisher; in fact, between the time of Columbus's original voyage and Richard Eden's pathbreaking *Treatyse of the Newe India* (1553), a span of sixty years, only one English work devoted to America seems to have been printed—in Antwerp.[3] If England had trouble keeping up with the news about the New World, it had an even harder time

seizing some of that world for its own. The hopes raised early on
by the voyages of John Cabot (1497–98) set the tone for English
enterprises in America throughout the next century, for they
ended in Cabot's disappearance; Cortés conquered Mexico some
sixty-five years before Virginia's first colonists gave up and went
home.[4] The invidious comparison between English and Spanish
expansionism did not, however, go unlamented. Richard Hakluyt,
the premier colonial advocate of his day, begins the dedication to
Sir Philip Sidney of his *Divers Voyages Touching the Discovery of
America* (1582) in dismay:

> I marvel not a little (right honorable) that since the discovery of
> America (which is now full fourscore and ten years), after so great
> conquests and plantings of the Spaniards and Portingales there, that
> we of England could never have the grace to set fast footing in such
> fertile and temperate places as are left as yet unpossessed of them.
> (8)

One wonders what sort of excitement English writers could have
absorbed. And indeed, the three most famous and oft-cited instances of the New World finding its way into English Renaissance
literature—More's *Utopia*, Spenser's *Faerie Queene*, and Shakespeare's *Tempest*—seem markedly ambivalent about the very fact of
America's discovery. More names his New World explorer Hythloday, or Well Learned in Nonsense, and his newfound land Utopia, or Nowhere; Spenser turns Europe's recently corrected ignorance about America into an oddly ironic proof of the existence of
Fairyland (*FQ* 2.proem); while Shakespeare places his American-
sounding island in the Old World's Mediterranean, far distant
from "the still-vex'd Bermoothes" (*Tempest* 1.2.229) it appears to
represent.

One explanation of this ambivalence would call it avoidance:
the English did not want to acknowledge that, in the race for New
World land, souls, and gold, they had been massively preempted.
Yet Hakluyt's wonder at the thought of England ignoring even
"unpossessed" American land suggests that his country is less un-
nerved by the New World than, oddly, indifferent to it. Such, at
least, is the view of England's colonial backwardness that Eden
(1555) had earlier adopted, along with an explanation for English
apathy that modern historians have by and large endorsed:[5]

> How much I say shall this sound unto our reproach and inexcusable
> slothfulness and negligence both before god and the world, that so
> large dominions of such tractable people and pure gentiles, not be-
> ing hitherto corrupted with any other false religion (and therefore
> the easier to be allured to embrace ours) are now known unto us,
> and that we have no respect neither for god's cause nor for our own
> commodity to attempt some voyages into these coasts, to do for our
> parts as the Spaniards have done for theirs, and not ever like sheep
> to haunt one trade. (*Decades*, 55)

This trade that the English are said to haunt "like sheep" is, of
course, a trade *in* sheep: during the sixteenth century, unfinished
woolen cloths increasingly dominated England's list of exports,
the woolens market became increasingly centered on the exchange
between London and Antwerp, and so English economic interests
saw little reason to look for business anywhere but to the east.
Moreover, what Eden calls "our parts" of America—North America—appeared in any case to lack the great prospects of those other
parts that had already been claimed: whereas the Spanish found
gold and extensive polities to conquer, the English could discover
only timber and fish. And finally, as any student of the period
might guess, the struggles over "false religion" within Tudor England provided ample matter to keep English minds busy at home.
By these accounts, in other words, the paucity of early English
publications on America would no longer seem much wonder at
all, nor would another otherwise curious bibliographic fact: that
besides being incidental, the first references to the New World
printed in England occur not in economic, political, or even geographical tracts but in imaginative literature, and then in association with idleness and folly. For instance, the title character of the
interlude *Hycke Scorner* (c. 1515–16) lies about his travel all over the
world, including those to "the new found island" (315) and "the
land of women that few men doth find" (323); while Alexander
Barclay's translation of Sebastian Brant's *Narrenschiff* (1494)—*The
Ship of Folys* (1509)—appends a discussion of America as the finishing touch to Brant's account "Of the foolish description and inquisition of diverse countries and regions":

> Ferdinandus that late was king of spain
> Of land and people hath found plenty and store
> Of whom the bidding to us was uncertain
> No christian man of them heard tell before

> Thus it is folly to tend unto the lore
> And unsure science of vain geometry
> Since none can know all the world perfitely.
>   (2.26)[6]

Born in this context of English indifference to America or satire inspired by it, the "new world" of More's *Nowhere* (1516) now seems an almost predictable English joke.[7]

Yet the odd truth about More's apparently dismissive meditation on America is that it contains perhaps the first Tudor attempt to elaborate a theory of colonization—according to D. B. Quinn, More in *Utopia* even "appears to be the first Englishman to use the word *colonia* in a Roman [i.e., imperialist] meaning" ("Renaissance Influences," 75).[8] And More's Utopian colonial theory, which turns the accusation that a land is "idle and waste" into a justification for colonizing it, came in fact to be repeated time and again in the American propaganda of Renaissance England. But what is perhaps most surprising in regard to More's ostensibly commonplace irony about the New World is the fact that, a year after the publication of *Utopia*, More's brother-in-law John Rastell actually attempted to colonize America himself. This chapter will take seriously the possibility that More's overtly fictional new world inspired Rastell to seek a real one.[9] Moving from More to an imperialist poem by Sir Thomas Wyatt that never even mentions America, I will try to explain how a literary tradition begun by *Utopia* that seems to reflect what some Tudors considered England's lamentable indifference to the New World[10] could nonetheless be taken, and intended, as colonialist propaganda. The paradoxicality of this literature stems from an ambivalent vision not just of distant lands, however, but of England itself. By assigning colonialism to Utopia, More seems to resist a policy that might threaten England's insular integrity. Yet Utopia too is an island, whose other-worldliness recalls not only the New World through which Hythloday first travels but also the New World of the ancients, the English island. I will argue that *Utopia* represents More's attempt to turn England's classical nowhereness into a way of seeing England and America as destined for each other; but because More cannot conceive of modern England as other-worldly in any positive sense, the utopical conjunction of England and America in *Utopia* remains obscure. Wyatt is more overtly imperialist, and his poem raises the question of empire in regard to an England even more like the classical view of it than More's England had been, but I will show that he too can only dimly suggest the imperial significance of English insularity: his poem contrasts Spain's golden empire to an island now excluded not only materially but also spiritually from both Old World and New. Finally, I will argue that, in highlighting the unworldliness of the literary as well as the insular medium that they use to signify England's imperial destiny, both More and Wyatt establish literature as a negative incitement to empire not just supplementing but, potentially, rivaling the utopic English isle itself.

I

The first book of *Utopia* inaugurates this series of expansionist paradoxes in an appropriately skewed way; for when the great debate of book 1 asks what "excellent men" ought to want, no one answers "empire." More the homebody, the counselor, argues for service to one's prince; Hythloday the wanderer, the philosopher, argues for freedom. But *Utopia* also advocates, as it were in silence, a third pursuit: to travel *and* serve, the life of More the diplomat whose business takes him to Antwerp, the scene of the debate; or of Vespucci the discoverer who starts Hythloday on his way to Utopia; or of the nameless sea-merchants for whom More negotiates[11] and who may own the Portuguese ships that return Hythloday to Europe (50/51). If this alternative seems practically absent from the first book, nowhere directly stated, it emphatically presents itself as soon as *Utopia* reifies absence, as soon, that is, as the opening debate goes Nowhere: in the second book, what had been fleeting references to travel-as-service in Europe become in Utopia the fully articulated national policy of colonization.

What keeps this alternative from more positive expression? One might assume that the covert presentation of travel-as-service in the first book represents an extremely subtle demonstration of the rhetorical method that More recommends to Hythloday during their debate, the "indirect approach": as More says, his "practical" philosophy gives up dogmatic assertion and instead "tactfully" "adapts itself to the play in hand" (98/99–100/101). Readers like Elizabeth McCutcheon have already found analogies to this "indirect approach" in "the processes of negation and opposites which typify so much of the *Utopia*"—for example, in recurrent stylistic devices like double negatives (litotes), that "speak of . . . a tendency to see more than one side of a question" ("Denying," 273). The negative presentation of travel-as-service could, in other words, be seen as merely another instance of More's winning urbanity throughout *Utopia*, of his apparent open-mindedness, moderation, and self-irony.[12]

Of course, a less sympathetic critic such as Hythloday might simply call it hedging, even though, in the case of travel-as-service, the equivocator would seem to be Hythloday himself. Perhaps the most salient feature of Hythloday's political critique throughout book 1 is his hatred of expansionism: in rejecting More's suggestion that Hythloday "would make an excellent member of any king's council," Hythloday contends that "almost all monarchs" would rather ignore his advice concerning "the honorable activities of peace," for "they care much more how, by hook or crook, they may win fresh kingdoms than how they may administer well what they have got" (*U*, 56/57).[13] Now no one, it seems, could mistake the discoverer for anything but an agent of expansionism; in his first letters patent for John Cabot (5 March 1496), Henry VII licensed Cabot and his sons to "subdue, occupy, and possess, all such towns, cities, castles, and isles, of them found, which they can subdue, occupy, and possess, as our vassals and lieutenants, getting unto us the rule, title, and jurisdiction of the same villages, towns, castles, and firm land so found" (trans. Hakluyt, *Divers Voyages*, 21). And yet not only is Hythloday strangely silent about this new and far balder kind of land grabbing; he also endorses Vespucci's voyages enough to become "his constant companion in the last three" of them (*U*, 50/51). Perhaps, as his behavior on the final voyage might lead us to believe, Hythloday truly does not recognize the expansionism in discovery: though he begins his American sojourn in a fort, the foothold of conquest, he soon strikes out with five other Europeans in search of "excellent institutions" (50/51–52/53). But, once again, what appears a blindness to travel-as-service in the first book becomes a vigorous advocacy in the second, when Hythloday praises Utopian colonialism.

The precise terms of Hythloday's praise seem to show, however, that a European struggle for power and a New World discovery represent, for him, categorically different pursuits. In one of his antiexpansionist diatribes, Hythloday reports how the Achorians won their prince another kingdom, but then "saw they would have no less trouble in keeping it than they had suffered in obtaining it" (88/89). Yet Henry assumed, and Cabot seemed to prove, that the land Cabot's license described as formerly "unknown to all Christians" would be cheap and easy prey: after Cabot's voyage the Milanese ambassador to England wrote home that "his Majesty here has gained a part of Asia, without a stroke of the sword" (Williamson, *Cabot Voyages*, 209). If Cabot's New World appeared then, to solve the practical problems of expansionism that Hythloday alleges, Vespucci's colonial fort seems intended to circumvent any ethical problem Hythloday might also have, since it apparently lays claim to land "unoccupied" not just by Christians but by anyone: though he befriends natives near the fort, Hythloday must travel "many days" from there before he finds "very populous commonwealths" (*U*, 50/51–52/53). This reassuring emptiness returns in *Utopia*'s second book as the central feature of the Utopian expansions that Hythloday lauds:

> If the population throughout the island should happen to swell above the fixed quotas, they enroll citizens out of every city and, on the mainland nearest them, wherever the natives have much unoccupied and uncultivated land, they found a colony under their own laws. . . . The inhabitants who refuse to live according to their laws, they drive from the territory which they carve out for themselves. If they resist, they wage war against them. They consider it a most just cause for war when a people which does not use its soil but keeps it idle and waste [*inane ac uacuum*] nevertheless forbids the use and possession of it to others who by the rule of nature ought to be maintained by it. (*U*, 136/37)

Yet, instead of canceling the accusation that the colonialism of *Utopia* is either equivocal or ambivalent, this difference between European and Utopian expansionism seems to confirm the charge. For More advocates colonialism only when it is associated with negatives, when it both derives from Nowhere and seeks, in the Utopian stipulation, land *inane ac uacuum*, idle and waste. And then not even these two negatives can turn colonialism into a fully English option. The Utopians choose wasteland "on the mainland nearest them"; as the Yale editors of *Utopia* point out, the nearest mainland to England was Europe, "but where were the waste places?" (More, *CW* 4:416). The answer is: in the opposite direction.

We seem back where we began. As at best a negatively positive response to questions concerning the practical and ethical feasibility of New World colonization, *Utopia* appears almost as resistant to America as the less subtle and extensive contemporary reflections on the subject. Indeed, *Utopia*'s negative formulations of travel-as-service would seem to suggest that More cannot escape questioning the very intelligibility of the idea. His professed distaste for ambassadorships—for example, "I never much liked the position of an envoy"; "You cannot believe how unwillingly I spend my time on [embassies]" (Erasmus, *Correspondence* 3:234, 5:158)—is a simple case in point. The Achorians reject expansionism after deciding that their king, "being distracted [*distractus*] with the charge of two kingdoms, could not properly attend to either" (*U*, 90/91); and in a letter to Erasmus (c. 17 February 1516) bemoaning the ambassadorial mission recalled in *Utopia*, More complains that an ambassador must prove equally distracted: "When I am away, I have to support two households, one at home and the other abroad" (Erasmus, *Correspondence* 3:234).[14] Such practical problems, and even the inevitable ethical problems of a career dedicated to what More later calls "the busy nothings of princes" (5:158), seem, however, only to exacerbate a more basic anxiety at the heart of ambassadorial life—homesickness: even though "away for a short time" only, ambassadors "are immediately haled back by longing for our wives and families" (3:234).[15] When Hythloday decides to travel, he forsakes his patrimony and declares, "From all places it is the same distance to heaven" (*U*, 50/51); but to travel in the interests of home ideally requires one to believe that one has never quite left it. A Utopian colony, for instance, is supposed to consider itself nothing more than home transplanted:

> If ever any misfortune so diminishes the number in any of their cities that it cannot be made up out of other parts of the island without bringing other cities below their proper strength . . . , they are filled up by citizens returning from colonial territory. They would rather that the colonies should perish than that any of the cities of the island should be enfeebled. (136/37)

More's homesickness as he presents it might make it very easy for him to consider any foreign residence temporary, but at the same time it also argues him incapable of adapting very well to such a residence in the first place. In fact, the closest it seems that More can come to feeling at home abroad is when he partakes of the foreign at home, either through news—Giles reports him "always most greedy to hear" of "unknown peoples and lands" (48/49)—or through things: "If he sees anything outlandish or otherwise re- markable, he buys it greedily, and has his house stocked with such things from all sources" (Erasmus to von Hutten, 23 July 1519, *Cor- respondence* 7:19). But why must the foreignness that More as home- body "greedily" consumes be as foreign as possible—not just dif- ferent from home but opposite to it, its negative, "outlandish" and "unknown"? Insofar as More's conception of home cannot be ex- tended beyond home, the foreign, it would seem, cannot help but figure as radically different—which makes More's residence abroad capable of threatening home not merely financially. In *Utopia*, talk with foreigners and about foreign lands causes More to *forget* home: Giles's "delightful society and charming discourse largely took away my nostalgia and made me less conscious than before of the separation from my home, wife, and children to whom I was ex- ceedingly anxious to get back" (*U*, 48/49). As *Utopia* opens, in fact, such absentmindedness quickly produces More's own negative, Hythloday, the man who has abandoned his home entirely; and *Utopia* itself, More's imagination of a new world, appears to have been begun during More's ambassadorial absence from home.[16] In other words, if the foreign can only with difficulty be conceived in the image of home, it can easily be imagined as home's replace- ment, a colony that becomes a home in its own right.

More's professed sedentariness, then, seems necessarily to transform him into only a negative advocate of travel-as-service; yet it would be a mistake to conclude that his temperament alone is what makes him suspect that ambassadors or colonists must al- ways suffer distraction. The discoverers about whom More must have heard and read do not prove More to be needlessly con- cerned with the relation between travel-as-service and one's sense of home; rather, they simply embrace homelessness as a positive boon. As Vespucci reports in the tract Giles says is read *passim*, everywhere (everywhere, that is, except in England), Vespucci came to Iberia originally as a merchant, but soon found himself on the one hand unable to make a good living and on the other aspiring to greater things—not simply large sums of money, as his future lies to some Indians suggest: "When they asked us whence we came, we answered that we had descended from heaven to pay the earth a visit" (*Navigationes*, 112). A lie about origins, denying both a mean birth and a place of birth, a connection to any earthly polity, this claim to godhead is characteristic of Vespucci not only as a relatively pure form of ambition but also as the kind of deception his ambition requires. For Vespucci did not pursue his discoveries in the name of his original home, nor even consistently in the name of any later one: he undertook his first two voyages for Ferdinand of Spain, his second two for Manuel of Portugal (85). In other words, mobility to Vespucci seems to depend on ambiguity. As he himself presents it, the decision to leave Ferdinand for Manuel looks unaccountable: it "was disapproved of by all those who knew me. For I was leaving Castile, where no small degree of honor had been shown me and where the King himself held me in high esteem. What was even worse was that I departed without taking leave of my host" (134). Yet his new allegiance to Manuel did not stop Vespucci on his third voyage from taking possession of a land "in the name of the most serene King of Castile" (136); the whole travelogue is in the end dedicated to Ferdinand; and, as if to sum up the studied ambiguity of his position, Vespucci concludes by reminding Ferdinand that "I am now living in Lisbon"—Portugal, that is—"not knowing what next your most serene Majesty will plan for me to do" (151).[17] In a later edition of the voyages, the one More probably read, Vespucci adds a dedication to still another king—René d'Anjou, King of Jerusalem and Sicily—in which he hopes that the novelty of the voyages (and perhaps of Vespucci's continually recreated affiliations) will afford René a sympathetic freedom from domestic responsibilities: "You will find in these pages no slight relief from the wasting cares and problems of government" (86).

Cabot too sees the gifts that rootlessness can bring. A Venetian in London writes home about his fellow Venetian's great successes away from home: "He is called the Great Admiral and vast honor is paid to him and he goes dressed in silk, and these English run after him like mad, and indeed he can enlist as many of them as he pleases, and a number of our rogues as well'' (Williamson, *Cabot Voyages*, 208). Nomads in particular become Cabot's disciples: the Milanese envoy to England says he has spoken with a Burgundian who

> wants to go back, because the Admiral, which is the name they give to Messer Zoane, has given him an island. He has given another to his barber, a Genoese by birth, and both consider themselves counts, while my lord the Admiral esteems himself at least a prince. (211)

But even mercenaries like these discoverers, turning homelessness to their advantage, cannot master the confusion it creates. Their radical desire not to be tied to any one home must finally be tempered into the desire only to be tied to more homes than one: untrammeled yet still in need of backing, the discoverer ends up not escaping allegiances but multiplying them. As Vespucci juggles Spain and Portugal, so Cabot tries to maintain loyalties to both England and Venice at once: he "planted on the land which he has found a large cross with a banner of England and one of St. Mark, as he is a Venetian" (208). But such attempts to claim more than one home have significant limitations: the Milanese ambassador adds that "this Messer Zoane, as a foreigner and a poor man, would not have obtained credence, had it not been that his companions, who are practically all English and from Bristol, testified that he spoke the truth" (209). Home may seem an arbitrary thing to a discoverer, but not to his patrons, and it therefore complicates travel for homeless and homebound alike.[18]

Yet even this final motive for More's baffled presentation of travel-as-service, the fact that the discoverer as well as More might find such a life difficult to embrace, cannot fully explain why *Utopia* seems characteristic of a nation's resistance to New World expansion. If More's apparently profound attachment to home makes his tentativeness concerning the travel in travel-as-service look exceptional, the discoverer's profound estrangement from home, and therefore from service, should render him equally exceptional. More's negativity in *Utopia* becomes less easily explained as mere eccentricity, however, as soon as one finds the same hesitations in an English contemporary of More who is not only as fully committed to the life of travel and service as a man could be, but is even exhorting his king to empire.

Robert Thorne was an English merchant resident in Spain, an intermediary between the Spanish, Portuguese, and English governments, and an investor in and proponent of discovery.[19] His famous letter to Henry VIII (1527) urging him to fund a northwest discovery, the first extant English writing of its kind, begins with very un-More-like directness: "Experience proveth that naturally all Princes be desirous to extend and enlarge their dominions and kingdoms." The corollary to this assertion, however, seems to suggest that the naturalness of the desire does not make it rational or right: "Wherefore it is not to be marveled to see them every day procure the same, not regarding any cost, peril, and labor, that may thereby chance; but rather it is to be marveled if there be any prince content to live quiet within his own dominions." This last evocation of a peaceful monarch is at once encouraged and undercut when Thorne now shifts imperialist desire from a naturally itchy prince to external pressures on him: "For surely the people would think he lacketh the noble courage and spirit of all other [princes]." Whoever does do the desiring, it is undeniable that kings "have in manner turned up and down the world," and what Thorne again calls a "natural inclination" for such troublemaking "is cause that scarcely it may be said there is any kingdom stable, nor king quiet, but that his own imagination, or other Princes his neighbors, do trouble him." If Henry were not at this point feeling queasy enough about his options, the next sentence, also the next topic in Thorne's argument, would clinch the matter: "God and nature hath provided to your Grace, and to your Gracious progenitors, this Realm of England, and set it in so fruitful a place, and within such limits, that it should seem to be a place quiet and aparted from all the foresaid desires" ("Declaration," 27–28)—divided from all the world, so divided from all desire to own it. Exhorting Henry to empire has come to seem instead like exhorting him to rein in his imperialist "imagination."

But the fact that Thorne is indeed exhorting his prince helps explain his wavering and slippery argument here, since Thorne is after all one of those subjects whom the prince must fear, unfavorably comparing Henry's quiescence to the great deeds that Spain and Portugal have already performed, and so politely warning him that "it will seem your Grace's subjects to be without activity or courage in leaving to do this glorious and noble enterprise" (31); Thorne knows that the only way to incite Henry safely is at the same time to praise him for maintaining England's stability. And it is also true that the more costly and dangerous Thorne makes imperialism look in general, the more his particular argument profits, for the same reason Henry's father, and presumably Hythloday, accepted New World enterprise while rejecting Continental forays: northwest discovery will "amplify and enrich" England "by a godly mean, with little cost, peril, or labor" (Thorne thinks the discovery will be easy, first because the northern route is the shortest to the open seas of the Pacific; second because the English ships will avoid the Atlantic ones of other nations; third because the English will travel in "perpetual clearness of the day" rather than "groping their way" in darkness as voyagers in lower latitudes must; and last—the implied base to all these considerations—because the heathens with whom the English will trade are easy marks).[20] These two very calculated motives for Thorne's ambivalence—his need to placate Henry and to make western discovery look more attractive—do not, however, cancel the possibility that Thorne cannot quite shake off a vision of England properly "quiet and aparted" from his own imperialist desires, or that he at least considers the vision to some degree ineradicable from Henry's mind. The next sentence highlights Thorne's dilemma marvelously: "One special cause" why England should seem its own world, uninterested in expansion,

> is, for that it is compassed with the Sea: by reason thereof it seems, this notwithstanding, their desires and noble courages have been most commonly like unto others: and with marvelous great labors, costs, and perils, they have traveled and passed the Seas, making war not only with kings and dominions nigh neighbors, but also with them of far countries, and so hath won and conquered many rich and fair Dominions, and amplified this your Grace's Realm with great victory and glory. (28)

"By reason thereof it seems," by reason of England's insularity, "this notwithstanding," notwithstanding England's insularity: to Thorne's mind, the same fact, the sea surrounding England, simultaneously opposes and promotes expansion.[21]

A Venetian visitor to England around 1500 claims that the English are in general much less ambivalent about their insularity than Thorne, for they "are great lovers of themselves, and of everything belonging to them; they think that there are no other men than themselves, and no other world but England" (Sneyd, *Relation*, 20–21). From this perspective, More's sedentariness looks like a national condition; if the English in general seem indifferent to the New World, perhaps that is because their island is all the world they desire. The Utopians, as colonizers, may appear less exclusively attached to their own island, yet it defines their national identity as surely as the Venetian thinks England's geography defines the English.[22] For Utopia becomes a separate world, a negative, a nowhere, only when it also becomes insular: by ordering a fifteen-mile excavation, the ancient conqueror Utopus converted a peninsula named Abraxa into the island of Utopia (*U*, 112/13). The story seems to glance at an apparently contemporaneous theory that England itself had once been a peninsula,[23] and therefore to hint as well at more extensive parallels between the English and Utopian isles. Erasmus was the first to assert that More in his newfound world "represented the English commonwealth in particular [*Britannicam potissimum effinxit*]" (*Correspondence* 7:23, *Opus Epistolarium* 4:21). But the very structure of More's work, its first book continually recurring to the subject of England, its second devoted to Utopia, already suggests the relation; and then *Utopia*'s marginal notes make the connection unmistakable: when Hythloday mentions the unusual currents of Anydrus, the river of Utopia's capital city Amaurotum, the note refers the reader to "The Identical Phenomenon on the River Thames in England"; and when Hythloday next describes a fine bridge over that river, the note adds, "In This Feature, Too, London Agrees With Amaurotum" (*U*, 118/19).[24] Later utopias may prove more explicit about identifying their new worlds with England, as in Joseph Hall's *Mundus Alter et Idem* (1605), *Another World and Yet the Same*, but they do not entirely surrender More's allusive manner in such identification, his "indirect approach"; see figure 1. Part of the reason that a utopia would avoid positive comparisons to England is, no doubt, the irony or evasiveness inevitable to a work that affirms the existence of a place it knows does not exist. But More's insistence that special signs of reference to England, such as London-like Amaurotum and Thames-like Anydrus, be negatives— "Shadow City" and "Waterless"—also suggests that what Utopia and England share is precisely the negativity constituted *in toto* by Utopian insularity. And in fact, when in the prefatory material to

Figure 1. Map of the world, from *Mundus Alter et Idem*, by Mercurio Britannico [Joseph Hall], Frankfurt [London], 1605. The absence of little England from the north yields an enormous new continent in the south. (By permission of the Houghton Library, Harvard University.)

Gallia
Rochel
Genoua
Baiona
HISPANIA
Seuilla
Roma
Sardina
Napoli
Sicilia
Corint
Constantinapolis
Mare Maior
Candia

Turchesta
Tenduc

ASIA

Cathaia

Indostan

Mare Rubru

Mare Mediter

Narsinga
Smagar
Si an

Malupar

C. Comori

Malaca

AFRICA

Anzica

Abassia

Mono motapa

Insula
Hermæphroditica

Insula
Beatica

Promontori Bonæ spei
Promontorium
Nigrum

Aphrodisia
Noua Gynia

PAMPHAGO
NIA

Nebauius flu.
calamiiu

IVRO
NIA

Nepenthes fluu

LOCANIA

Vel

Amazonia

Eugynia

MORONIA
FELIX

Lisonica gens

Plorauia

VSRAGINSA

Lingua dotia

MORON FATVA

Baueria

Tuberony
Colts

VARIANA
Vel Morion
Mobilis

Sbiocœia

Aspera Moronia
Orgila

FRVGIONA
Adhuc Incognita

Utopia "Anemolius" has Utopia say that "the ancients called me Utopia or Nowhere because of my isolation" (20/21), he cannot rightly mean Utopus's Utopia, about which the ancients knew nothing. Rather, he must be alluding to the classical conception of another island he wants to associate with Utopia, an island whose inhabitants Virgil's first eclogue calls *penitus toto divisos orbe*, wholly divided from all the world—England.[25] What Anemolius implies, in other words, is that "aparted" England has not only found its negative image in Utopia, but refound through Utopia its own negativity as both an island and an old Nowhere itself. "It is one of the curiosities of literary history," Josephine Waters Bennett remarks, "that, at the very time when the New World in the West was being explored, ancient notions about Great Britain as another world beyond the end of the earth caught the fancy" of English writers ("Britain," 114)—as if the discovery of a new New World prompted England only to turn its sights inward and backward, in the hope of "restor[ing] antiquity to Britain, and Britain to his antiquity," of recapturing England's past as the New World of old.[26] Even the Continental writers of the prefatory letters to *Utopia* seem led by the book to recall England's old otherworldliness: Desmarais praises *Utopia* as a product of the learning that now flourishes "among the British at the ends of the earth" (*U*, 26/27); and Busleyden addresses More as the "glory of your Britain and of this world of ours" (36/37).[27] But then, writing the "Letter to Dorp" (1515) while on the embassy depicted in *Utopia*, More had already styled himself *Morus apud toto divisos orbe Britannos*, "More among the Britons divided from all the world" (CW 15:126).

A preoccupation with celebrating England's own utopicality would indeed help explain why More has Hythloday so quickly traverse America in search of a utopic island; yet if *Utopia* indicates that the discovery of America caused More only to recall England's classical other-worldliness, why does More bother with a utopia even farther afield from England than America, and why, moreover, is that gratuitous island a colonialist power? In the Dorp letter, More fancies himself among the separate British while he is actually on the Continent, as if he can appreciate England's otherworldliness only from the external perspective that his Continental admirers possess. *Utopia*, begun by More while on the Continent and set in the time of his stay there, asks its readers to look westward both to England and beyond, thus highlighting the fact that America and England are equally aparted: each apart from, and between, the Old World setting of book 1 and the Utopia of book 2. More, it would seem, wants England and America to share in an otherness that the Utopian island both demarcates and names.

Later in the history of English imperialism, advocates of New World expansion will repeatedly ask the English to recall their own separateness from the world in order to recognize England's special, even providential incentives for occupying the New World. A broadside of the Virginia Company (1612) defends Virginia by a convenient analogy—"Who knows not England once was like / A Wilderness and savage place" ("Londons Lotterie," 24)—just as William Crashaw (1610) defends Virginia's wild inhabitants:

> For the time was when we were savage and uncivil, and wor-shipped the devil, as now they do, then God sent some to make us civil, others to make us christians. If such had not been sent us we had yet continued wild and uncivil, and worshippers of the devil: for our *civility* we were beholden to the Romans, for our *religion* to the Apostles and their disciples. Did we receive this blessing by oth-ers, and shall we not be sensible of those that are still as we were then? (*Sermon*, C4v)[28]

Utopia already does more, however, than suggest terms of rela-tion between England and America that later imperialists will ex-ploit. If More anticipates the notion that a comparable history of other-worldliness or utopicality should inspire England to occupy America, he also highlights the profoundly negative implications of such a claim. For Utopia too may colonize a land as other-worldly as itself, but to be other-worldly in this case is to be vacuous, *inane et vacuum*, either unreal or waste. And indeed, the imagina-tion of colonies in *Utopia*'s second book seems to follow on, to have required, the imagined wasting of England in the first. One of Hythloday's most celebrated tirades in book 1 concerns the practice of enclosing formerly common land, to which, Hythloday claims, English landowners have grown increasingly addicted: no longer "satisfied with the annual revenues and profits which their predecessors used to derive from their estates," and consequently lusting after the greater returns paid by wool, "they leave no ground to be tilled; they enclose every bit of land for pasture; they pull down houses and destroy towns, leaving only the church to pen sheep in." In short, they "devastate [*uastent*]" the country, turning "all human habitations and all cultivated land into a wilderness" (*U*, 66/67). Hythloday boasts that such rapacity and misery are unknown in Utopia, where "with equality of distribution, all men have abundance of all things" (102/3); communal ownership even prevents the sort of financial worries about home that make ambassadorships seem to More so heavy a burden (cf. 210/11, 238/39). In the narrative, of course, More thoroughly dismisses this glowing account of communism; but again *Utopia* answers an apparently intractable opposition with an alternative never overtly portrayed as such—property neither private nor communal but vacuous, the common ground that devastated England and empty America share. The unfortunate English tenants evicted by enclosures, the tillers who once caused the English isle to be "counted fortunate in the extreme" (68/69),[29] are not lost to the negative economy of *Utopia*. Rather, their evacuation is their passport, allowing them to resurface later under a new and more congenial regime—English farmers, *coloni* (66/67), become the occupants of Utopian colonies, *colonias* (136/37).[30] By conceiving the fates of England and America as intertwined, More in *Utopia* both raises and resolves the central problem of travel-as-service—how to leave home while retaining one's allegiance to it—yet he can positively formulate neither the question nor the answer: for *Utopia* argues that England will no longer seem to constrain, and America no longer seem to estrange, only when the English consider both places Nowhere.

II

Returning home two decades later from the Spanish ambassadorship for which More had apparently once been considered,[31] Sir Thomas Wyatt (1539) seems particularly determined to express the proper sentiments of an Englishman traveling in the interests of his country:

In Spain
Tagus farewell, that westward with thy streams
Turns up the grains of gold already tried:
With spur and sail for I go seek the Thames

Gainward the sun that showth her wealthy pride
And to the town which Brutus sought by dreams
Like bended moon doth lend her lusty side.
My king, my country, alone for whom I live,
Of mighty love the wings for this me give.
                    I flee

But Wyatt's apparent zeal is precisely what makes H. A. Mason call this "the strangest poem in the whole extant body of Wyatt's verse," because, as Mason rightly observes, "almost all his other reflections about life at the court of Henry VIII express only slightly less passionate disgust and repulsion" (*Wyatt*, 220).

At the time Wyatt was writing, of course, he had good personal reasons for sounding patriotic. In June 1538 the Pope had arranged a truce between Charles V of Spain and Francis I of France; in December he excommunicated Henry. As Henry's ambassador to Charles, Wyatt had the impossible task of preventing the alliance between Spain and France that shut England out.[32] Yet Wyatt had more to concern him than his failure: his fellow ambassadors Bonner and Heynes charged that it was deliberate. They claimed, among other things, that Wyatt resented his imprisonment in 1536 when Anne Boleyn and her alleged lovers had been executed; that he cared only "to please the emperor and Granvelle, and to be noted in the emperor's favor, whom he magnifieth above all measure"; and worst of all, when Henry rejected Charles's marriage plans for Henry and the Duchess of Milan, that Wyatt not only expected but desired his king to be "cast out the cart's arse"— expelled from Christendom like a piece of excrement or a criminal to be whipped and hanged.[33] Whether or not the accusations are true, they at least bear witness to the common understanding that Henry was in a bad way and, consequently, that treason was in the air. The arrest for treason soon afterwards of English lords associated with Wyatt signaled that both Henry's fears and Wyatt's own danger were, in fact, steadily increasing.[34]

In the light of these biographical details, it becomes easier to notice that Wyatt's effusion portrays him as overcoming a certain resistance. Wyatt envisions himself traveling not only toward England but away from the Tagus, which flows "westward"—that is, in the direction opposite to both Wyatt's homeward course and, implicitly, the course of the Thames (see figure 2). This curiously

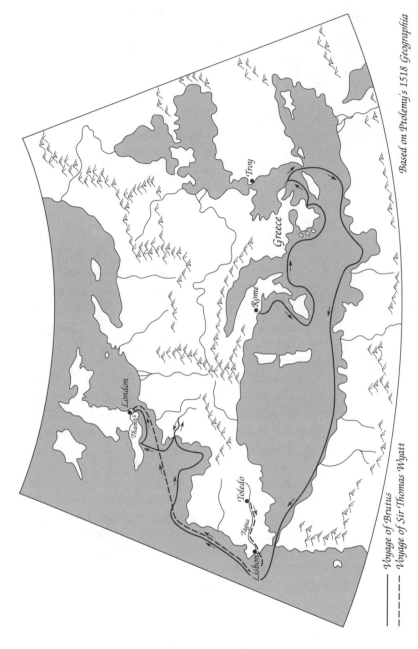

Based on Ptolemy's 1518 Geographia

Figure 2. A portion of the Ptolemaic world, showing England in the "utmost angle" and tracing the voyages of Wyatt and Brutus.

geographical counterpoint becomes still more mysterious when Wyatt describes his homeward journey in terms that make it seem doubly contrary, not just eastward but "gainward" or *against* the track of both the Tagus and the sun. In part, this depiction of himself voyaging as it were upstream helps Wyatt dramatize his homesickness: just as his impatience calls for "spur and sail" and finally "wings" to get him home, so it seems to exaggerate the obstacles in his way. But in other works by Wyatt a gainward voyage is a trope not of eagerness but of despair. One love poem, for instance, explicitly regrets the desire that leads, as in the Tagus poem, first to flight and then to a contrary eastward journey—

> Sometime I fled the fire that me brent
> By sea, by land, by water and by wind;
> And now I follow the coals that be quent
> From Dover to Calais against my mind.
> ("Sometime," 1–4)

—while others speak of Wyatt vainly striving "against the stream with all my power."[35] In fact, were the beloved toward whom Wyatt sails not king and country but a woman, one would be surprised to find Wyatt sounding anything but troubled. As even the most casual reader of his love poetry will notice, Wyatt invariably resists presenting his love life as either settled or chosen: instead, Wyatt the lover, like Wyatt the courtier, is constrained either to forsake, flee, or pursue. At the mercy of his "froward master" Cupid ("Mine old dear enemy," l. 1), Wyatt's loving is always thwarted, fromward.

Such is the case in the only other poem of Wyatt's beside "Tagus Farewell" that is headed "In Spain"—the canzone "So feeble is the thread." Wyatt complains in the poem

> That, when I think upon the distance and the space
> That doth so far divide me from my dear desired face,
> I know not how to attain the wings that I require
> To lift my weight that it might flee to follow my desire.
> (23–26)

Required to erase the distance between Wyatt and his object, the wings of mighty love here are not the only features of the canzone to recur in the different context of the Tagus poem[36] and therefore to cast doubt on Wyatt's desire for consummation in both works:

for when Wyatt in the epigram is finally about to cross the space dividing him from the beloved of his canzone, he abandons her as the professed object of his desire in favor of king and country, as if they reestablished the distance his journey would eliminate.[37] And in fact the Tagus poem imagines England itself as a scene of tantalizing division: though London and the Thames are joined, Wyatt presents their seemingly consummated love as the Thames only "lending" herself, and then only in the guise of a "bended" or crescent—a perpetually unfinished—moon.[38] What seems latent in the Tagus poem, in other words, are tokens of a dissatisfaction and resistance elsewhere typical of Wyatt, apparently tempered or suppressed in this case because here, paradoxically, Wyatt truly has reason to worry.

But why, if the poem does covertly manifest Wyatt's political anxieties, should Wyatt choose to associate the most prominent expression of resistance in the poem, his "gainward" voyage, not merely with the homeward direction of his travels but with their eastwardness? Some Tudors argued that every eastward voyage inevitably met resistance, sailing gainward not only the sun but the ocean's own following current;[39] yet why should Wyatt want to represent his political troubles under the guise of such travel difficulties, or conversely, what would make the westward course of the Tagus seem, for not just his oceangoing but his political career too, the path of least resistance?

As part of his argument to the city of Cordoba for improving navigation along the Tagus's southern competitor, the Guadalquivir, Hernan Perez de Oliva (1524) reminds his readers that, in the beginning, "dominion [*el Senorio*]" was held by the East, then by Asia, Persia, Chaldea, Egypt, Greece, Italy, and France; "now step by step approaching the West it appears in Spain [*agora de grado en grado viniendo al occidente parecio en España*]" (*Obras*, 134r). Not just empire, however, but the "world" itself has moved westward, so that "before we occupied the end of the world, and now we are in the middle of it [*antes ocupavamos el fin del mundo, y agora estamos en el medio*]" (133v). In other words, a New World has been discovered to the west and at the same time has been placed under the western dominion of the new Rome, Spain; by improving the Guadalquivir, Perez de Oliva maintains, Cordoba will be able to participate in the general good fortune of the empire, for "from these isles of the west will come so many ships laden with wealth, and so many will sail to them, that I believe they will leave a permanent imprint on the waters of the sea [*de estas Islas han de venir tantos navios cargados de riquezas, y tátos yrã, que pienso que señal hã de hazer enlas aquas dela mar*]" (135v).[40] Though Wyatt may well not have known Perez de Oliva, he could hardly not have heard about America. Towards the end of his ambassadorship, for instance, he had by special courier transmitted Sebastian Cabot's desire to leave his post as Charles's chief pilot and serve Henry instead.[41] But what must have made the New World particularly inescapable for Wyatt was the new Roman emperor's ownership of so much of it. The same month Wyatt left Spain, a triumphal arch in Florence honoring Charles showed him, in Roy Strong's words, "arrayed *à l'antique*, crowned with laurel and carrying the imperial sceptre, river gods at his feet, flanked, to his right, by the figures of Spain and New Mexico [*sic*], followed by Neptune, to show 'that the Western Ocean is dominated by his Majesty' " (Strong, *Splendour*, 79). Even Wyatt's bidding farewell to the Tagus implies his cognizance of America: since at least Roman times the river had served as a conventional synecdoche for the western bounds of the Ptolemaic world ("before we occupied the end of the world"),[42] yet now America had surpassed the Tagus both geographically and goldenly; and Charles's motto was *Plus ultra*, More beyond. The combination of map-tracing and resistance in Wyatt's poem begins to make more sense. If eastward for Wyatt is "gainward" the superseded Tagus—against the imperial union of gold and the sun that breeds it[43]—then the proper direction for Wyatt's journey must be west, the proper destination the golden Indies. And to turn away from this empire "without end" (Perez de Oliva, *Obras*, 133v), the *plus ultra* of an emperor whom Wyatt allegedly "magnifieth above all measure," means to turn instead toward an England excluded from Old and New World alike.

Now, it seems, the country Wyatt wants to "flee" is not Spain but England. This skeptical account of the Tagus poem does, after all, have the virtue of explaining why the poem adopts tropes of resistance from Wyatt's other work that appear to run contrary to the poem's overtly celebratory intentions.[44] Yet such an interpretation must itself suppress a striking feature of Wyatt's epigram— that, with the mention of Brutus dreaming, Wyatt's journey, however backward, assumes the shape of imperial prophecy. The great-grandson of Aeneas and the eponymous founder of Britain, Brutus in Geoffrey of Monmouth's *Historia Regum Britanniae* receives his "dreams" from Diana, who tells him that "beyond the setting of the sun" lies his true home, an island that will ultimately prove a second Troy far greater than Rome: "A race of kings will be born there from your stock and the round circle of the whole earth will be subject to them" (Geoffrey, *History*, 65). One might have thought that, as Waytt prepared to leave the capital of the largest European empire since that of Charlemagne, and to embark from the port to which Columbus's ships had first returned,[45] he would have been tempted to conclude that the Trojan home Diana had prophesied was not the one he would be sailing toward, but rather from. Yet instead, as with More in *Utopia*, an awareness of westward prospects seems to have led Wyatt back, gainward the sun, first to England's old status as itself a new world and then to a strange presentiment of England's future imperial power. Indeed, the comparison to More helps suggest how Wyatt's apparent negativity could actually represent an imperialist optimism. For if Wyatt's Brutus more directly represents English imperialist ambition than anything in *Utopia* does, it is also the case that, at the time Wyatt was writing, *Utopia*'s vision of a devastated and therefore potentially colonialist England had been realized in a manner too radical for even More to have imagined: England had been cast out of the community of the faithful, divided from all the Christian world.

In fact, the nearer England comes to seeming not only a separate world but a wasteland, the nearer it approaches the portentous island of Brutus's dreams. For to a degree neither Brutus nor modern commentators recognize, Diana as what Brutus calls the "terror of the forest glades, yet hope of the wild woodlands" (Geoffrey, *History*, 65)—the goddess of uncultivated ground—directs the course of Brutus's story throughout. Brutus is exiled from Italy for accidentally killing his father, Silvius, during a hunt (55); he aids fellow Trojans who, to escape slavery to the Greek king Pandarus, have fled to the woods (56); he defeats Pandarus in part by ambushing him in the woods (59–60); the first thing the Trojans do when they land at deserted Leogetia, the island where Diana prophesies a British empire, is to kill "all sorts of wild animals which they had discovered between the forest pastures and the woodlands" (64); trouble starts in Gaul when Corineus and his men go hunting in the king's forest (67); Corineus scatters the Gauls in a final battle by attacking from "a neighboring wood" in which he was concealed (70–71); and, except for "a few giants," Albion proves a deserted wilderness (72).[46] In short, the scene of the patricide continually recurs, each new instance retrospectively clarifying the transcendent rationale behind the original murder. The first stage of Brutus's journey (see figure 2), gainward the sun to Greece, transforms Silvius's death into the death of sylvan Italy as a home not just for the exiled Brutus but for all Troy: Brutus discovers that the woods of the Old World are only where Trojans hide from their conquerors. The trip to Leogetia, an island that "had remained uninhabited since it was laid waste [*vastata*] by a piratical attack in ancient times" (64), continues the reversal of Virgil's Trojan history back to the first flight from home; and it is in this setting reminiscent of Troy's ruins that Brutus learns of Diana's plans for a fresh Trojan start not in Italy but on an island "empty [*deserta*] and ready for your folk" (65). Surprisingly, the Utopian scruple about colonizing only wasteland turns up at the dawn of English history, when, as in *Utopia*, a representation of home devastated leads to a vision of new horizons. Here, the virginity of the power guiding Brutus gives this negative colonial connection a special point: Diana's decision to reveal her preference for a deserted island only after Brutus has reached a deserted island suggests that what she dislikes about Rome as a Trojan colony is the marriage of peoples arranged by Venus and then enforced by Juno, who demands that the Trojans mingle with and be submerged in Latin culture (Virgil, *Aeneid* 12.819–42). Just as Brutus had resisted the temptation to mix with the conquered Pandarus (Geoffrey, *History*, 62–63), so now, while heading westward (66), his battles with the Gauls end not in settlement but in further voyaging; and when he finally reaches the "promised island" (71) of Albion, only to discover a few giants still living there,[47] he quickly annihilates them. Finishing what the death of Silvius had begun, this murderous evacuation of England is what finally reinvents Troy's leader as not a wanderer but a founder, not sylvan Silvius but British Brutus. Now the same Trojans who were once forced into "the hidden depths of the forests" to maintain "the purity [*serenitas*] of their noble blood" (56) can truly raise a second Troy—not by escaping the wilderness of their defeat, however, but by embracing it as the positive condition of Troy's rebirth into something purer and thus, presumably, more powerful than the Roman blend. Wyatt, then, recollecting Brutus as he depicts himself sailing backward, pastward, from a new Rome and toward an England once again aparted, could be imagined reviving interest in an old, heroically empty promise still awaiting fulfillment, not "already tried."

Unfortunately, at the time Brutus too was in danger of being cast out the cart's arse. From a fairly canonical acceptance among medieval historians, the founder of Britain had in Tudor days lost much ground, most notoriously as a result of Polydore Vergil's *English History*, published five years before Wyatt wrote his poem. Much of the controversy surrounding Brutus replicates the political controversy of the day. Vergil the Italian disbelieved the Brutus story, in part because no classical source mentions it; while his critic Leland, an old friend of Wyatt's, considered that omission to be proof of a British history so dazzling that the envious Romans had tried to suppress it.[48] The imperial requirement that Britain be empty when Brutus arrives is, however, just the detail that led even English critics to accuse Geoffrey of lying.[49] In his preface to *The Pastyme of People* (c. 1530), John Rastell cites the opinion of "diverse great learned men" that, even if Brutus actually occupied Britain, it could not possibly have been uninhabited before him,

> considering that the rocks and mountains about Dover be so great and daily openly seen of them of Gallia and so small distance asunder and the sea so narrow that it may well be sailed in less than three hours and this country of Britain so fair so pleasant and so fertile that it is most likely that the people of Gallia should come over either to fish or for desire of knowledge of the land and to make some habitation therein and not to suffer it to be all desolate and unknown till the coming of Brute. (A2r)[50]

Rastell's history proper toys with the issue as it arises in Brutus's story: "Brute took shipping again and so sailing at the last arrived in the isle called Albion inhabited only with Brute beasts and giants where he took possession and called it after his own name Britain" (A2v). The mocking pun on Brute (which, of course, would also obtain in Geoffrey's Latin) suggests that the perfect allegorical fit between empty island and Trojan destiny is what makes Rastell skeptical; but skeptical about an historical claim, not necessarily about the English ideal represented.[51] A decade earlier, after all, Rastell had been one of the first English writers to discuss the real hidden world strangely anticipated by Geoffrey's fables about Britain: Experience in Rastell's *Interlude of the Four Elements* speaks of "new lands" found "westward" "that we never heard tell of before this / By writing nor other means" (ll. 737–39). While, unlike Brutus's Albion, these lands look inhabited, Rastell comments that the natives "as yet live all beastly" (780), and his subsequent evocation of an English colony in America demonstrates how, to him, the current brutishness of the natives makes them hardly count as inhabitants at all: after describing how a mutinous crew blocked his own New World voyage in 1517,[52] Rastell exclaims,

> O, what a thing had be then,
> If that they that be English men
>   Might have been first of all
> That there should have take possession
> And made first building and habitation
>   A memory perpetual!
>
> (762–767)[53]

Yet the English colony that Rastell imagines rising in the wilderness remains as fabled as Brutus's. Alluding to this passage, D. B. Quinn calls Rastell "the first man we know to make a plea for the systematic colonization of North America by Englishmen" (*New American World* 1:169), but Quinn's assessment mistakes Rastell's profoundly elegiac tone here, his sense that a miraculous English opportunity to give reality to Geoffrey's lie, to "have been first of all," is now forever lost.

Nevertheless, on a voyage to America in 1536, "M. Hore and diverse other gentlemen" (one of them Rastell's son, whose father died at around the same time in prison) do manage to enact the Brutus allegory, though with consequences far from imperial.[54] Reaching Labrador, apparently, the English look for savages but the savages flee; the New World empties itself to accommodate its conquerors. Unfortunately, the lack of savages means a lack of food, and the English begin to starve. The company mysteriously decreases, "and the officers knew not what was become of them," until

> it fortuned that one of the Company driven with hunger to seek
> abroad for relief found out in the fields the savor of broiled flesh,
> and fell out with one for that he would suffer him and his fellows
> to starve, enjoying plenty as he thought: and thus matter growing
> to cruel speeches, he that had the broiled meat, burst out into these
> words: If thou wouldst needs know, the broiled meat that I had was
> such a man's buttock. (*PN* 8:5–6)

Now the uninhabited land consumes its new possessors, fashions
out of the English the brutes they could not find. The captain
makes a long "notable Oration" against succumbing to such beastliness, whose only upshot—as famine increases—is that the English draw lots.

> And such was the mercy of God, that the same night there arrived
> a French ship in that port, well furnished with vittle, and such was
> the policy of the English, that they became masters of the same, and
> changing ships and vittling them, they set sail to come into En-
> gland. (6)

It would seem that the arrival of the well-stocked French, who like
their Gallic ancestors demonstrate a supposedly new world to
have been neither new nor all that alien, knocks the last bit of heroic potential out of the English story, and yet the narrator Hakluyt finds some relief at last in admiring a well-executed piece of
English treachery. For as Rastell explains, not to be "beastly" is to
be "cunning" (*Four Seasons*, 873). The only way such a failed confrontation with the wild can hope to call itself heroic, in other
words, is in escaping the New World and its beastliness, in returning home.

Back in England, the voyagers recuperate in the civilized security of Sir John Luttrell's castle. A gentleman unhappily associated
by name with the memory of American brutishness, one Mr.
Butts, "was so changed in the voyage with hunger and misery,
that Sir William his father and my Lady his mother knew him not
to be their son, until they found a secret mark which was a wart
upon one of his knees" (7). This apocryphal-sounding recognition
scene seems to have an earlier much-suffering homecomer in
mind, though how pathetically even in fabling their rediscovery of
England do the English make themselves heroes: the famous boar-
scar of Odysseus becomes a wart.[55] With the questionableness of
Brutus and the misadventures of Rastell and Hore in mind, it

again seems an indirect mark of dissatisfaction that Wyatt depicts himself as a Brutus going nowhere but to England.

Or at least a mark of half-satisfaction, as the moon of Wyatt's Thames is only half-achieved, lent. Like the other features of the poem that oppose England to Spain's imperial sun, this moon seems from one perspective to betray Wyatt's worries about an England that time has passed by, but from another to extend the imperial argument begun with Brutus, for the goddess of the wastelands who sends Brutus his dreams is also known as the goddess of the moon. Such an unstressed slide in the poem from one aspect of the triple Hecate to another helps account for Wyatt's interest in her: Diana, inhabiting three worlds at once, compensates for the geographical constraint toward which Wyatt drives. Brutus in Geoffrey's *History* celebrates the goddess for similar reasons; her three homes seem in his mind to qualify her as the best judge in matters of real estate:

> O powerful goddess, terror of the forest glades, yet hope of the wild woodlands, you who have the power to go in orbit through the airy heavens and the halls of hell, pronounce a judgment which concerns the earth. Tell me which lands you wish us to inhabit. (65)

But Wyatt's association of the moon with England also reflects an astrological tradition that imagined the moon producing in the English as unfixed a relation to the earth as the "lending" crescent of the Thames has in Wyatt's poem. To all appearances lacking the substance of other planets, made of mutability and borrowed light, the moon supposedly released the English from normal earthly bonds: as John Gower says,

> Bot what man under his [the moon's] power
> Is bore, he schal his places change
> And seche manye londes strange:
> And as this condicion
> The Mones disposicion
> Upon the land of Alemaigne
> Is set, and ek upon Bretaigne,
> Which now is cleped Engelond;
> For thei travaile in every lond.[56]

Apparently at odds with the Venetian who scorns England for thinking itself all the world, this astrological theory of English mobility actually follows from the idea of England's apartness also, and thus helps account for Thorne's own both insularist and expansionist view of his native island. England had seemed to the ancients another world—even at first "a fable and a lie" (Plutarch, *Lives* 5:25)—because it was not only separate from the Continent and barbarously distant from Rome but also too far north; to the ancients, that is, the always unsettled moon presided over a clime that itself appeared unsettleable.[57] If, then, Continental prejudice against England's habitability could explain the "lunatic" wanderlust of the English, even the confutation of this prejudice could also inspire the English to travel, for the mistake about England's habitability—a mistake of course particularly salient to the English—could suggest that other supposedly barren parts of the world would prove habitable too. Thorne, for example, employs such an argument in claiming that the northwest must be livable, and concludes in Utopian fashion, "Nothing in nature is made to be waste [*Nihil fit vacuum in rerum natura*]" ("Declaration," 50–51).[58] Again the apartness of England specially prepares it for occupying the American wasteland, and in fact the moon as the genius of this apartness figures even in More. Hythloday says that the island of Utopia, the negative of an older Nowhere, looks like a crescent moon, or more precisely, a moon *renascentis*, born anew; while its horns enfold "a wide expanse" of bay—that is, a void, an *inane* (*U*, 110/11). In Wyatt, the inverse image, the Thames as crescent and London its absent fullness, inscribes this incompleteness in England as the yearning for a consummation made possible only by England becoming less grounded, more moon and water.

Such a desire may look contrary, perverse, even inane, Wyatt's poem suggests, but only by the worldly standards of the Continent. Having explained that the Romans considered England's clime uninhabitable simply "because it was not inhabited [by them] at the time of the division into climes," Robert Anglicus (c. 1271) proceeds to quote Diana's prophecy to Brutus as, it would seem, proof not only that some ancients considered England eminently occupiable anyway ("Now it is empty and ready for your folk"), but also that England's supposed vacuousness at the time actually betokened an imperial promise greater than Rome's (Thorndyke, *Sphere*, 187/236–37). Three centuries later, Sir George

Peckham (1583) recalls how America too had once been "accounted a fantastical imagination, and a drowsy dream" (*True Reporte*, 449); here, one might think, was a new world that again argued the Old World nearsighted and at the same time, in fulfillment of Diana's prophecy, seemed to offer itself to the unworldly English as to the only conquerors truly capable of appreciating the sublime potential in vacuousness. Yet Wyatt's very dedication to his homeland, the conspicuous devotion that renders the tropes of resistance in his poem mysterious, seems as in More to keep England's contrary imperial hopes on the level of suggestion and "dreams" only.[59] In altering Wyatt's final line, "Of mighty love the wings for this me give," to "O mighty Jove the winds for this me give" (*Tottel's Miscellany* 1:81), Richard Tottel (1557) underscores the fact that Wyatt in his poem names no more transcendent a power or ambition than service, and profane service at that—not love of God, nor of Diana, nor of the imperial destiny Brutus's dreams foretold him; indeed, Wyatt never even explains the particular advantages or disadvantages of journeying gainward the sun.[60] Rather, just as Wyatt abandons voyaging westward and turns back within the bounds of the Ptolemaic map, so England's transcendent possibilities, Brutus dreaming, invert to the poet's submissive self—"My king, my country, alone for whom I live."

III

In the prefatory epistles to *Utopia*, More's Continental admirers describe him as a writer working under serious constraints. "Not only is he married," laments Erasmus,

> not only has he family cares to attend to, not only does he hold public office and handle an extraordinary number of legal cases, but he is distracted [*distrahitur*] by so many and weighty affairs of the realm that you wonder he finds time even to think of books. (*U*, 2/3)

Here learning replaces travel as the interest capable of drawing More from home,[61] while home conceived not just as domestic affairs but as aparted England threatens learning: "What would this wonderful, rich nature not have accomplished," Erasmus asks, "if his talent had been trained in Italy?" Erasmus believes, in short, that home has *wasted* More's literary powers—yet More has written *Utopia*, and the genius capable of producing it under such handicaps appears to Erasmus so unaccountable as to seem superhuman, *divinum* (U, 2/3).[62] The fact that the work thus miraculously produced should concern Nowhere only highlights the paradox of More's ability. More's own prefatory letter repeats the story of his distraction but turns his uncanny self-difference into a joke, his supposed ignorance about the location of the land he has created (38/39–42/43): as a place for which More himself cannot account, Utopia comes to represent, then, the apparent unplaceability of More's surprising powers. But More's invented island does more than register his ability to transcend distraction: it translates the nowhere that distracts into the very expression of More's transcendence. Powers wasted in the ostensible inanity of England not only prove that distraction a source of sublimity, but recreate inanity as itself sublime.

More's critic Germain de Brie (1520) prefers an unreconstructed view of More's own nowhereness: to him, More's Latin poems sound so unclassical and barbarous that they "are more reminiscent of poets indigenous to your Utopia" (CW 3:488/89); and he warns More that if Henry VIII "ever comes to perceive how enfeebled your Muse is in singing his praises, right then and there he will expel you from England and force you to move to Utopia" (494/95). What is interesting about this otherwise inevitable sarcasm[63] is that More's friends and even More himself beat Brie to the punch. In 1517 Richard Pace refers to More as "now I suppose more the Utopian not the Englishman" (Erasmus, *Correspondence* 5:57); but then More had introduced the idea very shortly after the publication of *Utopia*. A famous letter to Erasmus (1516) describes More's comical reaction upon hearing that his friend Cuthbert Tunstall admires *Utopia*:

> You can't think how I now fancy myself; I have grown taller, I hold my head higher, for I have continually before my eyes the perpetual office of prince which my Utopians are planning to confer on me. In fact I see myself already crowned with that distinguished diadem of corn-ears, a splendid sight in my Franciscan robe, bearing that venerable scepter consisting of a sheaf of corn, and accompanied by a distinguished company of citizens of Amaurote. (Erasmus, *Correspondence* 4:163)

This jeu d'esprit on the vanity of Nowhere and Shadow City, then on the vanity of More's pride in them, and finally on the vanity of his Utopian kingship, quickly modulates into an attack borrowed from *Utopia* on the inanity of real kings:

> Thus equipped, at the head of a long procession, I greet the envoys and the rulers of other countries, who are greatly to be pitied compared with us, however much they may foolishly pride themselves on their childish finery and the women's ornaments with which they are bedizened, loaded with chains of contemptible gold and made to look absurd with purple and gems and other such airy nothings [*bullatis nugis*].[64]

The sequence urbanely suggests, in other words, that More is specially cognizant of vanity because so elaborately entangled in it.[65] (As "Utopia" does for England, so More's own negative in *Utopia* names this exceptional inanity—Morus or "Foolish" becomes Hythloday or "Well Learned in Nonsense.")

But the publication of *Utopia* also makes More's special acuity available to others. Erasmus must have topics like the Utopian reduction of riches to *nugis*, trifles, in mind when he tells Antonius Clava (1517) that even the reader of *Utopia* risks becoming a Utopian: "You will feel that you have been transported into another world, everything there is so different" (*Correspondence* 4:223).[66] A poem "To the Reader" of *Utopia* by Cornelis de Schrijver takes Erasmus's claim one step further, and imagines the reader learning what it is like to be not simply from another world but otherworldly:

> Wilt thou know what wonders strange be in the land that late was
>   found?
> Wilt thou learn thy life to lead by diverse ways that godly be?
> Wilt thou of virtue and of vice understand the very ground?
> Wilt thou see this wretched world, how full it is of vanity?
>   (Robinson, trans., *Utopia*, 141)

"Vanity," *inane* (*U*, 30)—a vision of emptiness from emptiness, from the place that is no place. As the conclusion to More's letter is meant to demonstrate, such an airy perspective makes one sublimely liable to *contemptus mundi*: "I hoped to continue this delicious dream a little longer, but alas, dawn is breaking, and has shattered it and turned me out of my princedom, recalling me to my treadmill in the market-place. My only consolation is that I see real kingdoms do not last much longer" (Erasmus, *Correspondence* 4:164).⁶⁷

Now More's detractors, noting how smoothly such *contemptus* seems to lead him into a political career,⁶⁸ may once again call his negativity equivocation; but in fact the relation between More's worldliness and otherworldliness is stronger than the accusation of hypocrisy would allow, since a Utopian seeing the world as vacuous sees it colonizable. Like God when all the earth was *inane et vacua* (Vulgate Bible, Genesis 1.2), More envisioning the world's vanity does, after all, create his own new world. But then Utopia never escapes the conditions of its birth; rather, as Nowhere, it perpetuates the annihilation that spawned it. This paradox of an ironic detachment that itself falls prey to ironic detachment comes clearer not only in the endless critical debates about which of Utopia's features More seriously recommends but also in More's own assessments of his work. The letter to Erasmus, ostentatiously depicting More's Utopian vanity as modesty, had been anticipated in More's first letter to Erasmus (3 September 1516) on the subject of *Utopia*: "I send you my book on Nowhere [*Nusquamam*], and you will find it is nowhere [*nusquam*] well written" (Erasmus, *Correspondence* 4:66, *Opus* 2:339). The reply to Tunstall concerning Tunstall's letter of praise similarly stresses *Utopia's* inanity, calling the book a collection of "trifles [*nugas*]" (More, *Selected Letters*, 82, *Correspondence*, 85). Nothing, of course, is more traditional than this low estimation of a literary work, which is judged a "trifle" not merely on internal demerits but in its general uselessness to the real world. Sir Thomas Smith (1583), for example—sounding very much like More scolding Hythloday—claims that his *De Republica Anglorum* is no mere literary effort, for it anatomizes England

> not in that sort as *Plato* made his common wealth, or *Zenophon* his kingdom of Persia, nor as *Sir Thomas More* his *Utopia* feigned common wealths, such as never was nor never shall be, vain imaginations, fantasies of Philosophers to occupy the time and to exercise their wits: but so as England standeth and is governed at this day the xxviii of March *Anno* 1565, in the vii year of the reign and administration thereof by the most virtuous and noble Queen *Elizabeth*, daughter to King *Henry* the eight, and in the one and li year of mine age, when I was ambassador for her majesty in the court of France, the scepter whereof at that time the noble Prince and of

great hope *Charles Maximilian* did hold, having then reigned iiii
years. (144)

Yet, if it is perfectly conventional for John Marston (1598), say, to
imagine some "beard-grave" critic of his verse chiding, "Tut, tut,
a toy of an idle empty brain,"[69] More nevertheless embraces this
standard insult in a surprisingly thoroughgoing manner, by fash-
ioning the toy of his own *inane ac uacuum* brain as from the start
the "nowhere" vanity it might always be judged. Utopia, that is,
also reifies the conventionally impractical or unworldly character
of the literary work: in the most extraordinary assessment of his
trifle, More (January 1517?) calls it "a book which I think clearly
deserves to hide itself away forever in its own island" (*Selected
Letters*, 90, *Correspondence*, 88). The unworldly (literary) product of
an otherworld (England) that self-reflexively takes an otherworld
(Utopia) as its subject, *Utopia*, to More's mind, sublimely mocks
the worldly standards that would condemn it, but by the same
token acknowledges its sequestration from that world's positive
life.

With the slightness and dreaminess of his poem, Wyatt too
plays into the hands of graver opponents, his own flight from
gold suggesting, however, that, again like More, he disdains such
worldly critics in favor of an otherworldly system of value, where
"pride" alone is "wealthy." A professed antimaterialism is, of
course, a definitive feature of Wyatt's satires and psalms, and in
fact the more traditionally spiritual-minded "If thou wilt mighty
be" rewrites the Tagus poem's turning from gold and, implicitly,
from the New World in no uncertain terms:

> All were it so thou had a flood of gold,
> Unto thy thirst yet should it not suffice.
> And though with Indian stones a thousandfold
> More precious than can thyself devise
> Ycharged were thy back, thy covetise
> And busy biting yet should never let
> Thy wretched life, ne do thy death profit.
>
> (15–21)

Such a rejection of "Indian" riches crops up even in the love poems: the lyric "To seek each where," for instance, counterposes
the immaterial gift of Wyatt's heart to both "goldsmiths' work" (8)

and treasures for which one would search through "France, Spain, and Ind, and everywhere" (3). But in the Tagus poem, and quite unlike More, Wyatt suggests that he is mysteriously constrained to his otherworldliness, a driven Brutus. In part, I have argued, Wyatt's implied ambivalence mirrors what was a recent clarification of England's apartness, in which England had been cast out the world's arse (hence Wyatt's reluctance) and yet had also positively realized a destiny—and perhaps faith—separate from and superior to that world (hence Wyatt's desire). In another poem on his contrariness, however, Wyatt figures himself reluctantly pursuing no longer the trifle England but the trifle poetry, which he imagines an otherworld not merely evoked, like Utopia, but materially presented:

> Though I myself be bridled of my mind
> Returning me backward by force express,
> If thou seek honor to keep thy promise,
> Who may thee hold, my heart, but thou thyself
>   unbind?
> Sigh then no more, since no way man may find
> Thy virtue to let, though that frowardness
> Of fortune me holdeth. And yet as I may guess,
> Though other be present, thou art not all behind.
> Suffice it then that thou be ready there
> At all hours, still under the defence
> Of time, truth, and love to save thee from offence,
> Crying "I burn in a lovely desire
> With my dear master's, that may not follow,
> Whereby his absence turneth him to sorrow."
>   (*Collected Poems*, 25)

The first two lines nicely capture the mystery of Wyatt's restraint: does "bridled of my mind" mean bridled by my mind, in respect to my mind, or according to my mind? And whose is the "force express"? Still more striking in relation to the Tagus poem is another gainward journey, "Returning me backward"; yet here no geography accounts for Wyatt's awkward trajectory. Instead, the poem offers itself as an image of Wyatt's backwardness, for to be writing a poem—and one, moreover, addressed not to Wyatt's beloved but to his own heart—means that Wyatt must of necessity have turned from his beloved. In fact, the word that announces Wyatt's gainward journey here, *returning*, figures his backwardness as the continued poetizing or re-versing constituted by the second line. In place of the Tagus poem's outmoded Old World geography, in other words, is Wyatt's typography, the printed poetry that unaccountably returns backward from the right margin of one line to the left margin of the next; while here the "force" that keeps Wyatt within these strict yet inexplicable bounds—"Imprisoned in liberties" ("It may be good," l. 11)—remains mysterious, unspoken, because it resides in the absence of words, the blank spaces between which the island poem is compressed.

Of course, the poem's margins and allusiveness are, again, wholly traditional features of poetry in general; Bacon (1605) says that "poesy is a part of learning in measure of words for the most part restrained, but in all other points extremely licensed" (*Works* 3:343).[70] Yet in Wyatt the constrained incompleteness of literary work in this poem and of England in the Tagus poem—an incompleteness as it were more positively or materially (typographically and geographically) realized than in More—inversely suggests the spiritual freedom tacitly identified in the Tagus poem with Diana. The poem about Wyatt's bridling provides simpler explanations of this paradoxical relation between material constraint and spiritual liberty: by its compression and therefore portability the poem is able to speak its heart before the beloved, like the partial heart it bespeaks—only a part of Wyatt, yet therefore, in its entire dedication to the beloved, free. More crucially, however, Wyatt constrained to inhabit only these parts of himself suggests more of Wyatt than those parts can bear. And in fact this ennobling frustration appears in the Tagus poem as not just a political but also a poetical submission. For the Tagus traditionally marks the poet's surpassing power also. As the world's golden, westward end, it naturally came to represent the furthest reach of merely earthly good. In perhaps the most famous of the *Amores*, for example, Ovid declares:

> Verse is immortal, and shall ne'er decay.
> To verse let kings give place, and kingly shows,
> And banks o'er which gold-bearing Tagus flows.
> Let base-conceited wits admire vile things,
>   Fair Phoebus lead me to the Muses' springs.
>   (1.15.32–36)[71]

In the Tagus poem Wyatt turns away from this king-conquering poetic ambition (warranted by Apollo, the god of poetry and of the sun) just as he does from the New World—or rather, he turns both sublimity and New World *within*. Since at least the eighteenth century critics have emphasized the unexpressed, esoteric reach of this slight lyric. *Sprezzatura*—showing what seems to be less than one is capable of so as to hint at the existence of more—is a handy name for the strange mixture in Wyatt of what Tottel called deep-witted and C. S. Lewis considered after-dinner verse;[72] but Wyatt depends for his effect not merely on the effortlessness that Castiglione describes in his *Courtier*.[73] Rather, Wyatt stresses the gain-wardness of his journey (*gainward*, incidentally, appears to be his coinage), the need for spur and sail, the resistance encountered by his show of less: as if the *plus ultra* that might otherwise be thought available to Wyatt—imperial favor, American gold, immortal verse—were less sublime than the inexplicable force that turns Wyatt inward as if against his will, were less a transcendent mystery than his submission and constraint.[74]

In the Wyatt family, Wyatt's father seems to have pioneered this backward mode of self-idealization. The story goes that once, during the two years Richard III imprisoned, and occasionally racked, Sir Henry Wyatt for his allegiance to Henry VIII's father, Richard demanded of him, "Why art thou such a fool? Thou servest for moonshine in the water. Thy master is a beggarly fugitive. Forsake him and become mine. I can reward thee, and I swear unto thee I will" (quoted in Muir, *Life and Letters*, 1). What is so striking about the analogy between generations is the way Wyatt's poem apparently embraces a Richard-like characterization of loyalty.[75] Returning to his own "beggarly fugitive" of a master, Wyatt imagines the Thames "like bended moon"—like Richard's moonshine in the water; imagines his homeland sought "by dreams"; gives his dreamer, Brutus, a name no more, perhaps, than a fable; and finally consigns this strange expression of his patriotism to frivolous poetry. If, under such constraints, king and country come to resemble the trifles that England's more powerful enemies or a *contemptus* vision might consider them, Wyatt nevertheless presents himself as not only fleeing with the wings of freedom to their prison but also rediscovering their heroic potentiality. For it is by his submission to England's disappointing limits that Wyatt apparently hopes to begin translating himself into a Brutus and his aparted home into a limitless empire. Rather than journey beyond the Tagus either to the heavenly riches that one should prefer before "all the gold that the rivers Tagus & pactolus reverse and turn in their red sands,"[76] or to the new world of treasure in America, Wyatt finds his dream of empire arising from an otherworldly island within old-worldly bounds, from desires and powers transcendently constrained to the seemingly empty object of England so as to render them objectless, free, and yet with an object in view. This logic, too, is more familiar as a feature of Wyatt's love poetry. In "Mine old dear enemy," for instance, Wyatt complains of the perversity with which Cupid has afflicted him:

> He hath made me regard God much less than I ought,
> And to myself to take right little heed,
> And for a woman have I set at nought
> All other thoughts, in this only to speed.
>
> (29–32)

A Platonic Cupid replies that, on the contrary,

> I gave him wings, wherewith he might fly
> To honor and fame, and if he would farther,
> By mortal things, above the starry sky:
> Considering the pleasure that an eye
> Might give in earth, by reason of his love,
> What should that be that lasteth still above?
>
> (128–33)

To fly "by mortal things, above the starry sky": just as Wyatt finds a new world not outside the old map but within it, so to turn within bounds generally becomes for him the paradoxical means and expression of transcending them.

IV

When a few decades later Diana, or Cynthia, assumes the shape of England's queen, many of her subjects, my next chapter will argue, become far more straightforward than Wyatt in celebrating their confinement Nowhere. One Elizabethan in particular takes

Wyatt's sublime restraint, his trifling, to a positively literal extreme.

> The tenth of August [1576] a rare piece of work and almost incredible, was brought to pass by an Englishman born in the city of London named Peter Bales, who by his industry and practice of his pen, contrived and writ within the compass of a penny in Latin, the Lord's prayer, and creed, the ten commandments, a prayer to God, a prayer for the queen, his posy, his name, the day of the month, the year of our Lord, and the reign of the queen. And on the seventeenth of August next following at Hampton court he presented the same to the queen's majesty in the head of a ring of gold, covered with a crystal, and presented therewith an excellent spectacle by him devised for the easier reading thereof: wherewith her majesty read all that was written therein with great admiration, and commended the same to the lords of the council, and the ambassadors, and did wear the same many times upon her finger.[77]

The poor matter of the penny is made to bear the great spirit of religion and majesty; Bales, by his confinement to the penny's trifling bounds, demonstrates an "almost incredible" or nearly otherworldly ability; while he receives in turn, as the sublime correlative to that ability, the "great admiration" of queen, council, and foreign dignitaries. So remarkable a feat looks less exceptional, however, when one turns to the artists who were Bales's contemporaries; as Roy Strong notes, "England's greatest contribution to the art of painting during the Renaissance was the portrait miniature."[78]

If Bales and the miniaturists, then, more dramatically materialize their constraint than Wyatt does, other Elizabethans prove more explicit than Wyatt in discussing the value of such constraint. Roger Ascham (1570), for instance, justifying "why I, a man of good years and of no ill place (I thank God and my prince), do make choice to spend such time in writing of trifles," defends himself by way of a sublime authority who could work almost as well for Bales—"Homer, who, within the compass of a small argument of one harlot and one good wife, did utter so much learning in all kind of sciences as, by the judgment of Quintilian, he deserveth so high a praise that no man yet deserved to sit in the second degree beneath him" (*Scholemaster*, 54–55).[79] George Chapman reiterates these terms of praise when, like the commenders of More, he labels Homer "our divinest poet" not despite Homer's constraints but because of them. Describing Homer's poetry on the shield of Achilles as if Homer had literally confined himself to the shield's limits, Chapman (1598) maintains that "nothing can be imagined more full of soul and humane extraction: for what is here prefigured by our miraculous Artist but the universal world, which being so spacious and almost immeasurable, one circlet of a Shield represents and imbraceth?" (*Chapman's Homer* 1:543). Commenting the same year on his own poetry—his additions to Marlowe's *Hero and Leander*—Chapman can now overtly articulate the negative self-idealization that Wyatt only suggested: he speaks of himself as "being drawn by strange instigation to employ some of my serious time in so trifling a subject, which yet made the first author, divine *Musaeus*, eternal" (*Poems*, 132).

In his own writings Bales himself bears witness to the fact that, for an insular nation governed by a virgin queen, the embracement of restrictions seems to become an especially attractive aesthetic ideal. Elaborating the theory and practice of his alleged invention, "brachygraphy"—that is, shorthand[80]—Bales (1590, 1597) and his own commenders present his minutiae as not just materially but ideally prodigious, as in fact a powerful new form of *sprezzatura*. "Few words, much sense: few lines, the matter long: / In a little space much stuff contained is" (*Arte*, A4v), one commendatory poem claims; but Bales's conceits on his trifling are at once more modest and more fulsome: "Be it permitted me the least of thousands through your Honorable course of pardon," he writes Sir Christopher Hatton, "to offer up this small mite, proceeding from my slender capacity" (*Writing*, A2r, *Arte*, A2r). Later in the book Bales claims that shorthand paradoxically serves "an infinite number of uses" (*Arte*, B1v–B2r), one of which in particular will help England too in transforming smallness into magnitude, constraint into expansion: brachygraphy, explains Bales, is "greatly available for Ambassadors; Messengers, and Travelers into far countries, for the ready and speedy description of the place, manners, customs, policy and government of each nation" (*Arte*, B1v; cf. *Writing*, C1r). But then the report of Bales's penny in Holinshed had already followed an extraordinary instance of England extending its power by exploiting the ostensibly worthless: one of Martin Frobisher's men returning from their search for the Northwest

passage "brought from thence a piece of a black stone, much like
to a seacoal in color, which being brought to certain goldfiners in
London, to make a say thereof, found it to hold gold, and that
very richly for the quantity" (*Chronicles* 4:330).[81] In Elizabeth's otherworldly kingdom, what is a trifle to the rest of the world becomes a treasure.

Yet this new pride about trifling also makes the Elizabethans
more vulnerable than their predecessors to the charge of mere inanity. Thomas Nashe (1589) sees Bales's penny as an instance of
spirit depreciated, a folly more appropriate to the old English
world that had been darkened by papistry than to the new one
enlightened by truth:

> And here I could enter into a large field of invective against our
> abject abbreviations of Arts, were it not grown to a new fashion
> among our Nation, to vaunt the pride of contraction in every man-
> uary action: insomuch that the *Pater noster*, which was wont to fill a
> sheet of Paper, is written in the compass of a penny: whereupon
> one merrily affirmed that proverb to be derived, *No penny, no pater
> noster*. (*Works* 3:318)

To Nashe, rather than signal the essential disproportion of matter
to spirit, Bales's feat of "contraction" seems on the contrary to insist, in the papist's worldly manner, that spirit be equated with
matter, even the least matter possible: no penny, no pater noster.
The equivocality in trifling that Nashe highlights, its capacity to
exalt but also to debase, can make the Elizabethan expansionist as
well seem either wonderfully superior to practical obstacles or lu-
dicrously diminished by them.[82] Frobisher's voyage, for example,
ends badly: no more successful a colonizer than Cabot, he soon
finds that his miraculous piece of gold really was just a black stone
all along; and his most productive behavior toward the natives he
encounters is to capture one, who quickly dies.[83] Yet these New
World "brutes" whom Rastell considered incapable of real habitation anyway are not so much absent from English colonialist plans
as rather the absences upon which those plans depend. Eden
(1555) assures his readers that, unlike "the Jews and Turks who
are already drowned in their confirmed error," America's Indians
are open-minded about Christianity: in fact, "these simple gen-
tiles living only after the law of nature, may well be likened to a
smooth and bare table unpainted, or a white paper unwritten,

upon the which you may at first paint or write what you list, as you can not upon tables already painted, unless you raze or blot out the first forms" (*Decades*, 57).[84] The Indians, that is, are said to possess not only lands but minds that are *inane ac uacuum*—for the sublimely inane English, special prospects, because truly vacuous and therefore colonizable versions of the poet's idle empty brain.

2

Eliza and Elizium

Out from the world, yet on the ground,
Even in a place of bliss.
—Thomas Blenerhasset,
A Revelation (1582)

The year Elizabeth I came to power, England itself seemed to have lost its last claim to imperial grandeur, its sole remaining foothold on the Continent, Calais.[1] The accession at so awkward a time of a female prince, and an arguably bastard heretical female prince at that, made England's new isolation look all the more dangerous: the following year an Englishman at the court of Philip II likened England confronting the far greater Catholic powers of France and Spain to "a bone thrown between two dogs."[2] As Elizabeth began her rule, in other words, one would probably not have expected the next forty years to produce what has usually been considered England's greatest literature; and even modern criticism, with all the advantages of hindsight, has had a hard time accounting for the paradox. Those scholars interested in associating Elizabethan England's literary and political fates have offered basically two explanations for Elizabethan literature: what might be called an expansive and a repressive hypothesis, neither of which entirely fits the facts.

The first, the expansive hypothesis, is more obviously inaccurate. According to Sir Walter Raleigh the critic, "That marvelous summer time of the imagination, the Elizabethan age, with all its wealth of flowers and fruit, was the gift to England of the sun that bronzed the faces of the voyagers and of the winds that carried them to the four quarters of the world" (*English Voyages*, 151–52). But by the 1590s, the period of Elizabethan England's greatest literary activity, Elizabeth's voyagers had very little to feel expansive about: no one had found either a northeast or a northwest pas-

Figure 3. Medal of Queen Elizabeth I (obverse) and England (reverse), probably by Nicholas Hilliard, c. 1590. A bulging Elizabeth personifies little England's illimitable potentiality. The obverse is inscribed *"Ditior in toto non alter circulus orbe"* (There is no richer circle in all the world). The reverse inscription reads *"Non ipsa pericula tangunt"* (Not even dangers can touch). (By courtesy of the Trustees of the British Museum.)

sage; England's only New World colony (in Virginia) had failed, twice; and the most famous voyagers themselves—Drake, Cavendish, Frobisher, Hawkins—had all died at sea.

G. K. Hunter sees the same depressing fortune dogging the lives of the Elizabethan poets; for Hunter and the repressive hypothesis, Elizabethan literary sublimity is the product precisely of frustration, a sublimated expression of repressed anxiety about the political careers of both poet and nation.[3] The work of Frances Yates and her followers presents the bizarre cult of Elizabeth as the perfect illustration of a nation increasingly shunning the truth about the inconsequence it shares with Elizabeth: "The lengths to which the cult of Elizabeth went," argues Yates, "are a measure of the sense of isolation which had at all costs to find a symbol strong enough to provide a feeling of spiritual security in face of the break with the rest of Christendom."[4] Yet, in the manner of most psychologistic explanations of social phenomena, this repressive hypothesis exaggerates a likely response of some Elizabethans into the essential response of all. The limitations of Yates's position, for instance, become apparent as soon as one turns to a fan of Elizabeth's who is both foreign and papist, who is, indeed, the pope: "She certainly is a great Queen," exclaims Sixtus V,

> and were she only a Catholic she would be our dearly beloved. Just look how well she governs! She is only a woman, only mistress of half an island, and yet she makes herself feared by Spain, by France, by the Empire, by all.[5]

For Sixtus, Elizabeth's overt insignificance—her gender and her small dominion—is not an embarrassment to be hidden, but rather the very basis of Elizabeth's real claims to grandeur. This chapter will argue that the paradoxical literary ebullience of Elizabethan England derived in the same way not merely from a suppressed recognition of the inconsequence of country and queen, but also, and more definitively, from an embrace of that inconsequence. A poetry intimidated by classical and modern Italy, and more generally by a traditional contempt for its uselessness, came increasingly to perceive its common cause with a polity as marginal to the world of new Rome as it had been to the world of the old. In other words, poetry's poor reputation now seemed paradoxically to transport it into the heart of a depreciated nation's affairs. I will conclude by indicating how this coincidence of national and poetic marginality helps explain why what was perceived by many at the time as the major instance of Elizabethan literary sublimity, the epic declaring England an empire that "both first and second *Troy* shall dare to equalize," should have been a poem about a subject so ostensibly trifling as a fairy queen.

I

For the Elizabethans, the conception of England as an embarrassment was a very old one. In Virgil's first eclogue, as I have said, Meliboeus laments his exile to the ends of the earth, perhaps to *penitus toto divisos orbe Britannos*, the Britons wholly divided from all the world. *Divisos* here means more about England than its distance and barbarity relative to Rome;[6] quoting Virgil's line, Holinshed's *Chronicles* (1587) note that, because the ancients excluded England from their tripartite world, "it is not certain unto which portion of the earth our Islands . . . should be ascribed." Though in one sense simply a final indignity, this geographical ambiguity already begins to suggest an altogether different valuation of England. Holinshed elsewhere notes that when Aulus Plautius announced his plan to conquer Britain, "the soldiers hearing of this voyage were loath to go with him, as men not willing to make war in another world." The Otherworld, the land of spirits and of the dead, had often been presumed to lie in the western ocean; according once again to the *Chronicles*, England's westward location, along with the surprising, almost supernatural mildness of its climate, caused Plutarch to affirm "a part of the Elisian fields to be found in Britain."[7] England's otherness could, then, be construed either as barbarous or as heavenly; and one would naturally expect the English to incline toward the brighter side of the question: a medieval anecdote invoked by Camden (1590), Speed (1611), and Selden (1613), among others, relates how, when the pope "had elected *Lewis* of *Spain*, to be the Prince of those fortunate Islands [the Canaries], . . . our countrymen were verily persuaded, That he was chosen Prince of *Britain*."[8] Yet what is especially interesting about postclassical English history is the development of a tradition that refuses merely to reject the bad barbarous view in favor of the good heavenly one, but rather attempts to forge an essential relation between the two.

One catches an early glimpse of this paradoxical tradition in Bede's famous anecdote about the English-loving pope Saint Gregory. Before Gregory became pope, relates Bede, he encountered some boys for sale in a Roman marketplace, and asked

> what was the name of that nation, or people? And when answer was given, that they were called *Angles*, or english. Truly not without cause, quoth he, they be called *Angles*, for they have an *Angels face*. And it is meet such men were partakeners, and inheritors with the Angels in heaven. (*History*, 48v)

Barbarity and otherworldliness meet here not only in the narrative connection between slaves and angels but in a triple pun: angels as Angli, and Anglia as an England so named because located, as Spenser declares, in "the utmost angle of the world" (see figure 2).[9] Both sorts of loose relation—the narrative and punning connections—reappear on a more worldly level with Geoffrey of Monmouth's Brutus, the eponymous founder of Britain. As I explained in my previous chapter, Brutus journeys to the wilderness of England at first because, in obvious contrast to Rome's founder, pious Aeneas, he has been exiled from civil Italy as a patricide, but later because Phoebe promises him that "a race of kings will be born there from your stock and the round circle of the whole earth will be subject to them" (*History*, 65). These apparently disparate threads in Brutus's story are matched by contradictory associations in his name—either Brutus the noblest Roman or Brute the barbarian—that a Tudor writer like John Weever (1601) can nevertheless combine as if they were easily compatible: Weever defends England by arguing that "If we be brutish, you must it impute, / That we be so in memory of Brute" (*Whipping*, 431–32). Uncannily, a Lollard named Walter Brute, in a sermon reprinted by Foxe, is the first writer I have found who gives the ambiguity in Bede and Geoffrey, and the strange joke in Weever, a solidly explicable, indeed scriptural basis. Since "it is well known," Brute argues, "that this kingdom is a wilderness or a desert, because the philosophers and wise men did not pass upon it, but did leave it for a wilderness and a desert, because it is placed without the climates," then Britain must be the wilderness to which the woman of Revelation 12, the True Faith, flees.[10] Brute decides, in other words, that Britain's exclusion from the Roman, now corrupted papistical world, is precisely what constitutes its real heavenliness.

With the Reformation, and the excommunication of both Henry VIII and Elizabeth, the Tudors found this account of England's greatness as it were thrust upon them. But of course, Protestant Elizabeth in particular also seemed to vindicate Brute's faith in the English heterocosm, the sort of optimism that could lead George North (1581) to regard Gregory's Angle/angel pun as a prophecy that England would become "the place of [God's] elect" (*Stage*, 87).[11] First, it was said, Elizabeth reestablished England's otherness, both temporal and spiritual, by freeing England from the influence of Mary's Spanish and Catholic husband Philip II.[12] John Stubbs (1579) affirms that "it hath been always yielden unto her Majesty for the chief and first benefit done to this kingdom that she redeemed it, and yet not she but the Lord by her, from a foreign king" (*Gaping Gulf*, 36); while Nicholas Bacon (1571) considers "the first and chief" benefit of the queen's reign her "restoring and setting at Liberty God's holy Word amongst us" (D'Ewes, *Compleat Journal*, 138). (Naturally, English Catholics took a dimmer view of England's renewed otherness: for them, a nation "severed in faith and communion from the whole world [*a toto orbe fide & commu-*

nione distracti]" deserved to be considered "the desolate Isle of piti-
ful England."[13]) Second, Elizabeth brought England peace, a blessing that, as an orator before the queen in 1578 remarked, the Continent itself sorely lacked:

> There be that call England another world, which I think may be
> most true in this our age: for whereas all lands on every side of us
> are afflicted with most grievous wars, and tossed with floods of dis-
> sension, your Highness governing our stern, do sail in a most peac-
> able haven, and severed from the world of mischiefs, do seem after
> a sort to be taken up into a heaven of happiness.[14]

Most extraordinary about Elizabeth herself, however, was the virginity, the "impregnable virginity,"[15] that seemed not only to figure England's separateness and purity but actually to help preserve them, by literally fending off "foreign kings"; as Lyly in
Euphues' Glass for Europe (1580) declares about England's inviolabil-
ity, "This is the only miracle that virginity ever wrought, for a little
Island environed round about with wars, to stand in peace" (*Works*
2:210).[16] The miracle, one might say, was the very fitness of Elizabeth's virginity in relation to her other achievements, the astound-
ing contingency that this virginity (itself a type of contingency)
should appear at so apt a moment in English history. Elizabeth
could seem, in other words, the providential consummation of
England's efforts to realize itself *as* an island.[17] William Patten
(1575) lists "Ad Insulam" or "To the Isle" (*Calender*, 64r) as one
derivation of the queen's name; and Henry Constable boasts that
even if the seas surrounding England were to dry up, Elizabeth's
personal unattainability alone would keep England insular: "Thine
eye hath made a thousand eyes to weep / And every eye [a] thousand seas hath made / And each sea shall thine Isle in safety
keep."[18]

From the very start of her reign, Elizabeth herself made sure
that the story of her life—whose "whole course," North declares,
"is miraculous" (*Stage*, 95)—would seem to epitomize England's
struggle to free itself from Rome's dominion. Her triumphal procession into London in 1558 began from the Tower that had once
held her prisoner and now heard her thanksgiving prayer:

> I acknowledge that thou hast dealt as wonderfully and mercifully
> with me, as thou didst with thy true and faithful servant Daniel thy
> prophet whom thou deliveredst out of the den from the cruelty of

the greedy and raging Lions: even so was I overwhelmed, and only
by thee delivered. (*Queenes Majesties Passage*, 38–39)[19]

If her spectators missed the implicit analogy between Mary's reign
and the Babylonian Captivity, or between England's future and
Elizabeth's journey from her former prison to the rich pageants of
London, "her grace's loving behavior" toward the people, so opposite to Mary's aloofness, "indeed implanted a wonderful hope
in them touching her worthy government in the rest of her reign"
(16). This hope comprised, though as yet only vaguely, more than
the conviction that England's government had at last come home.
Representing in procession the active personification of England's
latent strength, Elizabeth by her winning condescension illumi-
nated the peculiar logic of that strength:

> What more famous thing do we read in ancient histories of old time,
> than that mighty princes have gently received presents offered them
> by base and lowly personages. If that be to be wondered at (as it is
> passingly) let me see any writer that in any one prince's life is able
> to recount so many precedents of this virtue, as her grace showed
> in that one passage through the city. How many nosegays did her
> grace receive at poor women's hands? how ofttimes stayed she her
> chariot, when she saw any simple body offer to speak to her grace?
> A branch of Rosemary given to her grace with a supplication by a
> poor woman about fleetbridge, was seen in her chariot till her grace
> came to westminster, not without the marvelous wondering of such
> as knew the presenter and noted the Queen's most gracious receiv-
> ing and keeping of the same. (*Queenes Majesties Passage*, 38)

Elizabeth can see the value in what the world deems valueless, the
worth in particular of "the poor and needy" who "may look for
[hope] at her grace's hand" (38), in general of poor excluded England; and primarily that value is, as the passage labors to establish, the very quality of vision exhibited by England's "worthy"
queen.

But then Elizabeth had a special incentive to read the value in
English poverty, for she herself was what the (Roman) world
deemed valueless—a bastard, a woman, and finally an excommu-
nicate. In a letter to Burleigh, Calvin demonstrates that even the
friends of Elizabeth could openly call her trifling, as long as at the
same time they attested to her providential value in improving
their own vision: while Calvin admits that he believes "the government of women . . . a deviation from the original and proper

order of nature, . . . to be ranked no less than slavery among the punishments consequent on the fall of man," yet

> there were occasionally women so endowed that the singular good qualities which shone forth in them, made it evident that they were raised up by divine authority; either that God designed by such examples to condemn the inactivity of men, or for the better setting forth of His own glory. (Quoted in Neale, *Queen Elizabeth*, 64)

By this account, it is Elizabeth's very immateriality that allows God to shine through her, and therefore the less powerful Elizabeth appears, explains William Lightfote (1587), the more powerful should be God's interest in her: "And forasmuch as thy glory is chiefly showed by bringing to pass thy will through weak means & feeble instruments, assist her we pray thee with thy spirit, that being weak in herself she may be strengthened by thy arm" (*Complaint*, I2r–v).[20] James Sanford (1576) accentuates the disparity between weak woman and godly might in another etymology of Elizabeth's name, which he follows with topoi of disparity already familiar to us:

> God surely preserveth her grace, having the name of ELIZABETH, to wit, *god's fullness*, god defendeth us *Angli*, as *Angeli*, according to saint Jerome's [Gregory's] allusion: God keepeth us, as if we were not of this world, for so Virgil calleth us *divisos orbe Britannos*. (*Houres*, A3r–v)

A virgin queen was, however, not simply more of the same old story about otherworldly England; the conflation of Elizabeth with older topoi made more pressing a particular interpretation of them. The corner of the world that classical England occupied had seemed to antiquity immense—Solinus, for example, asserted that England "deserveth the name almost of an other World" because of "the largeness thereof every way" (quoted in Bennett, "Britain," 115)—but the break with Catholic Europe, the loss of Calais, the extension of Spanish power throughout worlds old and new, and finally England's personification in an ostensibly trifling queen, increasingly committed the English otherworld to a sense of its own apparent inconsequence: as Anthony Marten (1588) says, "We be here removed in a corner from the rest of the world, and may be measured with a span, in comparison of all Christendom besides" (*Exhortation*, B2r–v). Significantly, perhaps the most extravagant praise of the queen, Edward Hellwis's *Marvell, Deciphered* (1589),[21] stresses again and again the weakness of both Elizabeth and her England. Hellwis adopts Walter Brute's reading of Revelation 12, though with crucial modifications.[22] The residence of True Faith in the English wilderness has now become a last-ditch defense: "This said Church of Christ and son of God, by the malice of Sathan, is brought unto her last decay, and left as desolate but only in an angle of the world, the engine of man being utterly incapable of all remedy or relief for the same" (*Marvell*, Bv). Yet Revelation's woman crying in pain is at the same time no longer simply the True Faith but the new Virgin, who "hath travailed to bring forth this man child Christ Jesus, notoriously in the sight of the world: which is to say, confessed, published, and advanced his holy laws, his sacred word, and most glorious Gospel" (6–7). England's material weakness, personified in the frailty and infertility of Elizabeth, has become a pledge of its spiritual strength.[23]

What makes Hellwis so confident about this strength is the fact that his commentary follows, and celebrates, England's victory over the Spanish Armada. No event, no seemingly providential realization of English insularity, better enabled the English to elaborate the traditional topoi of their disproportionate potentiality. The disparity in apparent strength between the Spanish and English navies became a set piece of English literature almost before the battle began. Daniel Archdeacon's *True Discourse* (1588) supposedly reproduces a pamphlet that Philip published in order to terrorize the English with the thought of "so many and mighty Monarchies against so small and little an Island: such huge ships against so small pinnaces" (11); but Archdeacon translates the pamphlet, he says, in order to display in turn England's scorn for Philip's vaunts, "so little account in respect of the Lord we make of the power of man" (10).[24] After the battle, Maurice Kyffen (1588) declares the Armada a victory by God in which "our Might and Means he did *exclude*, / That so himself most Gloriously may stand."[25] Elizabeth proved the inescapable figure both of these excluded means and of God's grace, or on a more worldly level, of an England eerily self-disparate, "like little body with a mighty heart" (*Henry V* 2.chorus.17). Before her troops at Tilbury, she herself exploited the propaganda value of her material insufficiency to the fullest:

> I know I have the Body of a weak and feeble Woman, but I have the Heart and Stomach of a King, and of a King of *England* too, and think foul Scorn that *Parma* or *Spain*, or any Prince of *Europe* should dare to invade the Borders of my Realm. (Quoted in Wilson, *England's Eliza*, 89)

The virgin's scorn for invasive princes becomes here a more general contempt for the power of mere body or matter per se.[26]

An unusual piece of post-Armada propaganda, James Lea's *Birth, Purpose and Mortall Wound of the Romish Holie League* (1589), nicely illustrates how the particular character of England's defeated enemy helped bring England's spiritual virtues into more striking relief. First, and inevitably, Lea notes that Spanish power seems, materially speaking, big: Philip had hoped to "swallow up little *England*, as the ravenous Crocodile doth the smallest fish in the seven mouthed River *Nilus*" (A3r). And what makes Spain look so big are two very different yet analogous modes of worldliness: on the one hand, papistry, the stocks-and-stones worship cementing the Holy League in the first place; and on the other, the American riches that have led Spain to occupy the New World and that stoke the fires of Philip's imperial ambitions. Lea envisions "*Philip* King of *Spain* made drunk and deceived with the superstitious cup of Romish abhomination, . . . whetted on according to his promise in the Holy League, champion-like to prepare his people, and discharge his abundance of Indian earth"; while the very pendants of Philip's ships bear witness to this double incitement, portraying "painted Saints, (sufficient guides for superstitious sots) full gaudily adorn'd with the finest gold, rak't out of wretched *India*'s Womb, whose senseless bowels the *Spaniards* (slave-like) ceaselessly tear out" (A2v–3r). Lea's map (figure 4), the centerpiece of his work, takes the sexual imagery here quite literally (L): the threat to Elizabeth is unmistakable, all the more since the map seems at first glance to have placed America where England (actually, where Norway) should be. And indeed, the fear that Spain might do to England what it had done to America galvanized Protestants from as early as Mary's reign. After recounting the atroci-

Figure 4. Frontispiece to *The Birth, Purpose and Mortall Wound of the Romish Holie League*, by I[ames]. L[ea]., London, 1589. Key:

A. Satan enthroned beside the pope; B. The Duke of Guise committing butchery; C. A papal nuncio pouring treasure at the duke's feet; D. Navarre, the Protestant champion; E. Queen Elizabeth; F. The pope and King Philip of Spain, whose gun shoots gold;

G. Exiled English Catholics shooting libels at Elizabeth; H. The Spanish Armada; I. Parma, the Spanish general; K. The outnumbered English fleet; L. America raped of her treasure by the Spanish; M. The Holy League languishing.

(By permission of the Folger Shakespeare Library.)

ties of the conquistadores in New Spain that Peter Martyr had described, the Marian exile John Ponet predicts that, if Spain invades England, as seems to Ponet ever more likely, the English will not only be enslaved like the Indians, but in fact "be by shiploads . . . carried into new Spain . . . [where] ye shall be tied in chains, forced to row in the galley, to dig in the mines and to pick up the gold in the hot sand" (*Shorte Treatise*, 91–92, 94, 165).[27] Yet the Armada demonstrates to Lea that the Spanish are the ones who have become "slave-like," brutalized by their hunger for gold and blood to such a degree that they encourage their ally the Guise to turn cannibal himself (B).[28] The poetical key to the map explains why Spain's wealth and power should not deceive England about its own very different strength. True, says Lea, God "makes our Land abound" with many goods "which other Nations lack":

> But yet a greater grace, we have his word in peace,
> God grant it may continue, and bring forth more increase.
> Let Spaniard then go delve and dig for hidden gold;
> Let him go rend rich *Indies'* bowels out.
>
> (Bv)[29]

And so England's queen, at the bottom of the map and almost off it, sits unruffled (E), while what in the earthly and victimized form of the Other World, America, represents the forced birth of material wealth, becomes in Elizabeth, America's virginal and otherworldly counterpart, the triumphantly free birth of spirit—breath and faith: *Unica spes mea Christus*, "My sole hope, Christ."[30] (Even Lea, however, is not without an almost instinctive ambivalence toward the idea of England's otherness, since the barbarian enemies of England all speak English, while England's sublime faith appears, oddly enough, in Latin.)

Yet such antimaterialism—a logical effect of England's classical otherworldliness, as I have tried to show—was not inevitably insularist. After all, as the papists delighted to point out, England's otherworld was not actually insular; commenting on a typical paean to "our *little Island*," Robert Parsons (1599) advises the author: "You must take in Scotland also, or else you err in Cosmography" (*Temperate*, 2).[31] Such a critique could find supporters even among some of Elizabeth's devotees, who believed that the antimaterialist articulation of an essential relation between England's material littleness and its spiritual greatness was only half the story, a story completed by the better material correlative of an empire. Once again, one need not have been English to appreciate the force of this argument, as the praise of Giordano Bruno (1584) for Elizabeth demonstrates: "If her earthly territory were a true reflection of the width and grandeur of her spirit," declares Bruno,

> this great Amphitrite would bring far horizons within her girdle and enlarge the circumference of her dominion to include not only Britain and Ireland but some new world, as vast as the universal frame, where her all-powerful hand should have full scope to raise a united monarchy.[32]

But as Bruno's oddly subjunctive rhetoric seems to betray, how can Elizabeth enact this materialization of her great spirit? Philip already owned the only new world in sight, and had, as Elizabethans less optimistic than Lea always complained, been applying the material treasure he found there toward his goal of conquering the Old World too. Lea might mock the bestiality of Spanish absorption in such worldly rubbish as gold, and celebrate England's spiritually centered integrity instead, but how was little otherworldly England to win the world?

It comes as no surprise that Elizabeth and her Privy Council, cognizant both of England's spiritual strength and of its material weakness, should have fallen victim so persistently to alchemical frauds—for example, by Edward Kelley, the assistant of John Dee who remained in Bohemia after Dee's mysterious sojourn there. Kelley somehow convinced Sidney's friend Edward Dyer that he, Kelley, had manufactured a powder capable of turning trifles into gold; Dyer told Burghley, who demanded Kelley's return to England; and Kelley naturally demurred. In a letter of Burghley's (1590?) that sounds slightly desperate—how, after all, is one to entice home a man who can spontaneously produce his own unbounded wealth?—Burghley plays his trump card, a lure transcending mere worldly value: he commands Dyer to remind Kelley that no impediment should "stay a man of his valor from the honoring of his sovereign; whom all princes honor; yea, whom the grand seignor, who despiseth others, hath reverence for her princely virtues and royal acts." As internationally standard a value as gold, miraculous Elizabeth represents the only possible correlative England can offer Kelley's powers; which is to say, she represents England's own alchemical "powder," capable, in Burghley's mind, of securing Kelley's, which is capable in turn of preserving little England. Burghley continues:

> But if I might have my wish, next to his coming home, I wish he would, in some secret box, send to her majesty a token, some such portion [of powder], as might be to her a sum reasonable to defer her charges for this summer for her navy, which we are now preparing to the sea, to withstand the strong navy of Spain, discovered on our coasts between Breton and Cornwall within these two days.[33]

Yet the very insufficiency of England's resources could itself seem to encourage expansion, in the same way that Hakluyt, beginning his *Principal Navigations* (1598), says King Arthur had been encouraged: "This kingdom was too little for him, & his mind was not contented with it" (1:6).[34] In other words, just as weak Elizabeth could seem to accentuate God's might, so the absence of any objective correlative to England's desires could seem to clarify and liberate those desires. When praising "the invincible minds of our English nation, who have never left any worthy thing unattempted, nor any part almost of the whole world unsearched," George Best (1578), for example, must speak of deeds for which England has as yet nothing to show, but which therefore seem promises of a greater, unfulfilled destiny: "We may truly infer, that the Englishman in these our days, in his notable discoveries, to the Spaniard and Portingale is nothing inferior: and for his hard adventures, and valiant resolutions, greatly superior" (*True Discourse*, 6–7).[35] Indeed, some claimed that the otherworldliness of the English, their material shortcomings and spiritual strength as the people *divisos orbe*, produced in English voyagers a peculiarity hybrid form of antimaterialism, a *contemptus mundi* that ended up enlarging the scope of their worldly desires. Writing to applaud Sir Humphrey Gilbert's first attempt at colonizing America, Thomas Churchyard (1578) describes Gilbert's adventurers as "more than men, half gods if I say troth," who from their superhuman vantage point "deeply look into these worldly toys" of quotidian life; and yet such otherworldly detachment turns out to indicate only how "whole kingdoms scarcely can suffice their minds and manhood both" ("A Matter," 231). Churchyard on the start of Gilbert's imperialist venture sounds like Prospero on the vanity of human wishes:

Now they have taken leave of worldly pleasures all,
That young and lusty were to live; and now to toil they fall
That finely were brought up; yea now they bid adieu
The glitt'ring court, the gallant town, the gorgeous garments new;
The bravery of this world, the pride and pomp of earth,
And look not backward any way to riches, race, or birth;
To worthy wife or friend, to babes nor nearest kin;
But only to the Lord above, and journey they are in.

(228)[36]

When one considered that spirit alone—the True Faith of which these adventurers were the proclaimed agents—had its own expansive power, prophesied by Christ himself, this demi-*contemptus* could seem surprisingly close to orthodoxy. In his advertisement for Gilbert's second, and this time fatal, American venture, Sir George Peckham (1583) encourages prospective colonists to "be of good cheer therefore, for he that cannot err hath said: That before the end of the world, his word shall be preached to all nations. Which good work, I trust is reserved for our Nation to accomplish in these parts" (*True Reporte*, 476).[37] A commender of Peckham imagines this process of conversion as itself alchemical, an exchange now of spirit for gold: the natives' "gains shall be the knowledge of our faith, / And ours such riches as the country hath" (440); or, as a later tract (1610) puts it, "[we] do buy of them the pearls of earth, and sell to them the pearls of heaven" (*True Declaration*, 9).[38] But England's otherworldly imperialists usually favored a more businesslike system of exchange, albeit one still as nearly antimaterialist and alchemical as possible, an economy once again requiring an especially deep vision into "toys": the English would hand the natives "trifles: As looking Glasses, Bells, Beads, Bracelets, Chains, or Collars of Bugle, Crystal, Amber, Jet, or Glass etc." (Peckham, *True Reporte*, 452), for which natives would give their goodwill, service, and ideally, gold. Marginalized by skeptical modern historians, this theory about the surprising power of English insufficiency actually dominated English colonialism at least through Jacobean times (as I will later show), so much so that in 1620, for example, while hundreds of Virginian colonists were starving, the treasurer of the Virginia Company

declared that the Commonwealth and State of the Colony in Virginia began generally to prosper so well as they did not desire any

more provision of Meal to be sent unto them but rather prayed that
the Company would be pleased to be at some charge to send them
a few trifling Commodities As Beads and such like toys whereby to
truck with the Indians for Corn and other necessaries to increase
and maintain thereby a Christian Commerce. (Kingsbury, *Records*,
1:423)

Against all odds—but then England's greatness had seemed to depend on such counterevidence—England like "another little
world" (Greene, *Friar Bacon and Friar Bungay* 4:7) was to be aug-
mented by trifling.

II

Now this expansive trifling was a conception to which, even aside
from the circumstances of their nationality, Elizabeth's poets were
in a sense professionally inclined. Sidney (c. 1581) adopts the
conventionally dismissive view of poetry when he describes his
Arcadia as filled with what was, coincidentally, standard ware to
trade with the Indians, "no better stuff than as in a haberdasher's
shop, glasses or feathers" (57); and yet this is the same writer who
elsewhere boasts that not Nature but "the poets only deliver a
golden [world]" (*Apology*, 15). George Chapman (1598) includes
both disparate positions—that poetry is less yet also more than
what the world values—in a single passage: he argues that poetry
was born when the soul, in disgust with "that worm-eaten Idol"
the body, devised

> another fruitless, dead and despised receptacle to reserve her ap-
> pearance with unspeakable profit, comfort and life to all posteri-
> ties—and that is this poor scribbling, this toy, this too living a pre-
> servative for the deathful tombs of nobility, being accounted in our
> most gentle and complemental use of it only the droppings of an
> idle humor, far unworthy the serious expense of an exact Gentle-
> man's time. (*Chapman's Homer*, 503)

Sidney and Chapman speak of poetry, in short, as other Elizabethan writers speak of England. Where Sidney claims that "Nature
never set forth the earth in so rich tapestry as diverse poets have
done," which proves that the poet, not "captived to the truth of
the foolish world," "doth grow in effect another nature" (*Apology*
15, 35, 14), Camden around the same time presents England as

Nature's own heterocosmic poem: "For Nature took pleasure in the framing thereof, and seemeth to have made it as a second world, sequestered from the other, to delight mankind withal" (*Britannia*, 4).

In other words, for the Elizabethans, both poetry and England could be understood as trifling *and* grand—a coincidence that England's poets could exploit in more or less conscious ways. At one end of the scale, trifling poetry could profit from the general enthusiasm about trifling England without having to acknowledge any debt; the idea that a nation could be at once inconsequential and sublime—"divided from the world as better worth" (Daniel, *Delia*, sonnet 44)—simply made more credible the notion that poetry, "not tied to the laws of matter," therefore participated in "divineness" (Bacon, *Works* 3:343). Just as ostensibly weak Elizabeth could be seen to overmaster her fellow princes, so could the English reader recognize what is to Samuel Daniel (1599) the equally miraculous potentiality of poetic Eloquence:

> Thou that canst do much more with one poor pen
> Than all the powers of princes can effect:
> And draw, divert, dispose, and fashion men
> Better than force or rigor can direct:
> Should we this ornament of glory then
> As th'unmaterial fruits of shades, neglect?
>
> (*Musophilus*, 945–50)

But then Elizabeth was "her selfe a peereles Poetresse" (Spenser, *Teares of the Muses*, 576), whose "excellent" poetry George Puttenham (1589) defines as not simply her verse but also her political alchemy, "by your Princely purse favors and countenance, making in manner what ye list, the poor man rich, the lewd well learned, the coward courageous, and vile both noble and valiant" (*Arte*, 4–5; cf. 63).[39] In the more sophisticated applications of England's grand littleness to poetry, poets could argue that as professional triflers— indeed, as trifles themselves: " 'Tis a pretty toy to be a poet' " (Marlowe, *Tamburlaine* Part 1, 2.2.54)—they, like their queen, were especially capable of seeing the value in English poverty, and thus should themselves be valued as the true defenders, even the prophets, of little England's great potential. Answering an attack by Philocosmus or World-Enamored on "neglected lays" (11), Daniel's Musophilus soon finds himself defending what Philocosmus considers equally "thrust from the world"—"this little point, this scarce discerned Isle" (427–28); while the later apostrophe to eloquence and its "poor pen" modulates into an extraordinary vision of otherworldly England's great potentiality—an empire of, and achieved by, supposedly "ungainful" (2) English poetry:

> And who in time knows whither we may vent
>> The treasure of our tongue, to what strange shores
>> This gain of our best glory shall be sent,
>> T'enrich unknowing Nations with our stores?
>> What worlds in th'yet unformed Occident
>> May come refin'd with th'accents that are ours?
> Or who can tell for what great work in hand
>> The greatness of our style is now ordain'd?
>
> (957–64)

Such an elaborate conception of the affinity between England and poetry informs Lyly's post-Armada play *Midas* (written 1589), whose title figure evokes the most obvious reason for considering both nation and poet mere triflers—their "ungainful" lack of gold. As my previous chapter noted, the last poem of the first book of Ovid's *Elegies* presents the classic defense of the poet on this score: Ovid does not lack gold, he disdains it. In the elegy, Envy can carp that Ovid's "time is spent so ill" on "fruits of an idle quill" because it misunderstands the nature of true value: "Thy scope is mortal," Ovid replies, "mine eternal fame." "Immortal" and therefore free from the quotidian standards that esteem gold the best that mortality has to offer, verse enables the poet to surpass the reach of even the most gold-intensive occupation: "To verse let kings give place, and kingly shows, / And banks o'er which gold-bearing Tagus flows." The Elizabethan poets never tired of reiterating the sentiment. Marlowe, for instance, whose translation of Ovid I have been quoting, may be less sanguine about poverty than his master, and may imagine the distance between poet and gold as a punishment inflicted on the patron of learning, Hermes, by the Fates; yet even as affliction the poet's poverty positively distinguished him for Marlowe from more earthbound wit:

> And to this day is every scholar poor;
> Gross gold from them runs headlong to the boor.
> Likewise the angry sisters . . .
>   . . . have concluded
> That Midas' brood shall sit in honor's chair,
> To which the Muses' sons are only heir.
>   (*Hero and Leander* 1.471–76)[40]

When Lyly devotes an entire play to Midas himself, one naturally expects a still more elaborate version of the inevitable argument: Ovid's account of the king foolish enough to proportion his desires solely to gold, and then foolish enough to favor Pan's over Apollo's music, seems for coherence's sake almost to demand an opposition between gold and true poetry that will work in poetry's favor. The surprise of Lyly's play, however, is that in his hands a myth ready-made for an argument about poetry becomes at the same time a contemporary political allegory—an argument about poetry *and* England.

Lyly's Midas is Philip II, who hopes his golden touch will make him "monarch of the world" (1.1.116–17), but who finds instead that his seemingly boundless worldly power—exemplified by his Armada—has mysterious limits: "Have I not made the sea to groan under the number of my ships: and have they not perished, that there was not two left to make a number?" (3.1.31–33). This reversal is all the more unsettling to Midas because the only thing that blocks his advance is as it were the very opposite of his might: the mere "Island" (47) of Lesbos, which is ruled by a "petty Prince" (51–52). Yet Midas realizes that the prince of this island—Elizabeth, obviously[41]—must only *look* petty, that pettiness inheres not in the ruler Midas cannot conquer but in the exclusively golden system of value that makes Elizabeth seem conquerable in the first place: "A petty Prince, *Midas*? no, a Prince protected by the Gods, by Nature, by his own virtue, and his Subjects' obedience" (52–54). This standard vision of little England's ungolden greatness—and standardly uneasy too, since Lyly cannot resist claiming later that the English (whom he imagines ruled by a king, not queen) are also "too rich" (4.2.41) to be troubled by Midas's gold[42]—marks the final stage of a revolution in Midas, who now decides to humble himself before the giver of his golden touch, Bacchus, in order to rid himself at once "of this intolerable disease of gold" and "that untemperate desire of government" (3.1.61–62). But Midas's overtly political change of heart leaves his troubles only half over. Bacchus cures him of his golden touch, but Midas then proceeds to wander into the midst of an argument between Pan and Apollo and win himself ass's ears by foolishly preferring the earthly to the heavenly god. This demonstration of a bestiality apparently deeper than the love of gold, deeper because unmotivated by hope of gain, actually reveals the continued yet indrawn power of that love; for Midas's ears quickly provoke him to lament his river-cure: "Is *Midas* that sought to be Monarch of the world, become the mock of the world? are his golden mines turn'd into water, as free for every one that will fetch, as for himself, that possessed them by wish?" (4.1.176–78). "Song" in Lyly's account represents, then, the touchstone of one's relative sophistication, which is inseparable from one's relative indifference to gold; and again higher powers of judgment get associated with England: mortified by his ears, Midas wonders, "What will they say in Lesbos?" (171).

In fact, Midas's final cure requires him to re-renounce his desire for both gold and England now in the context of what amounts to a kind of literary criticism. Midas decides he must seek the advice of Apollo's oracle, a course of action which his empire- and gold-loving councillor Martius rejects as "superstition" (5.1.38–39) about "a blind God" (5.3.16). But it is Martius, and then the rest of Midas's entourage, who reveal themselves as blind at the end of the play, when only Midas seems to catch Apollo's climactic pronouncement. For Midas this special access to Apollo's hidden wisdom represents a great change in sensibility. Before, he had preferred the univocality of Pan's pipe—associated with mere worldliness—to the "sweet consent" (4.1.96) of Apollo's voice, lute, and lute-strings, associated with the presence of a heavenly god on earth: "I brook not that nice tickling of strings," Midas had declared, "that contents me that makes one start" (129–30). Yet the oracle's verse, even though substituting the more rarefied doubleness of allegory for song, leads Midas nonetheless to a newfound appreciation of "Poesy's King" (136): "I see that by obscure shadows, which you cannot discern in fresh colors. *Apollo* in the depth of his dark answer, is to me the glistering of a bright sun" (98–100). What Midas has learned is the primary Renaissance apology for poetry, employed the same year as Lyly's play by Nashe in his *Anatomie of Absurdity*: "I account of Poetry, as of a more hidden & divine kind of Philosophy, enwrapped in blind Fables and dark stories, wherein the principles of more excellent Arts and moral precepts . . . are contained" (*Works* 1:25).[43] In other words, Midas sees the value in Apollo's oracle as Lyly has seen it in Ovid's myth and as Lyly's auditors should see it in Lyly's mythological play. And this better appreciation of the "superstitious" fables that seem to convict poetry of trifling[44] enables Midas to reach at last a more extravagant, though for us familiar, appreciation of England: "I perceive (and yet not too late) that Lesbos will not be touched by gold, by force it cannot: that the Gods have pitched it out of the world, as not to be controll'd by any in the world" (4.1.101–3). A "barbarous" (17) gold lover like Martius continues to believe both poetry and England mere trifles; kingly Midas learns to recognize the ostensibly petty as the actually divine; and the great-hearted English auditors of *Midas* come to see not only the likeness between England and poetry as divine trifles, but the inseparability of England's spiritual strength, its otherworldly worldliness, from the highest estimation of poetry.

Or, by the same token, from its lowest estimation: Lyly obliquely maintains that the love of England, as of poetry, will always seem to some a kind of superstition. This invidious view of England has, again, classical roots: as I noted in my previous chapter, Plutarch reports that "many ancient writers would not believe that it [England] was so in deed, and did make them vary about it, saying that it was but a fable and a lie" (*Lives* 5:25). And indeed, as an analysis of Renaissance nationalism, in particular of the cult of Elizabeth, the accusation of superstitiousness persists into our own century. According to influential historians like E. C. Wilson and Frances Yates, "patriotic Englishmen" in the sixteenth century "unconsciously half shifted their affection for a sacred Virgin to a profane" (Wilson, *England's Eliza*, 219).[45] But many Elizabethans were far less credulous in their virgin worship than these historians allow. Sidney's entertainment *The Lady of May* (1578/79?), for example, delights in the substitution of Elizabeth for the Virgin Mary as a chance to *feign* superstition. Presenting Elizabeth with "a chain of round agates something like beads," a pedantic character in the entertainment, Master Rombus, worries that the gift

betrays the degree to which its giver, Leicester, "is foully commac-
ulated with the papistical enormity":

> I have found *unum par*, a pair, *papisticorum bedorus*, of Papistian
> beads, *cum quis*, with the which, *omnium dierum*, every day, next
> after his *pater noster* he *semper* suits "and Elizabeth," as many lines
> as there be beads on this string. (*Miscellaneous Prose*, 31)

Unlike the papists who desire material props for their worship or
the puritans who fear "commaculation" from such props, however, Sidney's Leicester toys with "enormity," and thus presents
his love for Elizabeth as both devoted and urbanely detached.

Dekker's *Old Fortunatus* (1599) turns such feigning of superstition into a sophisticated worship not just of the queen but of England generally. The play begins with the entrance of "two old
men":

> 1. Are you then traveling to the temple of *Eliza*?
> 2. Even to her temple are my feeble limbs traveling. Some call her
>   *Pandora*: some *Gloriana*, some *Cynthia*: some *Belphoebe*, some *As-
>   traea*: all by several names to express several loves: Yet all those
>   names make but one celestial body, as all those loves meet to
>   create but one soul.
> 1. I am one of her own country, and we adore her by the name of
>   *Eliza*.
> 2. Blessed name, happy country: Your *Eliza* makes your land *Eli-
>   zium*.
>
> (Prologue 1–10)

Once again, as with Angle and Brute, England's surprising potentiality gets expressed in a pun—Eliza/Elizium—that represents not
only the value hidden in English trifles but the trivial means of
realizing that value: one need merely adjust one's vision. Yet now
overt superstition seems an essential component of more than the
partial or typological vision that figures the queen a pagan deity
like Cynthia; for the higher value that the partial name Eliza ultimately signifies is itself pagan, Elizium. One explanation of this
compounded superstition would be that Dekker wants to avoid
representing Eliza's potentiality as already fully realized, in order
to encourage instead the kind of expansive *contemptus* Churchyard
discerns in England's voyagers. That is, by characterizing otherworldly England as a heaven, and yet a heaven pagan and superstitious, Dekker may want to continue to excite a desire for tran-

scendence in Eliza's subjects even as they transcend appearances to celebrate their other-worldly bliss. A land both in and out of the world, Elizium by this account would be blessed insofar as its people have learned to enjoy and disdain the world at once.[46]

Such an interpretation of Dekker's apparent superstition seems to gain support from the fact that the pilgrim who praises Elizium is an actor, his identity as pilgrim already overtly disposable, just like the play-world that transforms the setting of its performance, Elizabeth's Court, into Eliza's temple. In other words, the play as a play already dramatizes how easily and with what sublime results one's vision may be adjusted, and yet at the same time how misguided one would be to accept this adjustment as final. The special self-consciousness encouraged by the play—a self-consciousness at once indulgent toward and detached from superstition—is, moreover, nothing other than what the fables of the poets can always seem to demand.

Yet the tenuousness of fables and play can just as easily seem to suit misgivings about the sublimity they represent. By questioning the status of Elizium in his epigram "In Elizabetham," John Weever (1599) can seem to highlight not only the hidden potentiality of ostensibly trifling England but a peculiar incompleteness and uncertainty, a negativity either instinctive or deliberate, that English optimism about trifles finds hard to avoid:

> If that *Elizium* be no fained thing,
> Whereof the poets wont so much to sing;
> Then are those fair fields in this Faerie land,
> Which fair *Eliza* rules with awful hand.
> (*Epigrammes*, 18)

III

If Dekker and Weever appear to demonstrate, then, how English trifling—and especially English poetical trifling—naturally gravitates toward an unstable alliance with superstition, just as Eliza seems naturally to entail her Elizium, they also provide a revealing name for the result: Weever calls England not just Elizium but "Faerie land," and one of Dekker's pilgrims refers to Eliza as the "Dread Queen of Fairies" (*Old Fortunatus*, Prologue, 55). Such allusions indicate the preeminence of one poet—Spenser—within the tradition of trifling, of combining England and poetry as transcendent trifles, that I have described. Just by apposing Elizium and Fairyland (as Gabriel Harvey does in his commendatory poem to *The Faerie Queene*),[47] one can already begin to grasp Spenser's centrality to this tradition. And indeed, an English Catholic named Anthony Copley, rewriting the first book of *The Faerie Queene* to suit his faith, decides that Elizium and Fairyland represent one and the same heresy.

The Argument to Copley's *Fig for Fortune* (1596) describes the Spenserian adventures of "an *Elizian* out-cast of Fortune, ranging on his jade *Melancholy* through the Desert of his afflictions," who encounters and then escapes the temptations of Despair and Revenge to find new hope in the teaching of a religious hermit. By depicting the hermit as surprised "to see a distressed *Elizian* in those parts," the Argument implies—orthodoxly for a reader like Dekker or Weever—that an unhappy Elizian is a contradiction in terms; but then the argument also deceptively defines the poem's evil Duessa-figure, Doblessa, as Fortune (A4r), whereas the poem itself makes quite clear that Doblessa also represents Protestantism:

> She had no Altar, nor no Sacrament
> No Ceremony, nor Oblation,
> Her school was Cavil, & truthless babblement
> Riot her Reign, her end damnation.
>
> > (70)

In fact, the term *Elizium* first crops up in the poem proper not in praise of Eliza but as the pagan ideal of Despair and Revenge (4, 7, 18); and when, as the Argument promises, the hermit Catechrysius expresses his surprise at the melancholy narrator—"Rare, yea all too rare are now adays / *Eliza*'s subjects seen to pass this ways"—he quickly adds that the narrator's troubles cast less doubt on the man than on his country:

> Belike ye are a Paradized people
> That so contain your selves in home-delights,
> As though that only under your steeple
> And no where else were all May-merry Rights:
> > A blessed people ye are, if it be so
> > And yet me thinks thou seem'st a man of woe.
>
> > (25)

The narrator tries to deflect this skepticism by dismissing himself as "The Rag of Fortune" (32), yet such self-stigmatization only underscores his theological errors. Just as Despair and Revenge have misled him from the true image of suffering, the Crucifixion, and from the matching knowledge that to "suffer for our Lord" is "more dear than sweetest Lullaby in Fortune's lap" (51–52), so Eliza's Elizium fools him into believing that worldly pleasure is bliss. As he guides the narrator to Mount Sion (in part, the Catholic Church), Catechrysius teaches him that

> Not all the flush of thy fore-frolic state,
> The worship of thy birth, thy rich revenue,
> Thy country's high applaud and estimate
> And all that fair *Elizium* can yield you,
>   Is of the worth to countervail this hap
>   Fallen from Fortune into Grace's lap.
>
>   (58)

In short, the poem inverts the terms of Dekker's and Weever's otherworldly patriotism; Copley claims that it is the English who love "the trash of earth" (28) and Catholics who are the true anti-materialists: "For we are no *Elizium*-bred wights / Nor have we such like merry days; / We have our joys in another kind / Ghostly innated in our soul and mind" (59).[48] But Elizium is not the only name for Protestant England that, to Copley's mind, unwittingly betrays English superstitiousness: the clear light of Sion helps some of Doblessa's followers realize the error of their ways and flee "the witch, as wak'd from out a dream / Of *Faery*" (78; my emphasis). Again, it would be a mistake to dismiss such accusations of superstition as merely partisan: we have seen that many English Protestants actively court the charge, and in equating Elizium with Fairyland the Catholic Copley only seconds the Protestants Dekker and Weever. But Spenser himself, I will argue, wants Fairyland to mean both less and more than Elizium. He, like Copley, attacks the Elizian view of England, and yet he embraces superstition more radically than either Dekker or Weever seems prepared to do.

Spenser, it could be said, takes his trifling more seriously. In fact, his works represent the most elaborate and influential attempt by an Elizabethan to combine the fate of poetry and England as trifles, even to model England's destiny on the course of his own poetical career, which was itself modeled on the career of Virgil. Spenser was, of course, not the only European poet at the time who hoped to do for his country "what Virgil had done for Rome" (Rathborne, *Spenser's Fairyland*, 128), but his choice of precursor also involved Spenser in two sorts of paradoxicality associated with Virgil that, I have tried to show, would have had special significance for an Elizabethan poet: on the one hand, the view, identified with Virgil's first eclogue, of England as either barbarous or heavenly, "divided from the world"; on the other hand, a more strictly literary tradition, also grounded in the *Eclogues*, that linked ostensible trifling to ultimate grandeur. This literary tradition has its own different though intertwinable threads: first, a pastoral thematics of disparity, of comparing great things to small (*Eclogues* 1.23), itself made portentous by the progress of Virgil's career from eclogues to epic;[49] and second, a faith in the allegorical nature of otherwise dismissable fables which finds its supreme evidence in the fourth, or "Messianic," eclogue's supposed prediction of Christ's birth.

After the work of Frances Yates, no scholar can forget that this Messianic eclogue, so useful in the defense of poetry, also possessed special political significance for the Elizabethans. The virgin—Astraea or Justice—whom Virgil describes returning from heaven with the golden age in tow (*iam redit et Virgo, redeunt Saturnia regna*, 6) could seem a prophecy come true with Elizabeth— "not the image or picture, nor by imagination, but a virgin indeed truly representing Justice, and effectually executing it."[50] This account of Elizabeth had, as Yates maintains, extraordinary implications for her, and therefore also for the Virgilian pastoral that could seem to have predicted her coming. Constantine identified Virgil's heavenly virgin with the Virgin Mary; Augustine with the true faith; and Dante with the world empire into which the true faith chose to be born. If Elizabeth as virgin mother of reformed religion seemed to extend two of these allegories, Yates argues, then why should she not have reawakened hopes about the third also, about a reformed world empire?

The suggestion seems plausible, though Yates oddly—and revealingly—omits citing the most likely source of evidence for her claim, the Elizabethan poem that actually offers to rewrite Virgil's praise of the Virgin in terms of Elizabeth, the fourth, or "Aprill," eclogue of Spenser's *Shepheardes Calender*:

> Tell me, have ye seene her angelick face,
>   Like *Phoebe* fayre?
> Her heavenly haveour, her princely grace
>   Can you well compare?
> The Redde rose medled with the White yfere,
> In either cheeke depeincten lively chere.
>   Her modest eye,
>   Her Majestie,
> Where have ye seen the like, but there?
>   (64–72)

On a strictly pastoral view, this "flowre of Virgins" (48) is merely "*Elisa*, Queene of shepheardes all" (34). But her "heavenly haveour" seems capable of evoking both Astraea and Mary, and the red and white mingled in her cheeks—an icon for "the uniting of the two principal houses of Lancaster and of York," Spenser's commentator E. K. reminds us—seem capable too of evoking a new golden age of empire, "because [the union] established *pax* under One Monarch, in place of discord and war under two rival houses" ("Queen Elizabeth," 51). The slimness of the evidence here would not necessarily defeat a Yatesian argument. After all, Virgil's own pastoral had not been particularly explicit about the imperial side of the golden age he envisioned; as Yates again notes (33), only in book 6 of the *Aeneid* does Virgil overtly attribute the new golden age of the fourth eclogue to Augustus's future world rule. In fact, Spenser's eclogue can seem more urgent than Virgil's about moving from pastoral to epic because it closes, as Virgil's eclogue could not, with two quotations from the *Aeneid*. At the end of "Aprill," Thenot's emblem asks Elisa *O quam te memorem virgo*, What shall I call you, virgin, how shall I properly understand you? and Hobbinol's emblem answers *O dea certe*, Surely a goddess—in the *Aeneid* (1.327–28), Venus, who guides Aeneas toward the founding of Rome. As Yates might maintain, such allusions to Elisa's unexpectedly sublime identity preview in trifling pastoral form the Elizabethan empire, and epic, to come:

But a third kingdom yet is to arise,
Out of the *Trojans* scattered of-spring,
That in all glory and great enterprise,
Both first and second *Troy* shall dare to equalise.

(*FQ* 3.9.44)

Yet these esoteric hints about Elizabeth's potentiality are resisted in Spenser's eclogue by other hints perhaps equally esoteric. For one, "Aprill" 's "laye / Of fayre *Elisa*" (34–35) is a song
that Colin, the *Calender's* hero, *used* to sing, before what E. K.
calls "that boy's great misadventure in Love, whereby his mind
was alienate and withdrawn not only from him, who most loved
him [Hobbinol], but also from all former delights and studies"; it
is Hobbinol, not Colin, who "records" the lay as proof of Colin's
now forsaken ability. In the light of Colin's unrequited love for
Rosalind, Hobbinol's decision to rehearse the Elisa song in particular looks almost comically ironic: what Colin can no longer celebrate, understandably, is virginity as an ideal. In fact, Colin's
frustration throughout the *Calender*, his new inability to see England as a paradise pristine and intact, threatens to fulfill not
Virgil's hopes but Meliboeus's fears, to make England seem a
land of exile.[51] "Januarie," Spenser's own first eclogue and a
monologue by Colin, even dismisses Tityrus's voice of content,
and presents exile as a fate on which Colin has already em-
barked:

A thousand sithes [i.e., times] I curse that carefull hower,
Wherein I longed the neighbour town to see:
And eke ten thousand sithes I blesse the stoure [i.e., fit],
Wherein I saw so fayre a sight, as shee.
Yet all for naught: such sight hath bred my bane.
Ah God, that love should breede such joy and pain.

(49–54)

Since E. K. identifies Tityrus as Virgil and the Meliboean Colin as
Spenser himself, Spenser the English pastoralist seems to be portraying himself as an exile both from Rome and from Virgil's sublime career as an imperial panegyrist.

Hobbinol's evocation in "Aprill" of the old Colin helps clarify
the surprising political implications of Colin's love-woe. He describes Colin's former praise of the queen as, again,

> his laye
> Of fayre *Elisa*, Queene of shepheardes all:
> Which once he made, as by a spring he laye,
> And tuned it unto the Waters fall.
>
> (33–36)

The lines depict the pristine complacence from which Colin's "madding mind is starte." The "laye," deriving from a stasis that it homonymously mirrors ("Which once he made, as by a spring he laye"), celebrated the virgin genius of this pristinity, and proportioned both the political order and the praise of that order to nature (Colin "tuned" the lay "unto the Waters fall"). Not only Colin's abandonment of the song but also Hobbinol's elegiac rendition of it break the fullness of relation, the perfect fit, that once obtained among poet, queen, and countryside,[52] and that Colin's admirers unwittingly threaten even in their celebratory emblems. Those emblems are, again, culled from the *Aeneid*'s first book, when Aeneas meets his mother Venus, who is disguised as a huntress, asks what name he is to call this maiden ("O quam te memorem virgo?") since she does not seem human, and then decides she is certainly a goddess ("O dea certe")—Diana, in fact, or at least a nymph. Aeneas's comic uncertainty and misapprehension, first in thinking his mother and the goddess of love a virgin, then the goddess of virgins, oddly reflects on Colin's erstwhile praise of Elisa as "the flowre of Virgins," with a face like Diana's other person, "like *Phoebe* fayre" (65). In other words, by their very appreciation of the queen, the emblems raise doubts about the fitness of describing Elizabeth as both a pastoral figure and a genius of virginity.

When Spenser turns in "October" to another unhappy poet, Cuddie, who has abandoned poetry for the baser and more traditional motive of poverty, dissatisfaction with England's political order becomes correspondingly more direct. If Cuddie's oaten reeds bring him no reward, Piers observes, then why not attempt some epic theme instead:

> There may thy Muse display her fluttryng wing,
> And stretch herselfe at large from East to West:
> Whither thou list in fayre *Elisa* rest,
> Or if thee please in bigger notes to sing,

Advance the worthy whome shee loveth best,
That first the white beare to the stake did bring.
(43–48)

Piers recommends, in other words, that Cuddie turn his alienation
from innocent pastoral into purposeful motion, so that his Muse
may imperially range "from East to West"; and this transformation
can be achieved, Piers assumes, by the ennobling praise of Elizabeth or Leicester (the name that E. K. supplies for Piers's "worthy"). Startlingly, Cuddie rejects the idea, and Piers accepts the
terms of Cuddie's rejection. England is no place to "rest," Cuddie
argues, because it has nothing to offer. The kind of epic singing
Piers proposes may have worked for Tityrus, who had a patron to
support him and a living hero (not to mention an empire) to inspire him,

But after vertue gan for age to stoupe,
And mighty manhode brought a bedde of ease:
The vaunting Poets found nought worth a pease,
To put in preace emong the learned troupe.
(67–70)

Piers does not, as one might expect, berate Cuddie for so thoroughly dismissing Elizabeth and her court—from what current heroic exploits *could* an English poet have derived inspiration?—but
shakes his head along with Cuddie and offers one more alternative:

O pierlesse Poesye, where is then thy place?
If nor in Princes pallace thou doe sitt:
(And yet is Princes pallace the most fitt)
Ne brest of baser birth doth thee embrace.
Then make thee winges of thine aspyring wit,
And, whence thou camst, flye back to heaven apace.
(79–84)

Cuddie defers to Colin on this, and the following eclogue sees
Colin helping poetry on its way; E. K. believes "November" "far
passing his [Marot's] reach, and in mine opinion all other Eg-
logues of this book." Yet this renewal and extension of Colin's vir-
tuosity seems only to ratify Cuddie's implicit correlation of resting
in Elisa with mankind's present shameful bed of ease, for Colin's
song has now become elegiac, and his alienation *contemptus mundi*.

What is worse, the elegy seems to be about Elizabeth. In the obvious sense that Colin's new preference for elegy marks the passing of his interest in paeans to Elisa, the mere fact of this change is an elegiac commentary on Colin's "Aprill" vision of the queen. The particular death that Colin laments, however, transforms the repudiation of "Aprill" into a revision:

> For deade is Dido, dead alas and drent,
> Dido the great shephearde his daughter sheene.
> ("November," 37–38)

E. K. is careful to dismiss the obvious but bizarre suggestion of the last line: the great shepherd, he cautions, "is some man of high degree, and not as some vainly suppose God Pan"—not, that is, the father predicated for Elisa in "Aprill" (51). And yet E. K.'s own discussion of the poem's argument, explaining as it does that "this Eclogue is made in imitation of Marot his song, which he made upon the death of Loys the french Queen," already implies the connection to Elizabeth; while the extensive formal and thematic similarities between "Aprill" 's lay of Elisa and "November" 's elegy[53] make it increasingly easy for the reader to "suppose":

> Sing now ye shepheards daughters, sing no moe
> The songs that *Colin* made in her prayse,
> But into weeping turn your wanton layes.
> (77–79)

"Aprill" haunts the final line here—what was once "tuned" to the "Waters fall" has now been "turn[ed]" to "weeping": "The flouds do gaspe, for dryed is theyr sourse, / And flouds of teares flowe in theyr stead perforse" (126–27). As Elisa "in her sex doth all excell" ("Aprill," 45), so Dido "for beauties prayse and plesaunce had no pere" ("November," 95); Elisa was "the flowre of Virgins," Dido "the fayrest flowre our gyrlond all emong" (75); Elisa "another Sunne below" (77), Dido "the sonne of all the world" now "dimme and darke" (67); and where the "Ladyes of the lake" (120) brought Elisa "of Olive braunches . . . a Coronall" (123),

> The water Nymphs, that wont with her [Dido] to sing and daunce,
> And for her girlond Olive braunches beare,
> Now balefull boughes of Cypres doen advaunce.
> (143–45)

One could say that these parallels kill Elisa in all but name, if it were not for the fact that Dido's other name in the *Aeneid* is Elissa.[54]

Yet Dido replaces, and in replacing kills, more than "Aprill" 's queen; the elegy per se also comprehensively erases Rosalind by refiguring the sign and motive of Colin's alienation, his "mourning" ("January," 48), to be the result not of Rosalind's disdain but of Dido's death. Indeed, the figure of Dido, elsewhere famous as queen and lover, seems to combine consideration of Elisa and Rosalind as lost causes.[55] "October" already suggests the possibility of this conflation. By revealing that the object of pastoral complacence (Elisa in whom one rests) can also be involved in desire (Elisa who loves a worthy), the eclogue raises a question that follows logically from Colin's dilemma. It is no wonder that love for Rosalind alienated Colin from the fullness of Elisa's virgin pastoral: "Shepheardes devise she hateth as the snake, / And laughes the songes, that *Colin Clout* doth make" ("January," 65–66). But what, "October" begins to ask, would happen to a shepherd's complacence if he were to fall in love with the benign genius of pastoral herself? Especially if Dido's beloved Lobbin is supposed to represent, as Malone suggests, "October" 's Robin Leicester, "November" answers the question by translating desire for the pastoral genius into her death, the deflowerer of "the fayrest floure" (75) whose wholeness kept pastoral intact: "shepheards wonted solace is extinct" (106); "Now she is gon that safely did hem keepe. / The Turtle on the bared braunch, / Laments the wound, that Death did launch" (137–39). Colin falls in love with Rosalind accidentally—he need not have visited her town, need not have seen her, need not have loved her when he saw her—and accidentally "cannot purchase" her ("Aprill," 159)—Rosalind just happens to loathe shepherds. But as the daughter of Pan and Syrinx (50–51), Elisa/Dido *is* pastoral and therefore an inescapable cynosure,[56] while her benignity that entertains all ("Ne would she scorne the simple shepheards swaine," "November," 97) and her virginity that bars all ("No mortall blemishe may her blotte," "Aprill," 54) make no contingent distinctions among potential lovers. After the incursion of desire, Elisa as a necessarily desirable and necessarily unobtainable object makes the pastoral ideal she embodies seem itself unpurchasable, so that by "November" frustration is perceived as the truth not just about loving a particular woman but about all worldly hopes:

> O trustlesse state of earthly things, and slipper hope
> Of mortal men, that swincke and sweate for nought,
> And shooting wide, doe misse the marked scope.
>
> (153–55)

Yet the shepherd's desire for Elisa is not, indeed by definition cannot be, abandoned; it survives as Dido does, though in new and unearthly form. Though the "layes" of innocent pastoral, its songs and its leisures, could no more resist the stain of mortality than Dido could, the best "in earthlie mould" (158), death ultimately frees Dido's soul from the taint of her "burdenous corpse" (166), and thus promises the triumphant realization of pastoral where Dido has gone:

> No daunger there the shepheard can astert:
>   Fayre fieldes and pleasaunt layes there bene,
>   The fieldes ay fresh, the grasse ay greene.
>
> (187–89)

During the course of *The Shepheardes Calender*, Rosalind's unpurchasability has, in other words, helped to clarify and then liberate the otherworldliness inscribed at the heart of the worldly pastoral Colin used to celebrate, the pastoral of the virgin Elisa:

> I see thee blessed soule, I see,
> Walke in *Elisian* fieldes so free.
>
> (178–79)[57]

Far from celebrating Eliza's England as a true Elizium, then, *The Shepheardes Calender* seems to attack the idea of applying the golden-age topos of Virgil's fourth eclogue to Elizabeth in any materially realized or realizable fashion. The poem appears to claim instead that both the empirical inadequacy of Elizabethan England to this topos, as in "October," and the logical incompatability of Elizabeth's virginity with material fulfillment, as in "November," should force Englishmen to turn their eyes heavenward: "Make hast ye shepheards, thether to revert" ("November," 191). Many Elizabethan writers make a similar case: that like the early Colin

the English generally have become enmired in the material benefits of the Elizabethan pax, have become like all pastoralists mere
triflers. Anthony Marten (1588), for instance, interprets the Armada threat as God's making trial "whether you more esteem
dainty fare, costly apparel, gorgeous buildings, and other vain delights of this world, than the loss of so happy a kingdom, of so
excellent a Prince, of so sincere a Religion, and of so pure a Gospel" (*Exhortation*, D3r–v). But Spenser appears to take Marten's antimaterialism still further, in the direction Copley also takes it, toward a repudiation of all worldly desires—even those concerning
England—as merely trifling. In imagining the Virgin Queen to
have already reconciled material and spiritual hopes, already embodied an Elizium in little, as if she were a "heaven on earth, or
earth that heaven contains,"[58] Elizabeth's worshippers, the *Calender* seems to claim, forget that the very word Elizabeth signifies not
her own fullness but God's, and that her value consists precisely
in her inadequacy to her own significance, a definitive lack that
frustrates the desire for material realization and encourages the
desire for a spiritual one. By proportioning Elizabeth and England
to its own inherent insufficiency, Spenser's pastoral seems to
stress the *contemptus* always latent in the Elizian ideal, along with
England's need to value that detachment exclusively.[59]

IV

The peculiar thing about *The Shepheardes Calender*, however, is that,
by making Elizabeth a crucial link in both the materially and the
spiritually directed views of England's potentiality, Spenser so ob-
scures his criticism of the queen as to turn the *Calender* into the
locus classicus of the view it seems to attack.[60] In fact, the poem
that "contains the first imitation of the *Shepheardes Calender* to appear in print"—Thomas Blenerhasset's *Revelation of the True Minerva* (1582)—champions England's material insufficiency from the
opening sentence of its dedication: "How far little England . . .
doth in perfect felicity surpass all the large kingdoms of the world,
that travel and small experience which I have had, hath sufficiently taught me" (v, *3r). Blenerhasset too styles himself a pilgrim, though he has erroneously wandered from an England *divisa*

ab orbe, and has thus recognized the otherworldly splendor he had otherwise failed to appreciate: "By travel I did think to climb up higher, / Thus not content in paradise to dwell, / seeking for heaven, I found out hateful hell" (B2r). The narrative proper begins with Mercury describing to an assembly of the gods a similarly misguided and fruitless search. An oracle has prophesied that the gods require a new Minerva "so all the world true knowledge will embrace" (A2v); Mercury sets out to find her, but following the westward course of empire—from Troy to Greece to Rome to Spain, through "the firm of all the world" (A3r)—he finds no one. What Mercury does not realize is that the world extends beyond the world, into the ocean, where the gods eventually meet the "true" Minerva—Elizabeth, of course—"ruling a world"—"*Troyno-vant*"—"at her will" (A3v, A4v). Not only the discovery of "little England's worthy Queen" (F3v) but also the means of her discovery vindicate littleness: ignorant how to find Minerva, the Olympians finally overhear a shepherd named Epizenes—"the Greek equivalent of [Blenerhasset's] pseudonym, Pilgrim," as Bennett notes (Blenerhasset, *Revelation*, viii)—who describes the English "*Eutopia*" (B2v) to Pan and some fellow shepherds. The gods follow Epizenes home, find Elizabeth beset by enemies like the pope and Mary Stuart, and then, in homage to the pastoral state Elizabeth keeps, rally round her with a fight song introduced in strikingly familiar pastoral terms:

> *Apollo* thou the best that ever played
> Take lute in hand, tune to the water's fall,
> *Minerva* lives, whom *Pallas* honor shall.
> (C4r)[61]

For Blenerhasset, at least, the "Aprill" vision of Elizian pastoral not only survives intact Colin's repudiation of it, but approaches nearer a claim even the happy Colin never quite made. In the *Revelation*, the prophecy, the transferral of empire, the true virgin, and now pastoral so knowledgeable and weighty as to enlist even Apollo in its cause, all suggest the English fulfillment of Virgil's golden-age eclogue that Spenser refuses to accept. If Colin's disruptive plight signifies at all for Blenerhasset, it is only as a threat Elizabeth has already avoided. The virginity that for Colin meant the lack at the heart of pastoral, the impossibility of worldly

satisfaction, now guarantees for Blenerhasset a paradisiacal fullness:

> Fancy shall build no nest
> Within her blessed breast,
>   the great increase
> of perfect love, and peace,
>   shall never cease.
>
> (D4r)

Two years later, George Peele's *Araygnement of Paris* likewise
imagines the Olympian gods bowing to a greater virgin goddess
in the west, and likewise finds Spenser at the heart of the conceit,
but Peele handles the potential problem of Colin more directly. For
Colin now surfaces as a character in the play, dying of the morbid
eroticism that is about to ruin Troy, a threat to which the new
western goddess, and consequently her pastoral kingdom, are
blessedly immune:

> There wons within these pleasant shady woods,
> Where neither storm nor Sun's distemperature
> Have power to hurt by cruel heat or cold,
> Under the climate of the milder heaven,
> Where seldom lights Jove's angry thunderbolt,
> For favor of that sovereign earthly peer
> . . . .
> That honors Dian for her chastity,
> And likes the labor well of Phoebe's groves:
> The place Elizium hight, and of the place,
> Her name that governs there Eliza is
> . . . .
> Ycompast round with a commodious sea:
> Her people are ycleped Angeli,
> Or if I miss a letter is the most.
>
> (5.1.1139–56)

It is, perhaps, no surprise that both Blenerhasset and Peele
should fail to recognize the "death" of Elizabeth in "November,"
but less understandable is their apparent indifference even to the
eclogue's unexceptional scruples about mortality. The Fates in the
Araygnement proclaim Elizabeth an earthly goddess whom they
have learned to spare (5.1.1231–33); the *Revelation* similarly declares the woman "who once was but a mortal Queen . . . / The
greatest goddess now on earth":

> She is not now as other princes be,
> Who live on earth to every tempest thrall,
> Desert hath crownd her with eternity.
>
> (Gr–v)

Blenerhasset's printer reminds the reader that it is "no heresy to affirm that every good man having the place of a Magistrate is a god"; borrowing a Catholic defense of saints, he adds that one worships "not the man, but the virtue" (∗v). The poem itself dramatizes this commentary by having Elizabeth lump Mercury with the heathen "Idols" that "I by God's spell did deface," until Mercury explains that he and his colleagues are only personifications: "*Saturn* doth signify / good government," "*Apollo* how divinely to endite," and so on (B3v–4r). Elizabeth can without offense come to seem immortal, then, insofar as she may be said to represent a "heavenly wisdom" (∗2r) that encomia like the *Revelation* will eternize—"her fame shall never fade" (Fv).[62] But the peculiar constitution of Elizabeth and England—the one an otherworldly virgin, the other a land "Out from the world, yet on the ground, / Even in a place of bliss" (A3v)—makes their materiality seem an essential part of their spiritual significance, makes them as it were actual allegories, material spirit, in which the abstracted allegories of the Olympians can find "the chiefest place of rest and quiet peace / upon the ground" (C4v). In other words, Elizabeth's immortality in the *Revelation* seems tacitly to depend on the identification of her as the *true* Minerva, the fulfillment to dim heathen previsions like Virgil's, just as England itself completes the westward march of empire. Freed from mutability in a poem that is, after all, the "Revelation" in "this the last and latter age" (A2v) of a virgin in the wilderness, Elizabeth and her England seem to look toward an earthly millennium—"on earth heavenly felicity" (F4v).

For Elizabethan theologians, however, a fully realized mediation between heaven and earth, a "carnal" reign of the blessed, was indeed superstition and heresy: rather than embrace Revelation 20 as a prophecy of Elizian England, "the vast majority of Tudor Protestant writers . . . interpreted the millennium of that chapter as a period in the past history of the church" (Bauckham, *Tudor Apocalypse*, 209).[63] In this light, the self-conscious pastoral trifling in Blenerhasset and Peele, like the "superstitious" machinery both writers share with Lyly and Dekker, seems to turn Spenser's own method in *The Shepheardes Calender* on its head. Where Spenser had highlighted Elizian immateriality so as to insist, it seems, on the exclusively spiritual nature of the ideal that Elizabeth represents, Blenerhasset and Peele use pastoral inadequacy as a way both to assert millenarianism and to detach themselves from it; indeed, for them the already realized paradise of Elizian England seems in part to consist of such theological freedom. Yet the negative method on which this freedom—or rather hedging—depends, the method to which the ostensibly trifling Elizabeth and England seem perfectly suited as both means and proof, betrays its inherent constraints when Blenerhasset and Peele turn to another, more traditional ideal than "Elizium," one in which they have a more obvious interest. Both writers call England "Troynovant," "a second Troy," and this belief in England's imperial destiny encounters the same problems in realization I described earlier. As long as Elizabeth's empire is of the spirit, like the one the pope condemns in the *Revelation*—"The Gospel now my mortal enemy / By means of her is preacht both far and nigh" (C3r)— England's slim material power can, with difficulty, be overlooked. But when Peele later in his career urges forward the expeditionary forces of Drake and Norris (1589)—"Whatever course your matchless virtue shapes, / Whether to Europe's bounds or Asian plains, / To Affrick's shore, or rich America, / Down to the shades of deep Avernus' crags, / Sail on, pursue your honors to your graves" ("A Farewell," 43–47)—either this hell-bent expansionism or the virgin pastoral that earlier constituted English bliss must suffer.

The disastrous conclusion to the Drake and Norris venture certainly made it easy for Peele to choose, and he does return in *Descensus Astraeae* (1591) to his previous vision of Elizabeth as a pastoral genius, but, as my next chapter will try to demonstrate, the pastoral conception of England that Peele helps promote also encourages the expansionist disasters, the honorable graves, that in turn reinforce it. A peculiar combination of imperialist ambition on the one hand and complacence about English pettiness on the other led Blenerhasset to extol England's military might only in a game of war, a joust (E2v–4r); and more than a decade later Peele finds himself able to reconstitute in a martial context his earlier celebrations of England's otherworldly worldliness only in describing an Accession Day tournament: his *Anglorum Feriae* (written 1595) implores the Muses to descend to "Eliza's Court, Astraea's earthly heaven," where "England's Empress," the "fair Queen of Brutus' New Troy," is also "England's lovely shepherdess" (8–9, 113, 44). But, it seems, the strains of the post-Armada years—the military setbacks, the death of one hero after another, the aging of Elizabeth, and finally Peele's own unprofitable career as Elizian England's panegyrist—occasionally force the game to appear more otherworldly and unreal than Peele overtly intends. When the sons of Sir Francis Knollys enter the lists, Peele imagines that "three of great King Priam's valiant sons / had left Elizium and the field of Mars / to celebrate Eliza's holiday" (266–68): the New Troy looks momentarily like the old one, the English Elizium like the classical land of the dead.

In fact, Peele's post-Armada poetry increasingly grapples with the pessimism of *The Shepheardes Calender* in particular, as if the *Calender* had indeed charted the inevitable course that a celebratory English trifling must take. In Peele's "Eclogue Gratulatory" (1589), for instance, two Spenserian shepherds, Piers and Palinode, debate first whether Piers as a mere shepherd should attempt a "lofty note" (12), and then whether the unsuccessful Drake and Norris voyage deserves such a note.[64] By insisting that his paean is proper both for himself and for the returning expedition, Piers only emphasizes rather than avoids the invidious conflation of pastoral and defeat. "The Honour of the Garter" a few years later (1593) recounts what could have been a subject of high jingoism, Peele's dream vision of past Knights of the Garter, and Peele at least sinks to sleep with an allusion to the Armada triumph (10–15); but the ghostly procession of former conquerors now merely "appointed well / For tournament" (42–43) produces even in the celebratory ending of the poem a very different sense of England's military prowess: the spirit of the order's founder, Edward III, heaves a sigh for the loss of France (350–53). The prologue to the poem shows more directly how Peele has come round at last to "October" and "November." Heroes and patrons like Sidney and Walsingham "are fled to heaven," and Peele wonders "why thither speed not Hobbin and his pheres" (38–39)—"Hobbin" presumably Peele's interesting mistake for Spenser. After cataloguing the other great poets England has failed to reward, Peele finds himself, like Colin, spiritualizing the pastoral whose material manifestation he now forsakes:

> Why go not all into th'Elizian fields,
> And leave this Center, barren of repast,
> Unless in hope Augusta will restore,
> The wrongs that learning bears of covetousness
> And Court's disdain, the enemy to Art.
> Leave foolish lad, it mendeth not with words,
> Nor herbs nor time such remedy affords.
> (64–70)[65]

By the decade's end, Peele and "Colin" both have made the pilgrimage Peele recommends; the procession of spirits swells with ever more recent heroes. But it is not until Elizabeth's own death and the elegies mourning it that Spenser's logic in *The Shepheardes Calender* seems to receive wider recognition, and the ideal of pastoral virginity, of Elizian insubstantiality, seems always to have meant a longing for an otherworld separate even from England: "Her Maiden-head with noble virtue crown'd, / Hath now attain'd the hav'n of her desire" (Nixon, *Memoriall*, A3r); "For sweet *Eliza* in *Elizium* lives" (Petowe, *Elizabetha*, A4r); "Reign ever there on that *Elizian* green: / *Eliza*, well may be *Elizium's* Queen" (Lane, *Elegie*, B1v–B2r).[66] Now "November" 's allegory looks transparent:

> Oh, come, and do her corse with flowers embrave,
> And play some solemn music by her grave,
> Then sing her Requiem in some doleful Verse
> Or do the songs of *Colin Clout* rehearse.[67]

V

Yet the ostensible subject of mourning in "November" seems by the evocative name Spenser gives her—Dido—to complicate Spenser's position on English worldliness as I have so far presented it, to suggest that Colin's separation from English pastoral and its lost genius is a step not only toward *contemptus mundi* but also, mysteriously enough, toward empire. We have already encountered this connection between *contemptus* and empire in More, Wyatt, and Churchyard; but a passage from John Dee's *General and Rare Memorials* (1577), a tract written in part to promote the New World voyages Frobisher undertook around the time of *The Shepheardes Calender*, makes the transition from otherworldly detachment to an enhanced desire for attachment especially clear:

> I have oftentimes . . . and many ways, looked into the State of Earthly Kingdoms, Generally, the whole World over: (as far, as it may, yet, be known to Christian Men, Commonly:) being a Study, of no great Difficulty: But, rather, a purpose, somewhat answerable, to a perfect Cosmographer: to find him self, *Cosmopolites*: a Citizen, and Member, of the whole and only one Mystical City Universal: And so, consequently, to meditate of the Cosmopolitical Government thereof, under the King Almighty: passing on, very swiftly, toward the most Dreadful, and most Comfortable Term prefixed.
>
> And I find . . . that if this British Monarchy, would heretofore, have followed the Advantages, which they have had, onward, They might, very well, ere this, have surpassed (By Justice and Godly, sort) any particular Monarchy, else, that ever was on Earth, since Man's Creation. (54)

If the movement here from spiritual liberation to material expansion sounds anticlimactic, however, if the vision of time sweeping to its final crisis seems also to magnify a sense of England's lost opportunities, as if Dee cannot decide whether he sees a door opening or closing, the source of indecisiveness would appear once again to be the theological trickiness, the potentially heretical superstitiousness, of basing an imperialist hope on an apocalyptic one.

Spenser's next Virgilian effort after *The Shepheardes Calender* looks even more uncertain about how to ground England's otherworldliness. Were Spenser to continue emulating Virgil's career as closely as he had begun, he would follow his own eclogues with georgics, which even in their name (from the Greek *geo-*, earth, and *organ*, work) imply an engagement with the world. The life of Virgil commonly included in sixteenth-century editions of his works added to this sense of the georgic as inherently worldly a more specifically political resonance, associating Virgil's georgics with the consolidation of empire: "It was related that Vergil joined Octavian at Atella, where the latter, returning victorious from Actium, was delayed by a minor illness. For four days Vergil and Maecenas read to Octavian the recently completed *Georgics*. The leader who had emerged victorious from what was to prove the last battle of the civil wars was thus confronted with the poet's fervent and hopeful celebration of the arts of peace" (O'Connell, *Mirror*, 3). Unfortunately, the years following the publication of

Spenser's eclogues *ended* peace for Elizabeth. Except for the re-
marks, mainly figurative, in agriculture's direction that appear in
"December" 's retrospective (73–126), Spenser omits writing about
such georgic "planting"; he describes his next work instead as
"wild fruit," from a land "through long wars left almost waste."[68]
And more fatal still, it would seem, to the imperialist project
"Dido" appears to announce, the contested ground about which
Spenser actually writes is Fairyland.

Yet *The Faerie Queene* begins with the story of an erstwhile fairy
peasant who discovers that his true identity is both English and
"georgic"—England's patron saint, George. If first eschewing
georgics and then offering the name George as the object of an
epic quest look like mixed signals, Spenser's choice of a saint for
his model of English heroism increases the confusion. To most
Protestants, the veneration of the saints seemed not only a misguided celebration of worldly life but even a kind of necrophilia.
For example, after enumerating some of the wonders of God's
power, Jean Veron in *A Stronge Battery Against the Idolatrous Invocation of the Dead Saintes* (1562) asks,

> But do not our adversaries most sacrilegiously, robbing god of his
> glory, attribute all those things to his dead creatures, I mean, to
> those that be already departed out of this world? what have they
> left unto god? what help what aid and succor that they have need
> of, do they not crave at the dead's hands? (A2v–A3r)

Help comes instead, says Veron, paraphrasing Romans 8.34, from
"Christ which is dead yea, rather which is risen again" (A6v); to
feel the need for the intercession of the dead means for Veron to
fear God's hatred of life, as if the dead were all He loved—to believe that "life . . . shall be able to separate us from the love of
God, which is in Jesus Christ" (Romans 8.38–39). The pagans personified their fear in their idols, and in Veron's account Saint
George figures as nothing but a new bloodthirsty pagan god: "The
English men had in stead of god Mars, whom the heathen worshipped for the god of Battles, that lusty knight Saint George of
Cappadocia" (A3r).

Spenser does more than appear indifferent to this kind of attack, however; he seems to dare his reader to think still worse
of him. As if choosing a saint for a hero were not enough of a
problem, Spenser further courts Protestant antagonism by placing

his English knight in a country that Protestants believed superstition had invented. Even E. K. reveals Spenser's perversity:

> The opinion of Fairies and elves is very old, and yet sticketh very religiously in the minds of some. But to root that rank opinion of Elves out of men's hearts, the truth is, that there be no such things, nor yet the shadows of the things, but only by a sort of bald Friars and knavish shavelings so feigned; which as in all other things, so in that, sought to nousel the common people in ignorance, lest being once acquainted with the truth of things, they would in time smell out the untruth of their packed pelf and Masspenny religion. (*V* 7:64)

In mocking elsewhere those "fine fablers and loud liars, such as were the Authors of King Arthur the great and such like" (*V* 7:44), E. K. moreover shows *The Faerie Queene* astoundingly on the wrong side of a third tradition of Protestant hostility, an animus this time against the Arthurian romances Spenser imitates and in which fairies so often figure.[69] The extremely popular Elizabethan homilist Edward Dering (1572) in fact manages to denounce saints, fairies, and quest-romances in one continuous tirade. Our forefathers, declares Dering,

> had their spiritual enchantments, in which they were bewitched, *Bevis* of Hampton, *Guy* of Warwick, *Arthur* of the round table, *Huon* of Bordeaux, *Oliver* of the Castle, the four sons of *Amon*, and a great many other of such childish folly. . . . And yet of all the residue the most drunken imaginations, with which they so defiled their Festival and high holydays, their *Legendary*, their Saints' lives, their tales of *Robin Goodfellow*, and of many other Spirits, which Satan had made, Hell had printed, and were warranted unto sale under the Pope's privilege, to kindle in men's hearts the sparks of superstition, that at last it might flame out into the fire of Purgatory. (*Briefe*, A2v)[70]

As so many "heathen fancies" that belong to the death of life without true faith, and that moreover lead to delusions about life after death, the saints, fairies, and romance so adamantly embraced by Spenser would seem to convict *The Faerie Queene* not of grounding Colin's *contemptus* but of falling victim to the ungroundedness that a *contemptus* may encourage. By this account, the trifling evasion of dualism in Blenerhasset and Peele that still ends up reducing English value to either the worldly or the otherworldly Elizium, to the English island or heaven, looks far less idle and delusory than Spenser's rejection of such a compromise. And yet, I have argued, Spenser seems to court such a critique, as if he has decided that the best way to avoid a debased trifling and instead reveal little England as both temporally and spiritually grand is to embrace superstition even more radically than his opponents—as Drayton described it at the time, "Colin . . . is to fayrie gone a Pilgrimage."[71] The advantages of this more extreme trifling, of basing an epic, and the imperial claims for England which that epic tries to articulate, on "such fabulous and ludicrous toys" (Harvey, *Discoursive*, 68–69) as fairies, romances, and saints, are not obvious. Poetry and England may meet—what Nashe (1589) calls the "feigned nowhere acts" of papist romance may assimilate *The Faerie Queene* to England's "nowhere" status in the European world[72]—but they meet only under what are apparently the worst possible conditions for both. This displacement of poetry and England to "nowhere" is, however, the key to Spenser's imperialist project even in the *Calender*, where Spenser attacks the reduction of England to the present materiality of its "Elizian" island. In *The Faerie Queene*, my next chapters will argue, Spenser decides to replace the heroic trifles of that island with the far more insubstantial heroic trifles of his poetry, so as continually to suggest England's transcendent spiritual *and* material potentiality without risking the absorption of that potentiality by any trivializing material embodiments.[73] Ironically engaging the skeptic's complaint about Fairyland in the proem to *The Faerie Queene* book 2—"Right well I wote most mighty Soveraine, / That all this famous antique history, / Of some th'aboundance of an idle braine / Will judged be, and painted forgery" (1)—Spenser goes on to claim that what looks like Nowhere actually represents a more other-worldly extension of Elizabeth's virgin power than even "fruitfullest Virginia": "And thou, O fairest Princesse under sky, / In this faire mirrhour maist behold thy face, / And thine owne realmes in lond of Faery" (4).[74] I will argue, in fact, that by exaggerating the traditional inanity of poetry, by composing an epic that, to the literal-minded, seems groundless, Spenser believes he can even substitute *The Faerie Queene* for Elizabeth as the more heroically "superstitious" motive to empire. For Spenser, Fairyland, not "Elizium," becomes the otherworldly weakness that liberates English strength.

3

Error as a Means of Empire

And surely seeing an Idol is nothing, it cannot infect the
creatures of God, but that the faithful may use them purely
and lawfully.
—Calvin, *Commentaries* . . .
upon . . . Acts (1585)

Now take my gnat, and try me in a toy,
Whether hereafter I may sing of Troy.
—Thomas Bastard,
Chrestoleros (1598)

So puzzling is Fairyland as an imperialist topic that critics have
tended to assume a true imperialism enters *The Faerie Queene* only
when Fairyland itself begins to crumble—as C. S. Lewis puts
it, "Spenser was the instrument of a detestable policy in Ireland,
and in his fifth book the wickedness he had shared begins to corrupt his imagination" (*Allegory*, 349).[1] Lewis does seem right to
insist on the relative invisibility of Spenser's colonial interests until the later books of the poem. Not until book 4, after all, does
Spenser explicitly exhort his countrymen to occupy any foreign
land;[2] while the famous mention of the Americas in the proem to
book 2—

Who ever heard of th'Indian *Peru*?
Or who in venturous vessell measured
The *Amazons* huge river now found trew?
Or fruitfullest *Virginia* who did ever vew?
(2)

—leads to an appeal not to colonize the New World but to believe
in the existence of Fairyland. If it seems peculiar for an Elizabethan
imperialist poem to have been diffident on the subject of America,
far more peculiar is *The Faerie Queene*'s early silence about the one

ongoing English attempt at expansion of the time, the Munster occupation, of which Spenser was a dedicated and profiting agent.

The bounds of genre or the lack of literary precedent cannot rightly be considered the real impediment to representation here. As Michael O'Connell points out, Camões in *The Lusiads* two decades earlier found no trouble naming actual names: a minor official in the Portuguese East Empire, Camões celebrates the voyage of Vasco da Gama that made his own colonial position possible. O'Connell decides that the moral of comparing Spenser to Camões is this: "*The Faerie Queene*, though undeniably patriotic, seems by its reticence toward specific historical deeds more skeptical—more Vergilian—than nationalistic" (*Mirror*, 5). Yet, the problematic equation of Virgil and political skepticism aside, O'Connell grants Spenser a freedom to imitate Camões that the Englishman may have possessed on literary grounds but hardly on historical ones: what epic founding comparable to da Gama's could Spenser have praised?[3] The comparison to Camões[4] in fact makes Spenser's "afflicted stile" (*FQ* 1.proem.4) in *The Faerie Queene* seem not so much skeptical or unworthy of its imperial argument as rather a function of that argument having no basis in fact.

The Shepheardes Calender had already highlighted the two handicaps to an Elizabethan epic—and Elizabethan empire—that seem to bother Spenser most: the relatively commonplace theological problem of reconciling the desire for empire to a proper *contemptus mundi*, and the more unusual political problem of extending the notion of "England" beyond the virginal ideal embodied by Elizabeth. These problems are both, significantly, ideological, not material; Spenser's epic will focus on single heroes, not on the more common epic subject of large-scale military expeditions, because he believes England will achieve empire only insofar as it fashions imperial-minded English gentlemen. And the first line of *The Faerie Queene* (1590), "A Gentle Knight was pricking on the plaine," turns Colin's unhappy exile from England and the world at the end of *The Shepheardes Calender* into the positive virtue Spenser wants his gentleman to desire from the start—mobility. The heroes England could claim were, after all, voyagers, men like Drake and Hawkins who had not only invaded Spain's New World but driven off her invading Armada. Richard Hakluyt (1589) celebrates "the principal navigations" of his countrymen, praising the English as the "stirrers abroad" par excellence (Taylor, *Original Writings* 2:399). In *The Spanish Masquerado* (1589), Robert Greene even interprets the Armada as God's signal that the overly complacent English should get moving: "Seeing how secure we slept, careless, reposing ourselves in that our own strength, for that we were hedged in with the sea, and had a long and peaceable time of quiet: made slothful by these his favors, his Majesty brought in these Spaniards to waken us out of our dreams" (*Works* 5:256). Yet the motion God requires is, in Greene's account, curiously circular, a way not to overgo but to reinforce the view that "God maketh ENGLAND like EDEN, a second Paradise" (287): the wreck of the Armada on the one hand and the successful return of Drake, Frobisher, and Cavendish from their American raids on the other show "that the Lord is on our side, that bringeth us home safe" (258). Greene's shortsightedness about excursions from England demonstrates that mobility is only the start of what the English imperialist-to-be must learn; his real enemy is the "Elizium" to which England's stirrers abroad feel they must return.

This chapter will argue, however, that even Spenser qualifies his impatience with English complacence: he believes the very limitations of a pastoral view of England make that view useful as a negative incitement to empire. Though *The Faerie Queene* begins by conventionally announcing its turn from pastoral, Spenser not only continues to call his poetry "rustic,"[5] but, I will show, returns to pastoral in the poem's first episode: he wants to establish empire and epic only by way of their difference from Elizium and pastoral. I will then briefly review the *Calender*'s sense that a pastoral view of England endangers England by fostering a theology and economy of trifling; yet, just as the Error episode uses pastoral trifling to dramatize the case for empire, so I will argue that Spenser's fellow imperialists plan not to eradicate England's trifles but to exploit them as a way to manipulate the pastoral sensibility of America's Indians. Finally I will explain how instances of pastoral in *The Faerie Queene* only highlight a continual process in the poem—and, ultimately, in Elizabethan culture—of defining ideals by their difference from trifles one can transcend. Yet these ideals prove so difficult to formulate otherwise that Spenser finds himself returning again and again to what has supposedly been transcended, until one begins to wonder whether pastoral in *The Faerie*

Queene has, as Geoffrey Hartman says, "swallowed both epic and romance" ("Nymph," 189)—and, finally, the dream of empire as well.

ERROR AS PASTORAL

As early in *The Faerie Queene* as its dedication, which styles Elizabeth the "Empress" of two countries, Ireland and France, over which the Elizabethans exercised little or no control (*V* 1:528), Spenser enables his readers to ask whether England's imperial pretensions can be said to fit the facts. The poem itself begins by raising analogous questions. In its first lines, which paraphrase one version of the *Aeneid*'s first lines, Spenser describes his Muse as previously having only "maske[d]" "in lowly Shepheards weeds" (*FQ* 1.proem.1); he goes on to wonder whether he is not "unfit" for the task of writing a Virgilian epic. A few stanzas later, in the first lines of the poem's narrative, Spenser introduces an armored knight who only a short time earlier had been "unfit through his rusticity" for any better seat at the court of the Fairy Queen than the floor (*V* 1:169), and who now only "seem[s]" "fit" for battle (*FQ* 1.1.1). This novice has, moreover, been given a surprisingly large commission: he must avenge those

> ancient Kings and Queenes, that had of yore
> Their scepters stretcht from East to Westerne shore,
> And all the world in their subjection held;
> Till that infernall feend with foule uprore
> Forwasted all their land, and them expeld.
> (1.1.5)

For an untried warrior who must both recapture a world empire and undo the Fall, the "hideous storm" (6) that begins the action of *The Faerie Queene* represents an appropriate test: itself a postlapsarian phenomenon, the storm derives from an "angry *Jove*" who seems to threaten the knight with no more than what he, like every other fallen creature, justly deserves. To evade this stricter sense of the fate that befits him, the knight retreats to "a shadie grove . . . / That promist ayde the tempest to withstand" (7). But the grove is an Eden that resists, rather than escapes, God's wrath—the trees hide "heavens light" (7), the birds "[seem] in their song to scorne the cruell sky" (8)—and in any case a pleasant grove in which to "shroud" (6) oneself is something less than the earth-spanning empire that the knight was supposed to secure, just as it is also less than the "trumpets sterne" that Spenser, the former pastoral poet, was now supposed to sound. The grove, that is, threatens to foreclose not only the imperial ambition of the red-cross knight but Spenser's equally untried poetical ambition to write an epic. But then Spenser's possible failure had already been suggested by the storm itself, which, in darkly alluding to Virgil's depiction of spring showers in the *Georgics* 2, stages the epic's first episode as a kind of miscreation, a devolution in the Virgilian poet's career.[6]

As the narrative continues, the substitution of grove for empire proves only the first in a series of contracted sights that climaxes in Redcross's strangulation: the sheltering "covert" (7) condenses to "a hollow cave" (11), the winding landscape to Error's "up-wound" (15) tail, soon murderously to be "wound" so tightly around the questing knight "that hand or foot to stirre he strove in vaine" (18). Half-woman, half-serpent, proleptically conjoining in herself the images of the fair lady who begins Redcross's quest and the dragon that will end it, the miscreative Error gives body and name to the logic that threatens quest and poem. Her entrance follows what had seemed a far happier combination of human and natural, first in the grove offering shelter, then in each of its prof-itable trees, like "the Eugh obedient to the benders will" (8–9)—which invoke another bit of the *Georgics*, Virgil's celebration of what "even sterile woods" provide for our use (2.440–53). Yet the trees are not used, only admired, or rather, the only use to which they are put represents a devolution even from georgic poetry: for the "shadie grove" in which Redcross and Una "shroud" them-selves recalls the "shade" in which Thenot and Hobbinol lay "close shrowded" ("Aprill," 32), the pastoral whose abandonment inaugurates Spenser's epic.[7] In its shrinking, then, the landscape registers a deepening involvement in the "lowly" (*FQ* 1.proem.1) poetic mode that the now heroic poet has supposedly left behind.

Error herself best figures both the involvement and its danger, for she travesties nothing other than Colin's "Aprill" ideal of pro-portion, of the kind of perfect fit between human and natural that Colin used to celebrate.[8] The transformation of her grove into a

labyrinth figures such trust in nature's hospitality to be a dangerous dependence. "They cannot finde that path, which first was
showne": the landscape assumes the agency of which Redcross
and Una feel themselves increasingly deprived, so that they
"doubt, their wits be not their owne." What first mirrored human
intention, human intention now mirrors: "so many pathes, so
many turnings" engender "diverse doubt" (1.1.10). As readers of
The Faerie Queene often notice, the battle between Redcross and Error elaborates this struggle over volition with almost mathematical
precision.[9] When Error's tail finally becomes "wound" about Redcross as it had been around "her selfe" (18), the two combatants
thus combined simply reproduce the chimera that Error has been
all along.

Glossing the earlier tree catalogue as "worldly delight" (*First
Commentary*, 2), John Dixon, a sixteenth-century reader of the
poem, alerts us to the potentially commonplace import of the
threat Error poses. According to Augustine, for instance, an interest in the things of this world must be a mistake, a loss, because
we are not of this world. Augustine's most famous formulation of
what is to him the essential error appears in *De doctrina christiana*
1.4:

> Suppose we were wanderers who could not live in blessedness ex-
> cept at home, miserable in our wandering and desiring to end it and
> to return to our native country. We would need vehicles for land
> and sea which could be used to help us to reach our homeland,
> which is to be enjoyed. But if the amenities of the journey and the
> motion of the vehicles itself delighted us, and we were led to enjoy
> those things which we should use, we should not wish to end our
> journey quickly, and, entangled in a perverse sweetness, we should
> be alienated from our country, whose sweetness would make us
> blessed. (Trans. Robinson, 9–10)[10]

The passage reads like a paraphrase of the Error episode, but for
two major differences: Spenser's "wandring wood" (*FQ* 1.1.13) is
not the world as such but only a certain spot on it; and Redcross
and Una have set out not to transcend the world but to reclaim it.
In isolating error as a mistake one makes on the way to empire,
the Error episode begins to suggest that what Augustine means by
worldliness is only what Spenser means by pastoral.

This distinction between an erroneous and an acceptable worldliness explains how Redcross frees himself from Error and gets

himself moving again. Unsurprisingly, perhaps, Redcross finds the strength to break Error's stranglehold on him only after Una reminds Redcross of his "faith"; he then follows Una's exhortation to "shew what ye bee" (19) by holding the monster at arm's length for a *contemptus*-like inspection. What's curious, however, is that Redcross in this distancing action still mirrors Error, "knitting" himself as she had gathered herself, strangling as she had strangled, as if her choking of him had been a necessary lesson. And in fact only when Error strangles Redcross, and Spenser objectifies the struggle—"God helpe the man so wrapt in *Errours* endlesse traine" (18)—does Una arrive to rally her knight, "sad to see" what, strictly speaking, she is unable to see: the oppressive cave that separated her from the battle has vanished, as if replaced as a "constraint" (19) by the collapse of identity between knight and monster. In other words, the reduction of Redcross to Error allows Una a *vision* of worldliness that helps Redcross "constraine" (19) his own vision, just as Spenser helps the reader see Error by restricting the phenomenon to one certain grove, and then to the verbal emblem of Redcross's struggle, complete with moralizing tag.

The questers after an English empire gain, that is, a privileged perspective on worldliness normally reserved for sky-dwellers like Urania, who, "loathing earth," must fly to heaven:

> Thence I behold the miserie of men,
> Which want the blis that wisedom would them breed,
> And like brute beasts doo lie in loathsome den,
> Of ghostly darkenes, and of gastlie dreed.
> (Spenser, *The Teares of the Muses,*
> 527, 529–32)

Indeed, their spectatorial position seems almost to end the battle. Error's consequent vomit or "parbreake" (a breaking through or thoroughly) widens the already saving breach between the monster and Redcross, forcing him not, as we might expect, to spit back at her, but rather to "turne him backe" from her (*FQ* 1.1.20). What has always astonished readers is the wildly disconnected variety of this vomit—"Blind, printed, and undigested!" Angus Fletcher exclaims. Yet Fletcher's dismay at Spenser's extravagance here helps clarify its thematic purpose. "One can hardly begin to tie the mistakenness of Errour to any particular fault or vice of knowledge" (*Prophetic*, 61): the sheer heterogeneity of Error's food blocks any binding, proportionate relation between it and the knight. The sheltering enclosure that has steadily shrunk, from lofty trees to claustrophobic cave to Error's stranglehold, now manifests itself to the removed Redcross as "lumpes," "gobbets," "bookes and papers," "frogs and toades," the "weedy gras" (*FQ* 1.1.20)—as minutiae, that is, to the man exalted by faith and Una above worldliness.[11]

But the stink of this "filthy parbreake" does affect the still ground-borne Redcross; he has been removed from the world only so far as to consider it not one small and loathsome den, but heterogeneous, *not one*. The excursus of the simile that follows, the first heroic simile of the poem (21), distances us both from Error's den and the hectic retaliations of battle while keeping us still on earth. The abrupt violence of "she spewd" slows to a seasonal change in a far, expansive setting: "As when old father *Nilus* gins to swell / With timely pride above the *Aegyptian* vale" (21). This old father's timely flooding refigures angry Jove's miscreative "tempest" (7) as originating from below, in the setting of a Captivity long ago escaped; while "fattie," "fertile," and "fruitful" positively separate the stanza from Error's loathsome vomit until the last line, which almost contradicts the description leading to it: "Such ugly monstrous shapes elsewhere may no man reed." This peculiar deferral of a necessary evaluative reflection, as it were loosening the poetry's own absorption in Error—an effect Harry Berger has called "conspicuous irrelevance"[12]—foreshadows the dispersal of Error into "her fruitfull cursed spawne" (22). When the action resumes, Redcross's actions continue not to mirror Error's; once again she is forced to represent, and so reduce, herself: the grove's enclosure finally sinks away from Redcross to the "serpents small" Error defecates from her "sinke," "Which swarming all about his legs did crall, / And him encombred sore, but could not hurt at all" (22).

Now, when the battle to end pastoral error has effectively been won, and almost to delay Error's inevitable destruction, an overt pastoral uncannily reenters Spenser's poetry.

> As gentle Shepheard in sweete even-tide,
> When ruddy *Phoebus* gins to welke in west,
> High on an hill, his flocke to vewen wide,
> Markes which do byte their hasty supper best;

> A cloud of combrous gnattes do him molest,
> All striving to infixe their feeble stings,
> That from their noyance he no where can rest,
> But with his clownish hands their tender wings
>   He brusheth oft, and oft doth mar their murmurings.
>   (23)

Just as Error ceases to overwhelm Redcross as soon as he grasps and sees it, so Spenser manifests the covert logic of the episode—pastoral—only when that logic has been relegated to a comparison with the scene it originally constituted, when pastoral, that is, can be visualized in and as a single stanza. Yet, if the stanza does in some sense retrospectively clarify the episode, the battle it depicts between a gentle shepherd and some gnats nevertheless disrupts our sense not only of the other fight's ferocity but of its stakes—now the human seems the offender. For the sweet eventide, the sunset, the hasty supper, and the marred soft song all evoke an elegiac spirit to which the shepherd stands opposed: he is high on a hill, his star is ascendant, he takes Phoebus's place. When we discover that John Dixon glosses the stanza by referring it to Matthew 4.8, a stage in Christ's temptation—"The devil showeth him all the delights of the world to entice," Dixon says, "but can not deceive" (*First Commentary*, 3)—the tonality of this truly Spenserian stanza comes to seem so mixed and peculiar as to warrant longer inspection.[13]

Though it is difficult to see how the details of the stanza might coalesce into the allusion Dixon finds there, the temptation on the mount, the culmination (in Matthew) of Christ's own wandering, has a certain dramatic propriety in relation to the Error allegory. A passage from More's translation of the *Life of Pico* (1510) automatically connects the two struggles: "Remember how cursed our old enemy is: which offereth us the kingdoms of this world, that he might bereave us the kingdom of heaven, how false the fleshly pleasures: which therefore embrace us, that they might strangle us" (*Works* 1:17). To such temptation Christ responded, "Avoid Satan" (Matthew 4.10); Petrarch atop Mont Ventoux found himself remonstrated by Augustine's lament that men go abroad to wonder at nature and yet leave themselves behind; but what in the shepherd's action recalls either Christ's repudiation or Petrarch's turning inward? Only, perhaps, his brushing gnats away, whose foremost iconographic association, ephemerality, does fit the *contemptus* theme: in the part of his *contemptus* litany immediately before the passage I quoted, Pico reminds his nephew that "the death lieth at hand. Remember that all the time of our life is but a moment, and yet less than a moment." The gnats also iconographically embody, and therefore distance and reduce, similarly worldly attributes of Error such as heresy, lechery, and even wandering,[14] and so suggest the possibility of at least a kind of Cynic *contemptus* in the stanza, the philosophy of Erasmus's Folly:

> If one (as *Menippus* did) looking out of the moon, beheld from thence the innumerable tumults, and businesses of mortal men, he should think verily he saw a many *of flies, or gnats, brawling, fighting, beguiling, robbing, playing, living wantonly, born, bred up, decaying, and dying*: So that it is scant believable, what commotions, and what *Tragedies*, are stirred up, by so little, and so short lived a vermin as this man is. (*Praise*, K3v)[15]

Yet, while such pagan *contemptus* may find its counterpart in the bathetic side of the shepherd's battle, the "noyance" from which "he no where can rest,"[16] the same features of the scene that weaken the suggestive connection between it and Christian virtue baffle this allegory also. Though high on a hill, the shepherd views neither gnatlike men nor worldly kingdoms but his flock; the gnats themselves, if comically miniaturized glories of the world below, are nevertheless atop the hill also; and their tender wings and murmurings generate a pathos that counters any repudiation of them. In sum, what blocks these allegorical readings, what keeps the stanza, for all its *contemptus* yearnings, earthbound, is the "lowly" character and setting Spenser and Redcross set out to leave behind them—the pastoral.

It looks misguided for a poet who announced his turn from pastoral and then proceeded to figure pre-epical modes as potentially deadly now to regret the loss of pastoral worldliness; but this final reduction, dislocation, and clarification of pastoral into a simile, the facing off of pastoral with its erroneous image, seems for Spenser to justify such nostalgia. The stanza's elegiac tone bespeaks more than the coming end of the episode itself. In the previous simile the characterization of father Nilus as old anticipated a turning back of the clock here also, the introduction of another old character: the gentle shepherd with his clownish hands recalls the clownish young men both Redcross and Spenser had been until only recently.[17] Surrounding the shepherd, circumscribing this old identity, the gnats refigure the collapse of Redcross into Error and therefore also the spectatorial distance granted Una and then Redcross himself. Indeed, they turn the discarded pastoral in upon itself, for their "tender wings" invoke E. K.'s company of pastoral poets, whose prior flights on "tender wings" Spenser in *The Shepheardes Calender* set out "every where" to emulate.[18] The bizarre Circean reduction of these poets to insects looks less surprising in the context of Virgilian poetics, which takes for granted that a poet should proportion his choice of subject to himself: if he is a fledgling, then his subject should be diminutive also, like the *Culex* Spenser translated as *Virgils Gnat*.[19] In representing pastoral poets *as* one of these small subjects—as gnats—the simile literally collapses an already metaphorically collapsible relation, and so substitutes the shepherd surrounded by gnats, and the gnats themselves, as a diffracted image of the strangulation Redcross just suffered. What the pathos of the stanza would seem to register, then, is Spenser's desire to hang onto a scene that he believes liberates both Redcross and himself by staging their erroneous past and so differentiating them from its constraint.

The thwarted *contemptus* of the stanza indicates how pastoral can go so far as to be divided against itself, as in *The Shepheardes Calender*, and yet fall short of transcendence. The simile begins hopefully. The Error episode introduced a pastoral-like grove, we recall, as a shelter from heavenly wrath, from the hideous storm; pastoral's far more typical reason for shelter is only the heat of the sun, and, in the simile, with the sun sinking in the west, the shepherd escapes even that slight inconvenience. Yet, though free now to leave the shade for a lofty hilltop vision of his world, the shepherd still labors under the pressure of a temporal "tempest" (*FQ* 1.1.7, 8), even when, or rather because, heavenly power seems to absent itself from the world. The vision comes only at this "hasty" moment, only when day is nearly done; the shepherd can contemn his world only, that is, when it is being eclipsed. And in favor of what would he despise it? The only other world to desire, heaven, the sun, is what's becoming absent; and if the shepherd's flock represents the paltry, fleeting vanities he might despise, appropriately metamorphosed into gnats, they, like a new grove, still encumber him, because until the death all shepherds ought to long for ("November," 182–92), he has no other place but his diminished world in which to live.

Redcross and Spenser, on the other hand, have only to discard pastoral in order to enact their own little apocalypse, sacrificing one kind of worldliness in order to save another. When Redcross severs Error's human head from her animal body, he explodes pastoral's strangling proportionment of human to natural, of self to place; with Error's head the trees of her grove (metonymically) fall as well, no longer required for shade but for the kind of use to which, say, the first tree mentioned, "the sayling Pine" (*FQ* 1.1.8), should be put. The death of Error even provides a final "sight" (26) of collapse: combining in themselves the shepherd's two cares, both the hungry sheep and the gnats "striving to infixe," Error's "scattred brood" have "flocked" (25) about their unhumanized mother and now "devoure" (26) her. As Error's blood and then her children's overstuffed bowels gush forth (24, 26),[20] a constraint or implosion once more turns outside, to the spectatorial freedom of Redcross simply watching his foes defeat themselves, or of "his Ladie seeing all" now approaching "from farre" (27). The microcosm that dies enemy to God—"cursed" Error and her "unkindly Impes of heaven accurst" (16, 26)—opens a worldly space, the "long way" Redcross travels, in which he can have "God to frend" (28) as well, a roominess subject only to the "happy starre" Redcross was "borne under" (27), distant in both space and time.

ERROR AS TRIFLING

Error appears to represent a mistake, however, that not just Spenser but England as a whole had recently escaped, a delusive ideal more clearly embodied in the second monster Redcross meets, though Archimago at first protests himself only a "silly old man," who, because he "lives in hidden cell, / Bidding his beades all day for his trespas," knows nothing of "worldly trouble" (*FQ* 1.1.30). In his youth Erasmus, of all people, spoke of monastic life in *De Contemptu Mundi* (1521, trans. 1532?) as a pastoral retreat, a covert to fend off the hideous storms of worldly existence: "Who (but he that is stark blind) seeth not that it is far more surer, more pleasant, and more commodious to journey through the pleasant green meadows without dread, than among so many images of death to be turned and went with perpetual vexation and trouble" (13r–v). Adapting passages from Virgil's *Eclogues*, Erasmus celebrates the monastery "like to Paradise of pleasure," where, among "orchards and greaves," "within these dens," "groweth the pople tree, to shadow us from showers" (13v–14r).[21] In Renaissance English versions of the Old Testament, however, "groves" figure as the idolatrous shrines that God repeatedly commands the Jews to "cut down" (e.g., Exodus 34.13); and Greene lauds the day England's "woodman" Henry VIII wounded the "Monster" Antichrist by demolishing its monastic hiding places: "flying to the text, whatsoever my father hath not planted, shall be rooted up by the roots, he suppressed their Abbeys, pulled down their sumptuous buildings, & scarce left one stone upon another" (*Works* 5:251).[22] The shattering of such pleasances "seeldom inward sound" (*FQ* 1.1.9) produced what many Protestants must have considered liberating catalogues of the rottenness and insubstantiality, the "pelting trash" (e.g., Derricke, *Image of Irelande*, 22), at their core: supposedly "holy relics" disgorged into the light as "stinking boots, mucky combs, ragged rochets, rotten girdles, pilled purses, great bullocks' horns, locks of hair, and filthy rags, gobbets of wood, under the name of parcels of the holy cross, and such pelfry beyond estimation."[23]

Spenser establishes the relation between Catholic worldliness and the pastoral ideal of proportion, and then reduces this subverted ideal to a literal trifle, first of all in *The Shepheardes Calender*'s tale of the fox and the kid. According to E. K.'s commentary on "Maye," the eclogue in which the tale appears, the interlocutors Piers and Palinode represent "two forms of pastors or Ministers, or the protestant and the Catholic." Piers wants to explain to the papist Palinode, "a worldes childe" (73), why Protestants would be foolish to make friends with papists, and so tells him a fable. The kid's mother leaves him at home for a while, warning him to keep his door locked. The "false Foxe" then comes to the kid's door disguised "as a poor pedler . . . / Bearing a trusse of tryfles at hys backe, / As Bells, and babes [i.e., dolls], and glasses in hys packe" (236, 238–40); "by such trifles," says E. K., "are noted, the relics and rags of popish superstition, which put no small religion in Bells: and Babies .s. Idols: and glasses .s. Paxes, and such like trumperies."²⁴ Pretending to be sick and lame, the fox lures the kid to unlock his door by presenting him a glass—the kid "was so enamored with the newell, / That nought he deemed deare for the jewell" (276–77). Once inside, the fox tells the kid

> many lesings of this, and that:
> And how he could shewe many a fine knack.
> Tho shewed his ware, and opened his packe,
> All save a bell, which he left behind
> In the basket for the Kidde to fynd.
> Which when the Kidde stooped downe to catch,
> He popt him in, and his basket did latch.
>
> (285–91)

The strangling collapse of pastoral proportion in *The Faerie Queene* here figures as a ludicrous mirroring in the little world of the glass; the false security of this mirroring is in effect what devours the kid. From the start the debate between Piers and Palinode had framed the kid's disaster in terms of failing to recognize one's enemies: the fox declares that "sicker I am very sybbe to you" (269), while his pretended lameness reinforces the false claim to kinship by making it seem impossible for him to have come from very far away. Because the kid is such a homebody, and so absorbed in the glass world that shows him nothing but himself, he cannot see the fox as the stranger, the Roman, he truly is.²⁵

Such blindness, the fox's peddling disguise suggests, ruins England not only theologically but economically. Tudor economists like Sir Thomas Smith often deplored England's habit of conducting its business "as though we had need of no other country in the earth but to live all of ourselves and as though we might make the market of all things as we list ourselves."²⁶ According to Smith, this ethos of self-sufficiency only breeds ignorance of foreign wiles, so much so that the English have become not only willing but eager to "pay inestimable treasure every year or else exchange substantial wares and necessary" for the superfluous "trifles" strangers sell (*Discourse*, 62–63). Clement Armstrong (c. 1533–36) complains about the foxlike "peddlers and chapmen . . . sitting on holidays and sundays in church porches and in abbeys daily to sell all such trifles, whereby all strangers in other realms hath work, and English men hath none" ("Treatise," 109); while William Harrison (1577) speaks of foreigners who brag "that they will buy the case of a fox of an Englishman for a groat, and make him afterward give twelve pence for the tail."[27] Although G. V. Scammel reminds us that "such doctrines were not peculiarly English and were equally prominent in France and Spain" ("Hakluyt," 20), Smith implies that England's insularity makes it peculiarly susceptible to exploitation: for Smith, in effect, England's homebodies cannot grasp the limitations of their island home, its smallness and its circumscription by the many enemies without who masquerade as kin. "Experienced" pastoral like the "Maye" eclogue may alert the English to the trifle-hawking papist enemy within, but it does nothing about the existence of an outside vastly greater than home, an outside now coalescing into the single huge threat of the Spanish empire.[28] Spenser represents the dilemma as the vicious irony and hopeless trap of a pastoral *contemptus*: even though one may gain a bird's-eye view of home's limitations, as the shepherd does in both "November" and *The Faerie Queene*'s pastoral simile, one is still left with home only—if not a credulous, at least a de facto proportioning between the kid and his baubles, the shepherd and his gnats, the self and its trifles. According to Spenser, in fact, Protestant England only continues to "delight" as Redcross and Una do (*FQ* 1.1.10) in another version of the danger it believes itself to have escaped. Like the "Aprill" Colin, Thomas Blenerhasset (1582) may praise Elizabeth as superior to those princes "who live on earth to every tempest thrall," and George Peele (1584) may celebrate Eliza's "pleasant shady woods, / Where neither storm nor Sun's distemperature / Have power to hurt";[29] but the English can never be safe, Spenser maintains, until they leave the false security of their trifle-world.

To England's colonial advocates, the solution seemed obvious—the New World, the perfect place to leave for, the storehouse that would supply all of little England's lacks.[30] But if colonialists saw America as an opportunity for England to dispense with its old trifling once and for all, they nevertheless continued to cherish trifles even in their new world trade. This time, however, the English became the clever foreigners. To writers like Sir Humphrey Gilbert (1576), for example, the *savage* avidity for trifles—for the very "glasses, puppets, rattles, and such things" that, in the context of Smith's *Discourse* (69), pestered England—had marvelous practical implications. Not only would these trifles readily persuade the savages to surrender their gold as the English had done, but by the production of trifles England's weaknesses at home would now be as it were alchemically transmuted into good. Gilbert trusts that by western voyages Englishmen will "have occasion, to set poor men's children, to learn handy crafts, and thereby to make trifles and such like, which the Indians and those people [the Chinese] do much esteem: By reason whereof, there should be none occasion, to have our country cumbered with loiterers, vagabonds, and such like idle persons."[31] A commender of Sir George Peckham's *True Reporte of the Late Discoveries* (1583) goes so far as to imagine all the lures of the foreign now available, no longer in the form, but for the price, of a toy:

> A bargain may you have, 'tis put into your hands,
> Of all commodities you have from other lands.
> And at so easy price you can not choose but gain:
> A trifle is the most, together with your pain.
>
> (442)

Spenser's shepherd simile outlines the sort of ideological gold that this trifling with savages was magically to produce: the facing-off of savage and trifle would free the English from their benighted past by staging it, continually reminding them of what they must leave behind, while at the same time already opening space for them by allowing them both to see another world (the savage mirror world) and to stand outside it. In fact, at the time Spenser was writing *The Shepheardes Calender*, Martin Frobisher employed on an Eskimo "a pretty policy" we have just encountered in Spenser:

> Knowing well how they greatly delighted in our toys, and specially in bells, he [Frobisher] rang a pretty Lowbell, making wise that he would give him the same that would come and fetch it. And because they would not come within his danger for fear, he flung one bell unto them, which of purpose he threw short, that it might fall into the sea and be lost. And to make them more greedy of the matter, he rang a louder bell, so that in the end one of them came near the ship side, to receive the bell, which when he thought to take at the Captain's hand, he was thereby taken himself. For the Captain being readily provided, let the bell fall, & caught the man fast, & plucked him with main force, boat and all into his bark, out of the Sea. (Best, *True Discourse*, 50)[32]

Frobisher's stratagem is pure fox, with, the English would say, two important differences. First, Frobisher only turns the fox's own wiles against him, "to deceive the deceivers" (50), for the natives have attempted some kidnapping of their own: one account of the duped native identifies him as the man responsible for the prior loss of five of Frobisher's own men (Stefannson, *Three Voyages* 1:162–65). And second, what the natives take, they eat. An English report of an uncannily foxlike maneuver by the natives themselves best demonstrates the English sense of savage versus civilized trickery. "One of them counterfeited himself impotent and lame of his legs, who seemed to descend to the water side, with great difficulty"; but far from being deceived by the malingering cannibal, the English once again adopt, at least in tone, the deception of the deceiver:

> Our General, having compassion of his impotency, thought good (if it were possible) to cure him thereof: wherefore, he caused a soldier to shoot at him with his Caliver, which grazed before his face. The counterfeit villain deliverly fled, without any impediment at all, and got him to his bow and arrows, and the rest from their lurking holes, with their weapons. (2:19)

The backfire of the trick in the native's face makes painfully evident how it had thwarted itself from the start, a "counterfeit pageant" that paraded its own deceptiveness, a false show making "(as it were) a full show of their crafty natures" (2:19). Simply, the English *see* better, and the shows they make are meant to demonstrate, both to themselves and ultimately to the natives, how savage, idolatrous, or cannibal vision is limited by its reflexivity: "when he thought to take . . . he was thereby taken himself" (2:19).[33]

The most straightforward experimental spectacle along these lines, turning the cannibal in upon himself in order to register his self-limitation, occurs on board ship as Frobisher conveys a second batch of captives, a man, woman, and child, back to England. George Best (1578) recalls the man's reaction to a kind of memento mori:

> When we showed him the picture of his Countryman, which the last year was brought into England (whose counterfeit we had drawn, with boat, & other furniture, both as he was in his own, & also in english apparel) he was upon the sudden much amazed thereat, & beholding advisedly the same with silence a good while, as though he would strain courtesy whether should begin the

speech (for he thought him no doubt a lively creature) at length, began to question with him, as with his companion, & finding him dumb & mute, seemed to suspect him, as one disdainful, & would with a little help have grown into choler at the matter until at last by feeling and handling, he found him but a deceiving picture. And then with great noise and cries, ceased not wondering, thinking that we could make men live or die at our pleasure. (*True Discourse*, 65)

The comedy of the native's mistake is as old as Narcissus, who in Golding's translation "like a foolish noddy / . . . thinks the shadow that he sees, to be a lively body" (Ovid, *Metamorphoses* 3.521–22); but this shipboard theater adds some English twists to the Ovidian story. In Ovid Narcissus wishes "I for a while might from my body part" (588) in order to embrace it. His image, in other words, makes painful the awareness that the self he loves is limited to one place, to the paradigmatic binding proportionment of self to space—his body.[34] A heathen version of Colin's dilemma (Colin is, we recall, a shepherd whose beloved hates shepherds, or a contemner of the world who cannot leave it), lacking even the lover's or the Christian's hope of future bliss, Narcissus's self-consciousness about the image as image not only fails to release him from its attractions but amplifies his woe. In the Eskimo's Narcissus-like case, his conversation with a mere image, investing that image with his own liveliness, presents a working model of idolatry as reflexive constraint. The difference from Narcissus is, of course, that the image is not the man's own, and that, like papist trickery, the superior mimetic technology of the English has staged the idolatrous occasion. (According to Erasmus in his *Peregrinatio* [1526], the pope's men could still go the English one better, by manufacturing a dumb image that could not only hold up his end of a conversation but dole out trifles: when Ogygius makes his offering to St. James at Compostella, "me thought he did laugh upon me, and beck at me with his head, & did reach to me this cockleshell" [115].[35]) By facing off the crafty cannibal with the "deceiving" picture—and a picture, no less, of the man taken by the bell, now dead and at last truly reduced to a trifle[36]—the English literalize the otherworldly perspective on wretched worldliness given them by their superior culture and their faith in God.

Unlike Colin's, the perspective is, crucially, fun: the native's comical anger with the picture, like the shepherd's annoyance with the gnats, puts trifling in proper perspective. Or conversely, savage admiration, which Best eagerly assumes to be due to the native's "thinking that we could make men live or die at our pleasure," construes the English as otherworldly gods. Best is peculiarly careful to specify the variety of pictures that the English had prepared for the viewing pleasure of their new guest, scenes of the previous guest "with boat, and other furniture, both as he was in his own, and also in english apparel."[37] In line with the long preamble to Best's *True Discourse*, which advances a number of arguments to settle English fears that the new lands were unfit for them (some believed, for example, that the warmer sun would blacken them), the paintings attempt to show the powers over identity that the English can command, powers that at least the voyagers recognize as resulting from their Redcross-like consciousness of the world's heterogeneity, their transcendence of the belief that there is only one way to dress,[38] only one culture, only one "world." And this new English cleverness about such trifles as bells and paintings, seeing round them as it were, never seems so clever as when it is contrasted with the credulity of strangers. Just as a Venetian once mocked the English for acting as if there were "no other men than themselves, and no other world but England" (Sneyd, *Relation*, 20–21), so Best now revels at the spectacle of another "savage and simple people," who,

> so soon as they perceived our men coming towards them (supposing there had been no other World, but theirs) fled fearfully away, as men much amazed at so strange a sight, and creatures of human shape, so far in apparel, complexion, and other things different from themselves. (*True Discourse*, 86)[39]

In freeing themselves from what Spenser considers the pastoral constraint of believing in only one world,[40] however, Elizabeth's voyagers find it increasingly difficult to plant themselves in any new world. If their superior vantage point on the savage trifle-world always places them outside, the home that continually beckons to such outsiders is the land they have just left, the world already *penitus toto divisus orbe*—"Elizium." Circumstances certainly conspire to make the New World less attractively otherworldly. Frobisher, for instance, plans but fails to colonize his "Meta Incognita," and succeeds only in making the same old English mistake, shipping home some 1,550 tons of fool's gold.[41] Yet even those Elizabethans most committed to settling America refuse to surrender the ideal of Elizian detachment entirely. A few years after Frobisher, Hakluyt (1584) may describe trifling as only a temporary colonial expedient, something to be used in America only "at the first," but he nonetheless imagines that the English will *"for many years* . . . change many cheap commodities of these parts, for things of high valor there not esteemed, and this to the great enriching of the Realm."[42] In fact, even as late as 1620, forty-five years after England's first American settlement failed, some Jamestown colonists complain that a "great scarcity" of georgic laborers, of "husbandmen truly bred" (Kingsbury, *Records* 3:256), has still kept Virginia from being planted on solid ground. The rest of the colony, meanwhile, having abandoned all efforts at settlement in favor of a new foreign trifle, tobacco (the subject of chapter 4),[43] seemed to imagine themselves living secure on the proceeds of their trifle sales to the Indians (the subject of chapter 5).[44] But this overseas English complacence displayed its own self-defeating reflexivity in the great massacre of 1622. Edward Waterhouse describes the day of the massacre:

> As in other days before, they [the Indians] came unarmed into our houses, without Bows or arrows, or other weapons, with Deer, Turkeys, Fish, Furs, and other provisions, to sell, and truck with us, for glass, beads, and other trifles: yea in some places, sate down at Breakfast with our people at their tables, whom immediately with their own tools and weapons, either laid down, or standing in their houses, they basely and barbarously murthered, not sparing either age or sex, man, woman, or child; so sudden in their cruel execution, that few or none discerned the weapon or blow that brought them to destruction. (*Declaration*, 13–14)

"With their own tools and weapons": the liberating vision of savage error encourages its own delusory pastoral, a new proportionment, to the supposedly credulous monster now smiling across the breakfast table.[45]

"THIS ANTIQUE IMAGE"

Like England's voyagers, Spenser in *The Faerie Queene* insists on revisiting not just pastoral but England's old foolish love of trifles in general, especially of papist ones. My previous chapter has already argued that such trifling is fundamental to Spenser's epic, dictating the choice of saints, fairies, and romance as the poem's subject matter; Michael Drayton notes with approval how the very title of *The Faerie Queene*'s first book, "The Legende Of The Knight

Of The Red Crosse, Or Of Holinesse," highlights Spenser's peculiar receptiveness to papist topoi:

> The word LEGEND . . . was anciently used in an Ecclesiastical sense, and restrained therein to things written in Prose, touching the Lives of Saints. Master EDMUND SPENSER was the very first among us, who transferred the use of the word, LEGEND, from Prose to Verse: nor that unfortunately; the Argument of his Books being of a kind of sacred Nature, as comprehending in them things as well Divine as Humane. (Quoted in Hamilton, ed., *Faerie Queene*, 27)

Not all readers of the poem, however, have been so sanguine about what C. S. Lewis calls Spenser's "humble fidelity to the popular symbols which he found ready made to his hand" (*Allegory*, 312). The poem's first reader, Gabriel Harvey, found such "fidelity" merely perverse—"*Hobgoblin* run away with the Garland from *Apollo*" (*V* 9:472).[46] Later readers such as William Nelson have lent credence to Harvey's critique by noting, for instance, the resemblance between Spenser's Arthur and Chaucer's "absurd" Sir Thopas; as Nelson observes, "the central action of a poem of such manifest seriousness as *The Faerie Queene*"—Arthur's quest—appears to derive "from a patent joke."[47] If the Chaucerian association looks too tenuous or incidental to undermine Arthur in the poem, one need only turn to a version of *A View of the Present State of Ireland* that explicitly derides those "vain *Englishmen*" who believe in the originary portion of *The Faerie Queene*'s British History, "the Tale of *Brutus*."[48] In fact, perhaps the most celebrated passage of Spenser's poem, his description of the Garden of Adonis, seems not only another instance of Spenser's paradoxical commitment to trifles but an allegory of that commitment. However ennobled by subsequent mythographers, the Garden, Erasmus explains, came to be "farre renowmd by fame" (*FQ* 3.6.29) as a proverb "for trivial [*leviculis*] things, which served no useful purpose and were suitable only for giving a brief passing pleasure"; or for " 'worthless, trifling men', born for silly pleasures—people like singers, sophists, bawdy poets, confectioners and so on" (*Adages* 1.1.4, in *Works* 31:51). In other words, the traditional association of the Garden with inanity—"The proverb is also known in the form: 'more fruitless than gardens of Adonis' "—seems paradoxically the very criterion that especially recommended it to Spenser as the nursery "of all things, that are borne to live and die" (*FQ* 3.6.30); and

Spenser's own bravura rendition of the Garden seems meant to vindicate the theory of trifling it obscurely expounds. That theory has a specifically English significance: *The Faerie Queene*, Spenser appears to imagine, will help free England from its embarrassingly credulous past, its former trifle love, not by destroying "fruitless" trifles but by *using* them, turning them, self-consciously and publicly, to a new profit.[49] Moreover, in converting trifles to gold, the poem's alchemical economy claims for both little England and its former "poor scholar" poet a power that, in otherworldly fashion, exceeds its ostensible means—as Galileo affirms, "to divine that wonderful arts lie hid behind trivial and childish things is a conception for superhuman talents" (*Discoveries and Opinions*, 1).

Harvey's reservations, however, become far more pointed and dangerous when focused on the papistry of Spenser's investment in trifles like St. George, an "error" central, I have argued, to both his project and the Elizabethan settlement as a whole. For the Elizabethans exploited Catholic practices in their most important celebrations of political authority. Roy Strong has described how, starting with Henry VII, the Order of the Garter became increasingly important to the Tudors; to follow Saint George's shifting role in the history of the order is to chart the course of Tudor religious policy in miniature: under Edward the saint was expunged from the ceremonies; Mary reinstated him; and Elizabeth silently retained him (*Cult*, 164–85 and 212–23).[50] As a highly visible aspect of Elizabeth's "religious ambiguity" (185), the saint reinforced her power either to alleviate partisan tensions or to offend both Catholic and Protestant alike. To a conservative like Stephen Gardiner (1547), for example, the continued use of the saint early in Edward's reign simply exemplified Protestant confusion: "If images be forbidden," he privately demanded, "why doth the King wear St. George on his breast?" (182). The Protestant King of Denmark, Frederick II, invested in the order in 1582, aimed for consistency: he "regarded the order as being somewhat popish and refused point-blank to wear the robes or to receive the Garter in the name of a saint" (178). By underscoring the less fastidious attitude of the Elizabethan regime, a Catholic propagandist like Sanders (1567) could transform the apparent exception, the anomaly of the saint's continuance, into a rule about the secular idolatry of the Elizabethans. He answers Jewel's attack on image worship by exhorting him to "break if you dare the Image of the Queen's Majesty, or Arms of the Realm . . . or token belonging to the honorable Knights of the Garter" (quoted in Strong, *Portraits*, 38). In Sanders's terms, then, Spenser's nostalgia for papist relics only reveals the queen-cultist's unbroken, though displaced, affection for idols.

Yet again, the shepherd simile seems to provide the opposite interpretation of such nostalgia: that Spenser preserves papist error in order to register his nation's and his own difference from it. This process of self-definition by negatives helps account not only for Spenser's archaisms or the "imaginative re-feudalization" generally of Elizabethan culture,[51] but also for Irenius's exaggeration in the *View of the Present State of Ireland* (c. 1596) that "it is but even the other day since England grew Civil" (*V* 9:118): Spenser wants the English to consider the past as nearly present as possible, to see themselves as nearly heterogeneous, not one, as possible. The *sprezzatura* incorporation of the archaic self continually suggests not just the detached urbanity of the modern self but the creative power of that urbanity. By virtue of the clarity gained from a detached or Roman perspective on old England, papists needed only trifles to exploit the nation; now, by adopting and maintaining a similarly detached perspective on themselves, the English learn the strength of mind over the matter they lack anyway, a strength tautologically demonstrated by this very transformation of their trifling past into value.

In *The Faerie Queene*, specific dramatizations of selves clarified as it were by self-distance—like Una and Saint George named only when her or his double appears (Hamilton, ed., *Faerie Queene*, 41, 46)—recall more precisely the lessons taught by the fox's captivating glass or Frobisher's deceiving picture. For it is Archimago who frames Una's double "of liquid ayre" (*FQ* 1.1.45), and so festoons himself that "*Saint George* himself ye would have deemed him to be" (2.11): the doubles, that is, are papist delusions. In being recognized as such, they first rescue Spenser's heroes from a binding proportion to anything but the "liquid ayre" that negatively identifies them, and, second, absorb whatever unreality might infect both those heroes and their ideals. In other words, the problem the doubles are supposed to solve is the possible emptiness of an allegorical or *sprezzatura* transcendence that can be figured only as what does not appear. Instead, the doubles, the papist or archaic selves, are what's empty, or, in the case of a figure like Duessa, they stigmatize the consciousness or theology that would believe whatever is invisible to be also absent.[52]

The climactic instance in book 1 of Spenser indulging a false image occurs on Contemplation's mount. Assuring Redcross, "thou man of earth," that the sight he is about to see "never yet was seene of Faeries sonne" (10.52), Contemplation pointedly recalls Despair's final words to Redcross a canto earlier:

> Die shall all flesh? what then must needs be donne,
> Is it not better to doe willinglie,
> Then linger, till the glasse be all out ronne?
> Death is the end of woes: die soone, O faeries sonne.
> (9.47)

The ominousness of the allusion carries over into Spenser's description of "the highest Mount" to which Redcross is led:

> Such one, as that same mighty man of God,
> That bloud-red billowes like a walled front
> On either side disparted with his rod,
> Till that his army dry-foot through them yod,
> Dwelt fortie dayes upon; where writ in stone
> With bloudy letters by the hand of God,
> The bitter doome of death and balefull mone
> He did receive, whiles flashing fire about him shone.
> (53)

This DeMille-like evocation of Moses answers all of Redcross's fears about the wrath "due" to him (50) while at the same time reducing those fears to the defectiveness, for a Christian, of any merely Old Testament vision. As the subsequent mention of the scene's New Testament antitype, the Mount of Olives, makes clear, the terrors of Sinai are also meant to foreshadow their own reversal in the divine love—all out of proportion to humanity's just deserts—that allowed Christ's sacrifice. By embracing a desperate imagination of things, both Contemplation and the simile reveal Despair as an image only, a constricted, cave dweller's misapprehension of the whole redemptive picture.

The surprise is that Despair's conventional mistake about earthly life matches an error about Redcross himself. When Redcross at last views the proper Elizium of the English Christian, the New Jerusalem, he learns at the same time that this sight never yet seen of fairy's son has still not been seen by one, because Redcross is actually "sprong out from English race" (60). While one might be tempted to write off Contemplation's original equivocation as artificial drama, his indulgence of Redcross's misconception up till the last moment is of a piece with the historian's claim that "it is but even the other day since England grew civil." The erroneous past must be preserved; and so the world in Redcross's eyes does not simply readjust to fit his newly acquired theology and erase the old, but instead splits in two: on the one hand, representing his false, archaic view, Fairyland, and on the other, arising with the truth about God, the ideal that must first be negatively identified, England. The Augustinian judgment of earthly life as an exile, the emptiness of either desiring (as in "innocent" pastoral) or fearing (as in "experienced" pastoral) to inhabit a world apart, is now absorbed no longer by a monstrous character like the double-being Duessa or the arch-image Archimago, but by Fairyland itself.[53]

Yet to keep Redcross from readopting his Error, to rescue England from coming to seem simply another Fairyland, Redcross also needs to learn how never to feel reductively proportioned to any one place again: his true and distant home, he discovers, is twofold, the New Jerusalem *and* England. In thanking Contemplation, who "hast my name and nation red aright, / And taught the way that does to heaven bound" (67),[54] Redcross pays tribute to the double knowledge he has received, yet without helping us to understand the connection between his earthly and heavenly loyalties. Neither does the previous dialogue between teacher and student clarify matters: even though Contemplation tells Redcross of the knight's two new homes almost in the same breath, only the loftier one at first interests the future saint. In his climactic temptation to contemn the world, when Redcross pleads, "O let me not . . . then turne againe / Backe to the world, whose joyes so fruitlesse are," Contemplation replies that Redcross cannot forgo Una "till from her cursed foe thou have her freely quit" (63), a condition Redcross accepts. What still bothers him, however, is why Contemplation "didst . . . behight me borne of English blood, / Whom all a Faeries sonne doen nominate?" (64), a resistance that highlights the apparent inconsequence of this news, and that seems due in part to Redcross seeing the New Jerusalem, while only hearing about England. I have argued that Spenser believes Redcross's nation requires this sort of tentativeness and ambiguity about England and its relation to the New Jerusalem as much as Redcross does, since the English must reject a premature, pastoral identification of their island with Paradise, in favor of a sense of England as completed only when God's work is, when that part of the world not English, and so estranged from God, has been apocalyptically returned to the fold. But for the orthodox Elizabethan, again, apocalypse does not yield the Millennium; to remain orthodox, in other words, Spenser has no choice but to remain ambiguous about the world to come. And so in a way the most revealing fact about the relation between Redcross's two homes is that he ostensibly travels to neither, but instead, to conserve Spenser's imperial, possibly millenarian hopes—which can only be "shadowed"—the quester returns to Fairyland.[55]

This return to a shadow world still might make the easiest kind of allegorical sense, as in Calvin's Ephesian assertion that earthly life "is like a place in battle array, wherein the Lord hath placed us, which we ought to keep till he call us away" (*Institution* 3.9.4, 169r), if Spenser had not already cast doubt on the sentiment by having Redcross employ it unsuccessfully against Despair (*FQ* 1.9.41). Heaven is not the only country to which Redcross must not yet travel; in order for the poem to retain a positive worldliness, part of the earth too, England, must paradoxically be closed to him. Yet if, properly speaking, the full material world of England does not yet exist, where on earth does the imperial Englishman stand? So little sense does the inevitable answer, "Nowhere," make that Spenser's contemporaries, and modern critics, often assume that Fairyland is nothing other than Greene's unforsakable island, the already realized ideal of otherworldly worldliness which, they believe, Spenser has celebrated right from the start— "Out from the world, yet on the ground, / Even in a place of bliss."[56]

Book 6 of *The Faerie Queene* does seem to admit the difficulty of living in a world unrealized, of being "tied," as the fairy king in Greene's *James IV* (c. 1590) brags he is, "to no place" (Chorus 1.7): for most readers, the book shows a Spenser so disillusioned with imperial prophecy that he reassumes his pastoral identity as Colin Clout and figures his imperial theme as destructive of a sublimer private visionariness.[57] Certainly the Colin Clout episode of book 6, where Sir Calidore interrupts Colin piping in the midst of "an hundred naked maidens" dancing in a ring (*FQ* 6.10.10–11), dramatizes the difference between pastoral poet and quester—but, I would argue, only in order to *save* the quest. For at heart the episode represents nothing other than a repetition of the Error episode and its gnat simile, with one striking difference: now Spenser more emphatically stages Fairyland's limitations by placing his own frustrated pastoral persona, along with conventionally pastoral fairies, inside the epic fairy world.[58] Unable to define his heroic project positively, Spenser increasingly indulges the pastoral that only negatively promises success. *Colin Clouts Come Home Again*, the pastoral Spenser published well after his epic's first installment, had already attempted to clarify Spenser's stake in pastoral by associating pastoral, as the Mutability Cantos will associate Fairyland, not with England or the New Jerusalem but with Ireland. Yet, as I will argue in chapter 5, by literalizing England's difference from the trifle shadowing it, Ireland also literalizes Spenser's attachment to trifles. And indeed, Spenser's life in Ireland kept him as close to England's trifling past as he could have wished: the four Irish monasteries he appropriated helped bring him a gentlemanly standing he might never have obtained at home, while the Irish barbarisms encumbering him, like the Irish horsemen dressed in the manner of Sir Thopas, supplied as London never could the everpresent trifling mementos of his own sophistication and sublimity.[59] One catches something of Spenser's oddly sentimental contempt for Ireland, a sense of roominess and mastery arising from the contemplation of dangerous old Irish "abuses," in the following request by Eudoxius that Irenius proceed in his complaints:

> Sith then that we have thus reasonably handled the inconveniences in the Laws let us now pass unto your second part which was as I remember of the Abuses of Customs in which me seems ye have a fair Champion laid open unto you, in which ye may at large stretch out your discourse into many sweet remembrances of Antiquities from whence it seemeth that the Customs of that nation proceeded. (*V* 9:81)

But like the shady grove, the trifles delude, encouraging dependence on themselves, seeming to demonstrate English power only

in order to strangle it, to reduce it to trifling. The shadows of Fairyland—"out of every Corner of the woods and glens they Came
Creeping forth upon their hands for their Legs Could not bear
them, they looked like Anatomies of death, they spake like ghosts
Crying out of their graves"—at last consume their shadower:

> *To the Queen. Out of the ashes of desolation and wasteness of this your
> wretched Realm of Ireland.* vouchsafe most mighty Empress our Dread
> sovereign to receive the voices of a few most unhappy Ghosts.[60]

4

Divine Tobacco

> My fruit is better than gold, even than fine gold; and my
> revenue better than fine silver.
>
> —Proverbs 8.19

Tobacco's first entry into English poetry doesn't strike the modern reader as a particularly auspicious one. In book 3 of *The Faerie Queene*, during a hunt, the fairy Belphoebe discovers the unconscious body of Prince Arthur's seriously wounded squire Timias:

> Into the woods thenceforth in hast she went,
>   To seeke for hearbes, that mote him remedy
>
> . . . .
>
>   There, whether it divine *Tobacco* were,
>   Or *Panachaea*, or *Polygony*,
>   She found, and brought it to her patient deare
> Who al this while lay bleeding out his hart-bloud neare.
>
> (3.5.32)

What could be more fleeting a reference? A plant growing in not only distant but fairy woods, and then only one of three alternatives for the herb Belphoebe actually does fetch; applied in the most unusual way, as a woundwort, not in a pipe; and Spenser's poetry never mentions the word, the novelty, again. Yet this seemingly offhand reference, and the newly introduced plant itself, had a surprising impact on later writers: no epithet for tobacco comes close to being as standard in later Elizabethan literature as Spenser's "divine,"[1] a fact almost as remarkable as the meteoric rise of tobacco smoking during the same period. In 1603, the first year for which official records of tobacco importation to England survive, 16,000 pounds of tobacco passed through official channels alone.[2] And a year after that, marking the new power at once of tobacco and king, James I issued his *Counter-blaste to Tobacco*, which denounced as England's ruination what Barnaby Rich

Figure 5.   An Indian rite, from Theodor de Bry's *America* part 3, Frankfurt, 1592. Cf. Nashe in his *Lenten Stuffe* (1599): "A pipe of Tobacco to raise
my spirits and warm my brain." (By permission of the Bancroft Library,
University of California, Berkeley.)

(1617) would later call "the most vain and idle toy, that ever was
brought into use and custom amongst men."[3] In fact, "as the literature of the day indicates," says tobacco historian Jerome
Brooks, tobacco "was nowhere more heartily taken up, after about
1590, than in England" (*Tobacco* 1:381). The paradoxical combination of inconsequentiality and power both in tobacco and in Spenser's reference to it seems perfectly foreshadowed by Spenser's
oxymoronic-sounding epithet itself—the weed is divine.[4]

What makes tobacco's rise to power even more impressive, and
helps in part to account for James's disgust, is the fact that the sole
owner of the New World from which tobacco came was the enemy, Spain. One would have expected the knowing Englishman
to shy away from tobacco as a constant reminder of England's be-
latedness in America: not only did Spain monopolize America's
treasures while England settled for a New World weed, but Spain

could further increase her fortune, and decrease England's, by selling that same weed to England. And yet tobacco in Spenser's passage represents not an exacerbation of a bad case but its cure.

A brief consideration of Spenser's allegory in the Timias and Belphoebe passage helps begin explaining how the English could accommodate tobacco's representation of their own inadequacies. For tobacco is only one of many grand trifles that figure in Spenser's passage. Neither Timias nor Belphoebe could be considered the most significant character in this or any other book of *The Faerie Queene*, and yet they represent what were in 1590 the two most prominent people in England: Spenser's patrons, Raleigh and the queen. And the rise to power of these figures—Raleigh the fourth son of a country gentleman; Elizabeth excommunicated, purportedly illegitimate, and female—could seem just as miraculous as that of tobacco, almost a pledge of England's own potentiality. A celebration of his small country's enormous spiritual and imperial claims, Spenser's poem matches the paradoxicality of its subject, here in the Timias and Belphoebe passage by the lowly pastoral meant "to insinuate and glance at greater matters" (Puttenham, *English Poesie*, 38), and everywhere by the epic representation of "our sovereign the Queen, and her kingdom in" the nothing of "Faery land" (*V* 1:168). But then "divine" Spenser himself,[5] the poor scholar turned laureate poet, testifies to the latent power of English trifles, producing with his contemporaries an extraordinary literature at a time when it would seem that imperial-minded Englishmen had little reason to exult.

These paradoxes are by now familiar, but what perhaps still surprises is the expectation by some Elizabethans that tobacco would not merely exemplify the divine potential of other English trifles, but actually help produce those divinities, even so far as to transform little England into a heaven on earth. Spenser's association of tobacco with Raleigh and Elizabeth suggests the real basis of England's hopes for an overseas empire, the American colony that Raleigh had already founded in Elizabeth's name—Virginia. This English foothold in the New World, its supporters claimed, would be different from Spain's American empire not only in location but in theory and practice. Thomas Cain has convincingly demonstrated that the Mammon episode in *The Faerie Queene*'s second book represents in part Spenser's warning about New World gold

(*Praise*, 91–101); according to Spenser, the Spanish, in their idolatrous fashion, have blinded themselves by worshipping an earthly god.[6] Cain oddly assumes, however, that Spenser is in particular warning Raleigh to "manage the gold of Guiana" temperately. The conclusion is anachronistic—Raleigh did not sail for Guiana till 1595—but, more important, misses Spenser's contrast between the gold-feverish Spanish colonies and "*fruitfullest* Virginia" (*FQ* 2.proem.2; my emphasis). The point of this chapter is to show what Spenser and his contemporaries take this contrast to mean, and why it is elaborated by talk about a smokable American "fruit." The first section of the chapter will briefly review the medical benefits tobacco was supposed to offer, and suggest why neither these supposed benefits nor tobacco's inherent pleasures can alone account for tobacco's popularity in the 1590s, precisely the period when England owned no New World empire from which to import tobacco and so was forced to buy it from the enemy who did; the second section will outline Raleigh and Elizabeth's crucial role in tobacco's popularization; and the final three sections will examine English claims about tobacco's divinity in relation to the literary tradition for tobacco inaugurated by Spenser and most fully worked out by John Beaumont's mock panegyric, *The Metamorphosis of Tabacco* (1602). In general, the advocates and critics of Elizabethan tobacco agree that the materially poor English are nevertheless Spain's ideological superiors, but disagree about whether tobacco will help or hurt this "fairy" superiority. The tobacco critic considers the imported weed pagan and earthly, qualities that infect England and lower its sights profoundly. A tobacco advocate like Beaumont counters that, with less persuasive claims to inherent value than gold, tobacco bespeaks the mind's power to create value, and so continually alerts the English mind (even physiologically, as I will show) to its own abilities. Later, in Stuart England, this idealism centering on tobacco would help foster a new economics of imperialism, one that began to displace gold as an imperialist preoccupation in favor of commodities previously understood as trifling.[7] But many Elizabethan propagandists of tobacco—drawn to medical and economic rationales for smoking yet pursuing such rationales only confusedly or ironically—were finally less concerned with tobacco's material than with its ideal import. Like the antimaterialists of my previous chapters, these writers believed that the immediate reward of gold had tricked the Spanish into equating imperial with economic success; tobacco was supposed to dramatize that, on the contrary, something like what we would now call ideology was true power. While the Spanish enslaved themselves to gold, tobacco taught the English to limit their ambitions to nothing—or, at least, to nothing but smoke.

I

Columbus sighted tobacco on his first voyage, but "the first original notice in English of the use of tobacco by the Indians" (Brooks, *Tobacco*, 1:17–18, 45) does not appear till 1565, in John Sparke's account of Sir John Hawkins's second slaving voyage. "The Floridans when they travel," observes Sparke,

> have a kind of herb dried, who with a cane and an earthen cup in the end, with fire, and the dried herbs put together, do suck through the cane the smoke thereof, which smoke satisfieth their hunger, and therewith they live four or five days without meat or drink, and this all the Frenchmen [Jean Ribault's men, about to be massacred by the Spanish] used for this purpose: yet they do hold opinion withal, that it causeth water & phlegm to void from their stomachs. (*PN* 10:57)

Such a report of tobacco's double, and as Sparke's "yet" signifies, slightly paradoxical power—at once to nourish and to purge—gets reiterated by English writers too many times to bother citing, though when William Harrison (1573) and the elder Hakluyt (1582) acknowledge that tobacco is now being planted in England, they naturally single out not its nutritional but its medicinal virtue as the benefit required by certainly well-to-do buyers: tobacco, they say, eases the rheum.[8]

Now the rheum—what we call an allergic reaction or the common cold—was enough of a worry in Tudor England to make a remedy for it seem marvelous indeed. Sir Thomas Elyot's *Castel of Helth* (1541), for instance, claims that "at this present time in the realm of England, there is not any one more annoyance to the health of man's body, than distillations from the head called rheums" (77v). Ever since the Tudor peace, Elyot believes, the disease has become more frequent, the English head more watery, as the English have increasingly devoted themselves to excess, like "banquetings after supper & drinking much, specially wine a little afore sleep" (8or). Indeed, in Elyot's account the rheum's symptoms—"Wit dull. Much superfluities. Sleep much and deep" (3v)—look just like its causes; one might conclude that the rheum not only mirrors but helps perpetuate the complacence and corruption of manners producing it.

Given this sociological understanding of the disease, however, tobacco seems an unusual choice for a remedy. If it is relatively easy to imagine a physical opposition between tobacco and the rheum, the rheum as cold and moist being driven out by tobacco as hot and dry, it is much less easy to see how an expensive novelty could help do anything but augment the intemperance Elyot decries.[9] "A Satyricall Epigram" in Henry Buttes's *Dyets Dry Dinner* (1599) mocks tobacco—though only its "wanton, and excessive use," a qualification to which I will return—as simply the latest foreign luxury helping to drown the English character: "On English fool: wanton Italianly; / Go Frenchly: Dutchly drink: breath Indianly" (P4r). Later, "Philaretes" in his *Work for Chimney-Sweepers* (1602) denounces tobacco not only as a foolish toy but as the devil's invention, a fact amply demonstrated, he believes, by the observations of the herbalist Monardes on tobacco's American heritage:

> The Indian Priests (who no doubt were instruments of the devil whom they serve) do ever before they answer to questions propounded to them by their Princes, drink of this *Tobacco* fume, with the vigor and strength whereof, they fall suddenly to the ground, as dead men, remaining so, according to the quantity of the smoke that they had taken. And when the herb had done his work, they revive and wake, giving answers according to the visions and illusions which they saw whilst they were wrapt in that order. (F4r)

(The devil aside, tobacco here even exaggerates the physical symptoms, the dullness and sleepiness, associated with the rheum: the priests fall down "as dead men.") The odd truth about this kind of argument, however, is that Philaretes' is the first full-scale attack on tobacco to be launched in English, some thirty years at the very least after its use in England began.[10] Even Monardes himself, in the herbal that proved to be "the most frequently issued book of overseas interest in the Elizabethan period,"[11] concludes that tobacco's superstitious application shows only how "the Devil is a deceiver, and hath the knowledge of the virtue of Herbs" (*Joyfull Newes* 1:86); by Philaretes' own account "Monardus" is one of the "many excellent & learned men" who "do commend this plant as a thing most excellent and divine" (*Work*, A3r). What was there about tobacco that enabled it for so long not only to escape the censure one would expect but to receive such lavish praise instead?

One answer is provided by Philaretes' anxiety about his pamphlet's reception. So strong are the voices for tobacco, and so rare the voices against it—"Many excellent Physicians and men of singular learning and practice, together with many gentlemen and some of great accompt, do by their daily use and custom in drinking of *Tobacco*, give great credit and authority to the same" (A3r)—that Philaretes feels he must embark on a disputation against Authority (citing Plato and Aristotle in his defense) before his tobacco argument can proceed (A4v). But to claim that tobacco prospered because the mighty took it under their wing[12] is only to rephrase the question: what enabled tobacco to win such powerful favor? The two most obvious explanations, that tobacco is inherently likable, not to say addictive, and that tobacco's novelty added luster to its intrinsic charm, fail fully to account for the particular circumstances of tobacco's reception in late sixteenth-century England. First, with the help of herbalists like Monardes, tobacco came to be regarded as not just a rheum distiller but an all-round wonder drug; since tobacco was not the only American herb celebrated this way, its own virtues, whatever they may be, would seem to say less about its identification as a cure-all than about its eventual ascendancy over other New World candidates for Panacea, such as sassafras. Second, the English craze for smoking, like the English taste for America in general, developed much later than on the Continent, later even than its introduction to England as a novelty.[13] Here the demonstrably false legend about Raleigh's introducing tobacco to England gains a certain credence: just as Raleigh hardly invented the idea of English colonies in America and yet was the first to start one, so we might imagine the most powerful Englishman in 1590 not as tobacco's original proponent but its most persuasive one.[14] The legend about Raleigh in fact derives from the 1590s—Buttes says "our English *Ulysses*, renowned Sir

Walter Raleigh . . . hath both far fetcht it [tobacco], and dear bought it" (*Dyets*, P5r–P6r)—though James himself lends greater authority to the claim:

> With the report of a great discovery for a Conquest, some two or three Savage men, were brought in, together with this Savage custom. But the pity is, the poor wild barbarous men died, but that vile barbarous custom is yet alive, yea in fresh vigor: so as it seems a miracle to me, how a custom springing from so vile a ground, and brought in by a father so generally hated, should be welcomed on so slender a warrant. (*Counter-blaste*, B2r)[15]

The denunciation makes sure that James's subjects understand tobacco's political significance: for tobacco to be attacked means for Raleigh to have fallen, and at the same time, though only implicitly here, for pathetic, unprofitable Virginia to have been confiscated by the Crown. I would like to turn now to the surviving evidence about Raleigh and tobacco in order to determine the attractions tobacco held for the man who focused England's attention upon it.

II

The first description and commendation of tobacco one can safely associate with Raleigh are the work not of Raleigh himself—indeed, Raleigh is for the most part above speaking on the subject—but of his servant Thomas Harriot, in Harriot's *Briefe and True Report of the New Found Land of Virginia* (1588).[16] The purpose of Harriot's tract—to advertise and justify Raleigh's American efforts—helps in an obvious way to account for both Harriot's praise of tobacco there and the many other claims about tobacco's medicinal wonders in general: if one wants to convince potential investors that Virginia "may return you profit and gain" (322), then a miraculous Virginian herb will come in very handy. What is less obvious is the close relation between the specific properties Harriot claims for tobacco and the kinds of economic returns he and writers like him expected America would bring to little England. The historian D. B. Quinn has called what he considers the most important of these expectations the supplementary economy, the complementary economy, and the emigration thesis.[17] The first, the supplementary economy, meant the hope "that North America could produce many of the products which England herself produced but in greater quantities" (Quinn, "Renaissance Influences," 83) and so could bolster and expand the limited homeland. Harriot is thinking this way when he lists potential Virginian commodities such as woad, "a thing of so great vent and use among English Dyers, which cannot be yielded sufficiently in our own country for spare of ground," but which "may be planted in Virginia, there being ground enough" (*Report*, 335). The second model foresaw the New World supplying the English, as Harriot says, "with most things which heretofore they have been fain to provide, either of strangers or of our enemies" (324). Renaissance writers generally assumed that the same latitude meant the same climate, and the same climate was all one country needed to produce the same commodities as another country; therefore Virginia, as "answerable" in climate "to the Island of Japan, the land of China, Persia, Jury [Jewry], the Islands of Cyprus and Candy [Crete], the South parts of Greece, Italy, and Spain, and of many other notable and famous countries" (383; cf. 325, 336), held out to England the hope that, in Quinn's words, "the English economy would . . . become virtually independent of imports from all but tropical lands" ("Renaissance Influences," 82). The final model, the emigration thesis, Quinn explains this way: "The tendency for population to increase after the mid-century, together with endemic unemployment associated with the decline of certain branches of the cloth trade, impressed—over-impressed—almost all those who thought about it with the idea that there was a surplus population which ought to be exported" (83). John Hawkins, in a prefatory poem to Sir George Peckham's *True Reporte* (1583), describes the impression more vividly:

> But Rome nor Athens nor the rest, were never pestered so,
> As England where no room remains, her dwellers to bestow,
> But shuffled in such pinching bonds, that very breath doth lack:
> And for the want of place they crawl one o'er another's back.
>
> (439)

It is with such hysteria in mind that Harriot extols "the dealing of Sir Walter Raleigh so liberal in large giving and granting land" in Virginia; "(the least that he hath granted hath been five hundred acres to a man only for the adventure of his person)" (Harriot,

Report, 385). In the light of these hypotheses about increased "home" production, freedom from the threat of foreign embargoes, and room in which to "vent" England's surplus, part of Harriot's description of tobacco's powers looks like a synecdoche for America's expected impact on the English body politic as a whole: tobacco, says Harriot, "openeth all the pores & passages of the body" (344), or in Hawkins's terms, lets England breathe.

The easiest way to grasp the economic constraints that tobacco-as-America might be imagined resolving is to think of them all as effects of one master problem—England's limitation to an island, in particular a northern island hemmed in by enemies. In his *Defence of Tabacco: With a Friendly Answer to Worke for Chimny-sweepers* (1602), Roger Marbecke traces to this source even England's peculiar susceptibility to the rheum: "but for that we are Islanders . . . we are by nature subject, to overmuch moisture, and rheumatic matter" (33).[18] Harriot's captain Ralph Lane, on the other hand, writes to Walsingham from Virginia that "the climate is so wholesome, yet somewhat tending to heat, As that we have not had one sick since we entered into the country; but sundry that came sick, are recovered of long diseases especially of Rheums" (Quinn, *Roanoke Voyages* 1:202). While Marbecke immediately goes on to agree with Elyot that excessive eating and drinking cause rheum also, these factors equally signal the predicament of a country unable to produce for itself, taking too much in—as it were, drowning for want of land.[19] With a whole world to themselves, the Indians, remarks Harriot, are moderate eaters, "whereby they avoid sickness. I would to god we would follow their example. For we should be free from many kinds of diseases which we fall into by sumptuous and unseasonable banquets, continually devising new sauces, and provocation of gluttony to satisfy our unsatiable appetite" (438). It is important to remember that in this dietetic case as in the case of the rheum, tobacco's cure is not merely figurative, representing the extra world little England hopes to acquire; tobacco smoke, said Sparke, "satisfieth their hunger," and Harriot classifies tobacco with other "such commodities as Virginia is known to yield for victual and sustenance of man's life, usually fed upon by the natural inhabitants, as also by us during the time of our abode" (*Report*, 337).

But no matter how convenient for understanding tobacco in relation to England's economic ills, this classification by Harriot actually forces consideration of some problems about Virginian tobacco that I have so far overlooked. If America is to help England by freeing it from the twin dangers of excessive importation and an unexportable surplus, one might have expected to find tobacco listed not only with the native foods that would support a displaced English population but with the "merchantable commodities" (325) that would feed and enrich home also—which is in fact where Harriot places that other panacea "of most rare virtues," sassafras (329).[20] Presumably Harriot knows something about the marketability of Virginian tobacco that he doesn't want to say directly, something like the "biting taste" that prevented Englishmen from becoming interested in colonial tobacco until John Rolfe imported Trinidadian seeds to Virginia in 1610–11;[21] most of the tobacco Englishmen "drank" before that time was indeed the enemy's—Spain's—so rather than alleviate England's trade woes, tobacco actually exacerbated them.[22] Good reason for sticking to tobacco's nutritional value; but the classification as food is problematic in its own way: Harriot never explicitly mentions the hunger-depressant power he could have found out about not only from the Indians, presumably, but also from such written sources as Monardes (*Joyfull Newes*, 90–91)—to whom, oddly enough, Harriot refers the reader in the case of sassafras, not of tobacco (*Report*, 329).[23] Whatever the real reason for Harriot's enigmatic silence here, he himself wants the reader to know both that his praise of Virginian tobacco has been cut short and that his reticence about it corresponds to his especially high regard for it: "We our selves during the time we were there used to suck it after their manner, as also since our return, & have found many rare and wonderful experiments of the virtues thereof; of which the relation would require a volume by it self." It is a regard the Indians share. "This *Uppowoc*"—Harriot's preference for the Indian instead of the well-known Spanish name is itself significant—

> is of so precious estimation amongst them, that they think their gods are marvelously delighted therewith: Whereupon sometime they make hallowed fires & cast some of the powder therein for a sacrifice: being in a storm upon the waters, to pacify their gods, they cast some up into the air and into the water: so a weir for fish being newly set up, they cast some therein and into the air: also after an escape of danger, they cast some into the air likewise. (345–46)

If I am right to say that Harriot has some difficulty *placing* tobacco in his colonial argument, this description of native or "natural" superstition, intended after all as a weak form of argument from authority, allows Harriot the liberty to speak of tobacco as a panacea without having to rationalize the claim in terms either of physiology or of England's peculiar needs.[24] Harriot does not use the Indians to show, in other words, that tobacco has some chemical or synecdochal relation to storms, weirs, or danger; according to Harriot, the Indians simply think that their gods like tobacco: one casts it on things, and things work.

Yet a more common colonial logic, more common even in Harriot's own tract, makes citing Indians as any kind of authority on value look strange. For the most salient fact about savages is that they always hold the wrong thing in "precious estimation"—not gold, for instance, but trifles. One could find Harriot's version of the first confrontation between Americans and Europeans in innumerable travel books:

> As soon as they saw us [they] began to make a great and horrible cry, as people which never before had seen men appareled like us, and came a way making out cries like wild beasts or men out of their wits. But being gently called back, we offered them of our wares, as glasses, knives, babies [i.e., dolls], and other trifles, which we thought they delighted in. So they stood still, and perceiving our Good will and courtesy came fawning upon us, and bade us welcome. (Quinn, *Roanoke Voyages* 1:414)

When Harriot speaks elsewhere of the Indians' powers of estimation, it is only copper "which they much esteem" (441), "which they esteem more than gold or silver" (425);[25] in other words, they "do esteem our trifles before things of greater value" (Harriot, *Report*, 371). While such notices of Indian misprision are meant no doubt to tickle Harriot's readers, and to demonstrate how cheaply Indian favor can be bought,[26] the savage love of trifles speaks directly to England's fears, once again, about its own extravagant trading habits. If, as I explained in my previous chapter, English economists could consider their European trade a delusion, the foolish English venting the solid good of bullion in exchange for mere pestering trifles, the still more foolish American savage represented the hope of turning passive victimization into active victimizing—of "buying for toys the wealth of other lands."[27]

The only catch in Harriot's case is that his credulous Indians don't *have* any gold; his prefatory letter warns the understanding reader to discount "as trifles that are not worthy of wise men to be thought upon" (*Report*, 324) the ill reports of such former colonists who "after gold and silver was not so soon found, as it was by them looked for, had little or no care of any other thing but to pamper their bellies" (323). In light of these disaffected gold hunters, with whom Harriot might reasonably expect a very large proportion of his audience to sympathize, Harriot's praise of Indian moderation takes on a colonial significance: if only the English could regard America as the Indians do, and learn to live in America as the Indians do, "free from all care of heaping up Riches for their posterity, content with their state, and living friendly together of those things which god of his bounty hath given unto them" (435). Once again, in the displacement of gold as a measure of value, Indian tastes assume a kind of authority.[28] Looking back on Harriot's interest in their "precious estimation" of tobacco, one might say that, for Harriot, tobacco supplies the lack of the precious metal; indeed, when he insists that a full relation of tobacco's virtues "would require a volume by itself," as if tobacco were a New World all its own, still awaiting discovery, he builds into tobacco not only gold's value but its very absence.[29]

It is a substitution that tobacco's critics later found the English people all too willing to make. Not only had a lack of Indian gold defeated expectations of happy returns from America: somehow even savages had managed to palm off a trifle on the ever eager English consumer. John Aubrey's life of Raleigh (c. 1669–1696) records how, near the turn of the century, the exchange of a trifle for a precious metal was quite literal: tobacco "was sold then for its weight in silver. I have heard some of our old yeoman neighbors say, that when they went to Malmesbury or Chippenham Market, they culled out their best shillings to lay in the scales against the tobacco" (quoted in Brooks, *Tobacco* 1:50). Thomas Campion (1619) later complains that such skewed powers of estimation have yielded the Spaniards profit:

> Aurum nauta suis Hispanus vectat ab Indis,
> Et longas queritur se subijsse vias.
> Maius iter portus ad eosdem suscipit Anglus,
> Ut referat fumos, nuda Tobacco, tuos:

Copia detonsis quos vendit Ibera Britannis,
  Per fumos ad se vellera cal'da trahens.

(The Spanish raider carries gold from his Indies and laments that he
has gone on long journeys. The Englishman undertakes a longer
way to the same parts so that he can bring back your smoke, un-
adorned Tobacco, which Spanish wealth sells, by this smoke strip-
ping and drawing to itself the hides from the Britons.)[30]

To its critics, tobacco even seemed to clarify the old fears about
England trading its solid commodities for nothing by dramatizing
the exchange in a way never before possible: whenever an Englishman lit his pipe,[31] he could seem to demonstrate unequivocally how "the Treasure of this land is vented for smoke."[32]

Yet a well-known anecdote about Raleigh first reported by
James Howell (1650) shows how the substitution of gold for smoke
could work in an Englishman's favor:

> But if one would try a pretty conclusion how much smoke there is
> in a pound of Tobacco, the ashes will tell him, for let a pound be
> exactly weighed, and the ashes kept charily and weigh'd after-
> wards, what wants of a pound weight in the ashes cannot be denied
> to have been smoke, which evaporated into air; I have been told that
> Sir *Walter Raleigh* won a wager of Queen *Elizabeth* upon this nicety.
> (Quoted in Dickson, *Panacea*, 172)

In another version of the anecdote the queen adds in paying,
"many laborers in the fire she had heard of who turned their gold
into smoke, but *Raleigh* was the first who had turned smoke into
gold" (Dickson, *Panacea*, 172).[33] The story compactly illustrates a
great deal of Raleigh's relation to the queen—the carefully staged
destruction of his property, like his muddied cloak or his melodramatically desperate posturings, bringing him greater wealth. But
this manner of enriching oneself via the New World and its products is crucially different from the colonial models and tobacco
uses I have specified: unlike a chemical or alchemical transformation of the English body or body politic, Raleigh's tobacco simply
wins him a bet; the gold comes neither from the New World nor
its inhaled representative but from Elizabeth. There seems nothing
about tobacco's place in the story, in other words, that some other
inflammable object might not fill—the operative term is, after all,
smoke.

But perhaps tobacco's replaceability here is what helps make its appearance in the story, and in the story of Raleigh's life, so inevitable: for the story must be about Raleigh, not tobacco, and it must show that what Raleigh does to tobacco, turning smoke to gold, is only what he has done to himself—as Stephen Greenblatt reminds us about Raleigh in his prime, he was "perhaps the supreme example in England of a gentleman not born but fashioned" (*Renaissance Self-Fashioning*, 285–86 n. 29). Contemporaries did not miss the correspondence, famously dramatized by Raleigh before his execution, between Raleigh's smoking and his pride, his aloofness; whether or not Raleigh smoked at the execution of his rival Essex also, the story sounded so plausible and epitomizing that, at his own execution, Raleigh was forced publicly to deny it.[34] Others quickly adopted the flourish a pipe could bring them. In his mock travelogue *Mundus Alter et Idem* (1605),[35] Joseph Hall "discovers" Raleigh and tobacco in Moronia Felix, or, in Hall's own gloss, the "land of braggarts, or of conceited folly" (93). Like Raleigh, everyone in Moronia Felix pretends to noble birth, though their claims, like their sumptuous buildings, "are exceedingly flimsy, and whatever their external splendor promises, on the interior they are sordid beyond measure" (94). Lacking funds and good sense, "most of the inhabitants feed neither on bread nor on food but on the fume" of their own vanity and of tobacco:[36] "and while their nostrils exhale smoke high in the air, their kitchens have passed completely out of use" (96). Joseph Beaumont (c. 1640s) will later denounce such high estimations of inanity in terms recalling Raleigh's wager: "Was ever *Nothing* sold by weight till now, / Or smoke put in the Scale?" (*Minor Poems*, 71). And indeed, the wager anecdote captures very well not only the insubstantiality of Raleigh's position as Hall sees it—"without a power-base of any kind, . . . Raleigh was totally dependent upon the queen" (Greenblatt, *Ralegh*, 56)—but also Raleigh's irritating or enviable ability to capitalize on that insubstantiality, to give it weight, to turn the smoke of his own bravura, and of Elizabeth's favor, to account.

If tobacco figures in the anecdote, then, as little more than the personal trademark of the queen's alchemist, Raleigh's America similarly distances itself from the national hypotheses about New World benefits that I have so far outlined. Even the primary advocate of such hypotheses, Richard Hakluyt, appears to abandon them whenever he helps Raleigh articulate his self-serving vision of America. In dedicating to Raleigh the newly edited *De Orbe Novo* of Peter Martyr, for example, Hakluyt (1587) praises Raleigh's

> letters from Court in which you freely swore that no terrors, no personal losses or misfortunes could or would ever tear you from the sweet embraces of your own Virginia, that fairest of nymphs— though to many insufficiently well known,—whom our most generous sovereign has given you to be your bride[.] If you persevere only a little longer in your constancy, your bride will shortly bring forth new and most abundant offspring, such as will delight you and yours, and cover with disgrace and shame those who have so often dared rashly and impudently to charge her with barrenness. For who has the just title to attach such a stigma to your Elizabeth's Virginia, when no one has yet probed the depths of her hidden resources and wealth, or her beauty hitherto concealed from our sight? Let them go where they deserve, foolish drones, mindful only of their bellies and gullets, who fresh from that place, like those whom Moses sent to spy out the promised land flowing with milk and honey, have treacherously published ill reports about it.[37]

The jolting reference to Virginia's imputed barrenness demands not only that the possibly vague or nominal comparison between Elizabeth and Virginia be taken seriously but also that the analogy be extended into what one might consider the most dangerous territory. Yet in similarly dwelling on the possible throwaway about Raleigh's "sweet embraces" with his "bride," the lavish sexual imagery that follows, the hidden beauty and the probe-able depths, shows that taking liberties is precisely Hakluyt's point: the racy language is itself part of the dalliance between Elizabeth and Raleigh that Virginia makes possible.[38] Like tobacco smoke, Virginia's whole beauty here in relation to Raleigh lies in its essential malleability, the ease with which it stands for a marriage, and the fruits of a marriage, otherwise impossible. But it is crucial to see that in allegorizing Virginia as a substitute Elizabeth, the passage drives toward claiming what Virginia's critics claim also, that Virginia has no attractions per se. And indeed Elizabeth will allow Raleigh to probe Virginia only if he stays at Court—near Elizabeth, certainly, but far from the vicarious deflowering.[39]

I do not mean to argue, however, that Raleigh's erotic American allegory is entirely at odds with other more nationally oriented New World views, or that Hakluyt himself, the writer here, does not also desire and enjoy this vision, as others would desire and enjoy Raleigh's smoking. After all, Elizabeth's virginity, or more negatively her barrenness, betokened national concerns not merely by analogy: since Elizabeth's foreign suitors represented the possibility of international alliances, since her favor meant money and power, and since her offspring, it was hoped, would ensure a peaceful succession, the queen's maidenhead would seem more than merely symbolic of both national isolation and the "want of place" at Court. By the same token, the logic of surrogacy that idealizes Raleigh's Virgin-ian colonialism would be useful not only to other colonialists trying to justify leaving England but to other courtiers trying to justify having interests besides Elizabeth: thrown into disgrace with the queen as a result of his actual marriage, the courtier Robert Cary, for instance, successfully redeemed himself by telling Elizabeth that "she herself was the fault of my marriage, and that if she had but graced me with the least of her favors, I had never left her nor her Court" (Nichols, *Progresses* 3:216).

In fact, as Hakluyt's allegory continues beyond the bridal motif, it demonstrates how the particular reduction of Virginia to a metaphor for an available queen only isolates a hidden tendency common to other more strictly economic colonial theorizing, a tendency to understand Virginia as nothing but a substitution, rather than a different place and, possibly, a different home. Hakluyt's comparison of the English people to the Jews highlights the problem of English attachment to England's island by ineptly running counter to that attachment: the switch from Raleigh and Elizabeth to Moses seems to leave Elizabeth behind—and Raleigh too, even if he is seen as Moses, for Moses, of course, never entered "the promised land"; but then Virginia as the promised land neither complements, supplements, nor relieves England but leaves the island, like the wilderness, behind altogether. In brief, the difference between Elizabeth and Moses in Hakluyt's allegory seems to be the difference between regarding England or Virginia as home. Yet Hakluyt can hardly be intending to suggest that England be abandoned. In calling Virginia the promised land he clearly overcompensates for *Virginia's* felt lack of intrinsic merit, a lack he at other times even helps, oddly enough, to publicize: the *Principall Navigations* (1589) records the verdict on Virginia of one more Raleigh underling, Ralph Lane again, who affirms "that the discovery of a good mine, by the goodness of God, or a passage to the Southsea, or someway to it, and nothing else can bring this country in request to be inhabited by our nation" (Quinn, *Roanoke Voyages* 1:273). On the other hand, Hakluyt can hardly mean that Englishmen should never settle Virginia. When, in his address to Raleigh, Hakluyt deplores, as Harriot will (*Report*, 323), those ex-colonists "mindful only of their bellies and gullets," it is the profiteering English view—that gold in hand is the only thing worth leaving home and probing Virginia's depths for—that he means, again like Harriot, to condemn. Hakluyt wants to say that Virginia supplies a "milk and honey" that satisfies something more than bellies, something like Raleigh's impossible desire for Elizabeth, which hopes to "occupy" both Elizabeth and Virginia at once, though in a far from literal way. A manna made "of conceited folly," of air—yet an air the Elizabethans thought substantial enough to "drink"—tobacco helps represent both the expansionist desire and its chimerical satisfaction.[40] Harriot's ambiguous position about tobacco/uppowoc, classifying it as nourishment to be exploited "there" while describing its use "here," begins to make more sense: requiring a volume all its own, tobacco helps suspend the question of Englishmen's true home, as if the metaphorical identification between England and Virginia were as good as, indeed better than, a soldier settlement.

III

Tobacco enters *The Faerie Queene* bearing this question of mediation, posed once again in terms of Raleigh's desire for Elizabeth. The dedicatory letter to Raleigh and the proem to *The Faerie Queene*'s third book identify Belphoebe in two ways. First, she is said to represent one aspect, or "person," of Elizabeth: "a most vertuous and beautiful Lady" as distinguished from "a most royal Queen or Empress" (*V* 1:168); or Elizabeth's "rare chastitee" as distinguished from "her rule" (*FQ* 3.proem.5). Second, Spenser claims to have fashioned her after Raleigh's "own excellent conceit of Cynthia" (*V* 1:168). By removing the impediment of Elizabeth's high station and presenting an Elizabeth after Raleigh's own conceit, Spenser's Belphoebe moves Elizabeth closer to Raleigh's desires in much the way Hakluyt's Virginian bride does. Tobacco strengthens the analogy to Hakluyt. With it, Belphoebe heals Timias's spear wound[41] but inflicts a love wound she cannot bring herself to cure: "But that sweet Cordiall, which can restore / A love-sick hart, she did to him envy" (*FQ* 3.5.50). This more desirable cordial happens to be "that dainty Rose" (51), "her fresh flowring Maidenhead" (54). Though Spenser's pathos here hardly figures in Hakluyt's passage (nor, for that matter, in Spenser's source),[42] the general allegorical point is basically the same: Raleigh is dying for Elizabeth's Rose, yet she grants him another flower, "divine Tobacco," as at once a demurral and a compensation; while the pastoral landscape that supports two classical herbs and an American one, and that presents the choice between them as almost indifferent, seems to show Spenser ignoring practical distances and distinctions (as far as he might safely do so) in favor of a less formidable gap, between not classes but states of mind— Timias's "mean estate" (44) and Belphoebe's "high *desert*" (45; my emphasis).[43]

This daring treatment of Raleigh's love for Elizabeth represents a step forward, or at least a new installment, in a debate about Elizabeth that Spenser had entered with the publication of *The Shepheardes Calender* a decade earlier. As my previous chapters argue, *The Shepheardes Calender* manifests Spenser's resistance to an increasingly popular view of Elizabeth that celebrated the Virgin Queen for keeping the English island separate and pure, an "Elizium." Faced with the problem of denouncing insularism as a political ideal while retaining Elizabeth as one, Spenser transforms Eliza's Elizium into an ideal that his alter ego, Colin, once celebrated but has now, for purely private and natural reasons, forsworn: what alienates Colin from pastoral complacency is, ostensibly, only his unrequited love for the shepherd-hating Rosalind. Yet the "November" eclogue, in which Colin returns as singer, underscores the political ramifications of his new melancholy by combining Eliza as pastoral genius and Rosalind as unattainable beloved in the figure of the dead Dido; Colin forsakes complacency about pastoral England to such a degree that he now longs only for the renovated "*Elisian* fieldes" ("November," 179) Dido seeks in heaven. If we take the epic reference in "Dido" seriously, however (and this is not the first such reference in the *Calender*), her death would also seem to mean, mysteriously enough, a gain for empire; the *Calender* leaves us wondering how Colin, the self-exiled Englishman, will find a compromise "England" between pastoral and the *contemptus mundi* that pastoral desire ultimately generates.

Compared to this esoteric argument about sexual frustration and Elizabeth, the *Faerie Queene* episode is quite striking in its directness, thanks to an even more striking development at Court: the rise to power and favor of "Colin's" exact contemporary and fellow adventurer in Ireland, Raleigh, has made it easier for Spenser to represent the unobtainable beloved as Elizabeth herself. Less obvious is the way the Timias and Belphoebe episode rewrites another feature of Colin's plight. In "December" Colin laments the fact that his pastoral lore cannot alleviate his love-woe:

> But ah unwise and witlesse *Colin cloute,*
> That kydst the hidden kinds of many a wede:
> Yet kydst not ene to cure thy sore hart roote,
> Whose ranckling wound as yet does rifelye bleede.
> (91–94)

This irony about herbal cures reflects the increasing transformation of Colin's frustrated desire into *contemptus mundi*; the "wede" becomes a synecdoche both for mere worldliness and for the pastoral "flowers" or poetry proportioned to that worldliness.[44] But when George Peele in his *Araygnement of Paris* appears to imitate Spenser, here in reference to Peele's own Colin—"And whether wends yon thriveless swain, like to the stricken deer. / Seeks he Dictamum for his wound within our forest here" (565–66)[45]—he pointedly separates Colin's frustration from the issue of Elizabeth's virginity. According to Peele, Colin despairs and finally dies because he is too worldly himself, too absorbed in his beloved to recognize the better, otherworldly worldliness embodied in the virgin Eliza, "in terris unam . . . Divam" (1230). Responding to such an interpretation of Colin's alienation, it seems, Spenser in the Timias and Belphoebe episode makes Eliza herself the purveyor of inadequate herb cures and therefore of the argument to despair.[46]

Spenser agrees with Peele, then, that the pastoral lover is too worldly, but he adds that the pastoral beloved is equally so: absorbing themselves in the disposition of Elizabeth's actual maidenhead and therefore reducing Elizabeth to the private person Belphoebe, Raleigh and Elizabeth, argues Spenser, debase the potentiality of a queen who, rightly understood, is as little a mere body as possible, a "Mirrour of grace and Majestie divine" (*FQ* 1.proem.4). Belphoebe treats her rose as if it were literal: she hides it in foul weather but in fair weather allows it to be "dispred" (3.5.51). The narrator, however, makes maidenheads sound figurative: he says they reside "in gentle Ladies brest" (52), and advises his female readers that such flowers should even "crowne" their "heades" (53). As for Timias, his response to Belphoebe does not, after all, differ much from the earlier reaction of the literalizing Braggadocchio, who

> fild with delight
> Of her sweet words, that all his sence dismaid,
> And with her wondrous beautie ravisht quight,
> Gan burne in filthy lust, and leaping light,
> Thought in his bastard armes her to embrace.
>
> (2.3.42)

Though nobler than "the baser wit, whose idle thoughts alway / Are wont to cleave unto the lowly clay," the languishing Timias nevertheless fails to aspire as the "brave sprite" should "to all high desert and honour" (3.5.1). If, then, Timias's degenerate precursor Braggadocchio helps reveal his own despair to be only a more genteel version of lust, Timias's master Arthur adumbrates the higher response to Elizabeth: he loves the queen as not the private Belphoebe but the public Gloriana. What's more, Arthur experiences less of Gloriana's physicality than either Braggadocchio or Timias does of Belphoebe's, for he meets the Fairy Queen only in a dream (1.9.12–15). Yet this dream is more than a fantasy. Determinedly ambiguous—material enough to have "pressed" the grass beside Arthur, though immaterial enough to vanish—Arthur's dream woman tantalizes him with just the right blend of corporeal and incorporeal inducements, of hope and despair, to keep him earthbound and yet always on the go.

Ultimately, however, not even Arthur's love proves fully separable from Braggadocchio's, for if Arthur seems less desperate than his squire, that is because he has no physically present beloved about whose body he can despair. In other words, like the reader of *The Faerie Queene* whose complacence Spenser expects to shake by "vaunt[ing]" of a fairyland Spenser "no where show[s]" (2.proem.1), Arthur escapes becoming absorbed in the queen's material person only because he "no where can her find" (2.9.7): it is the immateriality, the otherworldliness, the utopicality of both Fairyland and fairy queen that are supposed to keep both Arthur and the reader questing. By book 3, however, Arthur's inability to catch the fleeing Florimell has so aggravated his frustration about not reaching Gloriana that he begins to ride "with heavie looke and lumpish pace, that plaine / In him bewraid great grudge and maltalent" (3.4.61). The mere promise of some future consummation is no longer enough for him, and so it is that the next canto provides a more materialist version of Elizabeth—Belphoebe—in order to show us how catching her has its own problems.[47]

Raleigh himself articulates the pathos surrounding Elizabeth's admirers in these episodes when, in a portion of his *Ocean to Scinthia* (c. 1592) reminiscent of Wyatt's Tagus poem, he laments how his love for Elizabeth at once inspires and subverts his imperialist ambition:

> The honor of her love, Love still devising,
> Wounding my mind with contrary conceit
> Transferred itself sometimes to her aspiring,
> Sometime the trumpet of her thoughts' retreat;
> To seek new worlds, for gold, for praise, for glory,
> To try desire, to try love severed far,
> When I was gone she sent out her memory
> More strong than were ten thousand ships of war,
> To call me back, to leave great honors' thought,
> To leave my friends, my fortune, my attempt,
> To leave the purpose I so long had sought
> And hold both cares and comforts in contempt. (57–68)[48]

But the Timias and Belphoebe canto does more than reproduce Raleigh's "contrary" desire: it also offers a cure, suggested when Belphoebe first appeared in the poem. Upon Belphoebe's entrance in book 2, the narrator himself anticipates Braggadocchio's lustful absorption in her by devoting the longest blazon in the poem to her body (2.3.21–31); yet at the same time he stresses the saving insubstantiality of poetical leering when he adds, "So faire, and thousand thousand time more faire / She seemd, when she presented was to sight" (26). A climactic feature of every proem to

The Faerie Queene, this issue of Spenser's inadequacy at representing Elizabeth appears in narrative form later in book 2 when Arthur stops to admire the picture of the Fairy Queen on the shield of the knight of Temperance, Sir Guyon, and Guyon assures him that

> if in that picture dead
> Such life ye read, and vertue in vain shew,
> What mote ye weene, if the trew lively-head
> Of that most glorious visage ye did vew?
> But if the beautie of her mind ye knew,
> That is her bountie, and imperiall powre,
> Thousand times fairer then her mortall hew,
> O how great wonder would your thoughts devoure,
> And infinite desire into your spirite poure!
>
> (2.9.3)

An art figured as insufficient, "dead," to its referent turns out to mimic, and therefore properly underscore, the ontological insufficiency of Elizabeth's body to her mind.

Thus, when Spenser in the proem to book 3 ostensibly laments his ability only to "shadow" (3) Elizabeth, and imagines the queen possibly "covet[ing]" to see herself "pictured" instead in the "lively colours, and right hew" (4) of Raleigh's own poetry, he already begins the critique of "Cynthian" Belphoebe that will appear later in the same book. In fact, Spenser's depiction of Raleigh's "lively" art as lulling Spenser's senses "in slomber of delight" also recalls the critique of such art that had been developed in the preceding canto, where the artful Bower of Bliss proved so sufficient to nature as to be more prodigal in its worldliness than nature itself.[49] It is the pastoral art of "respondence" familiar from "Aprill" and the Error episode, in which "birdes, voyces, instruments, windes, waters, all agree" (2.12.70); and, when concerned with representing a woman in particular, it leads not to her enhancement but to her diminution, her reduction to and ultimately from her body, as when the magus Busirane forms the "characters of his art" with the "living bloud" (3.12.31) of Belphoebe's sister Amoret.

If Spenser argues, then, that his conspicuously inadequate or trifling representations of the queen are more faithful and consequently less damaging to Elizabeth's true beauty than Raleigh's iconic verse, he does not go so far as to insist that his own poetry is wholly insubstantial; rather, he depicts it as sharing the ambiguous status that Arthur accords his dream of Gloriana. When the muse Polyhymnia in *The Teares of the Muses* (1591), for instance, celebrates that "true Pandora of all heavenly graces, / Divine *Elisa*" (578–79), she also prays that "divinest wits" will "eternize" Elizabeth with "their heavenlie *writs*" (581–82; my emphasis). Polyhymnia stresses, in other words, not just the spiritual import of a truly Elizabethan poetry but its materiality, the actual writings or documents that Elizabeth's poets will produce; and these writings even surpass the bodies of Elizabeth and Gloriana *as* bodies in their ability to make lastingly present, to "eternize," what a normal body cannot. Yet how can one distinguish such acceptable poetic materiality from the worldly substantiality Spenser repudiates? Since the "writs" Polyhymnia describes are not Edenic, as in the Bower of Bliss (*FQ* 2.12.52), but "heavenlie," Spenser apparently believes that it is the oxymoronic "character" of this poetry, the allegorical disparity between its signs and its referents, that both saves it from mere worldliness and qualifies it to represent the equally oxymoronic divinity of the queen.[50]

In the Timias and Belphoebe episode, the "divine" similitude for a queenly "Mayd full of divinities" (3.5.34) is conceived so materially as to be called a flower, or in Spenser's more oxymoronic formulation, a "soveraigne weede" (33). But this poetical herb also has specific political implications. If Raleigh's romantic attachment to the queen enables a more directly critical treatment of her "insular" virginity in this episode than Spenser could muster in *The Shepheardes Calender*, another aspect of Raleigh's ambition—as unavailable to Spenser at the writing of *The Shepheardes Calender* as the royal love affair with Raleigh—has allowed Spenser to extend his critique. For the worldly herb that allegorically figures the limitations of worldliness can now be the flower of a pastoral transcending the English island and yet still English and earthly—Virginian tobacco. Shortsighted about their relationship, Timias and Belphoebe fail to recognize that the episode's conspicuously inadequate correlative to Belphoebe's maidenhead can mean more than its present materiality, can signify Virginia as both an otherworldly reflection of "the heavenly Mayd" (3.5.43) and an actual substantiation of her "imperiall powre." What "divine tobacco," a

posy of poesy, allegorizes, in short, is the possibility of Elizabethan expansion beyond the apparent material limitations of both
Elizabeth and England—the mystery of a royal Virgin bearing
"fruit."

IV

The surprising notoriety of "divine" as an epithet for tobacco
would seem to suggest, however, that Spenser's readers, and perhaps Spenser himself, see more in tobacco's divinity than a subtly
ironic literary-imperialist argument concerning the inadequacy of
pastoral to desire. No doubt the mere association of the queen
with this epithet helped popularize it, especially since tobacco requires divinity in the episode so as to render it more commensu-
rable, again, with "heavenly" Elizabeth. But if the divinity shared
by Elizabeth and Virginia in Hakluyt looks mysterious, what sense
can the assertion of tobacco's comparable divinity make? Tobacco,
it seems, must already have appeared a material expression of
spirituality for it to have conveyed, or seem to have conveyed, an
abstruse vision of Elizabethan otherworldliness so successfully; but
why? In part both Spenser and his subsequent imitators may echo
a Continental tradition about tobacco's divinity;[51] but then what
made Continental writers adopt this view? The influence of Indian
"estimation" seems once again difficult to deny, as James demanded his subjects to consider:

> Shall we . . . abase our selves so far, as to imitate these beastly *In-
> dians*, slaves to the *Spaniards*, refuse to the world, and as yet aliens
> from the holy Covenant of God? Why do we not as well imitate
> them in walking naked as they do? in preferring glasses, feathers,
> and such toys, to gold and precious stones, as they do? yea why do
> we not deny God and adore the Devil, as they do? (*Counter-blaste*
> B2r)[52]

If the charges against Marlowe, Raleigh, and Raleigh's followers
may be believed, the king's hysteria was not entirely unwarranted:
the infamous snitcher Richard Baines (1593) reported Marlowe's
assertion "that if Christ would have instituted the sacrament with
more ceremonial Reverence it would have been had in more admiration, that it would have been much better administered in a
Tobacco pipe"; and a lieutenant of Raleigh's was allegedly seen to
"tear two Leaves out of a Bible to dry Tobacco on" (quoted in Shir-

ley, *Harriot*, 182–83, 192). Philaretes comments, "Our wit-worn gallants, with the scent of thee, / Sent for the Devil and his company." To the tobacco hater, tobacco does not complement English values, it inverts them, hell for heaven; Philaretes too believes the comparison with Elizabeth explains tobacco, though not as her surrogate, a bride, but as her travesty, a whore: "O I would whip the quean with rods of steel, / That ever after she my jerks should feel" (*Work*, Br).[53]

The problem is the same one posed by Elyot's analysis of the rheum—how can a far-fetched luxury associated with the depths of superstition come to any good?—and yet some of tobacco's advocates not only excused tobacco but exalted it as England's "divine" savior from just that decadence and superstition it would seem to exacerbate. A poem attributed in Essex's lifetime to Essex offers the pathos Spenser associates with tobacco as tobacco's justification. The poem, "The Poor Laboring Bee" (1598),[54] laments Essex's singular and undeserved bad luck: "Of all the swarm, I only could not thrive, / yet brought I wax and Honey to the hive." Even before any mention of tobacco Essex invokes the terms of Timias's unhappiness—the other bees "suck" Elizabeth's flowers, the rose and eglantines—but the poem's conclusion makes Essex's debt to Spenser unmistakable: "If this I cannot have; as helpless bee, / Wished Tobacco, I will fly to thee" (the Egerton MS of the poem reads "*Witching* Tobacco," which moves the poem closer to Philaretes' pessimism about the exchange). Yet tobacco's cure works not by compensating for but by dramatizing and generalizing Essex's disappointment as the fate of all worldly desires:

> What though thou dye'st my lungs in deepest black.
> A Mourning habit, suits a sable heart.
> What though thy fumes sound memory do crack,
> forgetfulness is fittest for my smart.
>> O sacred fume, let it be Carv'd in oak,
>> that words, Hopes, wit, and all the world are smoke.

Calvin says that "not only the learned do know, but also the common people have no Proverb more common than this, that man's life is like a smoke."[55] And so Essex transforms Philaretes' attack on tobacco as "smoking vanity" (*Work*, Br) into the very basis of tobacco's claim to sacredness. Tobacco's insubstantiality, that is, leads Essex to a sublime view of the world as itself insubstantial, to *contemptus mundi;*[56] while in the same way the otherwise humiliating exchange of solid good for smoke—as a character in Dekker has it, "Tobacco, which mounts into th'air, and proves nothing but one thing . . . that he is an ass that melts so much money in smoke"[57]—here proves the taste for tobacco less delusory than the love of precious metals, "sweet dreams of gold."

Henry Buttes similarly turns tobacco's deficits to spiritual advantage, though more optimistically than Essex. The title page of *Dyets Dry Dinner* oddly takes for granted that a meal should be "served in after the order of Time universal," or to put it another way, that the ontogeny of one's banquet should recapitulate the phylogeny of human culture. Thus the meal begins with the food "Adam robbed [from] God's Orchard" (A7v)—fruit—then proceeds through dishes consequent on new developments in "humane invention," until our itch for "voluptuous delight" (A8r) leads us to that most odious of luxuries, sauces. It is at this point, as in Elyot, that the rheum arrives, the bodily counterpart to a superfluity, a running over, on two oddly correspondent scales of time, of a meal and of a human history that have both lasted too long:

> Thus proceeded we by degrees, from simplicity and necessity, to variety and plenty, ending in luxury and superfluity. So that at last our bodies by surfeeding, being overflown and drowned (as it were) in a surpleurisy or deluge of a superfluous raw humor (commonly called Rheum) we were to be annealed (like new dampish Ovens, or old dwelling houses that have stood long desolate). Hence it is that we perfume and air our bodies with *Tobacco* smoke (by drying) preserving them from putrefaction. (A8v)

Yet of course, as the phylogenetic scheme of the meal demands that we see, tobacco is the ultimate superfluity, and Buttes himself later spells out the rheumlike "hurt" tobacco can do: it "mortifieth and benumbeth: causeth drowsiness: troubleth & dulleth the senses: makes (as it were) drunk: dangerous in meal time" (P5v). Presumably his pharmacology is, then, homeopathic: a little more excess somehow eradicates excess altogether. But the moral is quite different from that of Essex, who prizes tobacco for dramatizing the true nature of all "voluptuous delight." Buttes's homeopathy cuts two ways. Fire to rheum's water, tobacco as afterdinner mint replaces the grand conclusion to our history, the conflagration that follows our punishment by deluge;[58] in other words, as at once the latest luxury and earliest apocalypse, tobacco homeopathically cures, in Buttes's mind, both our decadence and God's judgment upon it.

Though one is tempted to dismiss this conclusion, like so many other Elizabethan arguments about tobacco, as a particularly eccentric joke, Buttes's theology seems basically the same as Philaretes', who believes that the English are somehow in a peculiarly good position to mediate between worldly delights and a divine contempt for them. Philaretes' problem with tobacco is that it is too grossly of the world—its priestly user "dead sleeping falls, / Flat on the ground"—and so threatens to undo England's compromise between *contemptus* and carnality, heaven and earth: "But hence thou Pagan Idol: tawny weed, / Come not with-in"—not our Christian but—"our *Fairie* Coasts to feed" (*Work*, Br; my emphasis). Buttes defends tobacco's role in preserving this compromise by sidestepping overt theology and invoking instead what he considers commonsense physiology. According to Borde's *Breviary of Helthe*, for instance, rheum causes sleepiness by producing "great gravidity in the head," by weighing the head down ("The Extravagants," not by Borde, 18v). John Trevisa says it clogs one's "spirit":

> For sometime rheumatic humors cometh to the spiritual parties & stop the ways of the spirit and be in point to stuff the body. / Then cometh dryness or dry medicines. & worketh & destroyeth such humors. & openeth the ways of the spirit / & so the body that is as it were dead hath living.[59]

By this account hot and dry tobacco would seem, in other words, to oppose grossness; and so Marbecke argues even against Philaretes' interpretation of Monardes' report on tobacco's superstitious usage:

> For take but *Monardus* his own tale: and by him it should seem; that in the taking of *Tobacco*: they [the priests] were drawn up: and separated from all gross, and earthly cogitations, and as it were carried up to a more pure and clear region, of fine conceits & actions of the mind, in so much, as they were able thereby to see visions, as you say: & able likewise to make wise & sharp answers, much like as those men are wont to do, who being cast into trances, and ecstasies, as we are wont to call it, have the power and gift thereby, to see more wonders, and high mystical matters, then all they can do,

whose brains, & cogitations, are oppressed with the thick and foggy vapors, of gross, and earthly substances. Marry, if in their trances, & sudden fallings, they had become nasty, & beastly fellows: or had in most loathsome manner, fallen a-spewing, and vomiting, as drunkards are wont to do: then indeed it might well have been counted a devilish matter: and been worthy reprehension. But being used to clear the brains, and thereby making the mind more able, to come to herself, and the better to exercise her heavenly gifts, and virtues; me think, as I have said, I see more cause why we should think it to be a rare gift imparted unto man, by the goodness of God, than to be any invention of the devil. (*Defence*, 58–59)

Now smoke for substance is a godly exchange: the mind comes to herself, though still clogged and hamstrung by the body; carried up in ecstasies to a purer and clearer region, though still on earth.[60]

Freeing the English from the body's limitations as well as from England's small, rheumatic island, tobacco removes a secondary curb on the English mind—particularly, on English poetry. In light of the Renaissance theory that warmer climates are more conducive to mind than colder ones,[61] Harriot's list of the warm countries, like Greece and Italy, to which Virginia's climate is similar takes on a new significance: Virginia can be understood as opening for England not merely economic but intellectual and poetic vistas, vistas to which tobacco's own heat contributes. But to see Virginia's and tobacco's advantages in this light is to render finally untenable the reduction of tobacco's powers merely to synecdoches for Virginia's. In order to warm up the English the Virginian way, one must ship them many miles and latitudes hence; yet tobacco brings to the English Virginia's heat—what Beaumont will call the "Indian sun"—without their having to leave the comforts of home. But then all of tobacco's benefits, like its after-dinner annealing in Buttes, are immediate, and Virginia's only anticipated; insofar as those benefits are taken seriously, tobacco does not merely stand for the New World but stands *in* for it by transforming England into a new world all its own.[62]

Of course that is just the point tobacco's critics make also: Hall's name for Raleigh in the tobacco passage of *Mundus Alter et Idem*, Topia-Warallador, buries *Raleigh* in the name of the Indian cacique Raleigh met in Guiana, Topi-Wari, and the Spanish word for discoverer, *hallador*, so as to suggest how an Englishman's interest in America can un-English him. Richard Brathwait (1617), scandalized by the fact that the sign used to advertise a tobacco shop should be a black man smoking, called tobacconists *"English Moors"* (see figure 6).[63] The physiological side to this argument is that tobacco smoke makes an Englishman as black on the inside (inside the body, inside England's bounds) as the Indian is on the outside (on his body's outside, outside England).[64] But to the tobacco advocate smoke is precisely the key for proving that tobacco converts the New World into a disposable remedy—and now even Raleigh's self-aggrandizing bet, in which tobacco's smoke becomes his substance, seems to have its national correlative: tobacco purges the pent-up body, opens its pores, warms its brain, and helps it breathe, by itself going up in smoke. Opposing Philaretes' fear that tobacco will turn the English body into a torrid zone, Marbecke even denies that smoke has the power seriously to alter anything:

> The taking thereof, especially in fume, (which as your self granteth, *hath very small force to work any great matter upon our bodies*) can cause no such fiery, and extreme heat in the body, as is by you supposed, but rather, if it do give any heat, yet that heat is rather a familiar, and a pleasing heat, than an immoderate, extraordinary, and an aguish distemperature. (*Defence*, 19)[65]

The heat is familiar, so that England can become capable of New World powers without having to stop being England, can prove *alter et idem*: tobacco only helps the rheumatic English mind "come to herself."

V

If, as Francis Davison (1602) claims, some critics can insist that poetry too "doth intoxicate the brain, and make men utterly unfit, either for more serious studies, or for any active course of life" (*Poetical Rhapsody*, 4–5), a commendatory epigram to Sir John Beaumont's *Metamorphosis of Tabacco* (1602) can defend Beaumont by comparing his poetry to tobacco's self-consuming influence:

TO THE WHITE READER

> Take up these lines Tobacco-like unto thy brain,
> And that divinely toucht, puff out the smoke again.
>
> (*Poems*, 272)

Figure 6. Frontispiece to *The Smoaking Age*, by Richard Brathwait, London, 1617. The upper scrolls read *"Qui Color albus erat. / quantum mutatus ab illo. / Anglus in Æthiopium"* (whose color was white. / how much changed from that. / an Englishman into an Ethiopian). (By permission of the Houghton Library, Harvard University.)

Beaumont himself quickly implies that the primary metamorphosis of his title is tobacco's transformation into his poetry, a transformation unabashedly evoking the savage practice Monardes describes and Philaretes abhors:

> But thou great god of Indian melody
> . . . .
> By whom the Indian priests inspired be,
> When they presage in barbarous poetry:
> Infume my brain, make my soul's powers subtle,
> Give nimble cadence to my harsher style;
> Inspire me with thy flame, which doth excel
> The purest streams of the Castalian well.
>
> (276–77)

Where Marbecke tries to reconcile savage to Christian value, Beaumont characteristically insists on celebrating those features of Indian smoking, the superstition and barbarity, that most stand in the way of such a reconciliation. Beaumont's dedicatory poem to Drayton had warned readers that Beaumont would prove irreverent, since it emphasizes that the dedication is meant to be as much an affront to the powerful as a compliment to a friend: Beaumont claims he "loathes to adorn the triumphs of those men, / Which hold the reins of fortune, and the times." The Latin tag ending the dedication, from Catullus's dedication of his own work, embraces the poet's professed marginality less militantly, joking now about Beaumont's intellectual poverty: to whom better should I dedicate my poem, asks Beaumont, *namquam tu solebas / Meas esse aliquid putare nugas,* than you who used to think my trifles something. Yet with the rigor of a puritanical antagonist, Beaumont in his invocation completes the traditional assault on fruitless poetry by allying his poem not only with poverty and inanity but with superstition. For Beaumont subscribes to an alternative—in his view Spenserian—system of "estimation," whose genius is "the sweet and sole delight of mortal men, / The cornu-copia of all earthly pleasure" (275).[66] If poetry's influential critic Henry Cornelius Agrippa declares that poets *super fumo machinari omnia* (E1v), or, in the Elizabethan version, "devise all things upon a matter of nothing [*fumo,* smoke]" (33), then Beaumont will celebrate the "Castalian well" of *fumo*—tobacco.

After its invocation, in fact, the poem embarks on two myths of

tobacco's creation that celebrate tobacco's worth as against the religious and temporal orthodoxy separately scorned in dedication
and invocation but now combined in the figures of the Olympian
gods. In the first myth, Earth and her subjects frustrate their op-
pressor, Jove, by enlivening Prometheus's subversive creation,
man, with the flame of tobacco (Beaumont, *Poems*, 277–86). In the
second, less contentious tale, Jove courts a beautiful but standoff-
ish American nymph who outshines Apollo; Juno angrily transforms her into a plant—tobacco; but Jove retaliates by further
metamorphosing his former love into "a micro-cosm of good"
(286–304). While both myths associate tobacco's value with the victimized and profane, one last account of tobacco moves closer to
conformity, though only in order to attack still another kind of tyranny. This account takes the premise of the second myth further,
and decides that the gods must always have been ignorant of tobacco, or else, "had they known this smoke's delicious smack, /
The vault of heav'n ere this time had been black" (304). The more
the Olympians are imagined as prone to love "the pure distillation
of the Earth" (304), the more their powers and authority are blot-
ted out, blackened; for their love of tobacco assimilates them to
Harriot's Indian gods, and by implication, the pagan Greeks and
Romans to the pagan Indians.[67] In other words, Beaumont in-
volves tobacco in a rebellion now against not only religious or temporal authority but also "the purest stream of the Castalian well,"
the authority of the classics. Even the gods' ignorance of tobacco
damns the classical world, by reminding Beaumont's readers of
one of the first and most powerful intellectual reactions to America's discovery, the realization that the ancients had, for all their
intimidating genius, proven profoundly benighted—"Had but the
old heroic spirits known" (305)![68]

Yet Beaumont does not want the subversion of one orthodoxy
to become a triumph for another: he now explicitly asserts that
those "blinder ages" (306) were indeed wrong to worship Ceres,
for instance, but only because they ought to have worshipped tobacco instead. Modern times, he claims, have not abandoned superstition but discovered improvements on it:

> Blest age, wherein the Indian sun had shin'd,
> Whereby all Arts, all tongues have been refin'd:

Learning, long buried in the dark abysm—
Of dunstical and monkish barbarism,
When once the herb by careful pains was found,
Sprung up like Cadmus' followers from the ground,
Which Muses visitation bindeth us
More to great Cortez, and Vespucius,
Than to our witty More's immortal name,
To Valla, or the learned Rott'rodame.

(314–15)

To keep his distance from both orthodoxy and superstition, Beaumont now orthodoxly eschews *papist* superstition, "dunstical and monkish barbarism," yet in the name neither of humanism nor of the true church but of tobacco.

This last profanity derives a special bite from the fact that, to many of Beaumont's readers, the distinction between Indian and papist paganism would have seemed a nice one indeed. We have already seen how Marlowe conflates the two kinds of "ceremonial reverence" (and apparently some Catholic priests overseas felt the same temptation: in 1588 the Roman College of Cardinals was forced to declare "forbidden under penalty of eternal damnation for priests, about to administer the sacraments, either to take the smoke of *sayri*, or tobacco, into the mouth, or the powder of tobacco into the nose, even under the guise of medicine, before the service of the Mass"[69]). Chapman's Monsieur D'Olive mocks the similar views of Marlowe's enemies—here, a Puritan weaver reviling tobacco:

Said 'twas a pagan plant, a profane weed,
And a most sinful smoke, that had no warrant
Out of the Word; invented sure by Satan
In these our latter days to cast a mist
Before men's eyes that they might not behold
The grossness of old superstition
Which is, as 'twere, deriv'd into the Church
From the foul sink of Romish popery.
(*Monsieur D'Olive* 2.2.199–206)

The difference for Beaumont seems to be one of proximity: England has just escaped papistry's "dark abysm," while Indian superstition is at once too distant and too primitive a threat to be

taken seriously. The superior status of a blest age freed from papist barbarism now leads Beaumont to affirm that

> Had the Castalian Muses known the place
> Which this Ambrosia did with honor grace,
> They would have left Parnassus long ago,
> And chang'd their Phocis for Wingandekoe.
>
> *(Poems,* 315)

The wit of the final line depends on perceiving the two place
names, one Greek and one Indian, as equally outlandish and barbaric—on the suggestion, again, that the ancients were no better
than the Indians, or still more wishfully, that the authority of the
classics, as of the Indian "people void of sense" (315), depends on
the playful attribution of that authority by the enlightened English
reader.

One might say that the comical mixture of classical with Indian
subject matter focuses power on England as the excluded middle,[70] whose perfect representative would now seem to be "our
more glorious Nymph" (315), the virgin more successful than tobacco in withstanding the encroachments of the powers that be, of
superstition East and West—that "heretical" authority, Elizabeth.
Earlier in the poem Elizabeth had already enabled Beaumont to
make a provisional act of obeisance to the status quo: he had
claimed that, just as tobacco has replaced Ceres in the heaven of
the superstitious, so Elizabeth has replaced tobacco. Wingandekoe, the American home of the tobaccoan nymph, "now a far
more glorious name doth bear / Since a more beauteous nymph
was worshipt there": as Beaumont's note explains, "Wingandekoe
is a country in the North part of America, called by the Queen,
Virginia" (286–87). The moral would seem to be that Elizabeth outshines the dreams of the superstitious pagan; modern historians
of Elizabeth's cult would conclude that Beaumont wants to substitute worship of the queen for the cast-off "superstitions" not just
of paganism but of papistry, so that Elizabeth can absorb Catholi-
cism's displaced authority.[71] Yet here Elizabeth does not stand
apart, virginal, from the superstition whose authority she absorbs.
The terms of praise for Elizabeth that follow—the queen is, for example, "our modern Muse, / Which light and life doth to the
North infuse," "In whose respect the Muses barb'rous are, / The

Graces rude, nor is the phoenix rare"—sound if anything indistinguishable from the ones Beaumont previously applied to tobacco; in his poem at least, Elizabeth's authority, like the poem's itself, depends on highlighting its inseparability from *overt* superstition.[72] The comparison of queen to poet helps clarify the distinction: just as Beaumont refuses to name his own religion outright and instead presents his sophistication only negatively, masquerading as Indian or ancient barbarism, so Elizabeth's accomplishments are defined only negatively, by the degree to which she does tobacco or ancient Muse one better, and so, as Beaumont says, "exceeds her predecessors' facts." Beaumont nicely captures the paradox of Elizabeth's alliance to and difference from superstition when he asserts, "Nor are her wondrous acts, now wondrous acts" (315).

Such definition by negation may seem a little more explicable in an overseas context, as "the improvisation of power,"[73] when the English want the natives to love them and yet still to look foolish. Raleigh's lieutenant Keymis (1596) reports how, on his return to Guiana the year after Raleigh's visit, he found the natives constant in the devotion Raleigh taught them:

> Thus they sit talking, and taking Tobacco some two hours, and until their pipes be all spent . . . no man must interrupt . . . : for this is their religion, and prayers, which they now celebrated, keeping a precise fast one whole day, in honor of the great Princess of the North, their Patroness and defender.[74]

Of course, Catholic polemicists could ignore the distinction between the savage and civilized estimation of Elizabeth as easily as antitobaccoans ignored the distinction between savage and civilized smoking.[75] But leaving aside this problem, as well as the question of how deeply committed the Indians actually were to the queen, what practical benefits could Beaumont have thought that this Indian chapter of the cult of Elizabeth had yielded England? The purpose behind Beaumont's own version of the cult seems obscurer still when the one act of Elizabeth upon which Beaumont decides to elaborate is perhaps the most dubious one he could have chosen: he extols the queen for having

> uncontroll'd stretcht out her mighty hand
> Over Virginia and the New-found-land,

> And spread the colors of our English Rose
> In the far countries where Tobacco grows,
> And tam'd the savage nations of the West,
> Which of this jewel were in vain possest.
>
> (*Poems*, 316)

The last anyone had seen of England's single New World tamer at the time, the 1587 Roanoke colony, was more than fourteen years before, and the law presumed missing persons dead after seven; John Gerard's *Herball* (1597) musters as bright an optimism about the Lost Colony as could be expected when he mentions "Virginia . . . where are dwelling at this present Englishmen, if neither untimely death by murdering, or pestilence, corrupt air, bloody fluxes, or some other mortal sickness hath not destroyed them" (quoted in Quinn, *England*, 444). As the poem now turns to more strictly imperialist talk, Beaumont himself contradictorily emphasizes the hardships that still await English New World enterprises. Jove, he now says, hates tobacco "as the gainsayer of eternal fate," and so "this precious gem / Is thus beset with beasts, and kept by them"; besides, "a thousand dangers circle round / Whatever good within this world is found," and not the least of the dangers England continues to face are the Spanish, "far more savage than the Savages," who indeed "have the royalty / Where glorious gold, and rich Tobacco be" (*Poems*, 316–17). Beside the possibly apocryphal exportation of Elizabeth-idolatry to a small tribe in Guiana, then, the "acts" to which Beaumont must be pointing when he claims that Elizabeth has already tamed America are presumably speech acts such as Elizabeth renaming Wingandekoe Virginia, Hakluyt calling Virginia Raleigh's Elizabeth-like bride, Spenser placing Belphoebe in a tobacco field, and Beaumont himself writing this poem: in other words, the importation of barbarism, and especially of its representative "jewel," tobacco, into civilized discourse.

Again symbolic returns from the New World seem almost preferable to something more substantial, and again this preference gets elaborated, in the poem's climax, as esteeming tobacco more than gold:

> For this our praised plant on high doth soar,
> Above the baser dross of earthly ore,
> Like the brave spirit and ambitious mind,

Whose eaglet's eyes the sunbeams cannot blind;
Nor can the clog of poverty depress
Such souls in base and native lowliness,
But proudly scorning to behold the Earth,
They leap at crowns, and reach above their birth.

(317–18)

The sentiment, the contemning of mere fortune, is the same one introduced in the dedication to Drayton, but now oddly transformed from an antipolitical and individualistic pose to a national, imperialist argument: tobacco is the key to England's late and unlikely imperial hopes, "the gainsayer of eternal fate," precisely because it signals that the Spanish "have the royalty" of both it and gold, while the English have no empire at all. Both Beaumont's surprising metamorphosis and his peculiar theory here follow logically, however, from his disdain for those worldlings who, like Daniel's Philocosmus, declare of "trifling" poetry, "other delights than these, other desires / This wiser profit-seeking age requires" (*Musophilus*, ll. 12–13). Indeed, what in a contemporary work, the last of the *Parnassus* plays (1601–2), represents a poet's lament about contemptuous patrons, would in Beaumont's poem constitute a patriotic brag: "We have the words, they the possession have." (At one point in the plays another poet even imagines this envied "possession" to be "the gold of India"; as Dekker [1603] says, "Alack that the West Indies stand so far from Universities!")[76] Like the Virginia of Harriot and Hakluyt, poetry for Beaumont cannot please the material-minded; and by the same token Virginia requires "the brave spirit and ambitious mind" of the man professionally equipped to see the substance in what appears substanceless—the poet: "For verses are unto them food, / Lies are to these both gold and good" (Agrippa, *Vanitie*, 33).

But what inspiration is to be had from one's total outflanking by the enemy? A standard Christian explanation of the value of such trouble—here Calvin's explanation, in the chapter where he notes that "man's life is like a smoke"—seems at first miles apart from Beaumont's probable response: "For, because God knoweth well how much we be by nature inclined to the beastly love of this world, he useth a most fit mean to draw us back, and to shake off our sluggishness, that we should not stick too fast in that love" (*Institution*, 167v). But in justifying the imperial difficulties for which tobacco stands, Beaumont simply adjusts the sights Calvin sets. Gold has tricked the Spanish into making the literalizing, bestializing mistake of filling their bellies, while tobacco teaches the English instead a limited form of *contemptus*: "the clog of poverty" that tobacco represents—in short, England's limitation to its island home—does not "depress" Englishmen in their "base and native lowliness" because that clog is made of smoke (and imported smoke at that). Poor Englishmen harness the rarefying power of Apollo, the poet's god, and create a new golden age, not by embracing as the Spanish do the "terrestrial sun" of gold but by attaching themselves to something as nearly nothing as possible.

It is crucial to remember here, however, that in rejecting any binding, material correlative to its powers, the ambitious mind does not appeal instead to a heavenly correlative; though the idea of leaping at crowns and reaching above one's birth certainly suggests an aspiration, in spite of original sin, for a heavenly crown, tobacco smoke does not ascend that high: true, "our sweet herb all earthly dross doth hate, / Though in the Earth both nourisht and create," but when it "leaves this low orb, and labors to aspire," it ends up only "mixing her vapors with the airy clouds" (Beaumont, *Poems*, 318), which then drop "celestial show'rs" on English heads. Beaumont wants a crown somewhere between earth and heaven, both off the ground and of it, distinguished only from the frivolous low superstition that negatively defines its purview. Tobacco's limited, homeopathic dose of *contemptus*, its minor and embraceable conflagration, cures the pangs both of worldly trouble and of *contemptus* itself; it helps the ambitious mind, aware now of its own unfading substance, come to itself.

An alternative explanation of Beaumont's resistance to articulating his theology more clearly would note his multiple convictions for recusancy a few years later (Sell, *Beaumont*, 8–10), which raise the question whether any other tobacco advocate actually holds Beaumont's possibly anomalous position. It has not been my intention to demonstrate, however, that the writers I have discussed hold any one position about tobacco at all. Rather, they share assumptions about tobacco that are based on earlier physiological, economic, poetic, and theological claims, claims that are themselves analogous and cohere around premises concerning England the island, limited, rheumatic, and late; the analogies may or may not be pursued, or the writer may or may not recognize the consequences of those analogies he does pursue. Indeed, the primary value of tobacco for these writers is precisely its negativity, which enables it to mediate between normally opposed terms—between purging and feeding, high and low, trifle and jewel, superstition and religion, home and away, heaven and earth—by displacing both terms and substituting its own neither material nor spiritual essence, its "sweet substantial fume," instead.[77] The negativity of Beaumont's theological argument, for instance, substituting tobacco worship for either Protestant or Catholic polemic, may suit both his rebelliousness and his fears about recusancy convictions; but its efficacy, or danger, does not stop there. How does the imperialist reconcile his earthly ambitions to his heavenly ones? Beaumont's tobacco argument avoids choosing between worldly and otherworldly treasures by shadowing his aims in smoke.

Tobacco's critics perceive this shadowy negativity simply as negation, a problem to which Beaumont himself draws attention when at the end of his poem (in lines reminiscent of the end of *The Shepheardes Calender*) he asks his Muse, now suspiciously "clok'd with vapors of a dusky hue," to "bid both the world and thy sweet herb, Adieu": the poem too goes up (or down?) in smoke. But then the poem's motto, *Lusimus, Octave, &c.*, from Virgil's *Culex*—in Spenser's translation, "We now have played (Augustus) wantonly"[78]—has already cast this apparently wanton and excessive use of tobacco as itself dispensable, a mere fledgling poetic attempt soon to be transcended by a more properly imperial invention: for Beaumont, the tobacco pipe simply tunes the modern pastoral. Later, after England and the newly created Virginia Company had begun to pursue Beaumont's imperial goal more assiduously, Virginia's colonists tried to make the same argument about their own tobacco craze. Deploring the idea of a settlement based on a commodity that would "vanish into smoke" (*in fumu . . . evanitio*), John Pory (1620) asserts that "the extreme Care, diligence, and labor spent about it [tobacco], doth prepare our people for some more excellent subject."[79] "We affect not that Contemptible weed as an end," an official letter from the colony (1624) declares, "but as a present means" (McIlwaine, *Journals*, 26). My next chapter will show, however, that, long after Raleigh's early failures in Virginia, "contemptible" trifles like the conveniently replacing and replaceable tobacco refused to fade from colonialist view. In fact, it was only after all other plans for Jacobean Virginia seemed to its critics "vanished into smoke (that is to say into To-bacco)" (Kingsbury, *Records* 4:145) that the colony finally became profitable; the credulous savage so long anticipated by English colonialists, the one who was to buy trifles for gold and thus save the colony, turned out to be the English smoker.[80] By 1624, even James had to admit that Virginia "can only subsist at present by its tobacco" (*CSP Dom.* 11:290); and indeed, the more dependent on tobacco Jamestown became, the more ambiguous became even James's distaste. In 1619 the College of Physicians declared home-grown tobacco unhealthy, and James banned its production; but his decision turned on more than medical considerations: in exchange for the ban, the Virginia Company allowed the Crown much higher duties on the company's tobacco imports.[81] The colony that was supposed to expand the English economy by providing England the goods it could otherwise obtain only "at the courtesy of other Princes, under the burthen of great Customs, and heavy impositions,"[82] had been transformed by James, then, into simply one more foreign peddler of trifles, with James its extortionist lord—a king not of Fairyland but of thin air.[83]

5

The Triumph of Disgrace

> For I protest before God, there is none, on the face of the
> earth, that I would be fastened unto.
>
> —Raleigh on the rumors
> of his marriage (1592)

What appears to mark the end of "fruitfullest Virginia" as a colonial ideal during Elizabeth's final years—besides a colony vanishing and an American fruit going up in smoke—is the apparent de-
sertion, or rather defection, of two key Virginian advocates:
Raleigh sails to Guiana, and Spenser praises him for it. Raleigh's
change of heart seems particularly telling. As we have seen,
the colonialists in his service had already developed strong arguments to explain why the New World territory ripest for expansion was Virginia. It was, for instance, a world "not yet in any
Christian prince's actual possession" to which the Cabots had
given England "just Title" (Hakluyt, "Discourse," 222); it was
reachable by voyages "easy and short" that might "be performed
at all times of the year, and needeth but one kind of wind" (265);
and it was inhabited only by an easily vanquished naked people
who would anyway voluntarily "yield themselves" (318) to England's clement queen. Virginia was imagined, in short, the New
World most congenial to the English—"the best part of America
that is left and in truth more agreeable to our natures, and more
near unto us than Nova hispania" (279)[1]—so easy to assimilate to
home that it could paradoxically receive the name of the royal virginity that preserved England inviolate. Guiana, on the other
hand, lay in the very center of "Nova hispania"; as Raleigh's *Discoverie of the Large Rich, and Bewtifull Empyre of Guiana* (1596) records, Raleigh had to fight the Spanish (or at least run into them)
at almost every stage of his Guianan voyage, even kidnap a few of
them as guides, and include documents written by them as crucial

Figure 7. "C[aptain] Smith Bound to a Tree to be Shot to Death" and "Their Triumph About Him," enlargement from "A Description of Part of the Adventures of Cap: Smith in Virginia," in *The Generall Historie of Virginia, New-England, and the Summer Isles,* by Captain John Smith, London, 1624. (By permission of the Beinecke Library, Yale University.)

evidence in his Guianan propaganda. But still more revealing of the difference between Raleigh's new American venture and the old was the fact that Elizabeth never gave it her name. No longer could writers like Hakluyt so neatly epitomize England's special relation to North America by way of Raleigh embracing his surrogate virgin "bride"; for, as Raleigh's dedicatory letter to the *Discoverie* itself melodramatically emphasizes, Raleigh had already embraced a more literal, and also homebred, surrogate for Elizabeth—the woman he surreptitiously married in 1591, Elizabeth Throckmorton.[2] This romantic difficulty between Raleigh and the queen seemed, moreover, to have produced not just a change of venue but the most famous alteration in Raleigh's expansionist plans, a change in objective: for with the motive of marriage to a fruitful virgin lost, the American commodity peculiarly suited to figure that quasi-spiritual mystery—tobacco—also seemed to have vanished, replaced by Raleigh's obsession to placate Elizabeth with an empire now of gold.

In the second half of *The Faerie Queene*, published the same year as Raleigh's Guianan narrative, Spenser seems quickly to admit that the grounds for the tobaccoan or surrogate imperialism he had outlined six years earlier have now been undermined: book 4 continues the story of Timias (Raleigh) and Belphoebe (Elizabeth), but this time in order to represent Raleigh's disgrace (cantos 7–8). Yet the impact of the disgrace on Spenser has seemed to some readers more pervasive and injurious than the localized story of Timias's fall (and also recovery) would suggest: the later *Faerie Queene* begins darkly, at greater distance from Elizabeth, not only because it apparently alludes to the displeasure of Elizabeth's Lord Secretary, Burleigh, but because the proem to book 4 is the only one in the *The Faerie Queene* that fails to address Elizabeth directly (Hamilton, ed., *Faerie Queene*, 426). These ill omens, underscored at the end of the poem by Spenser's omission of the 1590 dedicatory letter to Raleigh, appear to crystallize near the end of book 4 also, precisely when Spenser invokes Raleigh's new New World. In the midst of cataloguing the rivers who have come to the wedding of the Thames and the Medway, after having just mentioned "that huge River, which doth beare his name / Of warlike Amazons, which doe possesse the same" (*FQ* 4.11.21), Spenser interrupts his fiction:

> Joy on those warlike women, which so long
>   Can from all men so rich a kingdome hold;
>   And shame on you, O men, which boast your strong
>   And valiant hearts, in thoughts lesse hard and bold,
>   Yet quaile in conquest of that land of gold.
>   But this to you, O Britons, most pertaines,
>   To whom the right hereof it selfe hath sold;
>   The which for sparing little cost or paines,
>   Loose so immortall glory, and so endlesse gaines.

(22)

If Elizabeth has any presence in this new America, it is only by association with "those warlike women" whom Belphoebe resembles, women who triumph over men (even the river that they "possesse" is male). Not only has the mysteriously liberal chastity of Virginia been turned into armed resistance, but Elizabeth's mirror in America has been reduced from the land itself to those who only "hold" it. As in Raleigh, then, the loss of fruitful relations between commoner and queen ends up widening the gap between England and its colonial object; and again this new alienation both produces the need for an English conquest in America and promises a new inherent value there—in a land no longer Elizabethan but golden. Yet how is it that Spenser has come to approve of gold fever, a motive for empire that—following More, Wyatt, Hakluyt, and Harriot—he had earlier seemed to deplore? In the proem to book 2, Raleigh's "fruitfull" American project had appeared so "agreeable" to Spenser as to represent a kind of precedent justifying his epic. The celebration of Guiana in book 4 would, in other words, seem to mark Spenser's surprising conversion not just to a new colonialism but to a new poetics.

As I noted in chapter 3, many, if not most, of Spenser's readers in the twentieth century have indeed considered the later *Faerie Queene* a different poem: as Michael O'Connell maintains, "the poem loses some of the moral complexity that characterizes the other books" (*Mirror*, 13). For O'Connell, the most thorough exponent of this view, what produces Spenser's narrowing of vision or his increasing "singleness of purpose" is his increasing investment in Elizabethan politics. During the years Spenser worked on the later books, O'Connell would have it, he grew less capable of transcending the brute facts of a history that no longer seemed to be going England's way, and as a consequence his allegory began to degenerate into a thinly disguised idealization of actual events: "Spenser abandons the allusive technique that characterized the introduction of contemporary elements in the first three books" (115); "the celebratory motive becomes apologetic and takes an unwonted precedence over the motive of moral judgment" (13); the poem's otherworldly fiction degenerates into so much "wish fulfillment" or "whistling in the dark" (158). For O'Connell, in short, *The Faerie Queene* becomes too literal; and the Guianan stanza seems to bear him out. There is, after all, a striking difference between Spenser's mere mention of Virginia's discovery or of "divine *Tobacco*" in the earlier books and his later exhortation to colonize America. And whereas Spenser earlier had made the value of Virginia difficult to construe—the fruit of a virgin, or by analogy to Fairyland, an empire hidden from "base" sight—now he makes America's value as literal as possible: gold. Though O'Connell never examines the Guianan stanza itself, he has strong reasons for associating Guianan colonialism with Spenser's fall into literalness: the Guianan enterprise reflects Raleigh's disgrace, and Spenser's representation of that disgrace in book 4 is, according to O'Connell, "the first time in the poem" that "the fiction is specifically constructed . . . to shadow a contemporary situation" (115). If O'Connell is silent about the reasons why Raleigh's disgrace should have been the first event to force its literalizing way into *The Faerie Queene*, perhaps that is because the reasons seem to him so obvious: how could discord between Spenser's two patrons not disturb Spenser,[3] especially when the trouble stemmed from Raleigh's insistence on a marriageable surrogate for Elizabeth—from his rejection, in other words, of the unconsummated love that continually motivates Spenser's "fairy" allegory?[4] Such love had seemed to motivate the Virginia colony as well; but now, in the face of Raleigh's difficulties, Spenser as allegorist and imperialist appears to abandon ideal alliances in favor of more literal, even businesslike arrangements: "But this to you, O Britons, most pertaines, / To whom the right hereof it selfe hath *sold*."

The question of Spenser's failing idealism and its relation to Raleigh's disgrace and the Guianan venture is, however, more complex than modern critics tend to allow. It is, after all, ingenuous to accept as evidence of decline the relatively frank admissions of a poet who inaugurates his epic career by having his proxy, Colin, abandon his pastoral pipe in despair. No self-characterization is as persistent in Spenser as the one exemplified by his pseudonym in *The Shepheardes Calender*, "Immerito," the Unworthy One; and consequently the nine cantos of book 4 that end with Spenser remarking on his failure to complete his work look rather more calculating than desperate.[5] As for Spenser's newly vexed relation to Elizabeth and its effect on his colonialism, Guiana seems less radically to supplant Virginia when one finds the mention of "fruitfullest *Virginia*" in book 2 immediately preceded by a reference to "the *Amazon's* huge river," and then discovers that the second edition of the poem, not the first, dedicates itself to the queen not just of England, France, and Ireland but of Virginia too (*V* 1:1). Raleigh's disgrace is indeed a pervasive subject in book 4; but Spenser makes it so, in order to pursue his own consistently critical views on what he considers the ultimately anticolonial relation between Raleigh and Elizabeth.

The actual account of Raleigh's fall in book 4 is framed by two obvious analogues to it, both of which interpret the disgrace afflicting Timias and Belphoebe less as Timias's apparent lust for a third character, Amoret, than as the original cross-class love between Timias and Belphoebe, a "disparagement" (4.7.16) itself driven by lust. In the framing episodes, the well-born Æmylia loves Amyas, the squire of low degree, and on her way to a tryst with him is met by Lust instead; the squire himself is similarly surprised and then held prisoner by another personification of lust, Corflambo, along with his proud and wealthy daughter Poeana, who falls in love with Amyas. Spenser then introduces a friend of Amyas, his look-alike Placidas, who, unbeknownst to Poeana, takes Amyas's place. After Lust and Corflambo have been killed and Arthur reunites the original lovers, nothing more is heard of them,[6] but Arthur convinces Placidas—a twin to Amyas, presumably, not just in looks but in status—to marry Poeana: "Thereto he offred for to make him chiefe / Of all her land and lordship during life: / He yeelded, and her tooke; so stinted all their strife" (9.15). According to these episodes, then, the only solution to the worldly desire of lovers separated by class is their equation in worldly terms, by a redistribution of wealth: the letter of means answers the letter of lust.

The Timias and Belphoebe episode only slightly modifies this seemingly debased moral. While hunting with Belphoebe, Timias discovers her twin sister Amoret in the clutches of Lust and tries in vain to kill the monster, only wounding Amoret in the process; Belphoebe appears, Lust flees, and Belphoebe succeeds in killing him; but she returns to find Timias kissing Amoret's wounds, and, after almost murdering the two, decides instead to repudiate Timias. Though more indirectly and discreetly than in the framing episodes, the lovers' encounter with Lust when they expect to find only each other clearly reflects on their own desires, and thus represents Timias/Raleigh's "brutish" dalliance with Amoret/Elizabeth Throckmorton as merely the carnal desire of Belphoebe/Queen Elizabeth and Raleigh displaced.[7] Moreover, just as in the frame episodes the transferral of wealth brings at least one pair of lovers together, so in the more genteel central story the ostensibly sentimental value of a ruby that Belphoebe had given Timias helps reunite the two. Once again the felt incommensurability of Timias to Belphoebe has produced a surrogate for Belphoebe; but unlike tobacco, which looks more figuratively and less literally valuable than a ruby, the surrogate seems little more than material, and smooths over the differences between the lovers as if those differences too were little more than material. In fact, insofar as the jewel that reconciles the lovers substitutes, as tobacco had, for Belphoebe's maidenhead specifically—a ruby for her "Rose" (3.5.51)—it suggests an even greater worldliness in the lovers than before. Amoret is just as much a virgin as her sister, and yet Timias considers her more available to his desires, as Raleigh thought Elizabeth Throckmorton to be more available than the queen; thus, the episode implies, Timias and Belphoebe are still blind to the larger possibilities of their love, but now because they see it as materially barred not just by Belphoebe's maidenhead but also by her wealth.[8]

In dropping tobacco from his allegory and replacing it with treasure, then, Spenser may have intensified his critique of Raleigh and Elizabeth, but he has also barred himself from using the miraculously "divine" potentiality of tobacco as a means to suggest an expansive construction of "Elizabeth" that does not itself appear literalist. When Arthur defeated Orgoglio in book 1 and occupied his castle, he, Redcross, and Una "did in that castle afterwards abide, / To rest them selves, and weary powers repair, / Where store they found of all, that dainty was and rare" (8.50);

but the conquest of Corflambo yields Arthur more substantial booty:

> Then gan they ransacke that same Castel strong,
>   In which he found great store of hoorded
>   threasure,
>   The which that tyrant gathered had by wrong
>   And tortious powre, without respect or measure.
>   Upon all which the Briton Prince made seasure,
>   And afterwards continu'd there a while,
>   To rest him selfe, and solace in soft pleasure
>   Those weaker Ladies after weary toile;
>   To whom he did divide part of his purchast spoile.
>   (4.9.12)

This apparently new indelicacy on Spenser's part has its counterpart in Arthur's unchaperoned travels with Æmylia and Amoret, which incur the wrath of Sclaunder and, Spenser expects, the "rash witted" reader (8.29); even Amoret herself is later said to stand "in fear of shame" (9.18). But Arthur behaves himself; the threat of debasement has become greater, it seems, only so that Arthur can more conspicuously vindicate his nobility. As Spenser comments when Arthur lifts Æmylia and Amoret "from ground" onto his horse, "No service [is] lothsome to a gentle kind" (8.22); the difference between a bad and a good character depends not on their respective proximity to baseness but on the "measure" each adopts toward that baseness.[9] Even the Guiana stanza attempts this compromise between material and ideal: the conquest of a golden land is said to be a matter for "hearts" and "thoughts," while the value Guiana will bring England consists not only of "endlesse gaines" but of "immortall glory." If the selling of "right" appears too great a compromise, however, it is nonetheless the continuing antimaterialism of Spenser's colonialism that stirs up trouble. For Spenser insists that Raleigh's character defines the American ventures he sponsors; by necessity, Raleigh molds Guiana into the image of his own disgraceful overliteralism. And indeed the Guiana stanza follows the Raleigh-like episodes in book 4 quite closely—only by taking treasure from the Amazonian women who possess it, the stanza says, can the English escape shame.

But then Spenser in book 4 does not consider the Guianan project England's only avenue for expansion. Feeling his misgivings about the cult of Elizabeth confirmed by Raleigh's marriage and the queen's scandalously revealing anger over it, Spenser in the years following the disgrace begins to elaborate an English colonialism more explicitly detached from Raleigh's literalist conception of Elizabeth and more explicitly centered on his own distant relation to the queen.[10] The year before *The Faerie Queene*'s second edition, Spenser in his *Colin Clouts Come Home Again* had already seized on Raleigh's disgrace as an opportunity to dramatize the difference between Raleigh and himself. (Though it is a critical commonplace to say that the discrepancy between Spenser's dating of *Colin Clout* [1591] and the poem's actual year of publication [1595] betrays Spenser's anxieties about celebrating a patron disgraced in 1592, it is just as plausible that the double dating is meant to suggest the continuity between Raleigh's pre- and post-lapsarian relations with the queen.) In the poem, Spenser's old persona, Colin Clout, recalls how he met the Shepherd of the Ocean, Raleigh, on the equal ground not only of poetizing—"He pip'd, I sung; and when he sung, I piped" (76)—but of Ireland, to which each had been brought by ill fortune in their loving. As a result of this complementarity, it would seen, Raleigh, says Colin,

> gan to cast great lyking to my lore,
> And great dislyking to my lucklesse lot:
> That banisht had my selfe, like wight forlore,
> Into that waste, where I was quite forgot.
>
>   (180–83)

The Shepherd of the Ocean then takes Colin to England and introduces him to Cynthia, who condescends to admire Colin and whom Colin comes to adore. At this point in Colin's story, a pastoral friend interrupts him with the question inevitably facing not only Spenser but Elizabethan colonialism in general:

> Why, *Colin*, since thou foundst such grace
> With *Cynthia* and all her noble crew:
> Why didst thou ever leave that happie place,
> In which such wealth might unto thee accrew?
> And back returnedst to this barrein soyle,
> Where cold and care and penury do dwell.
>
>   (652–57)

Colin's answer is that he has rejected not Elizabeth but her Court, which honors a literalist conception of value. Courtiers believe, for instance, that "highest lookes" correspond to "the highest mynd" (715), or that "arts of schoole" are "but toyes to busie ydle braines" (703–4); yet they themselves are of course the real triflers, who—like the kid in "Aprill"—will trade "all their wealth" only to "buy a golden bell" (724–25). The most revealing and comprehensive form of their debasement, however, is their attitude toward love, "for their desire is base, and doth not merit, / The name of love, but of disloyall lust" (891–92). Yet why should courtiers be so debased, especially when they spend their time so near the very "image of the heavens in shape humane" (351), the queen? Apparently, such nearness is itself the problem: courtly lust is not so much a dereliction from as an ardency for Elizabeth's "blessed presence" (661). What saves Raleigh in this case from the "disgraceful" charge to which Spenser elsewhere subjects him is the contingent fact that, as the story begins, Cynthia has "from her presence faultlesse him debard" (167). Colin, on the other hand, has voluntarily left the "presence" (332) into which Raleigh introduced him. If this sacrifice demonstrates both his superiority to lustful attachment and his higher appreciation of the queen's heavenly significance, it is nonetheless crucial to note that, once back "home," Colin also stops short of idealizing the queen altogether. Instead, he now mentally worships her presence: "My mind full of my thoughts satietie, / Doth feed on sweet contentment of that sight" (42–43).[11] Such an otherworldly meditation on Elizabeth's worldly body argues him capable, like Arthur, of a "measured" (rather than merely literal or metaphorical) relation to baseness, which means that he can attach himself to materiality— whether Elizabethan, English, or Irish—without debasing himself to it.[12] The difference in this characteristically equivocal conception of Elizabeth is that Spenser seems to accentuate it by means of Raleigh's disgrace. For nowhere in his poetry is Spenser more explicit about rejecting Elizabeth's corporeal virginity as an ideal than when Colin likens Elizabeth "to a crowne of lillies, / Upon a virgin brydes adorned head" (337–38): in thoroughly distancing or debarring Raleigh from Elizabeth, Raleigh's marriage has apparently inspired Spenser to counter the virginal insularism of Elizabeth-worship by envisioning the queen herself not just as an image of marriage but as a partial image, completed by spouses and sacraments to which she is only synecdochically related.

Spenser's use of Raleigh to justify his own better self-banishment from England might still seem, however, only one form among many of a more general self-justificatory process—the voluntary "disparagement," failure, or disgrace that I have called trifling. In chapters 2 and 3 I noted how Spenser tries to expand "England" first by associating it with pastoral, then by associating pastoral with Fairyland, and finally by associating Fairyland with Ireland; now, in *Colin Clout*, by combining all three "trifling" matters in the representation of himself as "a simple silly" Irish "Elfe" (371), Spenser manages to figure his literal attachments as both colonial and immaterial. Dramatized in Colin's adoring of Elizabeth's "shape" only in mind and from afar, such engaged detachment also manifests itself as Colin's mystifyingly equivocal relation to "home"—either Ireland, to which Colin (and Spenser) have returned from England; or England, to which Raleigh arranges Spenser's (and the *Calender* Colin's) return.[13] This strategy of unsettling is the same Spenser had previously applied to Redcross, who discovered himself affiliated to both England and the New Jerusalem; though now, unlike Redcross's, the two homes of Colin are quite literally distinct, and in book 4 of *The Faerie Queene*, when Spenser alludes to both "my mother Cambridge" (11.34) and "*Mulla* mine" (41), they become the radically disproportioning allegiances of the epic poet himself.

Yet, even though placing Spenser in a role previously filled by one of his heroes, these double homes in book 4 still also define Spenser by implicit contrast with Raleigh/Timias, whose own exile into the wilderness basely reflects Colin's: banished from Belphoebe's presence, Timias so devolves into "rude brutishness" (7.45) as to acquire an Irish peasant's "glib" of matted hair (8.12); and then even after his return to Belphoebe's favor he continues "all mindlesse" (18) of Arthur's quest.[14] Whenever Spenser wants to assure his readers that colonial life has not caused him to sacrifice the pursuit of glory, he rushes to compare himself, favorably, with one fellow colonizer in particular, the major sponsor of Elizabethan colonialism in both America and Ireland, Raleigh. And indeed, in order to demonstrate Spenser's freedom from material proportionment even in the worst case of erotic love, *Colin Clout* goes so far as to risk the particular form of Raleigh's disgrace: though Colin had earlier described Cynthia as "my lifes sole blisse, my hearts eternall threasure" (*Colin Clout*, 47), he later declares of Rosalind that "my thought, my heart, my love, my life is shee, / And I hers ever onely, ever one" (476–77). No doubt Rosalind is supposed to show only that Colin's love is blatantly twofold and contradictory;[15] Colin's concluding disquisition on her notes that she is anyway as absent as Cynthia (930–32), and that Colin recognizes he can never "love" her, only "honor" her (940–41). Yet when Spenser returns the same year, no longer as Colin but as himself, to celebrate his private beloved in the *Amoretti* and *Epithalamion*, he reveals her name to be the same as Raleigh's bride, Elizabeth (*Amoretti*, sonnet 74), and then marries her. Unlike Raleigh's marriage, of course, the ceremony takes place in Ireland, and the *Epithalamion* concludes with what in the context cannot help seeming a colonialist prayer, that Spenser's "fruitfull progeny" (l. 403) will "long possesse" "the earth" (418). But Spenser's continual dependence on Raleigh as an example of Elizabethan colonialism gone wrong has unmistakably affected Spenser's notion of such colonialism done right. That is, in attacking the error of Raleigh's literal attachment to Elizabeth, Spenser has been led increasingly to literalize his countervision of Elizabeth's expansive potentiality, until the imperial surrogate of fruitfullest Virginia seems reduced on the one hand to a neighboring island or on the other to a privately "Elizabethan" fruitfulness.[16] The Mutability Cantos will try again to rescue expansionism by suggesting more plainly that, as a surrogate for England, Ireland simply proves the English Otherworld an untenably insularist ideal. Having associated Fairyland with Ireland, these cantos next recall Ireland's ancient denomination as itself a *Sacra Insula* or "holy-Island" (*FQ* 7.6.37), a title whose irony in regard to "Elizium" will come out still more strongly in the *View*, when Irenius laments "the wretchedness of that fatal kingdom which I think therefore was in old time not Called amiss *Banno* or *sacra Insula* taking *sacra* for accursed" (*V* 9:145). Yet the surrogate imperialism that began as a mirror relation between Elizabeth and Virginia has, under the pressure of Spenser's counterpoint to Raleigh, become increasingly claustrophobic. Where the far less directly colonialist *Utopia* had managed to transfer English nowhereness to an island-negative and yet keep America's other world suggestively between the two utopias, the mirror relation between England and Ireland in Spenser seems instead to exclude America as an Elizabethan objective.

Even more than the Mutability Cantos, the *Prothalamion* (1596), the last work of Spenser's to be published in his lifetime, appears to acknowledge this threat of colonial restrictiveness or constraint. Implicitly paired with the *Epithalamion* and so dividing the idea of Spenser and marriage that the earlier poem presented, it has Spenser now in England, filled with "discontent of my long fruitlesse stay / In Princes Court" (6–7); the marriage celebrated is someone else's; Spenser is now also thoroughly, indeed doubly, English—both a native of London and a descendant of the Spencers of Althorp (128–31); yet, unlike the Irish-seeming Colin, he worries about English patronage, "whose want too well, now feeles my freendless case" (140). But then the primary difference between this poem and the Irish ones is that Spenser has no significant relation to an Elizabeth other than his "fruitlesse stay" at Court; he occupies the position of the disgraced Raleigh. For Spenser, it seems, the only way to escape the literalizing constraint of his identification with Raleigh—which mirrors, again, the prior constraint of surrogate colonialism supposedly exploded by Raleigh's disgrace—is to embrace the identification entirely and register his own failure. Hence the poem strangely moves from Spenser's personal frustration to the most millenarian-sounding lines in his poetry, an apparent anticipation of England and the New Jerusalem joined in imperial marriage: Spenser hopes that through Essex

> great *Elisaes* glorious name may ring
> Through al the world, fil'd with thy wide Alarmes,
> Which some brave Muse may sing
> To ages following,
> Upon the Brydale day, which is not long.
>   (157–61; cf. Revelation 19.6–9)

In the remaining sections of this chapter, I will begin to show that this peculiar association of apparent personal disaster and actual triumph figures prominently in the writings of later Elizabethan and early Jacobean colonialism. Just as Spenser increasingly embraces a failure that negatively signals a grander but as yet unrealized destiny, so will other imperialists emphasize the apparent

shortcomings of their exploits in order to intensify, not undermine, a sense of their colonial highmindedness. What makes this
extreme version of *sprezzatura*—a practice Sir Thomas Hoby translates as "disgracing" (Castiglione, *Courtier*, 46)—especially paradoxical is that it extends the Virginian colonialism whose end it
seems to proclaim. The figure of the disgraceful colonist becomes,
in short, the uplifting surrogate for a colonialism disgraced, which
can no longer be idealized through relations of surrogacy that involve the Virgin Queen more directly. I will try to demonstrate the
continuing virginalism of English colonial efforts in the years following Raleigh's disgrace by way of the two colonial advocates in
those years whom one might least associate with virginal Virginia,
and who also happen to be the most famous and influential writer-
voyagers of their day: Raleigh himself and Captain John Smith.

From the start of his *Discoverie*, Raleigh admits that he has returned to England carrying not buckets of American gold but only
a "bundle of papers" (3); yet, if Spenser in *Colin Clout* can represent
his colonial work as that of a shepherd singing about love rather
than a conquistador warring for gold, so Raleigh can maintain
throughout the *Discoverie* that an English empire must begin with
rhetorical, not material, gains. As the *Discoverie* has it, rather than
degrade himself by "spoil and sackage" (6), the properly fashioned
English imperialist must exhort his men, deceive the enemy, be-
guile the natives, and, most important, praise his queen. In fact, allegorizing the poor returns from his Guianan venture as a personal
triumph, a demonstration of the self-restraint he had previously
seemed to lack, Raleigh paradoxically celebrates virginity even more
than had the earlier Virginian writers. And yet, I will show, this
greater commitment to Elizabeth ends up exaggerating the paradoxicality of Raleigh's Spenserian imperialism in at least two respects.
On the one hand, forced to depict himself as suffering penance for
his earlier excesses, Raleigh repeatedly emphasizes the ungentle-
manly nature of the labors to which he submitted himself; while on
the other, by portraying Guiana's attractions as especially enticing
so that his resistance to them will look all the more chaste, Raleigh
raises the specter of a private erotic colonialism more detached from
Elizabeth and England, and also more disgraceful, than Spenser's
own. After Elizabeth's death, Smith will appear to embrace this
specter of debasement by presenting himself as Virginia's first
truly committed planter, a colonist apparently so enmired in settle-

ment that he not only labors for his bread but (in the first English instance of erotic colonial trifling) loves a savage princess. Yet the absence of Elizabeth as the trifler's guarantor will, in the manner of *Colin Clout*, help establish Smith's voluntary disgrace as the only proof available to the colonist of his own transcendent worth. The more disgraceful Smith's attachments appear, that is, the more detached he hopes to prove, until his failure looks so complete as to suggest his liberation not just from England, like Spenser, but from its colonies too—indeed, from all matter except those ostensibly trifling surrogates for American riches, his American books.

I

Far from suppressing the fact of his disgrace in *The Discoverie of Guiana*, Raleigh starts bemoaning it as early as his dedicatory letter. Addressing two lords of the Privy Council, Charles Howard and Sir Robert Cecil, he claims that the absence of Elizabeth from his life is precisely what caused him to embark on his voyage:

> It is true that as my errors were great, so they have yielded very grievous effects, and if ought might have been deserved in former times to have counterpoised any part of offenses, the fruit thereof (as it seemeth) was long before fallen from the tree, and the dead stock only remained. I did therefore even in the winter of my life, Undertake these travels, fitter for bodies less blasted with misfortunes, for men of greater ability, and for minds of better encouragement, that thereby if it were possible I might recover but the moderation of excess, and the least taste of the greatest plenty formerly possessed. (3)

As Raleigh represents it, the great difference of the Guianan project from Virginia—the lack of Elizabeth's support—is more than balanced by the continued centrality of Elizabeth to Raleigh's American ambitions. In fact, Elizabeth figures more prominently in Raleigh's travel account than in any Virginian narrative. Nowhere did Harriot say that he had mentioned Elizabeth to the Algonquians,[17] but again and again Raleigh tells us that he praised Elizabeth to the Guianans, at times coming to sound less like her propagandist than her priest. On Trinidad, for instance,

> I made them understand that I was the servant of a Queen, who was the great *Casique* of the north, and a virgin, and had more *Casiqui* under her than there were trees in their island: that she was an enemy to the *Castellani* [the Spanish] in respect of their tyranny and

oppression, and that she delivered all such nations about her, as were by them oppressed, and having freed all the coast of the northern world from their servitude had sent me to free them also, and withal to defend the country of *Guiana* from their invasion and conquest. I showed them her majesty's picture which they so admired and honored, as it had been easy to have brought them idolatrous thereof.[18]

The recording of such hyperbole and misrepresentation, in particular that Elizabeth had sent Raleigh and had sent him to liberate, seems to suggest the degree to which Elizabeth's absence has made her only that much more imposing—indeed, oppressive—a presence.

Yet the most extravagant advertisement in the *Discoverie* of Raleigh's greater subjection to the Virgin Queen is his new and seemingly most un-Virginian object, the gold of El Dorado. Rather than represent an alternative means to the wealth that Elizabeth now denies him (a possible interpretation of Raleigh's aims that Raleigh himself persistently raises), American gold becomes, strangely enough, a way for Raleigh to impoverish himself through service to his queen: "For I am returned a beggar, and withered, but that I might have bettered my poor estate, it shall appear by the following discourse, if I had not only respected her Majesty's future Honor, and riches" (4). Raleigh will explain that mining or warring for gold would have been a mistake, first because he had "neither men, instruments, nor time" (8), but more important because

(whereas now they [the Indians of El Dorado] have heard we were enemies to the Spaniards and were sent by her Majesty to relieve them) they would as good cheap have joined with the Spaniards at our return, as to have yielded unto us, when they had proved that we came both for one errant, and that both sought but to sack and spoil them, but as yet our desire of gold, or our purpose of invasion is not known unto [them]. (62)

Along with such exigencies of conquest, however, the personal significance of Raleigh's restraint is unmistakable. Four years earlier, shortly after his disgrace and imprisonment, Raleigh had already been forced to acknowledge how expensive the queen's favor could be: in the division of spoils from the "Great Carrack," the Madre de Dios, Raleigh claimed that he had sacrificed eighty thousand pounds to Elizabeth—"more than ever a man presented Her Majesty as yet"—as his "ransom" (*Letters*, 68). The *Discoverie* fashions Raleigh's forbearance in Guiana as only a more elaborate amends. The man who debased himself through the "brutish offence" of impregnating a surrogate Elizabeth decides he cannot remedy that error by way of the figurative surrogate Elizabeth had originally granted him, Virginia; to honor the ideal of virginity he seems to have repudiated, Raleigh must instead journey to a land over which the queen has no title, risk the slander that he intends once again to replace her in his affections ("They have grossly belied me, that forejudged, that I would rather become a servant to the Spanish king, than return," *Discoverie*, 4), and then show himself to have forgone, for Elizabeth's sake, all material satisfaction. It is to point this allegory of a voluntary restraint correcting the excesses responsible for his disgrace that Raleigh famously concludes, "*Guiana* is a Country that yet hath her Maidenhead"; and the reluctance apparent as he goes on to evoke the rape of a land "never sackt, turned, nor wrought"—"The face of the earth hath not been torn, nor the virtue of the soil spent by manurance, the graves have not been opened for gold, the mines not broken with sledges, nor their Images pulled down out of their temples" (73)— bespeaks not so much the pangs of colonialist guilt, as some critics have suggested, but Raleigh's new penitential chastity.[19]

Yet, no matter how Raleigh intends his restraint to be interpreted, one might think that the sheer prominence of gold as a motive for occupying Guiana runs counter to Virginian colonial policy, which, I have tried to show, defined itself as maintaining England's otherworldly integrity in opposition to Spanish gold hunger. Of course, the desire for gold had been a crucial part of the Virginian program nonetheless. As I noted in my previous chapter, Ralph Lane admitted about Virginia "that the discovery of a good mine, by the goodness of God, or a passage to the Southsea, or someway to it, and nothing else can bring this country in request to be inhabited by our nation" (Quinn, *Roanoke Voyages* 1:273); and no one needed more incentives of this order than Elizabeth. Harriot might try to entice other investors with the prospect of Virginian "fruits" like worm silk and sassafras, but in Raleigh's Virginian patent Elizabeth insists only on her traditional prerogative, "reserving always to us our heirs and successors for all services duties and demands the fifth part of all the ore of Gold and silver that from time to time and at all times after such discovery subduing and possessing shall be there gotten or obtained."[20] Yet even the proponents of Virginia's other assets had never meant to dismiss gold as a colonial objective entirely, only to defer it. In his "Discourse Concerning a Voyage" (1592?) to what is now New England, Edward Hayes speaks in familiar fashion of the need to confute "their error which hold those Countries of no value, unless that Mines of gold and Silver may there be found"; other "gross Commodities" exist that are "most needful for the State of England, to employ our people & Ships"—and, Hayes concludes, these will in the end "procure unto us both gold & Silver and also precious wares," by way of trade with Spanish America.[21] Others were far bolder in their plans for Virginia to lead the way to the gold it did not itself appear to possess; D. B. Quinn maintains, in fact, that the motive for colonizing Virginia "that was, perhaps, the most pressing one of all" was "the use of the settlement as a base for raids on Spanish shipping" (*Set Fair*, 53). Compared to the prospect of such raids, the idea of settling Virginia's fruitful land seemed to some colonists almost beside the point: one of Lane's men writing to Elizabeth from Virginia (1585) advises her only that the colony will enable her to "increase your navy by shipping made there, and be near upon every event, to possess king Philip's purse" (Quinn, *Roanoke Voyages* 1:225). Sir Humphrey Gilbert (1577) had long before outlined for Elizabeth how "by giving of license under letters patents to discover and inhabit some strange place" she could disguise her intention to attack Spanish shipping,[22] and it is this old strategy of colonialism as purposeful misdirection that Raleigh apparently enacts when, on the way to Guiana, he informs some Spaniards "that I was bound only for the relief of those english, which I had planted in *Virginia*, whereof the bruit was come among them" (*Discoverie*, 13). Just as the *Discoverie* is supposed to show that Raleigh's disgrace has not undermined his "Virginian" commitment to Elizabeth but strengthened it, so it demonstrates how, in turning to Guianan gold, Raleigh has, paradoxically, not abandoned the aims central to the idea of Virginia but rather embraced them more directly.

What's more, if Raleigh's Guiana only makes explicit the desire for gold that always implicitly fueled Virginian colonization, it also still labors to maintain the distance between England and gold that—for the practical, physiological, and ideological reasons I

have previously discussed—seems to so many English writers con-
stitutive of English otherworldliness. A contemporary apologist
for ventures like Raleigh's, William Covell (1595), represents English raids on Spanish gold as only a necessary evil:

> Is it not more honor for the rich *Indians* to contemn their gold, than
> for the greedy *Spaniards* so to covet it? which if it were not used to
> the prejudice of foreign princes, all countries could wish him to be
> glutted with it, and that the *Iberian* sands were like unto golden *Ta-
> gus*, and their little rivers, like unto *Pactolus* streams; but since he
> makes it the sinew of his war, and his war nothing but an intended
> triumph over the greatest Empires; it behooveth Princes to cross his
> *Argosies*, that goods lewdly gotten, may not be worse spent. (*Poli-
> manteia*, 139–40)

So Raleigh in the *Discoverie* repeatedly presents his desire for
Guianan gold in terms of the Spanish problem: England must invade Spanish America because Spain's "Indian gold . . . endan-
gereth and disturbeth all the nations of Europe" (9).[23] In his poem
"De Guiana," prefixed to Lawrence Keymis's account of a follow-
up voyage to Guiana the next year, George Chapman contributes
to this pragmatic argument by discriminating—in a manner almost
identical to the ostensibly gold-hating Sir John Beaumont—between kinds of gold quests.[24] He addresses those "*Patrician* Spirits" (l. 86) "that know you cannot be the Kings of earth, / (Claiming the Rights of your creation) / And let the Mines of earth be
Kings of you" (90–92). Here once again the justification for seeking
gold is the threat of that "*Iberian Neptune*" Philip, "whose *Trident*
he the triple world would make" (64–65); but Chapman also refers,
a good deal more mysteriously, to the threat of "earth" per se.
True English spirits "issue like a flame / On brave endeavors" (87–
88); they "scorn to let [their] bodies choke [their] souls" (106), by
which Chapman means that they refuse to allow their desires to
be constrained within the bounds not only of the flesh but of an
England described as "like a body numb'd with surfeits" (127).
Owing to such invidious conflation of homebodiedness with em-
bodiedness, and then of Old World gold-beds like Covell's Tagus
or Pactolus with worldliness generally ("Natures that stick in
golden-graveled springs, / In muck-pits cannot scape their swal-
lowings," "De Guiana," 144–45), quests for New World gold come
to seem oddly spiritual. The English know, Chapman says, that in

such ventures "the tract of heaven in morn-like glory opens" (89); they "renounce the course of earth, / And lift [their] eyes for guidance to the stars" (108–9). At the same time, however, gold as a heavenly matter prevents too radical a spiritualization of English aspirations. The poem begins with the epic question,

> What work of honor and eternal name,
> For all the world t'envy and us t'achieve,
> Fills me with fury, and gives armed hands
> To my heart's peace, that else would gladly turn
> My limbs and every sense into my thoughts
> Rapt with the thirsted action of my mind?
>
> (1–6)

Enticed by Guiana's gold from a Prospero-like contemplative isolation, antimaterialists like Chapman will in turn transform that gold from an end in itself to an earthly manifestation of spiritual power: "*Honor* having gold" will "rob gold of honor" (75).²⁵ The proof of Raleigh's honor is, as we have seen, his restraint in the face of enormous riches; and when he derides "those that only respect present profit" (*Discoverie*, 43), he could be said not just to renew but to refine the temperance of Virginian colonialists like Harriot and Hakluyt, who, much as they advocated abstinence in regard to gold hunger, could find no gold in Virginia from which to abstain.

In fact, not just Raleigh's restraint toward gold but his very desire for it help make the earlier colonial ideal of virginity a more prominent feature of the Guianan venture than it had been of the Virginian one. According to Raleigh, one Indian tribe that he befriended took the relation between his gold hunger and chastity quite literally: they urged Raleigh to help them "sack" another tribe, "and I asked them of what? they answered, of their women for us, and their Gold for you" (62). The Indians' sense that Raleigh's objectives differ from their own stems in part from Raleigh's care to represent himself, once again, as the servant of a virgin cacique:

> Nothing got us more love amongst them than this usage, for I suffered not any man to take from any of the nations so much as a *Pina*, or a *Potato* root, without giving them contentment, nor any man so much as to offer to touch any of their wives or daughters: which

course, so contrary to the Spaniards (who tyrannize over them in all things) drew them to admire her Majesty, whose commandment I told them it was, and also wonderfully to honor our nation. (44)[26]

But the singlemindedness of Raleigh's devotion to gold, represented as deriving most importantly from his chaste devotion to Elizabeth, itself has the curious effect of making him seem restrained in relation to Guiana's other prospects. He proves not only carnally but spiritually indifferent to the Indians, restricting a discussion of Guianan religion to its promising eschatology ("The *Orenoqueponi* bury not their wives with them, but their Jewels, hoping to enjoy them again"), and mentioning conversion only once, as a way to placate the Indians about robbing their graves (70). At the same time, he expresses little interest in what the Virginian advocate continually evoked, the extraordinary fertility of American soil. The land Raleigh stops to admire inspires him with visions not of georgic but of purely gentlemanly pleasures: having declared that, due to Guiana's gold, "the shining glory of this conquest will eclipse all those so far extended beams of the Spanish nation," Raleigh adds that "there is no country which yieldeth more pleasure to the Inhabitants, either for those common delights of hunting, hawking, fishing, fowling, and the rest, than *Guiana* doth" (71–72).[27] A paragraph later, he makes the implicit opposition here between gold and husbandry explicit: "Where there is store of gold, it is in effect needless to remember other commodities for trade"; and, while he does go on briefly to mention some commodities that the soil might bear, like dyes and cotton, he never notes, as Harriot did, what potential colonists might grow to sustain themselves. For gold not only does not require planting (though it does require digging, a point to which I will return), but it is a commodity one takes away; and so the geographical features finally most interesting to Raleigh are not lands on which to settle but rivers on which to move—which in Guiana seem almost more plentiful than land—like the one "we called the river of the *Red cross*" (36).[28]

As my previous chapters have argued, "chastity" helped make settlement a vexed issue in Virginia as well; and Chapman provides a striking image of the continuity with, but also the intensification of, Virginian colonialism in Guiana by depicting a sacral-sounding relation between colony and home no longer as bride and bridegroom but as two women entering a complicatedly asexual yet generative bond. Guiana

> Stands on her tip-toes at fair *England* looking,
> Kissing her hand, bowing her mighty breast,
> And every sign of all submission making,
> To be her sister, and the daughter both
> Of our most sacred Maid: whose barrenness
> Is the true fruit of virtue, that may get,
> Bear and bring forth anew in all perfection,
> What heretofore savage corruption held
> In barbarous *Chaos*; and in this affair
> Become her father, mother, and her heir.
>   ("De Guiana," 20–29)

This is not to say that heterosexual bonds have no place in Chapman's Elizabethan colonialism, but when they do appear, their eros has, for obvious reasons, been distinctly sublimated. The poem begins by evoking Raleigh's

> *Eliza*-consecrated sword,
> That in this peaceful charm of *England's* sleep,
> Opens most tenderly her aged throat,
> Offring to pour fresh youth through all her veins.
>   (9–12)

Not only is the consummation between Raleigh and Elizabeth noticeably displaced here, but the couple have been bizarrely transformed into Aeson and Medea, father-in-law (Elizabeth) and daughter-in-law (Raleigh).[29] Later, Elizabeth gets euphemized into corrupted "Nature," who by "her most lightning-like effects of lust / Wound[s] through her flesh, her soul, her flesh unwounded" (117, 120–21). The conceit, obscure even for Chapman, clearly betrays the difficulty that Raleigh's "lust" poses for both Guiana and the poet, though Chapman's Spenserian point seems to be that Elizabeth is the lascivious one: just as England's too embodied spirits "loose [their] souls" for gold and yet "loose gold" (70) by refusing to leave England, so Elizabeth, obsessed with the chastity both of the body and the body politic ("her flesh unwounded"), ignores the higher, more ideal chastity to which Raleigh is devoted and for which her own "barrenness" stands. Hence "Nature" quickly turns into England "like a body numb'd with surfeits," who does not feel Raleigh's "gentle applications"—from *within*, as England's "soul"—"for the health, use, & honor of her powers" (125–29). The interposition of this line of argument seems by the end of the poem to have cleared the way to a more familiar conceit: Chapman, now grown "prophetic," imagines Raleigh in proper Virginian fashion brought "Bridegroom-like" to his fleet (148–56). Yet Raleigh is said to be "espoused for virtue to his love" (157); the antimaterialism that got him off the hook of his disgrace has also barred him from a "fruitful" relation with either the Old World or the New.[30] For Chapman, all that Raleigh's chaste marriage can hope to generate is the matter of spirit, gold; and so the golden age Chapman now foresees arising for the English in Guiana has "plenty" crown not their fertile but "their *wealthy* fields" (168; my emphasis).[31]

In Virginia, such indifference to colonial plantation had had as its practical correlative a kind of pastoral-heroic imperialism that I have called trifling, the exchange of nothings for somethings that was supposed to rescue the English colonist from a debasing proportionment either to the native or to the land he exploits. Though the trifle was imagined by writers like Harriot and Beaumont as supplying the lack in Virginia of more extravagantly profitable gold, gold-filled Guiana as Raleigh understands it actually gives trifling the opportunity to realize its potentiality to the fullest. One of the Spanish documents appended to the *Discoverie* records a trade between the Spanish and the Guianans in which a hatchet was exchanged for "an Eagle that weighed 27 pounds of good Gold" (and the Spanish approach to this trade, incidentally, demonstrates that Raleigh's histrionic restraint was in reality a widespread commonsensical policy—"The Master of the Camp took it [the eagle], and showed it to the soldiers, and then threw it from him, making show not to regard it" (*Discoverie*, 83). But Raleigh is more optimistic about the exchange rate Elizabeth can expect:

> If there were but a small army afoot in *Guiana*, marching towards *Manoa* the chief City of Inga, he would yield her Majesty by composition so many hundred thousand pounds yearly, as should both defend all enemies abroad, and defray all expenses at home, and . . . he would besides pay a garrison of 3000 or 4000 soldiers very royally to defend him against other nations. (75)[32]

To Raleigh, in fact, Guianan gold appears not only an end for English trifling but a means, a better trifle. The possible identification of gold and trifle is not peculiar to him. When satires like *Utopia* reduce precious metals to *nugas*, or trifles, they are not so much inverting received notions of value as underscoring the inanity of those notions: the satires' claim, in other words, is that, far from being the opposite of the trifle, gold is rather the trifle par excellence. Even when speaking in gold's favor, economists like Sir Thomas Smith can somewhat endorse this satiric judgment. In his *Discourse*, Smith traces the invention of gold and silver coins to the problem of exchanging wares that were heavy, perishable, and difficult to proportion: "Therefore were the metals of gold and silver devised as wares of so little weight, most in value, and least cumbersome to carry, and least subject to detriment or hurt in the carriage thereof, and may be cut and divided in most pieces and portions without any loss, as the mean wares to exchange all other wares by" (71). The great efficacy inhering in such small and easily transportable "portions" of value as gold coins is part of what made the Spanish monopoly of American gold so frightening to the English: Sir Robert Cecil (1593), for instance, speaking to Parliament of the danger posed by Philip's influencing the Scottish nobility, points out that "it may be he hath sent thither no great Navy, and that her Majesty would not suffer him to do; yet do what she can, some one Paltry Fly-Boat may escape her Majesty's ships, and carry gold enough in her to make them Traitors, and stir them to Sedition" (D'Ewes, *Compleat Journal*, 472). This ostensible paltriness of gold is what enables Raleigh to imagine that Philip's "Indian" treasure "*creepeth* into Counsels, and setteth bound loyalty at liberty, in the greatest Monarchies of Europe" (*Discoverie*, 9; my emphasis); but at the same time it is what, to Raleigh's mind, will enable the conquest of Guiana alone to aid England so mightily. At times in the *Discoverie* Guiana figures as nothing but its gold, "the Magazine of all rich metals" (12), and seems as it were to geografy gold's extraordinarily compacted value: by itself, Raleigh claims, Guiana "shall suffice to enable her Majesty, and the whole kingdom, with no less quantities of treasure, than the king of Spain hath in all the Indies, east and west, which he possesseth" (10). Later, Raleigh becomes still more extravagant: he asserts that the conqueror of Guiana shall perform more than ever was done in *Mexico* by *Cortez*, or in *Peru* by *Pizarro*, . . . and whatsoever Prince shall possess it, that Prince shall be Lord of more gold, and of a more beautiful Empire, and of more Cities and people, than either the King of Spain, or the great Turk. (16)

Guiana is, in short, the mightiest trifle: "whatsoever Prince shall possess it, shall be greatest" (75). This is of course a standard valuation of little England; indeed, the difference between "little" gold and more traditionally conceived trifles is like the difference between the conception of little England as inherently grand and the conception of it as grand only by virtue of the godly power it signifies. Elizabethan colonialists depend on the second, less literal alternative—for them, England requires a New World colony in order to realize its own otherworldly potentiality; and Guiana serves this purpose only more immediately than Virginia had. Where "Virginia" could begin to magnify England while at the same time conforming to the image of England's sublime self-inadequacy (with savages beguiled by trifles, for example, or gold found only elsewhere), Guiana simply transfers to America the notion of England self-fulfilled (though this fulfillment, by virtue of the Spanish occupation and Raleigh's restraint, is itself also deferred). Just as his servants had imagined in the case of Virginia, so Raleigh speaks of a special, quasi-providential relation between England and Guiana: "it seemeth to me that this empire is reserved for her Majesty."[33] And the relation is demonstrated, as we have come to expect, by the special efficacy in Guiana of English littleness: Raleigh boasts that his Spanish predecessor in Guiana, Berreo, "hath spent 300000 ducats in the same, and yet never could enter so far into the land as my self with that poor troop or rather a handful of men" (23–24).

The most telling continuity between Guiana and Virginia, however, is one that the (momentarily deferred) immediacy of Guiana's rewards actually belies: Guiana, of course, has no gold either. Once again, in lieu of gold, an Elizabethan must invoke his queen; or more precisely, the mechanism of deferral built into a colonialism premised on Elizabeth's virginity once again helps to justify the absence of objective English grandeur—the scandal of Raleigh's marriage covers the scandal of his empty pockets.[34] If that marriage, and the Guianan venture it inspired, can be said to have changed the terms of virginal colonialism, it seems most accurate to say that Raleigh's disgrace only literalizes Elizabeth's continuing noninvolvement in America. This newly pronounced distance is nicely figured by the only gold that Raleigh can definitively argue Guiana possesses, the gold he brought it. Raleigh admits, "I gave among them many more pieces of Gold than I received of the new money of 20 shillings with her Majesty's picture to wear" (63): though in one regard simply another instance of Raleigh's impoverishing himself for the queen's sake, such gift giving not only reverses the trifling economy Raleigh wants to advertise but reduces Elizabeth's image in America from the womb of the land (whether fruitful or golden) to an imported trifle, from a world to a coin.[35]

However, in causing Raleigh himself to voyage to the New World and become by far the most prominent Elizabethan to publish a narrative of his American exploits,[36] the disgrace does make one significant difference to Elizabethan colonialism, in the idealization not of queen or country but of the colonist. Like Wyatt in his return to England, Raleigh presents himself as heroically constrained to make his voyage away from England, and, ultimately, constrained by love. Again and again Raleigh stresses his lack of enthusiasm not only for pillaging on his travels but for the act of traveling per se; for instance, sighting a series of waterfalls "above twenty miles off," Raleigh declares that "for mine own part I was well persuaded from thence to have returned, being a very ill footman, but the rest were all so desirous to go near the said strange thunder of waters, as they drew me on by little and little" (54; cf. 65). Like his restraint in regard to "pilfering," this reluctance too will form a part of Raleigh's defense about the gold he cannot produce: "It shall be found a weak policy in me," he maintains,

> either to betray my self, or my Country with imaginations, neither am I so far in love with that lodging, watching, care, peril, diseases, ill savors, bad fare, and many other mischiefs that accompany these voyages, as to woo my self again into any of them, were I not assured that the sun covereth not so much riches in any part of the earth. (55; cf. 9)

And then such physical suffering on his "painful pilgrimage" is what Raleigh clearly hopes will win him Elizabeth's pity. But these special effects of Raleigh's difficulties with the queen, difficulties that prompt him to dramatize the singularity of his labors in terms both of other voyagers and of his own history, also help to transfigure the received conception of the English colonial gentleman. In a bold though still only implicit comparison of his journeys in Guiana to the early days of his disgrace, Raleigh maintains that "there was never any prison in England, that could be found more unsavory and loathsome, especially to my self, who had for many years before been dieted and cared for in a sort far differing" (16). Raleigh's self-presentation here is complicated: he begins the *Discoverie* by attacking those critics who claimed "that I was too easeful and sensual to undertake a journey of so great travel" (4); yet he himself repeatedly invokes this criticism in order to suggest both his high social standing and the great pain to which his relationship with Elizabeth has subjected him. In other words, as a result of his disgrace, Raleigh promotes the representation of a colonist superior to the constraints of colonial labor who is nevertheless devoted to them.[37]

This change in the English colonist looks perhaps most dramatic when it seems to influence Raleigh's description of Guiana's other inhabitants. Whereas in Harriot the Indian oddly modeled the gentlemanly life that a prospective colonist could expect, a life of temperate ease, Raleigh's repudiation of ease, which begins to transform work into a sign of gentlemanliness, also helps to rescue the colonist from being equated with the idle savage, who now figures as the gentleman's intemperate opposite. The ostensibly Edenic Tivitivas—"They never eat of any thing that is set or sown, and as at home they use neither planting nor other manurance, so when they come abroad they refuse to feed of ought, but of that which nature without labor bringeth forth"—may love their tobacco as the Algonquians did, but Raleigh adds that "in the excessive taking [t]hereof," the Tivitivas "exceed all nations" (38–39). Other Indians are "marvelous great drunkards, in which vice I think no nation can compare with them" (21), or "the greatest carousers and drunkards of the world" (46). Entering one Indian village on a feast day, Raleigh and his men "found them all as drunk as beggars, and the pots walking from one to another without rest" (66). This strangely laborious idleness gets connected, in Raleigh's report, with the primary anomaly in Guiana's otherwise golden-age setting, the abundance of gold. Raleigh's objective,

Manoa, received its Spanish nickname El Dorado or "The Gold-man" from the manner in which its emperor supposedly "carouseth with his Captains, tributaries, and governors":

> All those that pledge him are first stripped naked, and their bodies anointed all over with a kind of white balsamum . . . [;] when they are anointed all over, certain servants of the Emperor, having prepared gold made into fine powder blow it through hollow canes upon their naked bodies, until they be all shining from the foot to the head, and in this sort they sit drinking by twenties and hundreds and continue in drunkeness sometimes six or seven days together. (21)

Here, then, is the purest version of the idle, body-loving "gold-made men" ("De Guiana," 78) whom Chapman despises. According to Raleigh, even less gold-rich Indians use gold only for another form of bodily indulgence; the Orenoqueponi tempt him to war upon their neighbors for gold, while they themselves war for women: their cacique Topiwari "complained very sadly (as if it had been a matter of great consequence) that whereas they were wont to have ten or twelve wives, they were now enforced to content themselves with three or four, and that the Lords of the *Epuremei* had 50 or 100" (*Discoverie*, 62). Guiana's third set of inhabitants, the gold-hungry Spanish, prove how infectious the native appetite can be: for the Indians also complain that the Spanish "took from them both their wives, and daughters daily, and used them for the satisfying of their own lusts, especially such as they took in this manner by strength" (44).[38]

Though Raleigh himself, the painful pilgrim, repeatedly wins such trials of the flesh, the need to document those trials in order to document his resistance makes Raleigh seem ambivalent in a manner even more startlingly new to the representation of the English colonist than is Raleigh's noble labor. Harriot, recording the Indians' perceptions of the English, adds incidentally, "they noted also that we had no women amongst us, neither that we did care for any of theirs" (*Report*, 379). Raleigh's version of sexual indifference is far more strenuous:

> But I protest before the majesty of the living God, that I neither know nor believe, that any of our company one or other, by violence or otherwise, ever knew any of their women, and yet we saw many hundreds, and had many in our power, and of those very young, and excellently favored, which came among us without deceit, stark naked. (*Discoverie*, 44)

The pressure of Raleigh's penitential allegory—the voyage away from his lust, in which, honoring and enriching his queen, he will touch nothing he desires—paradoxically inspires in the *Discoverie* the first wholly English notices of desirable American savages. Earlier in the *Discoverie*, this new interest not in a female America but in female Americans seemed a result, in fact, of Raleigh's anxieties concerning both his chastity and its allegorization. Raleigh mentions that the lascivious Spanish "buy women and children" from the final and most debased group of Guiana's inhabitants,

> the *Cannibals*, which are of that barbarous nature, as they will for 3 or 4 hatchets sell the sons and daughters of their own brethren and sisters, and for somewhat more even their own daughters: hereof the *Spaniards* make great profit, for buying a maid of 12 or 13 years for three or four hatchets, they sell them again at *Margarita* in the west Indies for 50 and 100 pesos, which is so many crowns. (33)[39]

Such transactions, uncomfortably close to Raleigh's own projected "payment" of Guianan gold to Elizabeth in exchange for his wife, lead Raleigh to stress not only his role in freeing some slaves but also his superior regard for the Indians he frees: "The master of my ship *John Douglas* took one of the *Canoas* which came laden from thence with people to be sold, and the most of them escaped, yet of those he brought, there was one as well favored, and as well shaped as ever I saw any in England, and afterward I saw many of them, which but for their tawny color may be compared to any of *Europe*." One of these exceptional Indian women does indeed return afterward, in exceptionally evocative guise; a cacique that Raleigh later meets

> had his wife staying at the port where we anchored, and in all my life I have seldom seen a better favored woman: She was of good stature, with black eyes, fat of body, of an excellent countenance, her hair almost as long as her self, tied up again in pretty knots, and it seemed she stood not in that awe of her husband, as the rest, for she spake and discoursed, and drank among the gentlemen and captains, and was very pleasant, knowing her own comeliness, and taking great pride therein. I have seen a Lady in England so like to her, as but for the difference of color I would have sworn might have been the same. (46–47)

Having left Elizabeth Throckmorton for the service of a still more distant Elizabeth, the disgraced Raleigh no longer encounters a land in the shape of his queen, and therefore desirable to any

Englishman; he encounters instead a literal royal woman—the queen, perhaps, but reduced by American proxy to the shape of an actual wife.[40]

II

The first returns from a Virginia no longer ruled by the Virgin Queen, the Jamestown settlement, struck officials of the newly created Virginia Company as putting Raleigh's golden dreams to shame. Writing to Salisbury about the "say" of Virginian gold that Captain Christopher Newport had brought home with him, Sir Walter Cope (1607) is ecstatic:

> If we may believe either in words or Letters, we are fallen upon a land, that promises more, than the Land of promise: In stead of milk, we find pearl. & gold in stead of honey. . . . There is but a barrel full of the earth but there seems a kingdom full of the ore you shall not be fed by handfuls or hatfuls after the Tower measure [a sarcastic reference, apparently, to Raleigh and Guiana[41]] But the *Elizabeth Jonas* & the *Triumph* & all the Ships of honor may here have the bellies full. (Barbour, *Jamestown Voyages* 1:108)

The next day, however, Cope rubs his eyes a little more determinedly: "Coming this day to Seal up under our Seals, the golden mineral till your Return It appeared at sight so suspicious That we were not satisfied until we had made four Trials by the best experienced about the city. In the end all turned to vapor" (111). This particular transformation of American trifling (a barrelful of earth yet a kingdomful of ore) into smoke was both cheaper and quicker than the Elizabethan delusions of Frobisher or Raleigh, and seems to have made the Virginia Company even more cautious in its public assertions than Elizabethan colonialists had been; but it did little good for Jamestown itself. Looking back over Virginia's recent history, William Crashaw (1613) sounds as exasperated as almost every earlier pamphlet on the colony when he asserts that "amongst the many discouragements that have attended this glorious business of the Virginian plantation: none hath been so frequent, and so forcible, as the calumnies and slanders, raised upon our Colonies, and the country it self" (Whitaker, *Good Newes*, A2r). The author of *The Proceedings of the English Colonie in Virginia* (1612)—either Captain John Smith or a group of his disciples[42]—is

Figure 8.   Some vengeful Indians pour molten gold down a greedy Spaniard's throat. From Theodor de Bry's *America* part 4, Frankfurt, 1594. (By permission of the Bancroft Library, University of California, Berkeley.)

more specific: the author, like Harriot, complains that not finding gold as the Spanish had is what "hath begot us (that were the first undertakers) no less scorn and contempt, than their noble conquests and valiant adventures (beautified with it) praise and honor" (Smith, *Works* 1:257).

From the start, in fact, Smith's *Proceedings* frames itself as an apology, though in the end the inability to find gold proves almost too distant a "defailment" (203) to excuse: the *Proceedings* has a hard enough time explaining why Jamestown had such trouble locating the one asset of which Virginia could supposedly boast, its fruit. The conquistadores were said to have gone hungry too, insatiably so, but as a plate in Theodor de Bry's *America* part 4 (1594) made famous, the Spanish had starved for gold (see figure 8). De Bry means of course to mock the Spaniards' "holy hunger" (Eden, *Decades*, 185);[43] yet for many English readers, a life "rich in gold, but poor in bread" (108–9) must still have seemed an enviable one. To Raleigh himself, for instance, gold remains the only American want that counts: at one point in his journeys, says Raleigh, "nothing on the earth could have been more welcome to us . . . than the great store of very excellent bread which we found in these *Canoas*"—nothing, that is, "next unto gold" (*Discoverie*, 43). The Jamestown settlers, however, were often reduced to a far more literal and all-consuming hunger. On one occasion, recorded only in George Percy's manuscript "Trewe Relacyon" (1612), it even drove the Indians to aggravate the particular indignity of de Bry's Spanish tragedy: "Lieutenant SICKLEMORE and diverse others were found . . . slain with their mouths stopped full of Bread being done as it seemeth in Contempt and scorn that others might expect the Like when they should come to seek for bread and relief amongst them" (265).⁴⁴

And yet the bulk of both the *Proceedings* and Smith's earlier *True Relation* (1608) concerns what one would have thought the humiliating subject of Smith's labors to secure food for the colony any way he could. Moreover, not only do the narratives occasionally acknowledge their pecularity in this regard—"Men may think it strange there should be this stir for a little corn, but had it been gold with more ease we might have got it; and had it wanted, the whole colony had starved" (*Works* 1:256)—but Smith at one point goes so far as to make the invidious Spanish comparison himself: "the Spaniard never more greedily desired gold than he victual" (212).⁴⁵ In fact, Smith and his disciples seem to consider his heroism comprised as much by his bravery in voicing the scandals that others suppress as by his more practical accomplishments. For honesty, Smith repeatedly claims, is the best colonial policy: having recounted a mutiny at Jamestown, he remarks, "These brawls are so disgustful, as some will say they were better forgotten, yet all men of good judgment will conclude, it were better their baseness should be manifest to the world, than the business bear the scorn and shame of their excused disorders" (212). At the same time, however, such boldness certainly irritated his enemies, and helped expose him to attack: according to the *Proceedings*, many disgruntled colonists "got their passes [home] by promising in England to say much against him" (275). But then Smith insists on outfacing slander against himself as well. At the start of the colony, for example, when he was held prisoner on suspicion of treason, his enemies

> pretended out of their commiserations, to refer him to the Council in England to receive a check, rather than by particulating his designs make him so odious to the world, as to touch his life, or utterly overthrow his reputation; but he much scorned their charity, and publicly defied the uttermost of their cruelty. (207)

Later in his life, as we shall see, the implicit correlation here between colonist and colony will become explicit: no longer Elizabeth or even James but the slandered Smith becomes, in his own writings, the best synecdoche for slandered Virginia.

It is no surprise, therefore, that Smith's policy of outfacing slander proves inseparable from his dedication to the dirty business of actual plantation. As prone as other colonial advocates to extolling Virginia—"Heaven and earth never agreed better to frame a place for man's habitation being of our constitutions"—Smith must always add a caution to dreamers—"were it fully manured and inhabited by industrious people" (144)—because the scandalous truth he believes most needs facing is that colonization requires work. Even before becoming the colony's president, for instance, Smith along with a cohort "divided betwixt them, the rebuilding our town, the repairing our pallisadoes, the cutting down trees, preparing our fields, planting our corn, and to rebuild our Church, and recover our store-house" (219). Smith's famous hostility toward the idle gentlemen of the colony, those "holding it a great disgrace that amongst so much action, their actions were nothing" (175), is matched on the gentlemen's side, however, by their identification of his "base" speech and views with his low social status: the courtly Edward Wingfield declares about Smith, for example, that "it was proved to his face, that he begged in Ireland like a rogue, without license, to such I would not my name should be a Companion" (Barbour, *Jamestown Voyages* 1:231). As a result, the contemptuous slander that seems most to beset Smith is the odd charge that he appears, in effect, too interested in settlement; he first becomes a prisoner, in fact, "upon the scandalous suggestions of some of the chief (envying his repute) who feigned he intended to usurp the government, murder the Council, and make himself king" (Smith, *Works* 1:206–7; cf. Percy, "Trewe Relacyon," 264).

For the gentlemen (and the Virginia Company) want, as always, something better than settlement.[46] Again and again Smith deplores the "golden promises" that allow the colonists "no talk, no hope, no work, but dig gold, wash gold, refine gold, load gold" (218); what debases a settler, to his mind, is not the "necessary business" of colonization thus "neglected" but the "dirty skill" of gold digging (219). And the best proof for Smith that the colony's gold lovers, not its laborers, are the ones made savage by colonial life is the gold lovers' inability to master the savages they encounter. Virginia's gentlemen seem to Smith incapable of appreciating that, just as they themselves will do anything for gold, so the equally "idle" Indians will do anything for "baubles of no worth" (257), on one occasion suffering "pains" for Smith that "a horse would scarce have endured, yet a couple of bells richly contented them" (73).[47] The gentlemen, that is, cannot fathom a naïveté they share. In fact, their own idleness makes them so addicted to trading for food rather than growing it that, like the foolish English consumer or conventional savage, they would willingly sacrifice their own valuables:

> Of . . . wild fruits the Savages often brought us: and for that the President [Smith] would not fulfill the unreasonable desire of those distracted lubberly gluttons, to sell, not only our kettles, hoes, tools, and Iron, nay swords, pieces, and the very ordnance, and houses, might they have prevailed but to have been but idle, for those savage fruits they would have imparted all to the Savages; especially for one basket of corn they heard of, to be at Powhatan's, 50 miles from our fort, though he [Smith] bought near half of it to satisfy their humors, yet to have had the other half, they would have sold their souls, (though not sufficient to have kept them a week). (264)

By this account, minds hungry for gold ultimately mean the same thing as souls reduced to a paltry half-basket's worth of "savage fruits."[48]

Smith himself, on the other hand, ostensibly proportioned to the baseness of scandal, labor, and ungentlemanliness, presents himself as simply indifferent to material representations of his own value. As he declares in the dedication of the work prefixed to the *Proceedings*, his *Map of Virginia*: "Though riches now, be the chiefest greatness of the great: when great and little are born, and die, there is no difference: Virtue alone makes men more than men: Vice, worse than brutes" (*Works* 1:133).[49] The practical upshot of this chaste idealism is that Smith, recognizing trifles for what they are, can most ably employ them. In a famous trading incident with the local Indian lord Powhatan, Captain Christopher Newport, the leading light of the colony's gold party,[50] makes grand gestures that, according to Smith, only reduce Newport to the savage's level: "Thinking to out brave this Savage in ostentation of greatness, and so to bewitch him with his bounty, as to have what he listed," Newport ends up getting corn from Powhatan "at such a rate, as I think it better cheap in Spain, for we had not 4. bushels for that we expected 20. hogsheads."[51] Smith, however, then

> glanced in the eyes of Powhatan many Trifles who fixed his humor upon a few blue beads; A long time he importunately desired them, but Smith seemed so much the more to affect them, so that ere we departed, for a pound or two of blue beads he brought over my king for 2 or 300 bushels of corn, yet parted good friends. (217)[52]

In one stroke, by the mere *pretense* of trifling attachments, Smith both acknowledges the scandalous hunger of the English and demonstrates their high-minded superiority to it.

Perhaps the most daring presentation in the *Map* and *Proceedings* of this particularly "disgraceful" brand of *sprezzatura* appears, appropriately enough, in some frivolous-seeming preliminary material, a brief vocabulary of Indian words (136–39). What looks frivolous about the vocabulary, besides the "savage" words themselves,[53] is that Smith lists too "few" of them to make the vocabulary useful,[54] makes jokes about the list (for instance, by inserting among the words for land, stone, water, and fish the Indian term for cuckold), and then ends with a peculiar dramatic dialogue between himself and an Indian[55] (I quote only the English lines):

> I am very hungry, what shall I eat?
> [W]here dwells Powhatan?
> Now he dwells a great way hence at Orapaks.
> You lie, he stayed ever at Werowocomoco.
> Truly he is there I do not lie.
> Run you then to the king mawmarynough and bid him come hither.
> Get you gone, and come again quickly.
> Bid Pocahontas bring hither two little Baskets, and I will give her white beads to make her a chain.
> (139)

It is not only by the mention of hunger that the passage seems to court the slander the *Proceedings* is meant to answer, for the reference to Pocahontas raises what the *Proceedings* treats as the most serious charge against Smith, the slander that he had proven himself so debased as to want to live not just like a savage but *with* one. Even the later passage recording this charge wavers between repudiating and entertaining it:

> Some prophetical spirit calculated he had the Savages in such subjection, he would have made himself a king, by marrying Pocahontas, Powhatan's daughter. It is true she was the very nonpareil of his kingdom, and at most not past 13 or 14 years of age. Very oft she came to our fort, with what she could get for Captain Smith, that ever loved and used all the Country well, but her especially he ever much respected: and she so well requited it, that when her father intended to have surprised him, she by stealth in the dark night came through the wild woods and told him of it. But her marriage could no way have entitled him by any right to the kingdom, nor was it ever suspected he had ever such thought, or more regarded her, or any of them, than in honest reason, and discretion he might. (274)

The similarity to Raleigh is striking, with the equally striking difference that now Raleigh's exceptional Indian woman has a name. The conclusion to the passage demonstrates just how closely Smith's professed ambivalence toward Pocahontas resembles Raleigh's self-restraint: "If he would he might have married her, or have done what him listed. For there was none that could have hindered his determination."[56] In the vocabulary itself, the interplay between hunger at the beginning and Pocahontas at the end increases the sense of Smith's indebtedness to Raleigh: where the disgraced Raleigh used the "threat" of intermarriage to help represent its alternative, gold lust, as chastity, Smith might be thought to dally with Pocahontas so as to distract his readers from his need for food. Yet, as Smith himself will admit, it is one thing to desire gold and another to desire food; and ultimately the difference between the two is only made more pronounced by Pocahontas's inclusion in the little narrative that Smith's hunger motivates. As the *Proceedings* will show, the entirety of the dialogue, not just its first line, concerns the colony's food problems: Powhatan moved to Orapaks in the hope of cutting the English off from his own provisions (147, 173, 256, 261); the baskets Smith wants from Powhatan's still obliging daughter are baskets of corn (212, 246, 250, 251, 255, 264); and the beads he promises Pocahontas are only "such trifles" as have always "contented her" (*True Relation*, 95).[57] Just as at one point Smith releases some Indian prisoners to Pocahontas, "for whose sake only he *feigned* to save their lives and grant them liberty" (221; my emphasis), so in the vocabulary's dialogue, it would seem, Smith only trifles with Pocahontas, as with all baseness, to his advantage.

Yet this otherwise plausible explanation of the passage discounts the real peculiarity of the Pocahontas line, whose change in tone and temporal inconsequence make it sound like a dreamy afterthought, connected to the previous dialogue only through information the text has yet to provide, and then still detached by Smith's evocation of merely "little" food baskets. One might claim that, by his pretense of affection for the savage girl he elsewhere fools, Smith is trifling with the reader. This view seems strengthened by the character of the epistle just prior to Smith's vocabulary, perversely dedicated by one T. A. "To the Hand": "Lest I should wrong any in dedicating this Book to one: I have concluded it shall be particular to none" (135). T. A.'s superiority to patrons soon becomes a flippancy toward readers in general: "If it [the book] be disliked of men, then I would recommend it to women, for being dearly bought, and far sought, it should be good for Ladies." The proverb here (Tilley, *Proverbs*, D12) invokes a whole field of antifeminist sentiment in which woman represents the naive trifler par excellence. In Robert Wilson's play *The Three Ladies of London* (1581), for instance, Lady Lucre grants her favor to the Italian merchant Mercatore only after he promises her "secretly to convey good commodities out of this country" for her sake:

> And for these good commodities, trifles to England thou must
>   bring.
> As Bugles to make baubles, colored bones, glass, beads to make
>   bracelets withal:
> For every day Gentlewomen of England do ask for such trifles from
>   stall to stall.
> And you must bring more, as Amber, Jet, Coral, Crystal, and
>   every such bauble,
> That is slight, pretty and pleasant; they care not to have it
>   profitable.[58]

But if T. A.'s use of the proverb suggests his disdain for the readers whom he considers either churlish or trifling, unable to appreciate the value of a book defending scandal-ridden Virginia, the rest of his epistle makes a surprising about-face on the subject not only of patronage but of trifle-loving women:

> When all men rejected Christopher Columbus: that ever renowned Queen Izabell of Spain, could pawn her Jewels to supply his wants; whom all the wise men (as they thought themselves) of that age contemned. I need not say what was his worthiness, her nobleness, and their ignorance, that so scornfully did spit at his wants, seeing the whole world is enriched with his golden fortunes. Cannot this successful example move the incredulous of this time, to consider, to conceive, and apprehend Virginia, which might be, or breed us a second India? hath not England an Izabell, as well as Spain, nor yet a Columbus as well as Genoa? yes surely it hath, whose desires are no less than was worthy Columbus, their certainties more, their experiences no way wanting, only there wants but an Izabell, so it were not from Spain. (Smith, *Works* 1:135)

Now there are two kinds of women: the ones idler than men, trading substance for the insubstantiality more appropriate to them; or the ones wiser (and richer) than men, recognizing the substance in what appears insubstantial, as they too are greater than they appear. If England has the heroes—preeminently, of course, Smith—who are capable of turning trifling Virginia to gold, it nevertheless lacks the patrons capable of believing in a colony that, like Smith himself, has been "traduced" as "base, and contemptible" (*True Declaration*, 6). "Only there wants but an Izabell, so it were not from Spain"—England, that is, only wants its "good Queen Elizabeth" (Smith, *Works* 1:403).[59] In light of this longing, the delicacy with which Smith treats the Indian princess in whom he supposedly feigns interest betrays the complexity of his position as a Jacobean colonist. Pocahontas, that is, combines the foolish and the royal woman:[60] already suggesting—as a virgin, not a virgin land—the constriction of special relations between England and America, Pocahontas as royal virgin seems also to figure the displacement of sublime trifling from England, while as a savage virgin she represents the impossibility of locating such potentiality in America. In other words, the only option for Jacobean trifling as Smith sees it seems to be its internalization in the figure of the unsettled colonist himself—the man John Davies of Herefordshire calls "Brass without, but Gold within" (*Poems*, 320).[61]

For the *Proceedings* is not content merely to excuse the shortcomings of the colonists: "Peruse the Spanish Decades, the relations of Master Hakluyt," it challenges, "and tell me how many ever with such small means, as a barge of 2 Tons; sometimes with 7. 8. 9, or but at most 15 men did ever discover so many fair and navigable rivers; subject so many several kings, peoples, and nations, to obedience, and contribution with so little blood shed" (258). So confident are Smith and his men in their own "small" abilities that they can risk invoking the possibility of their utter divorcement from England: angered by the company's replenishing Virginia only with delinquents, Smith exclaims, "Happy had we been had they never arrived; and we for ever abandoned, and (as we were) left to our fortunes" (269). The grandest manifestation of this self-reliant littleness is, of course, the lowly (and short) figure who comprehends the colony in himself (see figure 9). For Smith, indeed, the man best suited to colonial work is the one as beggarly-looking as he: "Who can desire more content, that hath small means; or but only merit to advance his fortune, than to tread, and plant that ground he hath purchased by the hazard of his life?" (343).

Yet this Spenserian intensification of trifling, which presents Smith as free from proportionment to objective correlatives such as gold or food or the English island, works in the end, as it had for Spenser, to undermine Smith's relation to any "ground" whatsoever. Though improvements on the laboring gentleman depicted by Raleigh, Smith's few planters maintain a crucial detachment from their work by its very voluntariness:

> Let no man think that the President, or these gentlemen spent their time as common wood-hackers at felling of trees, or such like other labors, or that they were pressed to any thing as hirelings or common slaves, for what they did (being but once a little inured) it seemed, and they conceited it only as a pleasure and a recreation. (238–39)[62]

Indeed, the only matter Smith admits to be truly pertinent to him is his own heroically errant body; as he declares in the dedicatory epistle to the *Map*, anticipating T. A.'s own dedication "To the Hand": "My hands hath been my lands this fifteen years in Europe, Asia, Afric, or America" (133).[63]

C.Smith taketh the King of Pamavnkee prisoner 1608

Figure 9. "C[aptain] Smith Taketh the King of Pamaunkee Prisoner 1608," enlargement from "A Description of Part of the Adventures of Cap: Smith in Virginia," in *The Generall Historie of Virginia, New-England, and the Summer Isles*, by Captain John Smith, London, 1624. The image of Smith dominating a larger Indian is echoed in the background by the image of English colonists, outnumbered, withstanding an Indian attack. (By permission of the Beinecke Library, Yale University.)

A few years later in Smith's career, however, this self-posses-
sion begins to look less satisfying: writing in the *Generall Historie*
(1624) about his experiences in both Virginia and New England,
Smith complains that "in neither of those two Countries have I
one foot of Land, nor the very house I builded, nor the ground I
digged with my own hands, nor ever any content or satisfaction
at all" (*Works* 2:326). The commendatory poems that once praised
Smith's contempt for riches can now as easily bemoan his lack of
reward: "Truth, travail, and Neglect, pure, painful, most unkind,
/ Doth prove, consume, dismay, the soul, the corpse, the mind"
(51).[64] Moreover, as a New World traveler superior to any grounds
for praise other than himself, Smith becomes increasingly unable
even to reach America, let alone possess it: leaving Jamestown due
to a serious injury in 1609, he briefly journeys to New England in
1614, sets out again in 1615 but is forced to return for repairs, tries
once more in 1615 but runs into pirates, then in 1617 his ships
prove unable even to leave Plymouth harbor—and he never sails
again.[65] As his "Prospectus" for the *Generall Historie* concludes, after "the expense of a thousand pound, and the loss of eighteen
years of time, besides all the travels, dangers, miseries and encum-
brances for my country's good, I have endured gratis," "these observations are all I have" (*Works* 2:16).

A version of this complaint, however, had already appeared in
the dedication to the *Map*: "Having been discouraged for doing
any more, I have writ this little" (*Works* 1:133). Yet, he adds, his
hands have always been his lands; even when he writes the *Map*,
in other words, the only reward that the self-reliant Smith claims
to expect proceeds from himself alone, from the hands that now
produce not deeds but books.[66] It would be a mistake to conclude,
therefore, that Smith turns to writing only as a meager compensation for a life of "defailments." He had written at least one book,
the *True Relation*, even as a colonist; and both the volume and the
frequency of his later literary efforts make his career as a writer
seem anything but an unnatural sequel to his career as a colonial
trifler. The only English voyager to America before Smith to publish more than one tract about his adventures was Raleigh, who
published two; yet Smith produced five wholly devoted to the
New World—*A True Relation* (1608), *A Map of Virginia* and *The Proceedings* (1612), *A Description of New England* (1616), *New Englands*

Trials (1620, 1622), and the *Generall Historie* (1624)—as well as one about his travels throughout the world—*The True Travels* (1630)—and three of advice to voyagers and planters generally—*An Accidence* (1626), *A Sea Grammar* (1627), and his last work, *Advertisements for the Unexperienced Planters of New England, or Any Where* (1631). Indeed, Smith proves almost as prolific a writer about America as the great editors Eden, Hakluyt, and Purchas, to whom he even prefers himself as an editor, on the basis of his actual colonial experience: "Had I not discovered and lived in most of these parts, I could not possibly have collected the substantial truth from such an infinite number of variable Relations" (*Works* 2:16; cf. 41, 44, and 3:288). At times, it is true, Smith worries that writing has taken the place of more vigorous labor on his part—as he says in a preface to the *Description*, "I confess it were more proper for me, To be doing what I say, than writing what I know" (*Works* 1:311; cf. 422)—and till the end he declares himself ready to make his words good, unlike those who "could better guide penknives than use swords" (*Works* 3:301). Yet he ultimately displaces the invidious comparison between his writing and his soldiering into the mouths of his inevitable detractors—"Envy hath taxed me to have writ too much, and done too little" (*Works* 3:141)—and decides instead that his books only complete the heroic picture of himself that his soldiering had begun. Conventionally modest about his literary abilities in the dedication of his *Generall Historie*, Smith wonders, "Where shall we look to find a Julius Caesar, whose achievements shine as clear in his own Commentaries, as they did in the field?" (*Works* 2:41); but a commendatory poem a few pages later declares, unsurprisingly, that one need look no further than Smith (50); and the identification becomes, in Smith's works anyway, a commonplace (317, and 3:47, 142, 145, 147)—he could not, after all, be a complete Caesar *without* his books.

In fact, the more Smith "disgraces" himself by merely writing, the more he grows to admire himself. "This great work [of colonization], though small in conceit, is," he declares, "not a work for every one to manage . . . [;] it requires all the best parts of art, judgment, courage, honesty, constancy, diligence, and industry, to do but near well" (*Works* 3:301; cf. 1:327–28). And, though Smith may, in exhorting James, claim that "nothing but the touch of the King's sacred hand can erect a monarchy" (2:43), he later asserts of Virginia, New England, and Bermuda "that the most of those fair plantations did spring from the fruits of my adventures and discoveries" (3:13).[67] According to his final work, the *Advertisements*, published more than twenty years after he last saw Jamestown, Smith's ostensible failure continues only to assimilate him to England's colonies all the more:

> Now if you but truly consider how many strange accidents have befallen those plantations and my self, how oft up, how oft down, sometimes near despair, and ere long flourishing; how many scandals and Spanolized English have sought to disgrace them, bring them to ruin, or at least hinder them all they could; how many have shaven and cozened both them and me, and their most honorable supporters and well-willers, cannot but conceive God's infinite mercy both to them and me.

As the passage continues, however, Smith so overtakes Virginia in misadventure that he takes center stage:

> Having been a slave to the Turks, prisoner amongst the most barbarous Savages, after my deliverance commonly discovering and ranging those large rivers and unknown Nations with such a handful of ignorant companions, that the wiser sort often gave me for lost, always in mutinies, wants and miseries, blown up with gunpowder; A long time prisoner among the French Pirates, from whom escaping in a little boat by my self, and adrift, all such a stormy winter night when their ships were split, more than an hundred thousand pound lost, we had taken at sea, and most of them drowned upon the Isle of Ree, not far from whence I was driven on shore in my little boat, etc. And many a score of the worst winter months lived in the fields, yet to have lived near 37. years in the midst of wars, pestilence and famine; by which, many an hundred thousand have died about me, and scarce five living of them went first with me to Virginia, and see the fruits of my labors thus well begin to prosper: Though I have but my labor for my pains, have I not much reason both privately and publicly to acknowledge it and give God thanks. (*Works* 3:284–85)

Oddly, and yet characteristically, the separation here between the "fruits" of the colonies and Smith's "labor" for them constitutes, in this context of Smith's glorious ills, not so much a lamentation as a boast. It stakes Smith's exclusive claim to the colonies at the same time as it frees him from any proportionment to them. If earlier in his career he had described the colonies, in terms marking his alienation from England, as "my wife" (and also "my children . . . my hawks, my hounds, my cards, my dice, and in total my best content, as indifferent to my heart as my left hand to my right") (1:434), this identification by the end of his life has come to mean that such "marriage" ties restrict everyone except the long-suffering (and otherwise bachelor) Smith himself.

In place of the material substance or "content" Smith persistently confesses himself to lack, however, actual women become more, not less, important to him. His ill fortune, that is, causes him increasingly to advertise his dependence on noble ladies, Isabells who see the value in ostensible poverty and so "record" his "worth" (3:145). As Smith explains to the Duchess of Richmond and Lenox, in a passage matching the list of his woes in the *Advertisements*,

> Yet my comfort is, that heretofore honorable and virtuous Ladies, and comparable but amongst themselves, have offered me rescue and protection in my greatest dangers: even in foreign parts, I have felt relief from that sex. The beauteous Lady Tragabigzanda, when I was a slave to the Turks, did all she could to secure me. When I overcame the Bashaw of Nalbrits in Tartaria, the charitable Lady Callamata supplied my necessities. In the utmost of many extremities, that blessed Pocahontas, the great King's daughter of Virginia, oft saved my life. When I escaped the cruelty of Pirates and most furious storms, a long time alone in a small Boat at Sea, and driven ashore in France, the good Lady Madam Chanoyes, bountifully assisted me. (*Works* 2:41–42)

"That blessed Pocahontas"—no longer, it seems, can Smith afford his former irony toward the women who supply Elizabeth's lack.[68] Yet the sheer number of these "incomparable" women continues to weaken Smith's attachment to any one of them in particular; if anything, indeed, the attachment is on the side of the woman, like Tragabigzanda, who hopes to make Smith her husband (3:186–88, 200), or Pocahontas, who later calls Smith her father.[69] A canny parody of Smith published the same year as the *Advertisements*, David Lloyd's *Legend of Captaine Jones* (1631), ridicules Smith's pose of embattled chastity by referring not only to Jones's "grace with thy great Queen Eliza" and then to "thy London widow next in love half-drown'd, / Which thou refus'dst with forty thousand pound," but, most tellingly, to "th'amorous ways / The Queen of No-land us'd to make thee King / Of her and hers" (16–17).[70] Yet in mocking Smith by transforming him into a Spenserian knight, Lloyd only reveals the extraordinary degree to which the chaste

Smith has indeed answered Spenser's call for an Englishman at once sublimely motivated by a transcendent love and yet not exclusively attached, either to Elizabeth or England—resisting even the Queen of No-land.

The problem is that Smith answers Spenser's call only too well, transforming every attachment into the semblance of one, into a proof of his own incomparable potentiality; one might say, in fact, that where Spenser hoped to see his books realized as colonies, Smith ends up realizing his colonies as books. If for some readers Smith's adventures could therefore look so detached from the material world as to seem "above belief," even "beyond Truth,"[71] for others such ungrounded mobility could also end up an ideal in itself: *The True Travels* arose, Smith says, when some noble readers asked him "to fix the whole course of my passages" not just incidentally, in a colonialist tract, but "in a book by itself" (*Works* 3:141). Even the tracts, however, reflect the increasing conflation of Smith's travails and writing that leads to these solitary "passages" of the *Travels*. A commendatory poem to the *Generall Historie* praises Smith for imparting America "to our hands," "There by thy *Work*, Here by thy *Works*" (*Works* 2:52), and Smith goes on to acknowledge the continuity between these two modes of colonial labor: "Thus far," he exclaims at the end of book 4, "I have traveled in this Wilderness of Virginia" (*Works* 2:333). Indeed, Smith later suggests that his writing is the greater labor of the two: continuing the history of the colonies in his *Travels*, Smith declares that "I have tired my self in seeking and discoursing with those returned thence, more than would a voyage to Virginia" (*Works* 3:215).[72] So untrammeled by a material relation to the colonies has Smith's indelicate labor for them become that he no longer requires any other field of honor as a colonist than the still more scandalous "lands" of his "hands"—not his work but his *Works*.

6

Distraction in *The Tempest*

Withal, that order that God annexed to marriage in his first
institution, viz. that married persons should leave father
and mother, and cleave each to other, is a good warrant of
this practice. For sometime there will be a necessity, that
young married persons should remove out of their father's
house, and live apart by themselves, and so erect new families. Now what are new families, but petty Colonies: and
so at last removing further and further they overflow the
whole earth. Therefore, so long as there shall be use of
marriage, the warrant of deducing Colonies will continue.
— John White,
The Planters Plea (1630)

For all the attention lavished on the idea that *The Tempest* is somehow about America, the countercharge advanced sixty years ago
by E. E. Stoll in "Certain Fallacies and Irrelevancies in the Literary
Scholarship of the Day" retains its force: "There is not a word in
The Tempest," Stoll argues, "about America or Virginia, colonies or
colonizing, Indians or tomahawks, maize, mocking-birds, or tobacco. Nothing but the Bermudas, once barely mentioned as a far-
away place, like Tokio or Mandalay" (487).[1] Stoll's incidental facts
are off—in act 2, scene 2 each of the "low" characters Stephano
and Trinculo momentarily imagines Caliban an Indian (34, 58)—
but his primary point is difficult to shake: if Shakespeare draws so
heavily on accounts of the shipwreck and miraculous survival of
Sir Thomas Gates and his Virginia-bound colonists on Bermuda in
1609, then why does he also go out of his way to establish that the
Bermudas are one place where his shipwrecked characters most
definitely are not? In the play no ship even wrecks: to Prospero's
question about the fate of the "brave vessel" Miranda saw "dash'd
all to pieces" (1.2.7–9), Ariel replies,

Safely in harbor
Is the King's ship, in the deep nook, where once
Thou call'dst me up at midnight to fetch dew
From the still-vex'd Bermoothes, there she's hid.
(226–29)

As Stoll demands that we see, the passage marks the Bermudas'
distance from, their irrelevance to, the present action in a number
of ways: as a far, inhospitable place one needs a spirit to reach; as
an obscurely motivated interest one previously had; and as a setting Ariel mentions only by the way, never referred to in the play
again.

What Prospero, and Shakespeare's play, seem to lack, in short,
is any colonial interest in America: where Gates had hoped to
"plant a Nation" (Rich, *Newes*, B2r), Prospero cares only to exercise his magic. Even the action on Prospero's Mediterranean isle,
controlled as it is by Prospero's magic, steadfastly resists the colonial analogy it nevertheless suggests: the "shipwrecked" men on
whom Prospero practices are Italians, overwhelmingly royalty or
nobility; they had been traveling east; they had been trying to go
home; only the lowest of them ever exhibit any intention of stay-
ing; and all do go home in the end.[2] But then, for all the success
that English colonialism had enjoyed over the previous century,
England's actual colonial enterprises in America might just as well
have been magical amusements, distractions, themselves; in other
words, at the time Shakespeare wrote *The Tempest*, he would have
had little reason not to assume that, like every other English attempt at colonizing America, the Jamestown settlement would
founder. This chapter will argue, in fact, that *The Tempest* constitutes an attack on what Shakespeare considers a magical and
therefore uncolonial view of American plantation. Part of what
causes the rather rigorous exclusion of colonialism in a play so
strongly suggesting the issue is, I will maintain, Shakespeare's
skeptical mimicry of a brand of imperialism I have associated particularly with Spenser's Fairyland, an antimaterialism holding that
the best way to win America is to raise the minds of one's insular
nation above the low thought of mere earthly possession; according to *The Tempest*, this virginal or utopic imperialism only lands
one on an island Nowhere, and converts empire, or the desire for

it, to irrelevance.³ But while Shakespeare's dramatization of the colonial antimaterialist as lord of little more than magic books may represent one mode of English expansion as self-destructive foolery or madness, as "distraction," it does not therefore eschew expansion altogether. What I will try to identify as the play's new and even more paradoxical imperialism finds its best image in the sort of marriage Spenser would deplore, one premised on the abjuration of expansionist desire—"All corners else o' th' earth / Let liberty make use of" (1.2.492–93)⁴—and yet that marriage ends up legitimately securing new territory for the abjurer. The sort of expansionism Shakespeare desires cannot help being obscure: he believes that the colony Gates set out to rescue will succeed as a colony only insofar as it forgets its purpose, imagining itself not as extending the power of its distant island home but as living at home in, truly marrying, Virginia. Yet how do the English come to consider Virginia no longer a fairy but a georgic land? *The Tempest*, I will argue, is a record of Spenserian antimaterialism trying to unthink itself—to renounce its magic and drown its book, to distract itself from its distraction.

I

Shakespeare's seemingly unusual combination of America and magical excursions actually figures in the first Jacobean masque (1604) produced by King James himself:

> On New Year's night we had a play of Robin good-fellow and a mask brought in by a magician of China. There was a heaven built at the lower end of the hall, out of which our magician came down and after he had made a long sleepy speech to the King of the nature of the country from whence he came comparing it with ours for strength and plenty, he said he had brought in clouds certain Indian and China Knights to see the magnificency of this court. And thereupon a traverse was drawn and the maskers seen sitting in a vaulty place with their torchbearers and other lights which was no unpleasing spectacle. The maskers were brought in . . . [and] presented themselves to the King. The first gave the King an Impresa in a shield with a sonnet in a paper to express his device and presented a jewel of 40,000£ value.⁵

By this account, the plot of the masque seems to allegorize the fact of the masque: that is, the Chinese magician who can produce knights and jewels from the other side of the earth seems only a dark, heterodoxical conceit for the greater and divinely legitimated power who has, after all, produced the "magician of China" in the first place.[6] Such a dramatization of the king's own "magical" influence does not obviously entail, however, the presentation of riches from China and the Indies,[7] especially when James is never said to be pursuing them in any way; and indeed, James in 1604 had little palpable connection to either land. It is as if the masque were claiming that, in comparison to actual expansionist ventures, James's apparent passivity was a more far-reaching mode of command.

Nine years later, even after Jamestown had given the king a genuine foothold in America, another court entertainment, George Chapman's *Memorable Masque* (1613), decides only to argue this mysterious claim more directly. Chapman's masque is a striking instance of what Frances Yates has called "The Elizabethan Revival in the Jacobean Age" (*Majesty*, 17–37), a militantly Protestant, Spanish-hating and imperialist movement that focused quite early in his life on the figure of Henry, Prince of Wales. To Henry's admirers, he seemed the quintessential man of action, whereas his father, the Venetian Paolo Sarpi, reported, "would like to do everything with words" (quoted in Strong, *Henry*, 76). Educated in part by Raleigh and a Spenserianism so strong as to compel even Jonson to dub him *Oberon, the Fairy Prince* (1611), Henry was, according to the one postmortem, the inspiration behind "all actions profitable or honorable to the kingdom . . . , witness the Northwest passage, Virginia, Guiana, The Newfoundland, etc., to all which he gave his money as well as his good word."[8] The same concern for expansion finds its way into the *Memorable Masque* for a number of reasons: Chapman had been a public advocate of New World ventures since his "De Guiana" in 1596; his masque was fashioned for the wedding festivities of Henry's sister Elizabeth and the Elector Palatine, who Henry's party believed would begin the end of papist dominion on the Continent; and the entertainment was "commanded by the Prince himself" (Strong, *Henry*, 178). Yet where one expects the masque to repudiate the mere verbalism and therefore stasis manifested in James's entertainment, it embraces instead only a more elaborate passivity. A character in the masque explains how it is that "the blind deity, Riches" has "miraculously arrived" in Britain:

For (according to our rare men of wit) heaven standing and earth moving, her motion (being circular) hath brought one of the most remote parts of the world to touch at this all-exceeding island; which a man of wit would imagine must needs move circularly with the rest of the world, and so ever maintain an equal distance. But poets (our chief men of wit) answer that point directly, most ingeniously affirming that this isle is (for the excellency of it) divided from the world (*divisus ab orbe Britannus*) and that, though the whole world besides moves, yet this isle stands fixed on her own feet and defies the world's mutability, which this rare accident of the arrival of Riches in one of his furthest–off–situate dominions most demonstratively proves. (ll. 35–48)

The imperialist magic of the masque no longer requires the interposition of a vulgar agent like the Chinese sorcerer, nor for that matter of any agency whatsoever—only the earth's turning; and Britain stands apart even from that impulsion, dilating in power by virtue of its isolation, filling with gold because golden colonies are what it lacks. Though perhaps made more extravagantly paradoxical by its unmediated transformation of spirit into gold, this strange allegory is indeed familiar Elizabethan material: Britain, Chapman maintains, represents an otherworld not for mere geographical or material reasons but "for the excellency" of "wit" that raises the nation's spirit above worldly entanglements, thereby rendering Britain capable of the specially imperialist imagination that Chapman's masque is supposed to exemplify. If England's poets are the "chief" exemplars of this otherworldly wit, its supreme embodiment is that kingly maker of "artful songs" (290), "our Briton Phoebus" (310), James—who can even teach some "Virginian princes" the error of their superstitious ways.

The same festivities that saw Chapman's masque, and in it the Elizabethan topos of English otherworldliness revived, also witnessed a performance of *The Tempest*. John Gillies notes how thoroughly Shakespeare's and Chapman's entertainments appear to clash:

Where Chapman's Britain is visited by a suitably opulent delegation of Virginian priests and knights, Shakespeare's only Virginian intourist is Trinculo's "dead indian." Where Chapman's native knights obligingly hand over their gold-mine, Shakespeare's intractably "salvage and deformed slave" curses his disinheritors with the gift of language. Even when benevolently inclined, Caliban is able to offer nothing more marketable than "young scamels from the rock" or, perhaps, himself, "a plain fish, and no doubt marketable."

. . . Shakespeare even seems to parody Chapman's cloudy gold mine with its El Doradoesque mythology of Indian riches, in Caliban's dream that

> The clouds methought would open, and show riches
> Ready to drop upon me; that, when I wak'd,
> I cride to dream again.

> ("Shakespeare's Virginian
> Masque," 674–75)

One need only recall James's "sleepy" masque with its own cloudy gifts to begin realizing how *The Tempest* reflects on the royal triumph in general. Indeed, an awed spectator (1604) describing one of the triumphal arches built for James's entry into London— a "pageant" so tall that "on the top you might behold, the sea Dolphins as dropping from the clouds on the earth"—sounds like a combination of the beastly Caliban on his dream and the princely Ferdinand on Prospero's own masque:

> But the glory of this show, was in my eye as a dream, pleasing to the affection, gorgeous and full of joy, and so full of show, and variety, that when I held down my head as wearied with looking so high, me thought it was a grief to me to awaken so soon.[9]

Filtered through its analogues in *The Tempest*, the spectator's bedazzlement here seems to expose the dreaminess of a power that manifests itself in such spectacles, a dreaminess from which one must sooner or later awaken to "grief": the "sweet airs" (3.2.136) that lead Caliban to recount his dreams of the heavens raining treasure, for example, so distract him that he himself eventually falls into a "pool" (4.1.182) not of condensed spirit but of "horse-piss" (199). A similarly deflating allegory appears to dictate Shakespeare's representation of Prospero—lord, magus, and also masque writer now explicitly combined—desiring and receiving from America only dew, as if this most immaterial and ephemeral of substances, not riches, were the only true correlative to a materially "baseless" (151) royal power.[10]

Yet, if *The Tempest* seems to attack the wishful imperialism of the Jacobean court, it appears no less critical of more practical-sounding approaches to expansion as well. The banquet masque that Prospero arranges in act 3, for instance, falsely promises easy pickings not to a naive dreamer but to the power-hungry King of Na-

ples, who had long ago backed Prospero's ouster in exchange for
Milan's vassalage, and who has recently married his own reluc-
tant daughter to the King of Tunis for, presumably, some political gain. That Prospero thinks even Alonso's imperialism wishful
or idealist seems demonstrated by the original punishment he
makes Alonso undergo, his running "aground" (1.1.4–5): Prospero wants to convince Alonso that his dualist confidence in the
power of his "authority" (23) has ultimately only exaggerated his
material limitations. Alonso must see, in other words, that in pursuing expansion he does not escape physical constraints but rather
falls more radically a victim to them: Sebastian complains that the
literally distracting "shipwreck" would never have occurred if
Alonso had allowed his daughter to stay at home (2.1.124–26); and
Ariel declares that, as punishment for supplanting Prospero,
Alonso must himself remain exiled "in this most desolate isle"
(3.3.80). Though this physical alienation ultimately reverses Alonso's expansionism to such a degree that he comes to experience
the internal estrangement of madness, Prospero also intends the
king's literal and spiritual "distractions" (3.3.90) as Alonso's cure:
like the good Gonzalo who, when faced with shipwreck, wishes
he could "give a thousand furlongs of sea for an acre of barren
ground" (1.1.65–66), Alonso, thinks Prospero, can save himself
only by learning to repudiate baseless roominess for grounded
constraint.

So thoroughly does Prospero construe Alonso's imperialism as
an effect of idealism, in fact, that his education of Alonso not only
tends to disregard the traditional political arguments against expansionism—for instance, Hythloday's contention that a "king,
being distracted with the charge of two kingdoms, [can]not properly attend to either" (More, *Utopia*, 90/91)—but instead continually underscores the fundamental material limitation of Alonso
and his party not just to Prospero's island but to their own bodies.
In the crude lessons reserved for the socially lower characters of
the play, Prospero makes the body painfully evident by means of
various small tortures: at the end of the play, for example, Stephano is forced to exclaim, "O, touch me not, I am not Stephano,
but a cramp" (5.1.286–87). Ariel, the spirit who can "divide, / And
burn in many places" (1.2.198–99), or whose airy body cannot be
wounded (3.3.60–66), alerts his viewers to the constraints of their

own bodies by a contrast that makes Ferdinand's hair stand on end. And Prospero has still other methods of embodiment at his disposal: paralyzing his victims, for instance, or making them hungry and sleepy, or forcing them to physical labor. Just as Alonso is supposed to recognize how his dualist policies backfire, only enmiring him further in what he believes he can transcend, so Prospero leads Alonso's son Ferdinand to associate his paralyzed, imprisoning body with an exclusively psychic self-perception: "My spirits, as in a dream, are all bound up" (1.2.487). Yet like the island on which the king's party founders, the body in Prospero's teachings ultimately represents not just a menace to idealism but its remedy. By the time of the play's third scene, the woebegone Alonso has already come to long for bodily limitation as a kind of release: watching his servants fall asleep, he laments, "I wish mine eyes / Would, with themselves, shut up my thoughts" (2.1.191–92).

Such a desire for corporeal self-imprisonment even helps cure the distracted Prospero himself. His own exile had, after all, also stemmed from a desire to escape material constraints, though Prospero had been intent not on enlarging his dominions but on "neglecting worldly ends" altogether, on "closeness and the bettering of my mind" (1.2.89–90). Yet Prospero's reaction to his own stagings of embodiment demonstrates that the mere recognition of material constraint can itself prove distracting. His dismay about the distance between Caliban's unredeemable "nature" (4.1.188) and the "insubstantial pageant" of his own magic leads Prospero to reject not only the manufactured extravagances—"the cloud-capp'd towers, the gorgeous palaces, / The solemn temples"—that his island lacks, but "the great globe itself" (4.1.148–58). In the light of such *contemptus mundi*, the New World dew that Prospero (only by way of Ariel) escapes his island's bounds to obtain looks like Prospero's purposefully ironic comment not so much on imperial greed as on the ephemerality of worldly goods generally. Like England's trifling voyagers, however, Prospero tries to temper this dualist or "distemper'd" (4.1.145) otherworldliness by displacing it onto others, proportioning them to the "enchanted trifle[s]" (5.1.112) of his self-consuming shows. By act 5, for instance, Gonzalo has been led to a far more panicky version of Prospero's earlier *contemptus*:

> All torment, trouble, wonder, and amazement
> Inhabitants here. Some heavenly power guide us
> Out of this fearful country!
>
> (5.1.104–6)

The reduction here of "fearful country" from the earth to only one island on it is familiar from Spenser's Error episode: by means of the spectatorial detachment gained in depressing such scapegoats as Gonzalo, Prospero transforms his island into a world he can leave without abandoning worldliness altogether.

Yet Prospero does not abandon his scapegoats either: rather, he ends the play having both revealed himself to his victims and expressed his wish not to quest after some new world but to return home. The difference between Spenserian and Prosperian trifling, it seems, is that Prospero's version admits its limitations. Indeed, Prospero appears to consider the sight of a victim proportioned to some trifling illusion as a show to which he himself is proportioned in turn: viewing the tears of Gonzalo that reflect Gonzalo's sight of Alonso's "frantic gesture" (5.1.57–58), Prospero exclaims, "Mine eyes, ev'n sociable to the show of thine, / Fall fellowly drops" (63–64). This "fallen" materialization of Prospero's previously abstracted vision into tears that reflect the tears he sees follows upon his acknowledgment of his own embodiment only in terms of his victims' constraints: he expostulates to Ariel,

> Hast thou, which are but air, a touch, a feeling
> Of their afflictions, and shall not myself,
> One of their kind, that relish all as sharply
> Passion as they, be kindlier mov'd than thou art?
>
> (5.1.21–24)

But then Prospero's own dualist distraction, previously figured in the separate persons of Ariel as airy expansiveness and Caliban as earthy limitation, is most fully "temper'd" when he now repeatedly makes himself sensible of his body by literally embracing the bodies of those who have already been made to perceive their own embodiment as a constraint (5.1.109, 121). That is, Prospero limits his distaste for a limitation to his body by making the feel of that limitation coincide with the feel of other bodies already "sharply" relished; he turns the perception of self-constraint into a basis for kinship. At the same time, he also reasserts his political identity, presenting himself "as I was sometime Milan" (85–86): in other words, his homeland is made to represent the geographical constraint that comes closest to seeming as inseparable from him as his body is; while this coincidence of his recovered embodiment with his recovered rule, his self-identification as Milan, grants him the expansiveness not only of fellow bodies but of the body politic he rules. Yet of course the materiality of both Prospero and Milan still makes a difference between them, just as the other bodies that Prospero embraces remain other, embraced only for a time, or (in what Prospero considers the archetypical dualism) as the "beating" blood now felt within Prospero's "mind" only comes and goes, like the tide[11]: if no longer seen as separable, Prospero and his homeland, Prospero and his fellow Italians, and even Prospero and his own body are not now seen as inseparable either. Throughout the play, after all, Prospero has insisted that the attempt to eliminate dualisms is itself dualist, and only exaggerates one's distraction. In finally acknowledging as self-constraints not just his body, his fellow Italians, and his political responsibilities but also that "thing of darkness" (5.1.275) Caliban, Prospero tries to ensure that his regained attachments will not prove as distracting as his detachment had once been: what is now "mine" for Prospero includes not just his own or a fellow body but a foreign one, a more self-evident scapegoat who both registers the disgraceful fact of embodiment and keeps that fact from fully absorbing Prospero's mind.

Indeed, the sight of this purposefully unstable resolution to Prospero's story seems to present a similarly useful collection of foreign bodies to Shakespeare's own audience. For Shakespeare's spectators, in other words, Prospero's theatrical lessons seem to recommend a trifling surrogate that can enable those spectators as well to achieve a temperate balance between attachment to and detachment from material limitation—namely, Shakespeare's own theater, the little Globe within England that one can leave without leaving either England or the great globe itself. Condemned by its critics for distracting the English from their work, their religion, and their proper place, the theater as Shakespeare implicitly presents it is at least homegrown estrangement, fulfilling Clement Armstrong's old dream of an England freed from its ruinous love of foreign trifles by itself manufacturing "all kind of artificiality

needful to suffice the whole realm" ("Treatise," 110). Such a distinction would presumably not mollify a theater-hater like Stephen
Gosson (1579), who complains that "were not we so foolish to
taste every drug, and buy every trifle, Players would shut in their
shops, and carry their trash to some other Country" (*Schoole*, 101,
D3r); but a foreign visitor to England in the 1590s is indeed struck
by the theater's role as a surrogate for more extravagant pursuits:
he describes the English "learning at the play what is happening
abroad; indeed men and womenfolk visit such places without
scruple, since the English for the most part do not travel much,
but prefer to learn foreign matters and take their pleasure at
home" (Williams, *Platter's Travels*, 170).[12]

   In *The Tempest*, Shakespeare tries to emphasize the saving familiarity in theatrical estrangement by depicting Prospero's abandonment of magic as the rejection not of theatrical shows but of
the theater's primary rival as material "art" (1.2.1)—the book.
Where Spenser had preferred the book to the body as a more conspicuously spiritual matter, Shakespeare takes the actual material
basis of the book more literally in order to associate it with one of
Spenser's own figures for the dualist conception of the body, the
tree. Representing the illusion that the body is radically distinct
from the spirit, merely natural, the tree in *The Tempest* can portray
the body as either the spirit's usurper or its slave. As a usurper,
the tree-body is a prison rooted in earth; as a slave, it can be uprooted and shaped into a vehicle—a boat, a butt of sack, a bottle,
or most valuable, a book—that the spirit supposes will both preserve and "transport" it.[13] Prospero stresses the power of his
books to liberate the spirit when, during the masque for Ferdinand
and Miranda, he explains that the masquers are

> Spirits, which by mine art
> I have from their confines call'd to enact
> My present fancies.
>
> (4.1.120–22)

Yet, in quickly disrupting the masque and expatiating on his mortality, he not only figures such art as distracting him from the real
bodily properties of his spirit—a "brain," for instance, that has
grown "old" (4.1.159)—but also exchanges the false purity of spiritual enactments for a performance in which "vex'd" (158) humans
like himself take part.[14] In other words, over the course of *The Tem-*

pest Prospero comes to favor an art that is literally embodied, specially able to limit its own distracting influence because temperately encouraging both the spiritual and the bodily participation of its audience.[15] True to his antidualist project throughout the play, Prospero in his epilogue directly addresses the fact of the Globe audience's participation only when certain conditions have been met: when his "charms" have ended, when he can admit the need for aid, and when this aid can entail the audience's feeling its own limitations in clapped "hands" (10) and lost "breath" (11) that will applaud but also shatter the dualist "bands" (9) produced by his enchantments. Like the "dew" of similarly homeopathic tobacco,[16] the play-world then vanishes into thin air; but the bodies within that world do not vanish; and their survival ("not a hair perished") might best seem to show how Prospero's temperately distracting lessons both derive from and tend toward home.

II

Yet of course attacks on wishful thinking and pleas for temperance had been dominant features of Virginian propaganda from its inception.[17] In the first publication to drum up support for the Gates voyage, *Nova Britannia* (1609), Robert Johnson sounds as if he is chiding Caliban when he reminds his readers that "the abundance of King *Solomon's* gold and silver did not rain from heaven upon the heads of his Subjects: but heavenly providence blessed his Navigations and public affairs, the chief means of their wealth" (17).[18] A tract by the Frenchman Marc Lescarbot, translated for the new Virginian venture at Hakluyt's instigation (1609), also emphasizes the need for hard work, arguing that "our felicity consisteth not in mines, specially of gold and silver, the which serve for nothing in the tillage of the ground nor to handicrafts' use" (*Nova Francia*, 14–15); "a Colony," writes the anonymous author of the Virginia Company's *True Declaration* (1610), "is therefore denominated, because they should be *Coloni*, the tillers of the earth, and stewards of fertility" (36). In their attempt to associate not georgic labor but gentlemanly idleness with "baseness of mind" (Johnson, *Nova Britannia*, 11)—only savages, says William Crashaw (1610), "cannot plow, till, plant nor set" (*Sermon*, D4r)—Virginia's apologists continually represent Chapmanian antimaterialism as "a golden dream" (Johnson, *Nova Britannia*, 11) that, like Caliban's, inevitably collapses into the grossest materialism. Again and again in the famous diatribes of Captain John Smith, as we have seen, "mere verbalists" with their airy talk of "fantastical gold" only smother the colony in "dirt" (*Works* 1:218–20). For Smith, in fact, the settlers become "distracted" (264)—torn from the proper business of plantation, torn by a dualist love of dreams and therefore unwittingly of dirt, and finally, even driven mad. Recounting the various causes of the massive death rate in Jamestown from 1607 to 1608 (and eerily foreshadowing some of *The Tempest*'s most famous lines), Smith concludes,

> But the worst mischief was, our gilded refiners with their golden promises, made all men their slaves in hope of recompense; there was no talk, no hope, no work, but dig gold, wash gold, load gold, such a bruit of gold, as one mad fellow desired to be buried in the sands, lest they should by their art make gold of his bones. (218)

Taking seriously the idea of an American background to *The Tempest*, Gillies notes the temperate strain in Virginian propaganda, and decides that "the Shakespearean motifs of temperance and fruitfulness [in *The Tempest*] derive from standard *topoi* in the discourse of Virginia" ("Shakespeare's Virginian Masque," 677);[19] yet Gillies concludes that Shakespeare's purpose in such borrowing is to construct "a conscious parody of the discursive portrait of Virginia" (683). According to Gillies, the play demonstrates how the temperate version of Virginia is just as wishful as its supposed opposite, just as much "a landscape of the mind"; one need only turn in the play to "a physical landscape of unimaginable strangeness and mystery—the landscape of Caliban," in order to recognize that, for Shakespeare, America remains "unassimilable" (702).[20] But it is Gillies's vision of radical or other-worldly difference in the play that seems wishful: his claim that Caliban "resists the attempt of the European mind to mythologize and control" (702) sits uneasily, for instance, with Caliban's closing declaration that he will "be wise hereafter, / And seek for grace" (5.1.295–96). Stronger evidence for Gillies's view (though he does not cite it) is that the Europeans do indeed fail to assimilate the otherworldly island, and simply leave it; yet even here Shakespeare's position can seem equivocal, for in the Gates analogue to the play, to leave an island paradise means finally to get down to the real business of colonization and settle Virginia.[21]

A reader like Gillies, intent on portraying Shakespeare as anti-imperialist, might counter that Shakespeare pointedly rewrites Gates's story, reversing the colonial voyage into a journey home; but then some temperately imperialist contemporaries of Shakespeare thought that all colonial ventures should be understood as homeward bound. In *An Encouragement to Colonies* (1624), for instance, Sir William Alexander ascribes Virginia's troubles to the greed of its "masters," who "have no care but how the best benefit may presently be drawn back from thence" because most "are strangers to the estate of that bounds, and intending to settle none of their Race there" (29–30). From this perspective the homebodies who Spenser thinks stand in the way of imperial expansion come to seem the perfect means of that expansion: for effective *coloni* Alexander recommends his own people, the Scottish, "naturally loving to make use of their own ground, and not trusting to traffic" (38). A colonialist interpretation of Prospero's homesickness becomes still more plausible when one considers the particular homes to which he and Alonso return, since, as many in *The Tempest*'s audience would have known only too well, neither Prospero nor Alonso really has a home to return to: from the early sixteenth century, *King of Naples* and *Duke of Milan* had been titles of the Spanish king.[22] And the road to these acquisitions, many assumed, had been paved by American gold: "With this great treasure did not the Emperor Charles get from the french king the kingdom of Naples, the dukedom of Milan, and all other his dominions in Italy, Lombardy, Piedmont, and Savoy?"[23] I have shown how, since at least Marian times, the English could fear Spain's American possessions not only as the major source of Spain's power—"his springs of gold, . . . that torrent which carried his subduing armies everywhere" (Greville, *Dedication*, 66)— but as the direst instance of the atrocities wrought by that power even on fellow Christians: Matthew Sutcliffe (1604) observes that "the Spanish government is very rigorous in *Spain*: but in *Flanders*, *Milan*, *Naples* and the *Indias* the same is most tyrannical and intolerable" (*Answer*, 81); "Consider what he hath done in the kingdom of *Naples* and in the *Indies*," warns William Lightfote (1587), "and trust him accordingly" (*Complaint*, G2v–3r).[24] "Temperate" colonial literature like that of Lescarbot and Alexander may denounce the love of American gold as preventing actual settlement, yet most colonial advocates also insisted that the only way to escape the calamity that had befallen nations like Naples and Milan was to intercept Spain's treasure fleets, or better, to wrest the Indies from Spain altogether; take America's gold away from the King of Spain, says Hakluyt (1584), and "all his Territories in Europe out of Spain [will] slide from him, and the Moors enter into Spain itself."²⁵ This larger purpose, not just the recognition of greed as an inevitable source of colonial backing, fostered in Virginia's apologists a curious ambivalence: on the one hand, a scorn for treasure seemed the only way to set the colony on its feet; on the other, the colony needed to be settled largely as a means to treasure.²⁶

In *The Tempest*, worries about England's security figure in more than references to a now-Spanish Italy. Prospero's tragedy results, after all, from his blindness to the treason and invasion that, in England's case, American gold seemed to make more likely. And his banishment to an island nowhere only literalizes his original insularism in Milan. As the play begins, Prospero now describes such insularism as dualistically or distractedly equivalent to its opposite, as a naive "confidence" in boundaries that was "sans bound" (1.2.97). By the same token, we learn that Prospero's newly literal isolation has not prevented a certain form of expansionism—Ariel's flight to Bermuda²⁷—and Prospero distracts Alonso to the island in order to represent even Alonso's imperialism as insularist too. Like the body in the spirit's illusion of detachment, the foreign to Alonso is radically different, and thus counts as either enslaved and paying "tribute" (1.2.124), or usurping; having married his "fair" (2.1.71) daughter Claribel to the black king of Tunis and then been shipwrecked on the voyage home from that marriage, Alonso laments the ruinous power that Tunis has exerted over him:

> Would I had never
> Married my daughter there! for coming thence,
> My son is lost and (in my rate) she too,
> Who is so far from Italy removed
> I ne'er again shall see her.
>
> (2.1.108–12)

Eventually, Prospero helps Alonso think of the foreign as not so drastically "removed," as neither wholly separable nor wholly inseparable from him, when he arranges for the otherworldly island to recover Alonso's son and discover a new daughter for him; yet how is the English audience supposed to "assimilate" this lesson, as Gillies might say, to think of home and away antidualistically? The answer seems to lie in *The Tempest*'s treatment of the New World, which, as I have said, the play repeatedly invokes only by allusion or, more precisely, by negation: in turning Gates's escape around, for instance, and pointing it toward homes that no one mentions have been expropriated by American gold; in insisting that Prospero's island is *not* Bermuda; in Miranda's famously mistaken identification of the Old World as the New. Shakespeare, it seems, wants to recommend American colonies as essential to England's well-being, and essential precisely because of the dangerous treasure those colonies may secure, but he must "remove" such motives and even America itself from direct consideration in order to promote the temperate homebodiedness without which, he believes, a colony cannot last.

Skillful at making travelers miserable, Prospero repeatedly suggests this homely moral, yet his magic leaves the positive lessons of colonial temperance only half-sketched. Ferdinand may find himself become a disgracefully laboring aristocrat after Smith's own heart, but the "baseness" (3.1.2, 12) of the Calibanic task he undertakes—to "remove / Some thousands of these logs, and pile them up" (3.1.9–10)—only inchoately approaches the husbandry Virginia requires (Frank Kermode highlights the determined absurdity of Ferdinand's log-bearing when he tells us that, in the episode's folk-tale analogue, the prince's task was "to chop down the wood as a preparation for the second task, which was to plough the ground," *The Tempest*, lxiii). Likewise, Prospero's masque begins an argument against Ferdinand's intemperate vision of the island as "paradise" by presenting "certain reapers, properly habited"—the only image of laborers, incidentally, in a Jacobean masque—and yet these *coloni* finally undo the georgic theme they raise when they "heavily vanish" (4.1.s.d). The essential airiness of Prospero's magic seems to stand in the way of his worldly aims.

In fact, Prospero's exhortations to temperance can succeed only when, as he himself repeatedly stresses, his idealist magic appears at the same time triumphant and defeated, when, for instance, his "soul" or "fine spirit" Ariel only "prompts" the chaste, yet embodied and rebellious, love of Ferdinand and Miranda. Sighting Ferdinand, the island-educated Miranda at first despairs that the "brave form" she sees is but "a spirit," "for nothing natural / I ever saw so noble" (1.2.412, 419–20), and Prospero exaggerates his fastidious distaste for material things in part to whet her appetite: "it eats and sleeps and hath such senses / As we have—such" (413–14).[28] Later, his compulsive demands that Ferdinand and Miranda rein in their lust similarly educe as much the carnality as the continence of a Ferdinand anxiously awaiting his wedding night, and it is Ferdinand's expression of both restraint and desire that seems to justify the georgic blessing of Ceres on the couple in the masque to come. In sum, the "distractions" (3.3.90) that Prospero has just inflicted on his enemies now find their temperate resolution in the "contract" (4.1.19) Prospero has helped arrange both within and between Miranda and Ferdinand, a contract made possible by his magic's having first "given" (3) his daughter away.

However, Prospero's warning that Ferdinand restrain his desire until "all sanctimonious ceremonies may / With full and holy rite be minist'red" (4.1.16–17) demonstrates Prospero's new insistence, arising with his new indulgence toward the flesh, that spirit no longer be a private matter. The home that Ferdinand and Miranda will forge out of previously antagonistic dominions depends not only on their combined will that it be a home but on the blessing of fathers, subjects, and, Prospero insists, the church that is missing from his island of ideal power. For, the play implies, without the church and the publication of spirit it both betokens and enacts, the temperate spirit—on the one hand superior to the distracting lust for riches—could not on the other hand extend itself to a material home beyond the bodies of the lovers. William Strachey (1610) boasts of various "Offices, and Rites of our Christian Profession" performed in Bermuda, what his editor Purchas (1625) will later call "the most holy civil and most natural possession taken of the Bermudas by exercise of Sacraments[:] Marriage, Child-birth, &c." (Strachey, "True Reportory," 38); while the Bermuda castaways who finally reach Virginia quickly refurbish the "ruined and unfrequented" chapel of their ailing colony and therefore also the ceremony on which their notion of civic spirit seems to depend:

> Every Sunday, when the Lord Governor, and Captain General goeth to Church, he is accompanied with all the Councilors, Captains, other Officers, and all the Gentlemen, and with a Guard of Halberdiers in his Lordship's Livery, fair red cloaks, to the number of fifty, both on each side, and behind him: and being in Church, his Lordship hath his seat in the Quire, in a green Velvet Chair, with a Cloth, with a Velvet Cushion spread on a table before him, on which he kneeleth, and on each side sit the Council, Captains, and Officers, each in their place, and when he returneth home again, he is waited on to his house in the same manner. (56–57)

Yet, since Shakespeare recognizes the need for a church only in the context of a marriage, and insists, moreover, that Prospero must arrange the love between Ferdinand and Miranda—not promise the construction of a chapel—before the distracted Italians can return home, it would seem that he envisions marriage as the fundamental component of a homely colonialism. A decade after *The Tempest* was first performed, the Virginia Company (1621) itself declared that "the Plantation can never flourish till families be planted, and the respect of wives and Children fix the people on the Soil" (Kingsbury, *Records* 3:493). But the different nationalities of Ferdinand and Miranda, along with Ferdinand's impression that Miranda is native to the island, suggest that Shakespeare imagines the English requiring even more drastic measures to "fix" themselves in America. Right from the start of Mexican colonial history, the Spanish king himself had encouraged alliances between colonists and colonized; and, while concubinage remained the rule in Spanish America, intermarriages did often occur.[29] In fact, as Anthony Pagden notes, "marriage into the Indian 'nobility' was at first seen to constitute a social advancement for some of the socially lower—and also for some of the not so low— members of Cortés's and Pizarro's armies" ("Identity," 67). Insofar as the Virginia Company had an official position on intermarriage, however, that position seems to have been unfavorable (as for fornication with Indians, it was, at least on paper, severely punished).[30] Finding the biblical source for the Virginian venture in God's commandment that Abraham leave his country, the preacher William Symonds (1609) admonishes the Virginian colonists that, like Abraham, they must "keep them to themselves. They may not marry nor give in marriage to the heathen, that are uncircumcised. . . . The breaking of this rule, may break the neck of all good success of this voyage" (*Virginia*, 35). A later and more temperate voice such as Sir William Alexander's, recommending "lawful alliances" between the English and the Indians as the surest way to colonial peace—"By admitting equality [they] remove contempt, and give a promiscuous off-spring, extinguishing the distinction of persons"—nevertheless cannot help imagining marriages even to converted savages as only "in some sort tolerable."[31] In fact, the famous marriage of John Rolfe to the Indian with whom Smith trifled, Pocahontas, represents the one "formal" alliance "recorded . . . during this period."[32] And Rolfe felt compelled beforehand to write an apology for the act, portraying himself less like a Ferdinand renouncing all other desires than like a Claribel—the one European in the play who actually marries outside her race—caught "between loathness and obedience" (*Tempest* 2.1.131): by Rolfe's account, he has decided to marry a woman "whose education hath been rude, her manners barbarous, her generation accursed," only for the sake of the colony and of Pocahontas's "unregenerate" soul (Hamor, *True Discourse*, 64, 67).

If English prejudice and its reflection in Claribel's lamented fate make it seem unlikely, then, that Shakespeare recommends literal intermarriage as a way to settle Jamestown, the play that stresses the importance of "sanctimonious ceremonies" might still seem to have a figurative mixture in mind. Imagined by both Alexander and Rolfe as the only way to make the prospect of colonially productive miscegenation more palatable, conversion, or the desire for it, suggests English interest in at least a spiritual marriage with the Indians. Elizabethan colonialists like Harriot had always spoken of the need for missionary work in America, but where England's enemy, "the Babylonian Enchantress," could boast of "six, eight, or ten millions, of Romish proselytes" in the New World (*True Declaration*, 13), the Elizabethans had trouble pointing to any savage converts of their own.[33] In part to end this embarrassment, to silence the papists' charge that "God would not suffer our schismatical and heretical Religion, to be infused into a new converted Region" (*True Declaration*, 66), the Virginia Company declared evangelism its highest priority: in the company's first charter

(1606), for example, the sole motive that James gives for establish-
ing the company is the "propagating of Christian religion" (Barbour, *Jamestown Voyages* 1:25). Gates indeed set sail during what
John Parker has called "the great crusade of 1609–10" ("Religion,"
270), when "to a degree never again equalled in the history of British overseas expansion the appeal [to colonize] was most forcefully
made by preachers, with a message essentially religious" (245).
Yet, Parker adds, "nothing in the 1609 charter [of the Virginia
Company], or in the church records that have been examined,
points to any administrative structure designed to support a major
missionary effort. . . . The Company's third charter, dated 12
March 1612, is elaborate in its plans for the civil government of the
colony, but utterly silent about religion in Virginia" (269–70). It
appears, in fact, that Jamestown had as much trouble importing
preachers as ploughmen: "Even in 1620 the colony had only five
clergymen" (268–69). What prevented the grand vision of conversion from materializing? The Spanish ambassador to London simply considers the godly aims of the Virginia Company no more
than a ruse enabling it to rake in "a good sum of money" (quoted
in Parker, "Religion," 251). Equally cynical, the Jesuit John Floyd
(1612) blames England's worldly Protestant preachers, who fear
"the miseries which the enterprise of converting Savages doth
bring with it, the wanting your native soil, friends and Gossips
wherewith now after Sermon you may be merry, the enduring
hunger, cold, nakedness[,] danger of death, and the like, but specially the want of the new Gospel's blessing, a fair wife, too heavy
a lump of flesh to be carried into *Virginia*" (*Overthrow*, 321). According to *The Tempest*, however, it is the carnal entanglements of
the savage that make spiritual contact with him impossible: Caliban's schooling ends up only imperiling his teacher's chastity,
and Prospero will "acknowledge" that "thing of darkness" his
(5.1.275–76) only after he has safely married his daughter to a
white man.[34]

The decisive anxiety in the play over the coupling of "black"
and "white" is hardly a new feature in Shakespeare's drama; one
need only recall the unfortunate loves of Aaron the Moor, Othello
(who in one version of *Othello* compares himself to a "base Indian"), and that Dido of Shakespeare's "anti-*Aeneid*," Cleopatra,
"tawny" and "black."[35] But Shakespeare does not always repre-

sent intermarriage as either so tragic or so literally interracial. For instance, Claudio in *Much Ado About Nothing* must wed at least the imagination of a black bride before he may have his white one: on his way to marry a woman he thinks he has never met, but who is actually the beloved he believes his lack of faith has helped to kill, Claudio pledges, "I'll hold my mind were she an Ethiope" (5.4.38). As an African, a woman betrayed, and yet also a "white Moor,"[36] Virgil's Dido would neatly fulfill all the conditions of Claudio's corrective wife here; and indeed Shakespeare seems to have perceived the *Aeneid*-like voyage of Gates as an opportunity to clarify his stake in intermarriage both actual and fanciful. One father in the play disastrously looses his daughter to a black African, while the other happily tests a prospective son-in-law by causing him to mistake his daughter for a native who, in Virgil, turned out to be no native at all: "Most sure, the goddess / On whom these airs attend!" (1.2.422–23, cf. *Aeneid* 1.327–28).[37]

Temperance as Prospero understands it begins, I have argued, with a stage-managed confusion of identity that happily distracts one from a more radically dualist notion of distraction: an image of the English audience that watches Italians speaking English, Ferdinand hearing his foreign goddess speak—"My language? heavens!" (429)—is both startled and reassured. In fact, the political alliance Prospero forges out of Ferdinand's sublime confusion has the *Aeneid* both ways: Ferdinand remains true to his Dido, and so loses an imperial interest in "all corners else o' th' earth," but his marriage must wait, as Aeneas waited for Lavinia, until he returns to Italy, where he will gain a new and legitimate empire. For Virgil either option—Dido in Africa or Lavinia in Italy—meant a kind of intermarriage, but Shakespeare, requiring a more familiar new world for his lovers, must treat both homeliness and foreignness more delicately. It is a delicacy familiar from Geoffrey of Monmouth's revision of the *Aeneid* and one that, again, the advocates and colonists of Virginia seem for the most part to have shared. As the sole instance of an Indian's marrying an Englishman, the wedded Pocahontas will retain the status she enjoyed when single—a "very nonpareil" (Smith, *Works* 1:274)—while the "nonpareil" (3.2.100) of Shakespeare's play demonstrates her singularity by transforming proposed marriage between whites into a kind of miscegenation everyone can bless.[38] Through its distracting con-

fusion of colonial dualisms, it seems, *The Tempest* encourages prospective colonists (in fact, "encouragement" implies more positive
formulation than Shakespeare's distracted colonialism allows) to
imagine themselves as the natives they marry—an illusion of con-
tracting with America that can be sustained only by the exclusion
from marriage of less attractive homebodies like Caliban who, in
their "dark" and "base" materiality, render the notions of native
and stranger too intractable.[39]

One can see the practice of this same brand of illusion, the trick
presentation of the European as both native and stranger, in a later
theatrical meditation on colonies, Fletcher and Massinger's *Sea-
Voyage* (acted 1622). Heavily indebted to *The Tempest*, *The Sea-
Voyage* not only engages many of *The Tempest*'s "colonial" topoi—
the Virgilian model, the new island as hellish and heavenly, slavery, cannibalism, a temperate disdain for treasure—but even manages to raise some distinctly American issues, such as human sacrifice, that Shakespeare omits. In fact, *The Sea-Voyage* is far more
explicit about its New World interests than its predecessor was.
The cannibalism in the play is a good case in point, figuring not as
an anagram of a character's name but as a real, if ultimately comical, threat:

MASTER.   They would have eaten her.
TIBALT.   Oh, damn'd villains!—
           Speak; is it true?
SURGEON.   I confess an appetite.

(3.1)

More important, every character in the play has participated in either a colony or a piratical expedition, and they like to speak of
heading "for happy places and most fertile islands" (3.1), "to seek
new fortunes in an unknown world" (5.4). Yet Fletcher and Massinger never introduce a single savage, nor even a character resembling one, like Caliban. Bolder than Shakespeare, they base
their plot on an unmistakably American atrocity, a people displaced by gold-hungry Europeans, but these uprooted natives are
actually a group of European colonists, "the industrious Portu-
gals," who had been living peacefully on "their plantations in the
Happy Islands" (5.2). As with Shakespeare, but now more radically, a dramatization in a vaguely New World setting of the evils

of usurpation and the rewards of temperance requires not the surrender of colonial ambitions but the exclusion of natives—or rather their incorporation, their cannibalization by the colonist distracted into usurper and usurped, newcomer and native.[40] Only when masquers such as Chapman exclude the temperate colonist himself can the Indian, now the superstitious yet convertible witness to England's otherworldly power, be licensed to appear.[41]

It is this banishment of the Indian from the temperate or antidualist conception of Virginia that perhaps most clearly betrays the dualism that even the homely English colonialist has trouble transcending, for both the otherworldly and the temperate imperialist ultimately insist on keeping their Englishness virginal, unmixed. In the English dream of colonial power—Brutus's old dream of an empty promised land—such exclusivity works like magic; but in moments of nightmare the magic is wielded Prospero-like by the "base Indian" whose home the English would call their own:

> Sir Thomas DALE making more invasions & excursions upon the Savages had many conflicts with them and one thing amongst the rest was very remarkable The which may be supposed to have been occasioned by the Savages' Sorceries and Charms for Sir Thomas DALE with Some of the better sort sitting in An Indian's house A fantasy possessed them that they imagined the Savages were set upon them each man Taking one another for an Indian And so did fall pell mell one upon An other beating one another down and breaking one of Another's heads, that Much mischief might have been done but that it pleased god the fantasy was taken away whereby they had been deluded and every man understood his error.[42]

Epilogue:
The Poem as Heterocosm

In the fairyland of fancy, genius may wander wild; there it
has a creative power, and may reign arbitrarily over its own
empire of chimeras.

> —Edward Young, *Conjectures on*
> *Original Composition* (1759)

It is an irony almost too appropriate to this study that the first
English text to imagine the Muse as steering an actual English poet
toward the New World should appear many years after Spenser's
death and in a poem that repudiates fairies. Abraham Cowley's
"To Sir William Davenant Upon his First Two Books of *Gondibert*,
Finished Before his Voyage to America" (1651) begins by attacking
earlier epic poetry while likening Davenant's better efforts to a
successful act of "plant[ing]"—that is, of colonization:

> Methinks *Heroic Poesy* till now
> Like some fantastic *Fairy-land* did show,
> *Gods, Devils, Nymphs, Witches* and *Giants'* race,
> And all but *Man*, in *Man's chief Work* had place.
> Thou like some worthy *Knight*, with sacred Arms
> Dost drive the *Monsters* thence, and end the *Charms*:
> In stead of those, dost *Men* and *Manners* plant,
> The things which that rich *Soil* did chiefly want.
>
> (1–8)

The depreciation of past heroic poetry as "some fantastic fairyland" unmistakably filters Cowley's generic vision of epic through
one medium in particular—*The Faerie Queene*; if Davenant is a good
"planter," Spenser is clearly a bad one. As the poem proceeds, this
talk of colonizing ability becomes literal. Davenant sails to America
in the service of Charles I's widow Henrietta Maria, and Cowley

hopes that the pragmatic imagination capable of putting heroic poetry on its feet can do the same for the New World:

> Sure 'twas this noble boldness of the *Muse*
> Did thy desire to seek new *Worlds* infuse,
> And ne'r did Heaven so much a *Voyage* bless,
> If thou canst *Plant* but *there* with like success.
> (37–40)[1]

Now the implication is that Spenser's Fairyland either failed to encourage colonization or revealed as mere fantasies those colonial ventures it supported.

A later commendatory poem by Nahum Tate, "To Mr. J. Ovington, On His Voyage to Suratt" (1696), tacitly extends the range of Cowley's attack from fairy epic to what Dryden (1691) had recently called "the fairy way of writing"[2] generally:

> Hard is our Task to Read with fruitless Pain,
> The Dreams of ev'ry Cloister'd Writer's Brain:
> Who yet presume that Truth's firm Paths they tread,
> When all the while through wild *Utopia*'s led,
> With Fairy-Feasts, instead of Science fed.
> As dreaming Wizards Midnight Journeys take,
> And weary with imagin'd Labor wake,
> So vain is *Speculation*'s fancy'd Flight:
> But search of Nature gives sincere Delight.
> (1–9)

For Tate, a literature of utopias, fairies, and wizards seems so far from "search of Nature" that he can use it to stigmatize the "dreams" of writers who have never traveled.

In one respect, this animus against "fairy" literature is almost as old as the literature itself. In *The Speeches at Prince Henry's Barriers* (1610), for instance, Jonson had advised the prince that, if he intended to quest "beyond the paths, and searches of the sun" in order to win a "world" (ll. 90–91), he must forget

> the deeds
> Of antique knights, to catch their fellows' steeds,
> Or ladies' palfreys rescue from the force
> Of a fell giant, or some score to un-horse.
> These were bold stories of our ARTHUR's age;
> But here are other acts; another *stage*

And *scene* appears; it is not since as then:
No giants, dwarfs, or monsters here, but men.
              (167–74)[3]

Yet where Jonson opposes only the extravagant form of chivalry that did, it seems, encourage Henry to develop the "many strange and vast conceits and projects" reportedly discovered among his papers after his death,[4] Tate simply considers fairy writing unreal. In his *Preface to Gondibert* (1650), Davenant himself wishes that Spenser had chosen "matter of a more natural, and therefore of a more useful kind"; so little relation to the actual world does *The Faerie Queene* seem to have for Davenant that he too considers it like "a continuance of extraordinary Dreams; such as excellent Poets, and Painters, by being overstudious may have in the beginning of Fevers" (7).[5]

This reduction of fairy writing to hallucination, something not just politically or spiritually but now also epistemologically unsound, has traditionally been ascribed to the rise of empiricism: in the terms of Cowley's later ode "To the Royal Society" (1667), philosophy, it is said, came to reject "Pageants of the Brain" (stanza 2) in favor of actual "things" (4).[6] But when one considers that the philosopher whom Cowley praises for having led England from unworldly "Errors" (4)—Bacon—was himself a utopian, the proclaimed antipathy of the empiricists to poetical chimeras begins to look somewhat misleading. In fact, Bacon's utopia, his *New Atlantis* (1626), conspicuously adopts topoi from the otherworldly tradition that Bacon supposedly helped to discredit: like aparted England, the utopic Bensalem is an island "beyond both the old world and the new" (*Works* 3:134), which the narrator of the *New Atlantis* likens to "a land of angels" (136). In some ways, moreover, the *New Atlantis* appears even less materialist than *Utopia*. Pious Christians whose conversion was begun by the miraculous appearance of "a great pillar of light" (137), the Bensalemites are consequently interested in possessing only the knowledge of other countries: "Thus you see we maintain a trade, not for gold, silver, or jewels; nor for silks; nor for spices; nor any other commodity of matter; but only for God's first creature, which was *Light*" (146–47). Elsewhere in his works, Bacon portrays himself as the explorer of a specifically "intellectual" New World (see figure 10);[7] in

New Atlantis he depicts ancient Mexico and Peru as the first imperialists, annihilated for their acquisitiveness by "Divine Revenge"
(142), apparently so that he can discredit a potentially materialist
or New World construction of otherworldliness and associate antimaterialism with an overtly fictional "new" Atlantis instead.

In other ways, of course, the Bensalemites do look more materialist than the Utopians, since they prize the precious metals and
fine linens that the Utopians so pointedly scorn. But like Chapman, Bacon in *New Atlantis* figures gold as a spiritual matter, bearing the color of the sun (155), and he seems to understand the rich
rewards that his utopian inventors receive (166) as providing the
necessary substantiation and prestige to a science that his readers
would otherwise disdain as trifling. At the start of the volume in
which *New Atlantis* first appeared, Bacon's editor, William Rawley,
notes how Bacon worried "that men (no doubt) will think many of
the experiments contained in this collection to be but vulgar and
trivial, mean and sordid, curious and fruitless" (*Works* 2:335); according to Rawley, Bacon defended himself by asking "whether
he were not a strange man, that should think that light hath no
use, because it hath no matter" (336). Even the down-to-earth
Cowley feels he must rebut the critics who think empiricism too
unworldly:

> The things which these proud men despise, and call
>   Impertinent, and vain, and small,
> Those smallest things of Nature let me know,
>   Rather than all their greatest Actions do.
>   ("Royal Society" stanza 8)

The most striking indication of a continuity between otherworldliness and the empiricism that seems to defeat it, however, is the
subversion of utopic fancies even in *New Atlantis* itself, a subversion that results precisely from Bacon's antimaterialism. By forbid-
ding commerce with other nations and keeping its existence secret, Bensalem has become other-worldly and thus otherworldly,
the most "chaste" of nations, "the virgin of the world" (Bacon,
Works 3:152). Yet the dedication to "light" that this apartness produces has by the end of the story led a leading Bensalemite to regret his nation's separateness and to violate its rules of secrecy:
after his relation of Bensalem's scientific wonders, he tells the nar-

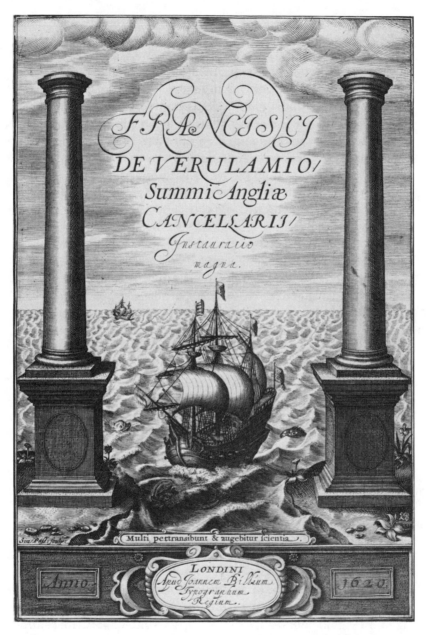

Figure 10.   Frontispiece to *Instauratio Magna (The Great Instauration)*, by Francis Bacon, London, 1620. Bacon's ship of knowledge sets out past the Pillars of Hercules, or beyond the known world. (By permission of the Houghton Library, Harvard University.)

rator that "I give thee leave to publish it for the good of other nations; for we here are in God's bosom, a land unknown" (166).

If Bacon's quest to enlarge "the bounds of Human Empire" (156) in part proceeds, then, from the same utopic tradition that produces fairy writing, that tradition also came increasingly under fire in the seventeenth century from other forces beside Baconian empiricism. Taking for granted the self-consuming tendency in utopic imperialism as I have so far outlined it, and narrowly focusing on the post-Jacobean reputation of *Utopia*, *The Faerie Queene*, and *The Tempest*, this epilogue will briefly consider what later religious and political changes caused these otherworldly texts to appear so radically unworldly, and then what new theoretical justifications for the literature developed as a result. Of course, in the manner of the fairy writers themselves, the later opponents of Fairyland may, to a certain extent, often simply extend the tradition when they signal its apparent failure: Cowley, after all, depicts the vanquisher of Spenser as a Spenserian knight, who "with sacred Arms / Dost drive the *Monsters* thence, and end the Charms"; while the character in Jonson's *Barriers* who advises Henry to reject romantic chivalry is none other than Merlin. In fact, as I will show, the same critics who denounce fairy writing for lacking "any foundation in truth"[8] will often elsewhere extol it as poetry's sublimest achievement—though only when the originally imperialist drift of More, Spenser, and Shakespeare has been not just reformed but forgotten.

I

An opening assertion in the anonymous *Golden Coast, or A Description of Guinney* (1665) highlights what are perhaps the two primary factors in the decline of otherworldliness as an approved national trait. The author celebrates the English for "being not now as of old, *divisi ab orbe Britanni, separatists* from the *Universe*, but commanding the commerce of all Nations; our *Negotiation* being not limited in a narrower compass than the whole Earth, and our dealing knowing no bounds but those of the world" (1–2). The central claim about English mobility recalls Hakluyt, who in his epistle dedicatory to *The Principall Navigations* (1589) had declared that "in this most famous and peerless government of her most excellent

Majesty, her subjects through the special assistance, and blessing of God, in searching the most opposite corners and quarters of the world, and to speak plainly, in compassing the vast globe of the earth more than once, have excelled all the nations and people of the earth" (Taylor, *Original Writings* 2:399). Yet Hakluyt did not feel as the *Golden Coast*'s author clearly does that the boundlessness of English voyaging and the apartness of England's island were mutually exclusive ideals; in fact, the *Golden Coast*'s stigmatization of separateness as separatism would probably never have occurred to him.

Only from the vantage point of the Restoration, that is, would a joke about utopian fanaticism seem pertinent to England generally. And yet the analogy between England and the Separatists was already telling before the Civil War. The Jesuit John Floyd devotes the last chapter of his *Overthrow of the Protestants Pulpit-Babels* (1612), an attack in particular on the Anglican minister William Crashaw, to proving "the impiety of the Protestant revolt from the Church of *Rome*, by the same four arguments wherewith *M. Crashaw* urgeth the *Brownists* for their Schismatical separation from the Church of *England*" (306–28). This identification of all Protestants as separatists becomes still more pointed in relation to a Protestant England priding itself on its otherworldliness. Defining his "true visible Church" as "a company of faithful people, by the word of God called out & separated from the world & the false ways thereof, gathered and joined together in fellowship of the Gospel, by a voluntary profession of the faith & obedience of Christ" (*Answer*, 196),[9] the separatist leader Francis Johnson (1600) not only echoes standard celebrations of Elizabethan England but improves upon them by stipulating that one's citizenship in the separatist Elysium is "voluntary" rather than simply an accident of birth. Even earlier in Elizabeth's reign, Protestant extremists may have begun, by association, to make a utopic view of England less attractive: Richard Griff or Griffin (c. 1590), for instance, criticizes "our disciplinaries, being the best name I can give them," who, "as though they lived in Plato's Commonwealth or Sir Thomas More's Utopia," have been emboldened "to desire and imagine a fantastical perfection."[10] By the 1640s, the growing strength of both a Puritan opposition and an overt millenarianism appeared to their enemies only to confirm such a charge.[11] Charles

I himself called his Puritan enemies Utopian;[12] and after Cromwell's death the characterization became a commonplace. The title
page of William Prynne's *Brief Necessary Vindication* (1659), for instance, demands "the restitution of our *Hereditary King and Kingly
Government*, not a *Utopian Republic*";[13] while Samuel Butler (1680)
later describes "a Republican" as "a civil Fanatic, an *Utopian* Sen-
ator" (*Characters*, 24; quoted in Gibson, *Bibliography*, 411), whose
fellows "were all Free-born in *Fairy-Land*, but changed in the Cra-
dle; and so being not Natives here, the Air of the Government
does not agree with them" (26).[14]

To some conservatives from Elizabeth's time on, the perfect way
to rid England of these disreputable utopians was to send them to
the lesser otherworld of America. As the anonymous "Verses on
the Puritan Settlement in America" (c. 1631) puts it,

> Let all the parisidean [paradisean] sect
> I mean the Counterfeit elect
> All Zealous bankrupts punks devouts
> Suspendent preachers Rabble Rout
> Let them sell all out of hand
> Prepare to go for new England
> To build new babel strong and sure
> Now called a Church unspotted pure.
>
> (37)[15]

Thomas Morton's *New English Canaan* (1637) reports how, when
finally ensconced in their paradisiacal new world, separatists do
indeed only realize their penchant for absurdity. In one chapter,
for instance, entitled "How the 9. worthies put mine Host of Ma-
re-Mount into the enchanted Castle at Plymouth, and terrified him
with the Monster Briareus" (288), Morton imagines the separatists
seeing themselves not just as romance heroes generally but as
Spenserian ones in particular: a tailor-preacher promises to sew his
congregation the garment-armor of a Christian man, which will
enable the Puritans "(like saint George) to terrify the great Dragon
error, and defend truth which error with her wide chaps, would
devour" (327–28).[16] Yet, while this risible new fairy England helps
to register by contrast the solidity of the old (and to explain why
the Royalists Davenant and Cowley should associate their attack
on fairy poetry with a military action against a Puritan-run colony
in America), it also suggests the degree to which English other-

worldliness and consequently English otherworldly poetry have begun to be undermined.

The Golden Coast is, however, more concerned with a positive reason for Restoration England's rejecting separateness as a national ideal: the English no longer simply "search" or "compass" the world, as Hakluyt would have it, but "command" a world trade. Thanks in large part to the success of a trifling expansionism in which commodities previously dismissed as useless had begun to turn huge profits, England's interests in the later seventeenth century could no longer be limited to its little island. The difference that this achieved expansionism made both to England and to English poetry can perhaps best be glimpsed in a later poem celebrating a state of affairs that is otherwise as Elizabethan as possible—peace established by a virgin queen. Alexander Pope published his *Windsor Forest* (1713) in support of the Treaty of Utrecht, which ended the War of the Spanish Succession and, according to modern historians, secured England's power, even hegemony, in the Atlantic. At the time, however, the Whigs believed that Queen Anne, the treaty's guiding spirit, had only ruined England's chance for complete victory. And their opinion of Tory backwardness seems confirmed by the start of Pope's poem (written, Pope claims, more than a decade before the treaty), which appears to celebrate England's renewed insularity under Anne. First, the poem deplores the fact that what Pope tellingly labels the "green Retreats" (1) of Windsor Forest had once been devastated by William the Conqueror—a figure uncannily revived, the poem implies, in the person of the previous monarch, the foreign and Whiggish King William III; and second, Pope tells the sad story of the virgin huntress Lodona, a former votary of Diana and Cynthia, who, "eager of the Chase" (181), leaves the "verdant Limits" (182) of Windsor Forest, is then herself chased by Pan, and escapes only by having Cynthia transform her into the river that flows back into the forest—a fable clearly representing both the threat of reversal in an "ever-increasing foreign war" and Anne's response to that threat.[17] Yet, if Pope imagines Anne countering the return of William the Conqueror, ending military excursions, and finally healing the divisions of civil war by resurrecting in herself the virgin protectress Elizabeth, he also sees her as harking back even further than William, and further afield.[18] For by formal allusions to Virgil, particularly at the end of his poem,[19] Pope represents his own effort as georgic, and therefore marks his confidence that the peace Anne has established will prove Augustan, imperial.

The apparent contradiction here—Pope's dedication to both an insular and an imperial ideal—is made salient in the poem by the fact that his dual allegiance seems to have rendered a Virgilian georgic thematically untenable. The pastoral bias of Pope's virginal insularism is signaled in minor ways early on, for instance by an epigraph from Virgil's *Eclogues* and a comparison of the forest to Arcadia (159); or more importantly, by the celebration of Windsor itself, which had already been the subject of Pope's *Pastorals* (1709).[20] Yet the inescapable token of Pope's distance from Virgil's *Georgics* appears at the end of the poem, the "imperial" section, when Pope celebrates the peacetime activity not of homely agriculture but of expansive commerce.[21] Why, then, does Pope even bother to associate a posttreaty England with georgics? Since commerce has at best a kind of metaphoric appropriateness to a literary form that mediates between pastoral and epic, one might say that Pope's praise of commerce and his formal allusions to Virgil identify his interest in georgics *as* formal. That is, by ignoring the agricultural basis of the georgic, emptying the literary form of its definitive thematic property, Pope seem to think he maximizes its formal property as the site of commerce between pastoral and epic, and therefore honors what is, to his mind, the real beauty of Anne's peace: its refusal to choose between epic and pastoral, between understanding England as either an empire or a pleasance.

The poem's celebration of the forest proper, "Where Order in Variety we see, / And where, tho' all things differ, all agree" (15–16), nicely figures Pope's confidence that such apparently contrary views of England can be reconciled. Entranced as Redcross and Una might be by Windsor's groves, which "like verdant Isles the sable Waste adorn" (28), Pope appears at first to abjure travel: "Let *India* boast her Plants, nor envy we / The weeping Amber or the balmy Tree" (29–30). Yet this threat of insular complacence proves illusory—we should not envy the Indies only "while by our Oaks the precious Loads are born, / And Realms commanded which those Trees adorn" (31–32). So fluidly does the sheltering forest metamorphose into an intimidating navy that the passage elides not only the differences between the two but also the georgic labor needed to convert one into the other;[22] if the forest "isles" will not prevent expansion, neither will expansion reciprocally exhaust them as England's conqueror once had, by laying the forest "waste" (44, 49, 80). This easy mobility between the woods within England and the world beyond it, between ease and "command," is still more strikingly associated with the issue of English military power in a later passage that marks the transition from a wood-land hunt to a foreign conquest by way of the *Georgics'* most fa-mous pastoral line (*Georgics* 4.176; *Eclogues* 1.23):

> Thus (if small Things we may with great compare)
> When *Albion* sends her eager Sons to War,
> Some thoughtless Town, with Ease and Plenty blest,
> Near, and more near, the closing Lines invest;
> Sudden they seize th'amaz'd, defenseless Prize,
> And high in Air *Britannia's* Standard flies.
>
> > (*Windsor Forest*, 105–10)

Controlled by the pastoral-georgic simile, the reversal here—lei-surely English hunters (including a spaniel) become the conquer-ors of a leisurely foreign town—is presented as anything but a re-versal; indeed, just as the simile's relegation of war to a metaphor for hunting tempers the Lodona-like eagerness of the soldiers it pictures, so their victory seems to depend on the sort of easy aban-donment of "Ease" that the simile enacts. By the Treaty of Utrecht, the passage suggests, Anne has replaced mere insularism and mere imperialism with a concept of England far more adaptive and therefore far more secure.

Spenser too had hoped to escape the dualism of island and em-pire, as he labored to convert English insularity into a trifling index of a more expansive potentiality; but for Pope, the Treaty of Utrecht will make England's expansion so effortless that it will even proceed without war: near the end of the poem, the Thames arises to predict that, after the treaty, "the shady Empire shall re-tain no Trace / Of War or Blood, but in the Sylvan Chase" (371–72). "The shady empire": with a single phrase, oxymoronically con-joining pastoral and epic, Pope rejects the island imperialism of both Elizabethan complacence and Spenserian disparity in favor of an imperial *concordia discors*.[23] Yet the phrase also indicates the degree to which, in abandoning Spenser, Pope, like Cowley, proves himself Spenser's inheritor: for the English island itself has been removed from Pope's equation, made positively "waste," like the georgic become a merely formal entity mediating the commerce between the shade of Windsor Forest and the empire that the forest commands. Where Spenser's imperialist celebration of his virgin queen proved unable to dissociate an otherworldly and therefore potentially mobile Englishness from the material separateness of England's otherworldly island, Pope has insularism "retreat" from the island itself to a still more trifling locale, the internal "isles" of Windsor, which "Monarch" and "Muse" (2) idealize into an internalized virginity preserving Englishness from the waste threatened by material ties both at home (complacence) and abroad (adulteration). It is no accident that Pope assigns the perception of England's new fluidity to a local deity who materializes England's island only to distinguish it from its earth—again, the Thames, whose "alternate Tides" (334) allow "whole Nations" both to "enter" (399) England and, presumably, to leave it.[24] Pope's insistence here on alternation is crucial to making sense of him as an anti-Spenserian Spenserian: the English can now internalize their island and therefore transcend it only when they already have somewhere else to go.

Pope wants to maintain, however, that soon the chaste English will no longer have foreign possessions as such, since Anne's treaty will replace conquest with commerce. And this saving substitution, like the reduction of war to hunting, will itself result from commerce, when, by means of the treaty, England will trade its more formal or fluid conception of itself with other nations. Hence the Thames foresees a time when even the least cosmopolitan of peoples, the natives of America's barbarous otherworld, will, in another tempered reversal, learn of England:

> Earth's distant Ends our Glory shall behold,
> And the new World launch forth to seek the Old.
> Then Ships of uncouth Form shall stem the Tide,
> And Feather'd People crowd my wealthy Side,
> And naked Youths and painted Chiefs admire
> Our Speech, our Color, and our strange Attire!
>
> (401–6)

This bravura contraction of the Thames's sights to England (where the Indians, significantly, do not land, but only "crowd" the Thames's "Side") is met by an expansion in the next lines:

> Oh stretch thy Reign, fair *Peace*! from Shore to Shore
> Till Conquest cease, and Slav'ry be no more:
> Till the freed *Indians* in their native Groves
> Reap their own Fruits, and woo their Sable Loves.
>
> (407–10)

But this concluding prayer for a millennial end to all disparity between nations belies the specific conditions of the peace Pope celebrates. Wasserman explains: "Although gaining little ground in the West Indies, England was granted the Asiento, or the lucrative monopoly to conduct the slave trade with the entire West Indies, and such valuable trade concessions that she would largely control the maritime commerce of those regions" (*Subtler Language*, 140); and yet, as if to demonstrate the effectiveness of Pope's casuistry, Wasserman never raises the issue of the Asiento in relation to Pope's peroration on Liberty.[25] Facing the problem, Maynard Mack simply assumes that Pope's moral vision surpassed the provisions of the treaty (*Pope*, 206). But, as we have in part already seen, the end of the poem deals exclusively with "feather'd people," "Peru," and "Mexico" (411–12): that is, with freed *Indians*, whose enslavement dramatically actualizes the constraints of having lived in a world apart. Commerce will indeed liberate them— by replacing them with England's newly acquired African slaves— but if the "sable" color of the Indians visibly marks the fact of this trade,[26] the traded Africans themselves drop from Pope's sight. For, as personifications of "the sable Waste" from which Windsor's "verdant Isles" save the extended nation, the Africans deny English commerce the chaste uncoerciveness that Pope wants to grant it. They show instead that the internalization of English insularity from an island to a state of mind depends on the simultaneous externalization of a foreign people from their own land and to the stigmatized blackness of their bodies; that England's insularity has become a human property only when the English have at the same time come into human property. In short, the suppressed African slaves betray the exclusivity denied by the suppression of England's island, the now expansive disparity between the shady empire and the world whose "trade" it commands.

II

If, then, a combination of religious divisiveness and imperial expansiveness in post-Jacobean England made celebrations of an England "divided from the world" increasingly less compelling, Pope shows us that English investment in the ideal of an otherworld did not for that reason disappear.[27] In fact, many of the writers who now resisted labeling England an otherworld simply found their otherworld elsewhere. Comparing his New World settlement to an Old World devastated by religious wars, a separatist such as William Bradford (c. 1654) could sound positively Elizian:

> From hence, as in a place secure,
> They saw what others did endure,
> By cruel wars, flowing in blood,
> Whilst they in peace and safety stood.
> ("A Word to New
> Plymouth," 33–36)

Even in England it became popular to think that America could take England's otherworldly place: a famous couplet from George Herbert's "The Church Militant" (1633), for instance, warns its readers that "Religion stands on tip-toe in our land, / Ready to pass to the *American* strand" (235–36). Indeed, the very same process that to some Elizabethans proved England's otherworldliness providential—the westward course of empire and spirit—is precisely what makes Herbert worry about the future of English religion. Having explained his own apocalyptic theory that "the course of things around must run; / Till they have ending, where they first begun" (*Motto*, D3v), George Wither (1621) wonders whether the Revelation passage that Walter Brute had applied to England's utmost angle might not instead refer to the new world farther westward:

> What if *America*'s large Tract of ground,
> And all those Isles adjoining, lately found?

(Which we more truly may a *Desert* call,
Than any of the world's more civil Pale.)
What then? if there the Wilderness do lie,
To which the *Woman*, and her *Son* must fly,
To space [scape?] the *Dragon's* fury; and there bide,
Till *Europe's* thankless *Nations* (full of pride,
And all abominations) scourged are,
With barbarism; as their neighbors were?

(D3v–4r)[28]

America was, moreover, not the only place in which to locate the otherworld that could seem no longer to fit England: the seventeenth century saw an increasing interest in theories concerning a land truly *penitus toto divisus orbe*, with no material ties to the earth at all—a world in the moon or the heavens. Thomas Traherne's "Shadows in the Water" (c. 1660s) goes so far as to transfer the language of New World propaganda to outer space:

Within the Regions of the Air,
Compass'd about with Heav'ns fair,
Great Tracts of Land there may be found
Enricht with Fields and fertile Ground;
    Where many num'rous Hosts
    In those far distant Coasts,
For other great and glorious Ends,
Inhabit, my yet unknown Friends.

(49–56)

As the companion poem to "Shadows," "On Leaping over the Moon," demonstrates, such utopic idealizations of other planets could also reflexively sublimate the earth itself. Where an Elizabethan could figure the English island as "out from the world, yet on the ground," Traherne takes the Copernican liberation of Earth from the drossy center to mean that every human occupies the Elizian's paradoxical position: "On heav'nly Ground within the Skies we walk" (51). And finally, though even a sketchy account of Milton's response to both Spenser and the new astronomy would require another chapter, one can note in passing that Galileo's investigations of other planets inspired Milton (1667) to imagine not England or America but the entire globe a "new world" and "happy Isle."[29]

But then these developments had, after all, been anticipated by

The Faerie Queene, which in the proem to book 2 associates Fairyland first with America and then with a world in the moon; one
might therefore expect that the fairy way of writing, though now
lacking "foundation" in England, could still come to seem
grounded in these other otherworlds. Later literary theorists, however, began to prize fairy writing more for its lack of reference than
for any new reference it gains. The same year that Pope was working on *Windsor Forest*, Joseph Addison (1712) starts *Spectator* no.
419 by asserting that

> There is a kind of Writing, wherein the Poet quite loses sight of
> Nature, and entertains his Reader's Imagination with the Characters
> and Actions of such Persons as have many of them no Existence,
> but what he bestows on them. Such are Fairies, Witches, Magicians,
> Demons, and departed Spirits. This Mr. *Dryden* calls *the Fairy way of
> Writing*, which is, indeed, more difficult than any other that de-
> pends on the Poet's Fancy, because he has no Pattern to follow in
> it, and must work altogether out of his own Invention. (*Spectator*
> 3:570)

The unnatural difficulty of fairy writing, already half-endorsed by
Addison's epigraph from Horace—"mentis gratissimus Error"
(*Epistles* 2.2.140), "the most gratifying delusion of my mind"—becomes by the end of Addison's paper a sublime capability: fairy
writing is now said to demonstrate that poetry "has not only the
whole Circle of Nature for its Province, but makes new Worlds of
its own, shows us Persons who are not to be found in Being, and
represents even the Faculties of the Soul, with her several Virtues
and Vices, in a sensible Shape and Character" (*Spectator* 3:573). In
The Mirror and the Lamp, M. H. Abrams labels this doctrine of poetry's otherworldly creativity "the poem as heterocosm," a critical
topos whose English history Abrams charts from Sidney until the
present, though he remains vague about its sources, especially its
native ones (272–85). Yet More's self-deprecating joke that *Utopia*
should hide itself away in its own island shows how directly the
Tudor conflation of England and America as heterocosms helped
to displace trifling poetry into new worlds;[30] and then the subse-
quently weaker and stronger heterocosmic theory that I have outlined—weaker because less pertinent to England politically and
spiritually; stronger because more radically actualized in extrater-
restrial worlds—only accentuated the supernatural elements of an

otherworldly tradition already in place. In fact, so entangled with this tradition was later heterocosmic literary theory that even the lapse of interest in an English otherworld did not entirely bar heterocosmic poetry from seeming to play the nationalist role it originally hoped to fill. Addison, for one, continues to think fairy writing a specially English phenomenon: "Amongst all the Poets of this Kind our *English* are much the best. . . . For the *English* are naturally Fanciful, and very often disposed by that Gloominess and Melancholy of Temper, which is so frequent in our Nation, to many wild Notions and Visions, to which others are not so liable" (*Spectator* 3:572). Not just Spenser but now the Shakespeare of *The Tempest* too is considered a national poet,[31] and in such terms as Spenser might almost approve—as the master of an "Error" representing the internalization of England's material detachment from the world; except that where this internal dissociation had formerly been seen as a precondition of empire, it has now been reduced to a national propensity for hallucinations, for "wild" distraction.[32]

And indeed, as Addison himself demonstrates, the disparity, the trifling grandeur in otherworldly poetry that Spenser had purposefully embraced now inspires a more uncontrolled ambivalence.[33] In his *Account of the Greatest English Poets* (1694), Addison criticizes Spenser for the very immateriality that he himself would later call "gratifying":

> We view well-pleas'd at distance all the sights
> Of arms and palfries, battles, fields and fights,
> And damsels in distress, and courteous knights,
> But when we look too near, the shades decay,
> And all the pleasing lanschape fades away.
> (*Miscellaneous Works* 1:31–32)

Conversely, in Cowley's "Muse" (1656), the same poet who earlier celebrated Davenant's fidelity to nature can now glorify poetry for its ability to transcend nature, in not just mastering new worlds but creating them:

> Whatever *God* did *Say*,
> Is all thy plain and smooth, uninterrupted *way*.
> Nay ev'n beyond his *works* thy *Voyages* are known,
> Thou 'hast thousand *worlds* too of thine *own*.

Thou speakst, great *Queen*, in the same *style* as *He*,
And a *New World* leaps forth when *Thou* say'st, *Let it be*.
                                            (30–35)[34]

In Spenser, a poetry divided from the world had always seemed
at odds with itself; but for the sometimes dismissive, sometimes
enthusiastic Cowley, that division has only been exaggerated, into
the utopia of either an erring dreamer or a creating god.

Notes

Works have generally been cited by the author's name and a short title; full details can be found in the bibliography. Works frequently cited have been identified by the following abbreviations:

CSP	*Calendar of State Papers, Domestic Series*
CW	More, *Complete Works*
FQ	Spenser, *The Faerie Queene*
PN	Hakluyt, *Principal Navigations* (1598–1600)
Suppl.	Brooks, *Tobacco, Supplement*
U	More, *Utopia*
V	Spenser, *Variorum Edition*

INTRODUCTION

1. "England's Forgotten Worthies," 446. For Froude, the relation between the voyagers and the literature is causal in a surprisingly direct way. "We wonder at the grandeur, the moral majesty of some of Shakespeare's characters," writes Froude, but in fact "the men whom he draws were such men as he saw and knew" (445)—preeminently, Froude's essay implies, "the Elizabethan navigators," who were not merely heroic but "full for the most part with large kindness, wisdom, gentleness, and beauty" (462).

2. *Elizabethan Conquest*, 33; for more on the policy, see 32–34, 48–50, 62–63, 105, and 113. The anonymous writer of "Of the Voyage for Guiana" similarly recommends that the English have "the Inga of Manoa [i.e., of El Dorado] by the consent of his Lords and Casiques surrender the ensigns of his Empire to her Majesty to be returned to him again to be holden in chief of the Crown of England" (Raleigh, *Discoverie*, 146).

3. Throughout this study, I use the terms *savage* and *Indian*, rather than *Native American* or *Amerindian*, in order to emphasize that I am describing English conceptions of Native Americans, not Native Americans as they were in fact.

4. *Pilgrimes* 18:497–98; quoted in Smith, *Works* 1:237 n. 9. In every text I cite, excluding titles and Spenser's poetry, I have modernized spelling (and silently corrected obvious typographical errors). Even in the case of titles and Spenser, I have changed *i* to *j* and *u* to *v*.

5. *Pilgrimes* 18:494; quoted in Smith, *Works* 1:234 n. 2. For another angry reference by Smith to the coronation, see 2:189.

In a broadside publicizing the coronation, the Virginia Company ("Considering . . . ," 1609) declares that Powhatan "hath granted Freedom of Trade and Commerce to our English people," "witnessing the same by accepting a Copper Crown presented unto him, in the name of King *James*, and set upon his head by Captain *Newport*." Cf. *True Declaration*, 11. The specification that the crown was copper would seem to indicate that the company believed the coronation was itself a sophisticatedly trifling action. As later pronouncements from the company show, it came still closer to Smith's position; cf., e.g., the references to the Indians "glutted with our trifles" in Barbour, *Jamestown Voyages* 2:266 and *True Declaration*, 40.

6. Hakluyt, "Discourse," 263; for an introduction to the "black legend" of Spanish atrocities in the New World, see Maltby, *Black Legend*.

7. Writing for the Virginia Company after the massacre, Edward Waterhouse (1622) explicitly recommends the adoption of Spanish colonial methods, which include the use of "Mastiffs to tear" the Indians (*Declaration*, 24). In his essay "Of Plantations" (1625), also published after the massacre, Bacon too rejects trifling, but only because he believes it is not benign enough: he advises that "if you *Plant*, where Savages are, do not only entertain them with Trifles, and Gingles; But use them justly, and graciously, with sufficient Guard nevertheless" (*Essayes*, 108).

8. Strachey, *Historie*, 26; cf. Smith, *Works* 3:276.

9. Quoted in Strathmann, "Raleigh," 265; cf. Strachey, *Historie*, 93.

10. For an exceptional instance of skepticism regarding the standard explanations for the Renaissance, see the first chapter of C. S. Lewis's *English Literature in the Sixteenth Century*.

11. From the prayer concluding the epistle to the reader in the Geneva Bible (***4v). Unless otherwise noted, I quote the Geneva version throughout.

12. Quoted in Masson, *Drummond*, 120, cited (though misascribed) in Sheavyn, *Literary Profession*, 157–58; my emphasis.

13. Parker, *Books*, 94; for the central role in Tudor colonial advocacy of what Parker calls a "literary-nationalist tradition" (82), see Parker, passim.

14. Sidney and Puttenham are drawing on Horace in *De Arte Poetica*, ll. 391–401; for other Tudor references to this allegory in a literary-critical context, see Smith, *Elizabethan* 1:74, 231, 234, and 297.

15. For the literary-theoretical topos of Orphic power turned into a colonialist topos, see, e.g., Parmenius, *De Navigatione*, 178–92; Raleigh, "Observations," 33–34 (which expands Botero, *Cities*, 2); Barbour, *Jamestown Voyages* 1:233; and Lescarbot, *Nova Francia*, 186. George Chapman (1596) expects to see "a world of Savages fall tame" before Raleigh's adventurers in Guiana "as if each man were an *Orpheus*" ("De Guiana," ll. 165–66).

16. Fulke Greville (c. 1604–1614) claims that Sidney became interested

in another rivalry, between little England and equally little Holland: "they without any native commodities (art and diligence excepted) making themselves masters of wealth in all nations; we, again, . . . exporting our substantial riches to import a superfluous mass of trifles" (*Dedication*, 84). But the belief that Holland was using littleness rather than being used by it gained currency primarily with the Jacobeans, beginning, e.g., with Greville's "Treatise of Monarchy," 414–16. For a short bibliography of Jacobean works on Holland as a mercantile and possibly colonial power, see Shammas, "English Commercial Development," 167 and 172.

17. Warner also mentions Philip's impresa here; for other invidious references to it, see Lea, *Answer*, 25 and Keeler, *Voyage*, 245. Hakluyt is at times less optimistic than Warner about the limitations of Spanish gold: in his "Discourse" he says that Martyr "truly prognosticated" when he declared to the young Charles V that from America "shall instruments be prepared for you whereby all the world shall be under your obeisance" (244–45, quoting Eden, *Decades*, 64). Hakluyt later quotes Oviedo: "God hath given you these Indies . . . to the intent that your Majesty should be the universal and only monarch of the world" (311–12). The most famous expression of this belief appears in Ariosto (1532), who moves from an account of the discovery of America to an apocalyptic prediction concerning Charles:

> God means to grant him all this earthly Isle,
> And under this wise Prince his dear anointed,
> One shepherd and one flock he hath appointed.
> (*Orlando Furioso* 15.22–26;
> trans. Harington 15.14–18)

18. For a fine recent discussion of this old chestnut about Elizabeth, see Montrose, "Shaping Fantasies."

19. See Bacon, *Works* 8:387–88, for the critical debate concerning the relation of the entertainment to Raleigh. The inability of scholars to decide whether the entertainment supports or derides Raleigh reflects my point.

20. Chamberlain, *Letters*, 1:64–65; for Spenser matched with Virgil in his own lifetime, see, e.g., Wells, *Spenser Allusions*, 7, 29, 36, 41, 60, and 63.

21. For the possibility of the pun, see Richard Stanyhurst in his "Description of Ireland" (1577) on a community within the English Pale: "But Fingall especially from time to time hath been so addicted to all the points of husbandry, as that they are nicknamed by their neighbors, for their continual drudgery, Collonnes, of the Latin word Coloni, whereunto the clipt English word clown seemeth to be answerable" (4). Cf. Jonson's *Tale of a Tub* (acted 1633) 1.3.30–47; the editors' note (*Jonson* 9:280); and a Jamestown figure, George Percy, who spells *colony* "Colline" ("Trewe Relacyon," 267). Colin Clout is, of course, not even a husbandman: his mere association with coloni-alism will become a feature of the red-cross knight's identity, as I show in chapter 3.

CHAPTER 1. AN EMPIRE NOWHERE

1. Early in the century, two knighted Shakespeareans—Sir Walter Raleigh and Sir Henry Lee—made the discovery of America seem fundamental to England's literary renaissance. Later writers such as Robert Ralston Cawley, Howard Mumford Jones, and Frank Kermode continued to examine the New World from a literary perspective (for an extensive survey of literary allusions to America during the English Renaissance, see Cawley, *Unpathed Waters*, 275–395), but the topic of America's influence on Renaissance literature was never significantly reevaluated, nor did it regain the general critical attention of Renaissance scholars, until the publication in the 1970s of Stephen Greenblatt's book on Raleigh, his first essay on *The Tempest*, and the articles now composing *Renaissance Self-Fashioning*. Though far less well disposed to Tudor expansionism than his predecessors, Greenblatt has not made clear whether his analyses of discursive or epistemic continuities between that expansionism and English literature support or subvert the strong view of American influence that Raleigh and Lee helped make commonplace. For the New World work of all these writers, see my bibliography (I am indebted to Sara Norman for the reference to Lee's *Great Englishmen*). It is an interesting question why literary critics should for so long have lost interest in examining the New World more thoroughly—no doubt the demise of an overt imperialism and the rise of the New Criticism were major factors—but I will not pursue that question in this book.

Subsequent to Greenblatt, the most notable work on the New World by literary critics has been Todorov's *Conquest of America* (which basically elaborates Greenblatt's claim about the "improvisational" superiority of the European over the Indian); Mullaney's two articles "Strange Things" (1983) and "Brothers and Others" (1987); and Hulme's *Colonial Encounters* (1986). None of these writers directly addresses the question of influence.

2. *Old World*, 8; see *Old World*, passim, and also Elliott, "Renaissance."

3. The year after Columbus's voyage saw at least twelve European editions of his letter: at Barcelona (one), Rome (three), Antwerp (one), Basel (one), Paris (three), plus three editions of Dati's Italian versification (one at Rome, two at Florence); see Sanz, *Bibliotheca*, 18–21.

The Antwerp book is entitled *Of the Newe Landes*. Eden refers to "a sheet of printed paper, (more worthy so to be called than a book) entitled of the new found lands" that had "chanced of late to come to my hands" (*Treatyse*, 5); if this tract is something other than the Antwerp volume, it has not survived.

4. Cortés's own extremely popular letters fared no better than Columbus's in England; see Cortés, *Letters*, lx–lxvii.

5. See, e.g., Quinn and Ryan, *England's Sea Empire*, 19, and 12–18 for a bibliography of writings on "Commerce and Colonialism."

6. A later translator of the *Narrenschiff*, Henry Watson, also adds America to the same portion of his *Shyppe* (1517); and the Scottish poet

William Dunbar invokes "the new found Isle" in the similarly sarcastic context of his poem "Of the Waraldis Instabilitie" (before 1513). For quotations, see Quinn, *New American World* 1:130–31.

Cf. also the fragment of a morality play, *Old Christmas or Good Order* (1533), in which Riot and Gluttony are banished from England:

> RIOT.   Alas Gluttony what shall we then do
> GLUTTONY.   In faith to the newfound land let us go
>   For in england there is no remedy.
>
>   (75–77)

7. For Utopia called a "new world," see *U*, 106/7 and 196/97; twice the prefatory letters also describe Utopia as in the new world (14/15, 42/43).

8. Eden in 1555 seems to consider the term *colony* unfamiliar enough to require glossing; e.g., "their new colony or habitation" (*Decades*, 110). As Quinn notes ("Renaissance Influences," 77), Ralph Robinson in his translation of *Utopia* (1551) eschews the term altogether, preferring instead the simpler "foreign towns" (70).

9. It is well known that, in New Spain in the 1530s, Vasco de Quiroga tried to set up Indian communities patterned after Utopia; see Zavala, "Sir Thomas More."

10. In the dedicatory letter to his tract on the existence of a northwest passage, *A Discourse of a Discoverie for a New Passage to Cataia* (1576), Sir Humphrey Gilbert, for example, begins by differentiating his project from More's: "Sir, you might justly have charged me with an unsettled head if I had at any time taken in hand, to discover Utopia, or any country feigned by imagination: But Cataia is none such" (Quinn, *Gilbert*, 1:134). The *True Declaration* (1610) answers those critics who think reports about Virginia "to be but Utopian, and legendary fables" (33)—critics like Jonson, Chapman, and Marston in their *Eastward Ho!* (1605):

> Why, man, all their dripping-pans and their chamber-pots are pure gold; and all the chains with which they chain up their streets are massy gold; all the prisoners they take are fettered in gold; and for rubies and diamonds, they go forth on holidays and gather 'em by the seashore to hang on their children's coats, and stick in their caps, as commonly as our children wear saffron-gilt brooches, and groats with holes in 'em. (3.3.25–32; cf. *U*, 152/53)

Though Lawrence Keymis (1596) distinguishes the Guiana project from "hope of a new found Utopia" (*Second Voyage*, 445), he claims that Columbus showed how ventures sounding merely Utopian can nevertheless bear inestimable fruit.

11. See Surtz, "St. Thomas More"; appropriately, More never mentions so specific a reason for his embassy.

12. Cf. Richard Sylvester, "Si Hythlodaeo Credimus," which proposes that the apparent standoff in book 1 between the two main debaters, More and Hythloday, and then between the debate itself and Hythloday's lengthy exposition of Utopian policies in the second book, represents More's attempt to avoid dogmatism. For Sylvester, divisiveness in *Utopia*

is less an expression of ambivalence on More's part than "a plea for both engagement and detachment, both dialogue and monologue, in matters that concern the best state of a commonwealth" (301). Unfortunately, what makes this via media difficult to accept as such is the fact that flexibility represents no compromise between the debaters but rather More's position in the debate right from the start.

13. A marginal note also declares that "Today the Desire for Expansion is the Curse of All Commonwealths" (*U*, 112/13).

14. For More's financial problems resulting from his embassies to Bruges and Calais, see Marius, *Thomas More*, 190–91, 198.

15. Erasmus's prefatory letter to *Utopia* stresses both More's sedentariness and its disruption by the embassy recorded in *Utopia*: "He has never left his native England except twice when serving his king on an embassy in Flanders" (*U*, 2/3). For evidence that Erasmus exaggerates, see *U*, 268, and Marius, *Thomas More*, 51–52.

16. Erasmus tells von Hutten that More wrote the second book of *Utopia*, the discourse on Utopia, "when at leisure" (*Correspondence* 7:24), and J. H. Hexter argues that this leisure time could only have been supplied by More's stalled embassy (*U*, xv–xvii). (Hexter goes on to make even more specific claims about the timetable of *Utopia*'s composition, though on the basis of very tenuous evidence that discounts the possibility of More's rewriting; see xvii–xxiii.)

Not coincidentally, it would seem, the two other early Tudor works that raise the issue of English enterprises in America—Rastell's *Four Elements* and Robert Thorne's "Declaration of the Indies," both of which I examine—also seem to have been composed outside England. For indications that Rastell wrote his interlude in Ireland, see Reed, *Early Tudor Drama*, 202–3; Thorne, an English merchant resident in Spain, appears to have transmitted his letter to Henry VIII by way of Sir Edward Lee, England's ambassador to Spain; see Hakluyt, *Divers Voyages*, 33.

17. Cf. Cabot's son Sebastian, who worked for both England and Spain, sometimes concomitantly, and, as the Spanish ambassador to England in 1550 says, "tried to make his profit out of both sides" (quoted in Quinn, *England*, 153; see 131–59).

18. Of course, Cabot's disappearance adds a further complication to the idea of rootlessness: as Polydore Vergil says, Cabot "is believed to have found the new lands nowhere but on the very bottom of the ocean" (quoted in Williamson, *Cabot Voyages*, 225).

19. For an account of Thorne and the English merchant community resident in Spain, see Connell-Smith, *Forerunners*.

20. Nevertheless, Thorne is one of the few Renaissance writers to allow that a savage disregard for gold and love of "trifles" make sense: both novelty and usefulness, Thorne argues, recommend a knife or nail over precious metal ("Declaration," 34).

21. More's Polylerites seem meant to highlight by contrast this ambiguous apartness of islands: "They are far from the sea, almost ringed round

by mountains, and satisfied with the products of their own land, which is in no way infertile. In consequence they rarely pay visits to other countries or receive them" (*U*, 74/75). Yet not even this landlocked island can escape the rest of the world, for "it pays an annual tribute to the Persian padishah."

22. In fact, Sir Thomas Smith mistakenly associates *Utopia* with isolationism: "Well a man may change the name of things, but the value he cannot [change] in any wise to endure for any space, except we were in such a country as Utopia was imagined to be that had no traffic with any other outward country" (*Discourse*, 105).

23. The Elizabethans credited John Twyne with this theory (see Ferguson, *John Twyne*, 30–32), though More's joke would seem to suggest that it had been current earlier than Twyne. Cf. Richard Verstegan (1605), who, while expounding the view that England was once joined to the Continent (*Restitution*, 95–112), declares in a marginal note, "*Sir Thomas More* in his *Utopia* seemeth so to understand of our country of *England*" (96–97; cited in Kennedy, "Additional References," 22–23).

24. Apparently composed by either Erasmus or Giles; see *U*, 280–81.

25. Actually, the poem says that Utopia received its name because it was *infrequentiam*. The Yale editors comment: "The allusion must be to the rare visits of foreigners to the island . . . —so rare that people wondered whether it actually existed anywhere" (*U*, 279). But the Utopian chronicles mention only one classical visit, a shipwreck, of which no report ever reached the Old World: "Some Romans and Egyptians were cast on shore and remained on the island without ever leaving it" (*U*, 108/9).

Samuel Daniel (1612) notes that before the Roman conquest of Britain, "as it lay secluded out of the way, so it seemed out of the knowledge of the world" (*Works* 4:86).

26. This is the project that Camden (1586) says Ortelius suggested and Camden undertook in *Britannia* ("To the Reader," 4), which begins with a disquisition on Britain as another world. Parker notes that the discovery of America also apparently sparked an increased interest in classical geographies—that is, in geographies that do not mention America (*Books*, 134–35).

27. In his prefatory letter William Bude imagines Utopia "one of the Fortunate Isles, perhaps close to the Elysian Fields" (*U*, 12/13), which is again a classical conception of England: see Bennett, "Britain," 117–24.

28. Cf., e.g., Johnson, *Nova Britannia*, 14; Strachey, *Historie*, 6; and the Virginia Company's broadside "Declaration." Arthur Ferguson claims that John Twyne in his *De Rebus Albionicis* (written c. 1530s) "was probably the first English scholar to make this sort of connection" ("John Twyne," 34–35). The earliest instance that I have found of England's former barbarity becoming a colonial incitement is in a letter of Sir Thomas Smith (1572) concerning the colonization of Ireland: "This country of England, once as uncivil as Ireland now is, was by colonies of the Romans brought to understand the laws and orders of th'ancient orders [*sic*]" (quoted in

Canny, *Elizabethan Conquest*, 129). For Spenser's version of this appeal, see the third part of my chapter 3.

29. The only reference in *Utopia* to England as an island occurs here, when that island is being imagined a wasteland.

30. By 1609 William Symonds can make this relation between enclosures and colonization explicit: thanks to enclosures, "the true laboring husbandman . . . can hardly scape the statute of rogues and vagrants" (*Virginia*, 20), and therefore would be better off in America. Interestingly, the wool trade in these cases does not block consideration of America but rather provokes it.

31. See Roper, *Life*, 207, and Marius, *Thomas More*, 210.

32. See Muir, *Life and Letters*, 44–45. Wyatt is reported to have complained to the Spanish, "Perhaps by not mentioning my master in the treaty the object was to show that he is not a Christian king?" (quoted in Muir, *Life and Letters*, 63).

33. For Bonner and his accusations, see Muir, *Life and Letters*, 63–69. Cromwell apparently suppressed this attack on his favorite, but after Cromwell's fall in 1541, Bonner's letter was unearthed and Wyatt was arrested. The ex-ambassador wrote a declaration (178–84) and speech (187–209) in his defense—"arse" is his more colorful version of the "tail" Bonner reported—but he seems never to have stood trial.

34. At the time the Marquis of Exeter and Lord Montague were arrested, Wyatt's presumed mistress Elizabeth Darrell was questioned about Wyatt (Muir, *Life and Letters*, 82–85). In a letter to Cromwell from Spain (28 November 1538), Wyatt remarks: "I have had it told me by some here of reputation that peradventure I was had in suspect both with the king and you, as they said it was told them." He adds rather unconvincingly, "I take it light" (86).

35. "To wish and want and not obtain," l. 6; cf. "Most wretched heart," l. 27 and "Patience, though I have not," l. 6.

36. For instance, Wyatt devotes four lines in the canzone (17–20) to describing the sun's journey—only in these two poems does he use the word *westward*; his beloved is "absent wealth" (58); her transcendently golden hair "doth surmount Apollo's pride" (69); her eyes emit "lively streams" (70); Wyatt longs for "the resting place of love" (93); and the final word in each poem expresses Wyatt's desire to "flee."

37. Certainly nothing divided Wyatt from his erotic desires so extravagantly as Henry. Whether or not Wyatt loved Anne Boleyn, he suffered imprisonment and nearly death for the possibility. Besides Henry's many other interests, he seems also to have courted Wyatt's wife, yet a condition of Wyatt's release from his second, near-fatal imprisonment was that he return to the wife he loathed. Henry commanded that if Wyatt should "not lead a conjugal life with her, or should he be found to keep up adulterous relations with one or two other ladies that he has since loved, he is to suffer pain of death and confiscation of property" (Muir, *Life and Letters*, 13–36, 212, 209). These facts add depth to Joost Daalder's explanation

about the "other will" in the poem that Wyatt says fills him with "deep despair" (88): Wyatt, Daalder claims, "probably refers to the King's will that Wyatt was to stay in Spain" (Wyatt, *Collected Poems*, 90). Yet, as I have noted, Wyatt always represents his actions as unchosen, the will that chooses as relentlessly other. He is ever restless, as Surrey's epitaph maintains, because he cannot have his will.

Mason suggests a simpler reason for the beloved's replacement in the Tagus poem: Wyatt's "loyalty and patriotism" may be merely "a mask for his love for his mistress" (*Wyatt*, 222). But the question remains: why would Wyatt feel the need for such a mask?

38. Though less radically than Wyatt, Michael Drayton also describes the Thames's crescent shape as an image of erotic fulfillment and yet constraint: according to Drayton, Brute decides to place his city

> where fair *Thames* his course into a Crescent casts
> (That, forced by his tides, as still by her he hasts,
> He might his surging waves into her bosom send)
> Because too far in length, his Town should not extend.
> (*Poly-Olbion* 16.325–28)

39. See McCann, *English Discovery*, 173–75.

40. Cited in Elliot, *Old World*, 73, from whom I borrow the last translation. What prevents westward-traveling empire from next leaving Spain and heading for America is, Perez de Oliva maintains, the sea.

41. "Item, to remember Sebastian Cabot, he hath here but three hundred ducats a year, and he is desirous if he might not serve the king, at least to see him as his old master. And I think therein. And that I may have answer in this" (Muir, *Life and Letters*, 81).

42. Cf. the epitaph of Pico della Mirandola (died 1494): "*Iohannes jacet hic Mirandula, caetera norunt / Et Tagus, & Ganges, forsan & antipodes*" ("Here lies *Mirandula*, *Tagus* the rest doth know, / And *Ganges*, and perhaps th'*Antipodes* also," trans. Hakewill, *Apology*, 217)—that is, Pico's fame extends from west to east and possibly south.

The difference between England and a Continental nation as ends of the earth is explained by John Speed (1611): "*Virgil* surely (of all Poets the most learned) when describing the Shield which *Vulcan* forged (in *Virgil's* brain) for *Aeneas*, he calls the *Morini* (people about *Calais*) *the outmost men*, doth only mean that they were Westward, the furthest Inhabitants upon the Continent, signifying withal that Britain as being an Island, lay out of the world" (*Theatre*, 1). Such a distinction does not prevent competition: Perez de Oliva, for example, asserts that Homer thought Cordoba and its environs, not otherworldly England, "the Elysian fields" (*Obras*, 132r).

43. For this theory of gold's origins as it crops up in early Tudor travel literature, see McCann, *English Discovery*, 163–67.

44. Cf. the far more straightforward celebrations of London as "Troynovant" by William Dunbar (1501) and Robert Fabyan (1516) (quoted in Manley, *London*, 52–57), not to mention the more straightforward dis-

missal of the Tagus in Sylvester's paean (1605) to England ("The Colonies," ll. 463–64, in *Bartas*).

45. This port is, of course, Lisbon—the capital of Portugal, not Spain. But Wyatt appears to ignore this distinction, first by heading his poem "In Spain," and second by addressing the poem to the river itself, which rises in Spain. Even if Wyatt does imagine the Tagus flowing toward both the Spanish and the Portuguese empires in America, however, my point remains unchanged: he still has to picture an imperial expansiveness from which England is absent.

46. Tatlock does note the prominence of woods in Brutus's story, but ascribes it to the influence of the hunt-loving Norman kings on Geoffrey (*Legendary*, 358–59).

47. Brutus's counterpoint to Aeneas supports the allegorical speculation that these giants represent distorted, vestigial images of the old "heroes" who lost Troy: Italy, Aeneas's final destination, is also the land of his ancestors (*Aeneid*, 3.167–68).

48. Leland, *Assertio*. For Polydore considered a Roman, see Millican, *Spenser*, 31–32; John Bale (1549) in another context complains that "for so little esteeming our true Antiquities, the proud Italians have always hold us for a barbarous nation" (quoted in Millican, *Spenser*, 33).

The best appraisal of the controversy remains Kendrick's, in *British Antiquity*; see particularly 34–44 and 78–98.

49. Polydore Vergil says of Geoffrey that he "hath extolled them [the British] above the nobleness of Romans and Macedonians, enhancing them with most impudent lying" (*English History*, 29). Cf. John Twyne (c. 1530–50), who calls Geoffrey "that Homer, or father of lies" (*ille Homerus, ac mendaciorum pater*) (*De Rebus Albionicis*, 13).

50. Cf. Polydore Vergil, *English History*, 31–32 and Twyne, *De Rebus Albionicis*, 16.

51. Rastell suggests this interpretation when he refuses to deny or affirm the Brutus story. His interest in Brutus is, he claims, less historical than moral: he wants to preserve the "many notable examples" of good and bad princes, God's wrath, and so forth, that Brutus's story contains (A1v).

52. For relevant documents, see Quinn, *New American World* 1:161–68.

53. William Bradford shows how little difference a century of contact with the Indians could make to this view of America as empty: "The place they had thoughts on was some of those vast and unpeopled countries of America, which are fruitful and fit for habitation, being devoid of all civil inhabitants, where there are only savage and brutish men which range up and down, little otherwise than the wild beasts of the same" (*Plymouth*, 25).

54. For primary documents on Hore's voyage, see *PN* 8:3–7 and Quinn, *New American World* 1:209–14; for a detailed commentary, see Quinn, *England*, 182–89; for Rastell's imprisonment, see Rastell, *Four Elements*, 10.

55. Stephen Gosson (1582) associates this kind of story with romance, and mocks the trifling proof of identity as it appears in plays: "Sometime you shall see nothing but the adventures of an amorous knight, passing from country to country for the love of his lady, encountering many a terrible monster made of brown paper, & at his return, is so wonderfully changed, that he can not be known but by some posy in his tablet, or by a broken ring, or a handkerchief, or a piece of cockle shell" (*Playes*, 161).

56. *Confessio Amantis* 7.746–54; cited in Zacher, *Curiosity*, 142. Cf. Sir John Mandeville, who translates the moon's lack of substance into lightness and therefore speed:

> we been in the seventh climate that is of the moon, and the moon is of lightly moving and the moon is *planet of way*. And for that skill it giveth us will of kind for to move lightly and for to go diverse ways and to seeken strange things and other diversities of the world, for the moon environeth the earth more hastily than any other planet. (*Travels*, 119–20)

Caxton (1490) cites the moon's special relation to England in order to explain why England is so linguistically divisive: "For we english men / been born under the domination of the moon. which is never steadfast / but ever wavering / waxing one season / and waneth & discreaseth another season / And that common english that is spoken in one shire varieth from another" (*Prologues and Epilogues*, 108; cited in Zacher, *Curiosity*, 142).

57. According to the highly influential *Sphere* of Sacrobosco, for instance, the habitable world is divided into seven climes; beyond the seventh "there may be a number of islands and human habitations, yet whatever there is, since living conditions are bad, is not reckoned a clime" (Thorndike, *Sphere*, 112/140). A thirteenth-century English commentator, Robert Anglicus, explains: "The last clime ends . . . where the altitude is 50½ degrees, and this is hardly across the English channel, so that almost all England is outside a clime" (ibid., 187/236). For the history of the theory of climes, see 16–18 n. 88.

58. Cf. George Best (1578) on the habitability of the north above the forty-eighth parallel: "How then can such men define upon other Regions very far without that Parallel, where they were inhabited or not, seeing that in so near a place they so grossly mistook the matter" (*True Discourse*, 39–40). Anglicus anticipates this line of argument when he asserts that the mistake of past authorities about England disqualifies them from ruling on the habitability of the equatorial regions (Thorndike, *Sphere*, 192/241).

59. Cf. Thorne, who in a postscript warns the English ambassador to Spain that "to move" Thorne's northwest project "amongst wise men it should be had in derision. And, therefore, to none I would have written nor spoken of such things but to your Lordship, to whom boldly I commit in this all my foolish fantasy as to my self" ("Declaration," 53).

60. Nor, on the other hand, does he mention such quotidian reasons for his return to England as politics, money, fear, the weather, or simple homesickness: see Muir, *Life and Letters*, 54–55, 87. (Wyatt did indeed abhor the Spanish climate. The heat blocked any literary exercise especially.

In a letter to Cromwell, Wyatt complains: "I have such a pain in my head that it grieveth me to write or read. This town of Toledo is dangerous for the head" [Muir, *Life and Letters*, 91]. Later chapters will return to the issue of climate in English poetry and imperialism.)

61. It is, again, the company of learned men that enables More the ambassador to forget home (cf. Erasmus, *Correspondence* 3:235–36). In discussing the reception of *Utopia*, More concludes that the favorable opinion of Erasmus "will be more than enough for my judgment. We are 'together, you and I, a crowd'; that is my feeling, and I think I could live happily with you in any wilderness [*solitudine*]" (Erasmus, *Correspondence* 4:116–17, *Opus Epistolarium* 2:372)—that is, in the wilderness of learning exemplified for More by his Nowhere.

But the oppositions aligned with relative clarity here grow too complicated elsewhere for such easy systemization. After all, service, the opposite of travel, is what takes More away from home, not only on embassies but in England. According to More's son-in-law and biographer, William Roper, Henry VIII so enjoyed More's company at supper that More "could not once in a month get leave to go home to his wife and children" (*Life*, 202) (and, in the end, Henry imprisoned and then beheaded him). But then More can imagine home itself as separating him from his true home in heaven (cf. 242, 253), a belief manifested in "the New Building" More constructs "a good distance from his mansion house" so that he may frequently "sequester himself from worldly company" (211). What these shifting oppositions show is that More under any circumstance figures himself distracted. This predilection appears more starkly in Roper's More as a characteristic figure of speech that associates the realization of More's desires with his own injury or demise: for example, "Now would to our Lord, son Roper, upon condition that three things were well established in Christendom [viz., universal peace, uniformity of religion, and "a good conclusion" to Henry's marriage problems], I were put in a sack and here presently cast into the Thames" (210; cf. 223, 224, 227, 245).

62. Giles follows Erasmus's lead, calling More "a man distracted [*distractus*] by a mass of public business and domestic affairs" and yet also "of superhuman and almost divine genius" (*U*, 22/23); while Desmarais later marvels at More "among the British at the ends of the earth" "much distracted [*distractus*] by public and domestic affairs" (26/27). Cf. Robert Whittington (1519) on the marvel of More as homebound author: "Ulysses' long voyages brought him the wisdom / More in *Utopia* managed to tell" (quoted in Sullivan, *Supplement*, 120).

63. Polemicists fantasize the exile of opponents to Utopia throughout the English Renaissance: for example, Foxe (1570) suggests that malcontents "which neither live here like Angels, nor yet remember themselves to be but men amongest men, are to be sent *ad republicam Platonis*, or to *M. More's Utopia*, either there to live with themselves, or else where as none may live to offend them" (quoted in Wooden, "Unnoticed," 91; cf. Sullivan, *Supplement*, 15 and 102). John Grange (1577) tells his coy mistress

that "sith you think your beauty such, as none enjoys the like: / To *Plato's* City, fairies' land, or to *Utopia* wenne" (*Golden*, E1v; cf. Gibson, *Bibliography*, 403, and Sullivan, *Supplement*, 98).

64. Erasmus, *Correspondence* 4:163–64, *Opus Epistolarium* 2:414. For *nugis*, cf. *U*, 152/53.

65. Cf. More's prefatory letter to the second edition of *Utopia* (1517), in which he jokes with Giles about a critic who has detected "some rather absurd elements" in the book: "Why should he be so minded as if there were nothing absurd elswhere in the world?" (*U*, 248/49).

66. Cf. Giles, who says in his prefatory letter that, reading More, "I am as affected as if I were sometimes actually living in Utopia itself" (*U*, 22/23).

67. In his prefatory letter William Bude imagines Utopia a "Hagnopolis," or Holy City, detached from the earth but not in heaven either, "leading a kind of heavenly life which is below the level of heaven but above the rabble of this known world" who engage in "empty" [*inanibus*] pursuits (*U*, 12/13).

68. For a measured assessment of More as politician, see Elton, "Thomas More."

69. *The Scourge of Villanie*, satire 10, ll. 23, 21.

70. Cf. Richard Rich on his versified *Newes From Virginia* (1610): "I must confess, that had I not debarred my self of that large scope which to the writing of prose is allowed, I should have much eased my self, and given thee better content" (A3v).

71. Translated by Marlowe. For evidence of Wyatt's familiarity with the *Amores*, see Nelson, "Note." John Skelton in *Phyllyp Sparowe* seems to have Ovid in mind when he hopes for Apollo's grace, "To whom be the laud ascribed / That my pen hath enbibed / With the aureat drops, / As verily my hope is, / Of Thagus, that golden flood, / That passeth all earthly good" (871–76). Poetry is equal rather than superior to the Tagus here because Skelton means his praise of Jane Scrope to be worldly: "And as that flood doth pass / All floods that ever was / With his golden sands, / . . . / Right so she doth exceed / All other of whom we read, / Whose fame by me shall spread / Into Perce and Mede, / From Briton's Albion / To the tower of Babylon" (877–79, 883–88).

72. Tottel's (1557) and Lewis's (1954) remarks are conveniently reproduced in Thomson, *Critical Heritage*, 32 and 180, respectively; Tottel actually speaks of "the weightiness of the deep-witted Sir Thomas Wyatt the elder's verse." Thomas Warton (1781) refers to the poem's "great simplicity and propriety, together with a strain of poetic allusion" (quoted in *Critical Heritage*, 45); George Nott (1815) allows that the lines "prove Wyatt's mind to have been well stored with reading. But what constitutes their chief merit is a certain air of truth which shows them to have been the spontaneous effusion of feeling" (quoted in *Critical Heritage*, 58). Most recently, Mason says that "we are drawn into mysterious depths of feeling by the body of the poem" (*Wyatt*, 221).

73. In imagining the perfect courtier, one of Castiglione's interlocutors says he finds

> one rule that is most general, which . . . taketh place in all things belonging to a man in word or deed, above all other. And that is to eschew as much as a man may, and as a sharp and dangerous rock, too much curiousness, and (to speak a new word) to use in every thing a certain disgracing [*sprezzatura*] to cover art withal, and seem whatsoever he doth and saith, to do it without pain, and (as it were) not minding it. (*Courtier*, 45–46)

For a useful account of *sprezzatura* in Castiglione, see Rebhorn, *Courtly*, 33ff.

74. The gainwardness of Wyatt's journey even suggests a parallel between himself and a heavenly body: for the view that the lesser astronomical spheres moved eastwardly, a direction "repugnant" to the westward-moving first heavenly sphere, see Wyatt's very obscure poem "When Dido feasted" and the commentary by Rebholz (*Complete Poems*, 490–94). Lucan anticipates Wyatt in transforming this heavenly contrariety into pathos, though he attributes that pathos to "the sorrowing Sun . . . driving his steeds harder than ever against the revolution of the sky, and urging his course backwards, though the heavens whirled him on" (7.2–3). In fact, contrariety yields sublimity even in the preeminently worldly case of the Tagus, whose westward-moving water "turns up" the resisting gold.

75. Here too, however, Sir Henry anticipates his son by making his own loyalty to Henry seem as arbitrary as possible: he answers Richard, "If I had first chosen you for my master, thus faithful would I have been to you."

76. Erasmus, *De Contemptu Mundi*, 20r, a possible source for Wyatt cited in Mason, *Wyatt*, 223. Cf. Chaucer's translation of Boethius: "Alle the thinges that the ryver Tagus yeveth yow with his goldene gravayles, or elles alle the thinges that the ryver Herynus [Hermus] yeveth with his rede brynke, or that Indus yeveth that is next the hote party of the world, that medleth the grene stones with the whyte, ne sholde nat cleeren the lookinge of yowre thowht, but hyden rather yowre blynde corages within her dyrknesse" (*Boece* 3.10.11–19). Silius Italicus also mentions the Tagus in combination with the Pactolus and the Hermus (*Punica* 1.155).

77. Holinshed, *Chronicles* 4:330. Stow's *Annales* (1592) partially reprints this account, and follows it with the report of a similarly trifling display:

> Also about the same time *Mark Scaliot* black Smith born in London, for trial of workmanship, made one hanging lock of iron, steel, and brass, a pipe key filed three square, with a pot upon the shaft, and the bow with two esses, all clean wrought, which weighed but one grain of gold or wheat corn: he made also a chain of gold of 43. links, to the which chain the lock and key being fastened and put about a flea's neck she drew the same, all which lock, key, chain and flea, weighed but one grain and a half. (1164)

Scaliot appears in Holinshed under the year 1579; Stow adds here, "A thing almost incredible, but that my self (amongst many others) have seen it, and therefore must affirm it to be true" (4:406).

78. *Miniature*, 6. For an analysis of the relation between Elizabethan poetry and "the miniature craze" in Elizabethan England, see Fumerton, "Secret Arts."

79. The classical precedent for Bales's feat does in fact involve Homer. "Keenness of sight," says Pliny, "has achieved instances transcending belief in the highest degree. Cicero records [in a lost work] that a parchment copy of Homer's poem *The Iliad* was enclosed in a nutshell" (*Historia Naturalis* 7.21). Certainly Bales was aware of Pliny's story, for he apparently matched it, though with the difference, once again, of tying poor matter to great Christian spirit: his book "within an English Walnut no bigger than a Hen's egg, seen and viewed [?] of many thousands with wonderful admiration," is "the English Bible" (Harleian MS. 530, art. 2, f. 14).

For Bales analogized to poets, see Rowlands, *Letting*, A3r.

80. For the authenticity of this claim, see Nashe, *Works*, 4:427–28 and 5:suppl. 64.

81. When Frobisher later returns to the island from which the stone was taken, he can find no other,

> so that it may seem a great miracle of God, that being only one rich stone in all the island, the same should be found by one of our countrymen, whereby it should appear, God's divine will and pleasure is, to have our common wealth increased with no less abundance of his hidden treasures and gold mines, than any other nation, and would that the faith of his Gospel and holy name should be published and enlarged through all those corners of the earth, amongst those Idolatrous infidels. (Best, *True Discourse*, 57)

82. Speaking before the House of Commons in 1601, Robert Cecil thus mistakenly associates *Utopia* with a disdain for farmers (in *Utopia, coloni*): "excepting Sir *Thomas More's Utopia*, or some such feigned Commonwealth, you shall never find but the Ploughman is chiefly provided for" (D'Ewes, *Compleat Journal*, 674; cited in Gibson, *Bibliography*, 411). For the related, and more arguable, notion that More is interested in rationalizing agriculture so as to release the Utopians from "rural bondage," see Gury, "Abolition."

83. Writing about these two prizes, George Best (1578) establishes a kind of proportion between them in more than number: the accounts of their taking occur within a paragraph of each other; both are obtained against enormous odds; and Frobisher takes both for the same reason, because he is "desirous to bring some token thence of his being there" (*True Discourse*, 50).

84. The analogy derives from Martyr: "For like as razed or unpainted tables, are apt to receive what forms so ever are first drawn thereon by the hand of the painter, even so these naked and simple people, do soon receive the customs of our Religion, and by conversation with our men, shake off their fierce and native barbarousness" (Eden, *Decades*, 106). Cf. Strachey, *Historie*, 18.

Both Hakluyt and Stow retell a story from *The Great Chronicle of England* that eerily exemplifies this conception of the Indian:

This year also [September 1501 to September 1502] were brought unto the king iii men taken In the New found Isle land. . . . These were clothed In beasts' skins and ate Raw flesh and spake such speech that no man could understand them, and In their demeanor like to brute beasts whom the king kept a time after, Of the which upon (ii) years passed (after) I saw ii of them apparelled after English men In westminster palace, which at that time I could not discern from English men till I was learned what men they were, But as for speech I heard none of them utter one word. (Williamson, *Cabot Voyages*, 220–22)

For the conception of Indians as bestial because linguistically deficient, see Greenblatt, "Learning."

CHAPTER 2. ELIZA AND ELIZIUM

1. In his address to both houses of Elizabeth's first parliament, the Lord Keeper, Sir Nicholas Bacon, demanded (1559), "Could there have happen'd to this Imperial Crown a greater loss in Honor, Strength and Treasure than to lose that piece, I mean *Calais*?" (D'Ewes, *Compleat Journal*, 13).

2. Quoted in Wernham, *Making*, 26.

3. *Lyly*, 34; Hunter is attacking the "Whig" notion that "the 'spaciousness' of Elizabeth's reign is a setting for a new-found freedom of the human spirit" (3).

4. Yates, "Queen Elizabeth," 59.

5. Quoted in Neale, *Queen Elizabeth*, 294. Cf. "The second voyage of Master Laurence Aldersey" (1586): "They brought us to the house of the Cady, who was made then to understand of the 20 Turks that we had aboard, which were to go to *Constantinople*, being redeemed out of captivity, by sir *Francis Drake*, in the west *Indias*, and brought with him into *England*, and by order of the Queen's Majesty, sent now into their Country. Whereupon the Cady commanded them to be brought before him, that he might see them: and when he had talked with them, and understood how strangely they were delivered, he marveled much, and admired the Queen's Majesty of England, who being but a woman, is notwithstanding of such power and renown amongst all the princes of Christendom" (Hakluyt, *Principall Navigations* [1589], 224).

6. For example, Roger Ascham (1570) recalls how "once it pleased" Cicero "to rail upon poor England, objecting both extreme beggary and mere barbarousness unto it, writing thus unto his friend Atticus: 'There is not one scruple of silver in that whole isle, or anyone that knoweth either learning or letter' " (*Scholemaster*, 150).

7. William Harrison, "Historicall Description" book 1, cap. 1 (Holinshed, *Chronicles* 1:3); Holinshed, "The Historie of England" book 3, cap. 19 (*Chronicles* 1:481, first in 1577 ed.); Harrison, "Historicall Description" book 1, cap. 18 (*Chronicles* 1:183).

8. Camden, *Britannia*, 4; cf. Speed, *Theatre*, 1 and Selden's notes to *Poly-Olbion* (1612) in Drayton, *Works* 4:15–16. Bennett's "Britain among the

Fortunate Isles," which lists these references and notes their source (119), is a useful compendium of the *alter mundus* topos in Renaissance England; many of my references may be found in her article.

Characteristically for the dialectic I am describing, the "Fortunate Isles" story is not unequivocally in England's favor. Hakewill, for instance, cites it as evidence of "the ignorance of former ages" (*Apology*, 232–33).

9. The Angle/angle pun may not seem operative in Bede's account, but it was certainly available to Gregory, as the Renaissance knew. In a letter to Eulogius, Archbishop of Alexandria, announcing the mission to England launched by Gregory, Gregory refers to "the tribe of the Angles placed in an angle of the world [*gens Anglorum in mundi angulo posita*]" (*Registrum Epistularum* 2:551). The greatest popularizer of the Angle/angle etymology was Higden's *Polychronicon*: "Anglia hath that name as it were an angle and a corner of the world [*Anglia dicitur ab angulo orbis*]" (2:4–5 [1.39]). In his translation of Virgil's *Eclogues*, Abraham Fleming explicates the pun in relation to the *divisos* line (*Bucoliks*, pp. 3–4).

10. Quoted in Bauckham, *Tudor Apocalypse*, 86. For the classical theory of climates that assumed the area of the world in which Britain lay to be uninhabitable, see chapter 1.

11. Cf. the revenging ghost Gorlois's closing prophecy about Elizabethan England in *The Misfortunes of Arthur* (1588): "Gorlois will never fray the *Britons* more. / For *Britain* then becomes an Angels' land, / Both Devils and sprites must yield to Angels' power, / Unto the goddess of the Angels land" (Hughes et al., 195–96; quoted in Wilson, *England's Eliza*, 103 n. 29). See also Averell, *Mervailous Combat*, E1v.

12. The English Catholic Nicholas Sanders (1585) asserts that Mary married Philip primarily because he "would be a help to her in bringing the kingdom back again to the faith and obedience of the Church" (*De Origine*, 222). For the Protestant view that Philip was ultimately responsible for the loss of Calais, see, e.g., Nedham, "Letter," 124–25, Wheeler, *Treatise*, 40, and Sutcliffe, *Answer*, 86, 174; the Catholics blamed the loss on "heretical treason" (Parsons, *Warn-word*, 80v).

13. Sanders, *De Origine*, 205/288; *Supper* A3v. For Catholics too, Gregory I seemed a figure prophetically pertinent to modern England; they liked to compare Gregory XIII to his predecessor, and thereby encourage him to believe that "he may be canonized for delivering us from heresy as St. Gregory has been for delivering us from heathendom" (quoted in Meyer, *England*, 283; cf. Bacon, *Works* 8:18–19).

14. Nichols, *Progresses* 2:158. Cf. the mayor of New Windsor to the queen in 1586:

> How (in a manner) miraculous a thing it is, that while the whole world (as I might say), even the Kingdoms, and Countries round about us (to us a world), stand at this day garboiled and oppressed with troubles and stirs; we, even we alone, here in this our England (as it were a little Goshen), neither feeling dint of sword, nor hearing sound of drum, nor fearing either slaughter or depilation of the Oppressor, sit us still every man in his own

home, having freedom at the full to praise God in his sanctuary, and safety at the full to follow our affair in the Commonwealth. (2:478)

15. Quoted in Wilson, *England's Eliza*, 388, from *A Chaine of Pearle* (1603). Some believed this hyperbole about Elizabeth's virtue to be literally true, as in the rumor reported by Jonson "that she had a Membrana on her which made her uncapable of man" (*Jonson* 1:142).

Even the Catholic Parsons accepts the relation between England's otherness and Elizabeth's virginity, but argues that both are equally effects of English heresy: "The principal cause of her grace's not marrying is to be presumed to have proceeded of the different Religion of foreign Princes, who desired the same on the one side: and on the other, the inequality of blood in her own subjects, for such advancement" (*Temperate*, 8).

16. Cf. Greville, who describes the Armada victory as Elizabeth's "virgin triumph over that sanctified and invincible navy" (*Dedication*, 124).

17. For the tradition that England was originally not an island at all but a peninsula, see *FQ* 2.10.5 and chapter 1.

18. "To the Q: After His Return Out of Italy" 12–14; Constable never published the poem.

19. Cf. North, *Stage*, 89–90. For the most influential account of Elizabeth's imprisonment and deliverance, see Foxe, *Acts* 8:605–24.

20. Cf. Elizabeth in 1601: "Should I ascribe any thing to my Self and my Sexly Weakness, I were not worthy to live then" (D'Ewes, *Compleat Journal*, 660).

21. The mad William Reynolds provides unusual testimony to the power of Hellwis's praise: Reynolds believed that the Privy Council had published works like *A Marvell* and *Venus and Adonis* so as to make him fall in love with Elizabeth (Hotson, *Shakespeare's Sonnets*, 141–47).

22. Bauckham, *Tudor Apocalypse*, 179–80 notes this connection.

23. For the related tradition that celebrates the Virgin's little womb as paradoxically able to contain "that which the whole world cannot hold" (*quem totus orbis non capit*), see Hunter, *Dramatic Identities*, 75–78.

24. Cf. Greene's *Spanish Masquerado* (1589) on the massive force of the Armada—enough "to threaten ruin to the greatest Monarchy of the whole world"—as "bended against a little Island, a handful in respect of other Kingdoms" (*Works* 5:255).

25. Quoted in Stone, "Sad Augurs," 473. Anthony Marten (1588) deduces from the Armada's defeat that "if all the world fret and rage never so much against you, the Lord will fight for you. He will give the victory, and ye shall but look on" (quoted in Bauckham, *Tudor Apocalypse*, 177).

26. I say "mere body" because Elizabeth describes her great spirit as materialized in the "Heart" and "Stomach" of her body politic, which was itself supposedly incorporated within her body natural. As I will later show, Spenser opposes this material conflation of the queen's two "persons" (*V* 1:168). Cf. Montrose, "Elizabethan Subject," 315–16. In a later speech to the House of Lords (1593), Elizabeth again "acknowledge[s]"

her "Womanhood and weakness" (and, implicitly, her virginity), though this time as a reason why "my Mind was never to Invade my Neighbors, or to Usurp over any" (D'Ewes, *Compleat Journal*, 466).

27. The belief that Spain hoped to inflict American cruelties on England surfaced particularly in relation to the Armada: Archdeacon writes that King Philip, "having with *Nimrod*, like beasts hunted men with Dogs in *India*, would fain use the like practice here in England" (*True Discourse*, 8). Cf. Thomas Deloney's "A New Ballet of the strange and most cruel Whips which the Spaniards had prepared to whip and torment English men and women: *which were found and taken at the overthrow of certain of the Spanish Ships*, in July last past, 1588" (*Works*, 479–82; and Vaughan, *Golden-grove*, K1v–2r.)

28. Anthony Pagden notes that "parts of butchered Huguenots had been sold publicly in Paris and Lyon in 1572" (*Fall*, 84).

29. Cf. Nichols, *Progresses* 2:158, and Anthony Nixon, *Memoriall* (1603):

> If all the costly Mines of th'Indians,
> Which secretly lie hid within the ground:
> If all the precious stones which in the sands
> Of *Lybia* land most plenteously abound:
> If all the joys of human heart's content,
> Which seated are under the Firmament,
>
> Should be transported to our English coast,
> And here enjoyed as our proper own;
> Of them we might not half so truly boast,
> As of this sacred truth amongst us sown.
>
> (Br)

30. Cf. Mother England in John Aylmer's *Harborowe* (1559), after she lists (as Lea does) England's "plenty of all things" (P4r):

> Besides this God hath brought forth in me, the greatest and excellentest treasure that he hath, for your comfort and all the world's. He would that out of my womb should come that servant of his your brother John Wycliff, who begat Hus, who begat Luther, who begat truth. What greater honor could you or I have, than that it pleased Christ as it were in a second birth to be born again of me among you? (Rv)

Lea continued his propaganda campaign the next year with *A True and Perfecte Description of a Straunge Monstar* (the Holy League again).

31. Jonson in fact refused to celebrate England as a separate world until the accession of James, who at least provisionally combined England and Scotland by renaming his dominions Great Britain. See *Part of the Kings Entertainment in Passing to His Coronation* (1604), ll. 41–45 and *The Masque of Blackness* (1605), where Jonson declares that "with that great name BRITANIA, this blest Isle / Hath won her ancient dignity, and style, / A world, divided from the world" (246–48). Cf. *The Masque of Queens*, 395, *Love Freed*, 189–90 and 285, and *Pleasure Reconciled*, 198–200.

32. Quoted in Yates, "Queen Elizabeth," 85–86 from *Le Cena de la Ceneri*, which in another, more straightforward version remains wistful: "If

the empire of fortune would correspond to and would match the empire of the most generous mind and spirit, [Elizabeth] would be the sole empress of this terrestrial sphere, and with fuller significance that divine hand of hers would sustain the globe of this universal monarchy" (trans. Jaki, 83).

33. Strype, *Annals* 3:618, 620; letter noted and affair discussed in Fell-Smith, *John Dee*, 201–13. Cf. the queen's involvement in two other frauds, by Cornelius de Lannoy (1565–67) (*CSP* 1:249, 275–77, 289, 292), and Roloff Peterson (1593–97) (*CSP* 3:376–77, 422–23, 435, 558; 4:17–18, 31, 105, 119–20, 219, 518–19, 539, 543).

34. In the 1589 edition, 245.

35. Hakluyt (1598) later elaborates Best's immediately subsequent claim that Spain's apparent triumphs in navigation had all along been too materially grounded to betoken any real spirit: "For admit that [Spain's] way [to America] was much longer" than England's,

> yet was it never barred with ice, mist, or darkness, but was at all seasons of the year open and Navigable; yea and that for the most part with fortunate and fit gales of wind. Moreover they had no foreign prince to intercept or molest them, but their own Towns, Islands, and main lands to succour them. . . . And had they not continual and yearly trade in some one part or other of Africa, for getting of slaves, for sugar, for Elephants' teeth, grains, silver, gold, and other precious wares, which served as allurements to draw them on by little and little, and as props to stay them from giving over their attempts? (Taylor, *Original Writings* 2:437)

36. The matching complaint of Thomas Hacket (1568)—"But alas, the greater number of men are given to idleness and sensuality" (Thevet, *New Found Worlde*, *3r)—was one of the most persistent features of New World propaganda in the English Renaissance. Cf. Captain John Smith's famous attack (1612) on those former settlers who slandered Jacobean Virginia:

> because they found not English cities, nor such fair houses, nor at their own wishes any of their accustomed dainties, with feather beds and down pillows, Taverns and alehouses in every breathing place, neither such plenty of gold and silver and dissolute liberty as they expected, [they] had little or no care of any thing, but to pamper their bellies, to fly away with our Pinnaces, or procure their means to return for England. (*Works* 1:176)

The attack copies almost verbatim Thomas Harriot's account (1588) of the first Virginian colony (*Report*, in Quinn, *Roanoke* 1:323), which itself echoes in part Richard Eden's dedication to the first collection of New World voyages printed in England, *A Treatyse of the Newe India* (1553) (AA4r).

37. Writing on the same voyage, Edward Hayes (c. 1583) seconds the idea that the English will, indeed must, convert the Indians, as evidenced

> by the revolution and course of God's word and religion, which from the beginning hath moved from the East, towards, & at last unto the West, where it is like to end, unless the same begin again where it did in the East, which were to expect a like world again. But we are assured of the contrary by the prophecy of Christ, whereby we gather, that after his word preached

throughout the world shall be the end. And as the Gospel when it descended Westward began in the South, and afterward spread into the North of Europe: even so, as the same hath begun in the South countries of America, no less hope may be gathered that it will also spread into the North. (Quinn, *Gilbert* 2:388)

This Gospel version of the westward march of empire became very popular in Jacobean times: see Lovejoy, *Religious Enthusiasm*, 16–20.

38. Raleigh nicely flatters such hopes when he reports a Spanish story that certain Indians "now admitting of Christianity and obedience to the king of Spain" had sent Philip their idol, "a Giant all of Gold," "in token they were become Christians, and held him for their king" (*Discoverie*, 84). More rigorous antimaterialists may condemn this model of colonial exchange, but they nevertheless accept it as what happens in America. Thomas Bastard (1598), for example, considers gold a trifling reward for spirit:

> *Indie* new found the Christian faith doth hold,
> Rejoicing in our heavenly merchandize.
> Which we have chang'd for precious stones & gold
> And pearl and feathers, and for Popingyes.
> Now are they loving, meek and virtuous,
> Contented, sweetly with poor godliness.
> Now are we salvage, fierce and barbarous,
> Rich with the fuel of all wickedness.
> (*Chrestoleros*, 85–86)

Cf. Herbert's "The Church Militant," ll. 249–58.

39. James was, of course, even more conspicuous a poet: during Elizabeth's reign, Gabriel Harvey (c. 1598–99) refers to him as "the sovereign of the divine art" (*Marginalia*, 231).

40. For an extensive treatment of the poverty of poets, see the three Parnassus plays (c. 1598–1602); as their editor J. B. Leishman notes, the first play specifically alludes to *Hero and Leander* (at 1.63–64 and 76). The complaint about patronage is in particular a pastoral topos derived from Theocritus's *Idyll*, 17. Eclogue 3 of Thomas Lodge's *Fig for Momus* (1595), for instance, portrays Lodge as the shepherd "Golde" (*Works* 3:23), himself a treasure who does not receive the literal gold due him. I will, shortly, treat the most famous instance of this topos, the "October" eclogue in Spenser's *Shepheardes Calender*.

41. For Lesbos as England, see Hunter, *Lyly*, 180, who notes that Sapho in *Sapho and Phao* is a general compliment to Elizabeth, "and Sapho in Ovid appears as the Queen of Lesbos."

42. Though devoted to a satire on greed, Richard Barnfield's mock-panegyric "The Encomion of Lady Pecunia: or The Praise of Money" (1598) nevertheless cannot resist praising Elizabeth, and even true religion, in the terms it otherwise denounces:

> The time was once, when fair *Pecunia*, here
> Did basely go attired all in Leather:

> But since her reign, she never did appear
> But richly clad; in Gold, or Silver either:
>   Nor reason is it, that her Golden reign
>   With baser Coin, eclipsed should remain.
>
> And as the Coin, she hath repurified,
> From baser substance, to the purest Metals:
> Religion so, hath she refined beside,
> From Papistry, to Truth.
>
> (90–91)

43. For Sidney, the fact that the oracle of Delphi should choose to prophesy in verse already constitutes a defense of poetry: "For that same exquisite observing of number and measure in words, and that high flying liberty of conceit proper to the poet, did seem to have some divine force in it" (*Apology*, 11). The defense is traditional: cf. Horace, *Ars Poetica*, 400.

The conventional excuses for poets making wisdom look trifling range from fear of reprisal (e.g., Smith, *Elizabethan* 1:65), consideration for simpleminded readers (66), contempt for simpleminded readers (2:203), and hopes to make wisdom memorable (ibid.).

44. In Agrippa's influential attack on poetry, "trifle" and "fable" are almost synonymous: cf., e.g., *De Incertitudine*, 33–34. Stephen Gosson cites the poets' addiction to mythology as the best proof of their trifling. Either the mythological divinities are themselves merely trifles mystified—for example, the ancient poets made "gods of them that were brute beasts, in the likeness of men, divine goddesses of common harlots" (*Apologie*, 127)—or else the gods "delight in toys" (132), like material sacrifices and "light huswifes" (*Schoole*, 87).

45. Yates, it is true, at first imagines the substitution as "half-unconscious" ("Queen Elizabeth," 78), by which she means that the Elizabethan state in part exploited the connection, but she finally decides that "it would be, perhaps, extravagant to suggest that, in a Christian country, the worship of the state Virgo was deliberately intended to take [the] place" of the cult of the Virgin (79). I do not deny that the cult of Elizabeth may have fostered idolatry or the exploitation of it, only that Mary's replacement by Elizabeth depended primarily on the transference of actual superstition, "unconscious" or otherwise.

46. For another instance of an overtly superstitious pilgrim involved in the defense of England "from the world sequestered all alone" (16), see Weever, *Whipping*.

47. "Hobynoll" celebrates "that fair Island's right / Which thou doest veil in Type of Fairy land / Eliza's blessed field, that *Albion* hight" (*V* 3:186).

48. The criticism that the Elizians mistake temporal for spiritual good fortune would, no doubt, have seemed to Copley supported by assertions like G. D.'s in his *Briefe Discoverie* (1588): "Let *God's* especial favors therefore miraculously showed unto *her Majesty*, and his exceeding blessings abundantly poured out by him upon her Country, be unto you (as it is

indeed) an assured argument, that her *Religion* is the true *Religion* acceptable unto God, and conformable to his word" (119).

49. Cf., e.g., Abraham Fleming (1589) calling the *Eclogues* "even a pearl in a shell, divine wit in a homely style, shepherds and clowns representing great personages, and matters of weight wrapt up in country talk" (*Bucoliks*, A2v).

50. Barckley, *Discourse*, ∗3v. See Yates, "Queen Elizabeth."

51. Cf. Patterson, "Re-opening," 64.

52. As E. K.'s headnote suggests, the other homogeneity from which Colin's heterosexual desire proves alienating is Hobbinol's homoerotic love. See William Webbe's *Discourse of English Poetrie* (1586) for evidence that readers did indeed notice "the motion of some unsavory love" in the *Calender* (in Smith, *Elizabethan* 1:264–65; quoted in Wells, *Spenser Allusions*, 9).

53. Palgrave (*V* 7:395), Greg (398) and Renwick (401–402) discuss the marked similarities between the stanzas of "Aprill" and "November."

54. Noted by Malone (*V* 7:402). Following Malone on this and on his identification of Dido's lover Lobbin as Robin Leicester, Mary Parmenter concludes that Dido is indeed Elizabeth, who, in the words of the *Variorum*, "is now figuratively dead to Leicester by reason of the threatened French marriage" (404). Paul McLane supports this analysis, noting, for example, that Gabriel Harvey had a year earlier complimented the queen by calling her Elissa, and that the "Aprill" nymphs recur in "November" (*Study*, 47–60). While the connection with Alçenon makes sense, the decoding by Parmenter and McLane is nevertheless reductive, and collapses the distinction obtaining, as I will try to demonstrate, between Elizabeth and a certain view of her which "Dido" represents.

55. Cf. Montrose: "Colin's elegy for Dido is a displacement of the Rosalind-Elisa problem in which Spenser attempts a radical solution by symbolic means: kill the lady, thus sending her spirit to heaven, where the lover's spirit might hope eventually to join her in a communion free from the accidents and constraints that characterize earthly life—life within the body and the body politic" ("Perfecte," 54). In my account, Spenser ultimately does not endorse such *contemptus mundi*.

McLane (*Study*, 27–46) maintains that "Rosalind" too has all along meant Elizabeth, but Spenser's question is, again, what does "Elizabeth" mean? McLane's reductive claim must overlook the differences in character and status between Rosalind on the one hand and Eliza and Dido on the other. It is important to note that Spenser is less nervous about figuring Elizabeth as a private person when that person is also a fairy—Belphoebe; see chapter 3.

56. "If we follow out the Ovidian logic of the [Pan and Syrinx] myth, which E. K. retells concisely in his gloss, it becomes obvious that Elisa is also a personification of pastoral poetry: the 'offspring' of the love chase and the nymph's transformation were the reeds from which Pan created his pipe" (Montrose, "Perfecte," 40). As Montrose notes, the presence of

this myth behind Eliza makes Colin's song seem an expression not of virginal innocence but of "sublimated eroticism" (50).

57. McLane, *Study*, 60 notes the pun on *Eliza* here.

58. Sidney, "The 7. Wonders of England" (written c. 1580); cited in Wilson, *England's Eliza*, 248.

59. For the view that "the longing for paradise" is "the fundamental object of Spenser's criticism" in *The Shepheardes Calender*, see Hamilton, "Argument," and Berger, "Mode" and "Orpheus." MacCaffrey covers similar terrain, though she oddly contradicts her developmental account of the *Calender* by ending with "Aprill," which she believes shows how "the arts of government can unite antagonists and create another Eden" ("Allegory," 106).

"Aprill" 's waterfall topos, perhaps the most widely imitated topos in the *Calender*, epitomizes for Spenser how the innocent ideal of presence rests on a latent awareness of absence. That is, the waterfall seems to legitimate an ideal of presence not in avoiding but in overmastering absence, presenting change as continuity and motion as stasis. By "November," however, the fall in the waterfall begins to take precedence, when songs of praise are, again, no longer tuned to the waterfall but turned to weeping (79). Spenser's earliest and so potentially most innocent published poems, his translations of Petrarch and Du Bellay, also characterize the waterfall topos as ultimately apocalyptic. In "The Visions of Petrarch," the poet watches as Muses and Nymphs "tune their voyce / To the soft sounding of the waters fall" (48–49); "But while therein I tooke my chiefe delight, / I saw (alas) the gaping earth devoure / The spring, the place, and all cleane out of sight" (51–53). The sight of this and other disasters persuades Petrarch to "loath this base world, and thinke of heavens blis" (96). "The Visions of Bellay," with their "virgin faire" who "to falling rivers thus tun'd her sobs" (127, 130), simply compress the recurrent narrative. For interesting reflections on the waterfall topos in Spenser and its subsequent history, see Hollander, "Footing," 22–28 and "Undersong," 12–19.

60. Among modern readers Michael O'Connell typifies this mistake when he claims that Colin's abandonment of political praise highlights the degree to which that praise had all along been an "idealization," and yet "the actual Elizabeth falls short of the ideal Eliza" only "owing to the fallen human condition" for which Colin's "love melancholy" is simply an apt metaphor. In other words, O'Connell believes that there is nothing wrong with the repudiated ideal as it stands, and he eventually works himself round toward celebrating the inadequate "actual" too: Spenser wants "to show to men within the fallen state the points of connection between their actual ruler and the ideal of which she is merely the human participation" (*Mirror*, 6–7). Montrose agrees that "Colin's *April* encomium is an ideal image toward which Elizabeth may aspire," and considers Spenser so confident of Elizabeth's proximity to this ideal that Spenser advances the encomium as indeed "an English and Protestant fulfillment of Vergil's fourth eclogue" ("Perfecte," 43, 40).

61. Bennett notes that "the third quarter of the *Revelation* is a ringing of changes upon the lay of "Aprill" (Blenerhasset, *Revelation*, xi).

62. In the poem Elizabeth seems worried by this claim about her immortality:

> The life (quoth she) of every living thing
> Must perish quite, for death will it deface:
> But death to death by due desert to bring
> Such death on earth is life everlasting,
> I know right well such immortality
> you have obtaind, and such remains for me.
> (Fr)

Yet I would argue that the almost hermetic abstractness of this demurral indicates Blenerhasset's resistance to making Eliza's immortality merely ideal.

63. See Bauckham, *Tudor Apocalypse*, Christianson, *Reformers*, Firth, *Apocalyptic*, and Olsen, *Foxe*, all of whom dispute William Haller's claim in *Foxe's 'Book of Martyrs'* that the Elizabethans imagined their nation as a millennial triumph.

64. In the manner of "October," Palinode is extraordinarily explicit about doubting whether Essex as a participant in the expedition deserves praise: "I see no Palm, I see no Laurel bows, / Circle his temples, or adorn his brows, / I hear no triumphs for this late return, / But many a Herdsman more disposed to mourn" (94–97).

65. Sidney's death seems for Peele to epitomize his new doubts about England's potentiality; compare "Eclogue," 61–77, and *Polyhymnia*, 108–14, 224–26. "Augusta" is, of course, the queen, for whom Peele must invent a new pseudonym in order to *avoid* the connection with "Elizian fields."

66. Cf. Thomas Goodrick and Edward Kellet, respectively, in the collection of elegies called *Sorrowes Joy* (1603): "Eliza to *Elysian* fields is gone" (6); "Eliza was a flower / Worthy alone to deck the Elizian plain" (26). Interestingly, John Weever's elegy for Spenser makes a similar point about "Colin": "Colin's gone home, the glory of his clime" (*Epigrammes*, 101).

67. Cf. Richard Niccols (1603): "Where's Collin Clout, or Rowland now become, / That wont to lead our Shepheards in a ring?" (*Expicedium*, B3r). For other allusions to Spenser in elegies for Elizabeth, see Wells, *Spenser Allusions*, 92–96.

68. Dedicatory sonnet to Ormond (V 3:193); my emphasis. The opening lines of *The Faerie Queene*, an imitation of what were once considered the opening lines of the *Aeneid*, underscore by omission this lack of georgics in Spenser's career. Spenser says he now leaves "oaten reeds" for "trumpets sterne"; Virgil, that he left pastoral for georgics (*et egressus silvis vicina coegi / ut quamvis avido parerent arva colono, / gratum opus agricolis*), which he now leaves in turn for epic (*at nunc horrentia Martis*).

69. For the opposition to romance among the first generation of humanists—More, Erasmus, Vives—see Adams, "Bold Bawdry"; for the

pertinence to Spenser of such opposition, see, e.g., Bennett, *Evolution*, 74–77. Perhaps the most famous association of chivalric romance with the "standing pool" of "Papistry" appears in Ascham's *Scholemaster*, 68–69.

70. Cf. John Harvey (1588), who asserts that "Legendaries" like "the tales of Hobgoblin," "king Arthur," and "Orlando furioso," were intended "to busy the minds of the vulgar sort, or to set their heads awork withal, and to avert their conceits from the consideration of serious, and graver matters, by feeding their humors, and delighting their fancies with such fabulous and ludicrous toys" (*Discoursive*, 68–69; quoted in Thomas, "Hobgoblin," 421).

71. From the third eclogue of *Idea The Shepheards Garland* (1593) (*Works* 1:55).

72. Nashe is denouncing what he takes to be the recently manifested atavism of English publishers: "What else I pray you do these bable [i.e., bauble, babble, Babel] bookmongers endeavor, but to repair the ruinous walls of *Venus* Court, to restore to the world that forgotten Legendary license of lying, to imitate afresh the fantastical dreams of those exiled Abbey-lubbers, from whose idle pens proceeded those worn out impressions of the feigned no where acts, of Arthur of the round table, Arthur of little Britain, sir Tristram, Huon of Burdeaux, the Squire of low degree, the four sons of Amon, with infinite others" (*Works* 1:11).

73. Even before *The Faerie Queene* Spenser imagines fairies a cure not only for materialism but for the *Calender's contemptus* as well. His *Prosopopoia. Or Mother Hubberds Tale* begins where *The Shepheardes Calender* leaves off, with the departure of Astraea:

> It was the month, in which the righteous Maide,
> That for disdaine of sinfull worlds upbraide,
> Fled back to heaven, whence she was first conceived,
> Into her silver bowre the Sunne receeved;
> And the hot *Syrian* Dog on him awayting,
> After the chafed Lyons cruell bayting,
> Corrupted had th'ayre with his noysome breath,
> And powr'd on th'earth plague, pestilence, and death.
>
> (1–8)

This heavenly wrath sets Spenser's "weake bodie . . . on fire with griefe" (15), until his raconteur friends come to cheer him:

> Some tolde of Ladies, and their Paramoures;
> Some of brave Knights, and their renowned Squires;
> Some of the Faeries and their strange attires;
> And some of Geaunts hard to be beleeved,
> That the delight thereof me much releeved.
>
> (28–32)

Increasingly ironic, the lines present fairies as simply the next step in absurdity after knights. Yet Spenser seems to appreciate his friends' "nowhere" stories precisely because they are "strange" and "hard to be beleeved," and therefore able to absorb despair about a world apparently alienated from or emptied of God.

74. Whether a consequence of modesty (Chettle) or vanity (Jonson), Elizabeth's reputed distaste for actual mirrors complements Spenser's antimaterialism here; see Jonson, *Jonson* 1:141–42, 166.

CHAPTER 3. ERROR AS A MEANS OF EMPIRE

1. For an earlier view that Spenser is consistently imperialist, however, see Greenlaw, "Spenser." Impressed by the fact that the first fairy king is said to have ruled India and America (*FQ* 2.10.72), Michael Murrin claims that Fairyland simply "is" India and America, and "thus a dream of empire" that "compensates for [England's] political weakness" (*Allegorical*, 137–40). But Murrin never answers the central question raised by doubting critics, which is how Spenser's depiction of fairyland may be said to enact such imperial "wish fulfillment" (139). More persuasively, Greenblatt in his own discussion of Spenser as "our originating and preeminent poet of empire" relates Guyon's destruction of the Bower of Bliss to the colonization of both America and Ireland (*Renaissance Self-Fashioning*, 169–92); but he never explains why, if the Bower is a figure for colonies, Guyon ends up abandoning it.

2. In a passage I will later discuss, Spenser urges the occupation of Guiana (*FQ* 4.11.22). I do not mean to say that Spenser shows no sign of imperialism before book 4—see, e.g., 2.3.41, 3.3.22–23, and 3.9.44—only that his exhortations to empire are rarely direct.

3. In his *Sir Francis Drake* (1596), Charles Fitz-Geffrey does insist that Drake is a hero of epic proportions. If Drake had "been born in *Agamemnon's* age," Fitz-Geffrey maintains, "all poets would have written in his praise / Their *Æneads*, *Iliads*, and *Odysses*" (*Poems*, 23); and Fitz-Geffrey advises Spenser, among others, to give up singing about any other subject: "Let famous RED CROSS yield to famous DRAKE, / And good Sir GUYON give to him the lance" (22). But the tedious repetitiveness of Fitz-Geffrey's praise betrays the fact that he has no epic action to celebrate. Like his list of England's voyagers, which ends up bemoaning the death of every contemporary hero he names (67–78), Fitz-Geffrey's praise of Drake continually turns to elegy: for example, "Had he surviv'd, *Tempe* had been our land, / And *Thames* had stream'd with *Tagus'* golden sand" (40).

For similarly troubled Elizabethan claims concerning the potentially epic grandeur of voyagers like Drake, see Warner, *Albions England* 12:71, Segar, *Honor*, 58–59, and a very revealing eclogue, possibly by Edward Fairfax, entitled "Ida and Opilio." In the eclogue, Opilio begins praising English voyagers by first describing Drake's successful circumnavigation; he then turns to Frobisher, who, though heroic, failed to find the northwest passage or actual gold; next he alludes to Gilbert, who "lost himself when his light frigate sank"; then he bemoans the voyagers to Russia who were either frozen or lost—at which point the poem breaks off.

The voyagers were not the only potential heroes of Elizabethan epic. Samuel Daniel in *The Civill Wars* (1599) irritatedly wonders why Spenser bothers with "fained *Paladins*" when he "may give glory to the true designs / Of *Bourchier, Talbot, Nevile, Willoughby*" (5.4)—but these are *past* imperial heroes, and their epics do not get written. William Alabaster began an epic on the life of Elizabeth, his *Elisaeis* (c. 1590), but it breaks off after Princess Elisa enters the Tower.

4. Elizabethan readers were certainly capable of making such a comparison. During the years Spenser was composing *The Faerie Queene*, a number of translated histories of the Spanish and Portuguese conquests began appearing for the first time since Eden's lonely Marian edition (1555) of Peter Martyr: for example, Gomara, *Pleasant Historie* (Spanish ed. 1552; trans. 1578); Zarate, *Strange and Delectable History* (1555; trans. 1581); Lopes de Castanheda, *First Book* (1551; trans. 1582); Las Casas, *Spanish Colonie* (1552; trans. 1583); and Hakluyt's own Latin edition of Martyr, *De Orbe Novo* (1587). The first known translation in any language of another Camões-like epic, Ercilla's *Araucana* (1569–90), is itself Elizabethan, *The Historie of Araucana*, once attributed to Burghley but now to George Carew (1555–1629), a close contemporary of Spenser who, like Spenser, spent many years in Ireland (*Historie*, vii–viii n. 1). It is interesting to note, however, as Pierce does, that Carew's sketchy prose translation shows Carew unconcerned with the epic pretensions of Ercilla's historical account.

Other heroic poems about voyagers also preceding *The Faerie Queene* include Gambara's *De navigatione Christophori Columbi* (1581), Stella's *Columbeidos* (1585) (published first in London and dedicated by Jacobo Castelvetro to Raleigh), and Lobo Lasso de la Vega's *Cortes valeroso* (1588). For a general account of the Columbus poems, see Bradner, "Columbus."

5. See *FQ* 3.proem.5, and the dedicatory sonnets to Lord Grey de Wilton (*V* 3:194) and Raleigh (196).

6. Noted in Hamilton, ed., *Faerie Queene*, 31. The storm has other Virgilian parallels: namely, the tempests in *Aeneid* 1 and 4 that threaten Aeneas's own epic quest by driving him into Dido's arms. But Spenser's reference to Jove and his lover's lap is specifically georgic—*tum pater omnipotens fecundis imbribus Aether / coniugis in gremium laetae descendit* (*Georgics* 2.325–26)—and forces these generically more appropriate allusions into the background.

7. Cf. Hobbinol in "September," requesting Diggon in typically pastoral manner to "sitte we downe here under the hill: / Tho may we talke, and tellen our fill, / And make a mocke at the blustring blast" (52–54); and see too the storms, blasts, shade, and heat of "Januarye," 23, "Februarie," 1–2, "June," 2, "Julye," 25–26, "August," 47–48, "October," 116, and "December," 2 and 5. For the cave as a pastoral pleasance, see Virgil's *Eclogues* (1.75, 5.6, 5.19, 9.41) and the "shepheards den" (96) and "darkesome caves" (117) of *Virgils Gnat*.

In other writers the tree catalogue itself is often overtly pastoral: Sannazaro's *Arcadia* opens with such a catalogue, for instance, and another appears in the last eclogue of Sidney's *Arcadia* book 1. Ovid's oft-cited version of the tree catalogue belongs to an episode in the *Metamorphoses* with an obvious pertinence to the Error episode generally: through the attractive power of his song, Orpheus manages to convert a plain into a shady grove (10.86ff.). Spenser demonstrates that he associates even this scene with pastoral when he transfers the burden of Orpheus's song, the death of the lovely boy Cyparisse, to the more obviously pastoral woodland setting of canto 6. (The setting in fact recalls "Aprill" specifically: "singing all a shepheards ryme," the woodgods worship Una "as Queene, with olive girlond cround," 13.)

8. For the corresponding theological allegory of Error, see Cullen, *Infernal*, 25–26; Nohrnberg, *Analogy*, 135–51; and Klein, "Errour." The term *proportion* is E. K.'s; he describes the twelve eclogues as "proportioned to the state of the twelve months" (*V* 7:10; see also 113).

The later Fradubio episode (*FQ* 1.2.30–44) represents this problem more directly than the Error episode does by replacing the trees that fit human intention with humans (or at least elves) who have been transformed into trees.

9. In noting the mirror relation between Redcross and Error, Paul Alpers, for example, calls the battle "a genuine psychomachia, an expression of conflicting potentialities within a single mind" (*Poetry*, 337).

10. For a brief history of this conception of Error from the Bible to the Middle Ages, see Zacher, *Curiosity*, 42–44.

11. For this analysis of a mirror relation thwarted by miniaturization, I am indebted to Steven Knapp's examination of the Narcissus topos in Wordsworth (*Personification*, 112–16).

12. See *Allegorical Temper*, 120–60.

13. Cf. the far more straightforwardly heroic simile from *The First Part of the Tragicall Raigne of Selimus* (acted c. 1590), which borrows Spenser's imagery here: "A matchless knight is warlike *Selimus*, / And like a shepherd mongst a swarm of gnats, / Dings down the flying Persians with their swords" (Greene, *Works* 14:287; noted in Wells, *Spenser Allusions*, 38; see also Greene, *Works* 14:289).

For other instances in Spenser of elegiac similes that defer a monster's destruction, see *FQ* 4.7.30 and 5.8.43.

14. For gnats, see A. B. Chambers's article on Donne's "Canonization" ("Fly," 254, 255, 257); and Lucian 1.191. Chambers's helpful survey oddly omits the fly iconography that would seem the most immediately appropriate to Donne's poem: the fact that the fly is considered, as Lucian says, "the creature of a day" (87).

15. Menippus actually compares men to ants (Lucian 2.301). Erasmus would seem to have substituted flies or gnats in order to exploit their associations with ephemerality.

16. For such "noyance" provoking *contemptus*, see Spenser's "Visions of the worlds vanitie" (esp. stanzas 2 and 10), which incessantly draws the moral, "Let therefore nought that great is, therein glorie, / Sith so

small thing his happines may varie" (111–112). For the persistent relation in Spenser's mind of flies or gnats to the deflation of vanity, see also *Virgils Gnat; Muiopotmos: or The Fate of the Butterflie*; and, in *Two Other, Very Commendable Letters*, the Latin poem to Harvey (*V* 10:10, ll. 174–75).

17. Noted by Hamilton, ed., *Faerie Queene*, 36.

18. *V* 7:10. It would be a mistake to dismiss the echo as accidental or merely a second instance of a stock image: in Spenser's eighty-eight uses of the word *wings*, he applies the adjective *tender* to it only this once. The similar "tender plumes" occurs in *Colin Clout*, 422, where Colin praises Samuel Daniel as a fledgling poet along the lines E. K. had earlier spoken of Colin himself. For possible sources, see *V* 7:239.

19. Renwick (*V* 7:240) notes that the locus classicus for this theory is Vida: "[A youngster], unskilled in matters [poetic], ought not to venture to compose long *Iliads*, but should gain experience little by little, making his debut by playing on the shepherds' slender pipes. Soon he will be able to tell in verse of the fearsome fates of a gnat, or of how in boundless battle the murderous mouse dealt death to the croaking troops of marsh-loving frogs, or weave a tale of the stratagems and webs of the subtle spider" (*De Arte Poetica* 1.459–465).

The interchangeability of flies and persons is dramatically realized in the next episode, when Archimago transforms two sprites "like little Flyes" into the images of Una and a squire (1.38). Later, Redcross in Orgoglio's dungeon, "all his flesh shronk up like withered flowres" (8.41), becomes a gnatlike murmurer (38).

20. Note that "wound" (25), gash, replaces "wound" (18), enveloped, in this open mode. For suggestive remarks on the "radical openness" of Spenserian narrative generally, see Parker, *Romance*, 54–113.

21. Cf. *Eclogues* 9.39–43, noted by Rummel in her edition of *De Contemptu*.

22. Greene's "text," Matthew 3.10, comes closer to Spenser's emphasis on inutility as the outward sign of monastic evil: "And now also is the axe put to the root of the trees: therefore every tree, which bringeth not forth good fruit, is hewn down, and cast into the fire." The comparison of the monasteries to these scriptural trees was a popular one. Cf. the member of Parliament (1536) who argued that, in dissolving the lesser monasteries, Parliament should remember that "these were as thorns, but the great abbots were putrefied old oaks" (quoted in Wright, *Three Chapters*, 107); or Foxe, who refers to Cromwell's plucking the monasteries up by the roots (*Acts* 5:368 and 378). For extended jokes on this comparison, see Hall, *Union*, 825–26, retold in Foxe, *Acts* 5:179–81; and Harington's translation of Ariosto, *Orlando Furioso*, pp. 6–7.

The Catholic Nicholas Harpsfield (c. 1553–58) also relates monasteries to woods, but in a much more favorable light: "What is the decay of woods and the cause of the excessive price of wood," he asks, "but the suppression of the said monasteries, which did carefully nourish, supply, and husband the same?" ("Treatise," 299).

23. Frere and Kennedy, *Visitation Articles* 2:59–60. For the topos of the relics' nearly overwhelming number and variety, see "Declaration of the Faith," 39, Wright, *Three Chapters*, 226–27, and the prefatory epistle to the English translation of Erasmus's *Peregrinatio* (c. 1536–37), which declares that Erasmus "hath set forth to the quick image, before men's eyes, the superstitious worship and false honor given to bones, heads, jaws, arms, stocks, stones, shirts, smocks, coats, caps, hats, shoes, mitres, slippers, saddles, rings, beads, girdles, bowls, bells, books, gloves, ropes, tapers, candles, boots, spurs (my breath was almost past me)" (104–5).

24. Cf. Averell's *Mervailous Combat* (1588), which refers to "that peddler the Pope, that continually unloadeth his pack to make some sale with us of his Popish trash" (D4r); and warns that papists "will make you believe they are friends, but they are deadly enemies." "Beware the Fox," he concludes, "that shape of lamb retains" (E1r). Calvin makes the fox sound more specifically Erroneous when he deplores those papists who "busied their heads about pelting trifles, and would needs make meritorious deeds of them, and in the meanwhile did cast men's consciences into so strait bonds, as was enough to choke them" (*Sermons*, 217r).

25. Hume argues that the distinction between wolves and foxes in "September," 154–55, suggests that the wolf represents a straightforward papist and the fox "a secret papist who presents himself as a Church of England pastor" (*Spenser*, 21–23). Whether overt or covert, however, the fox remains "Roman"; as Tyndale (1530) said of all papist prelates, "They be one kingdom, sworn together one to help another scattered abroad in all realms" (*Practice of Prelates*, 441).

26. Cf. Higden's *Polychronicon*: "Of all lands' riches this land hath need to none; / All lands moot [i.e., must] seek help needs of this alone [*Insula praedives, quae toto non eget orbe, / Et cuius totus indiget orbis ope*]" (2:20–21 [1.41]).

27. "Historicall Description," 397; see also 371, 395, 396. For more on Armstrong, see Bindoff, "Armstrong"; for the attribution of the *Discourse* to Smith, see *Discourse*, xx–xxvi. While Smith considers the chief cause of England's economic troubles to be not England's trifling but its "debasing or rather corrupting of our coin and treasure" (*Discourse*, 69), he ascribes this problem also to English insularity: "If men might live within themselves altogether without borrowing of any other thing outward, we might devise what coin we would; but since we must have need of other and they of us, we must frame our things not after our own fantasies but to follow the common market of all the world, and we may not set the price of things at our pleasure but follow the price of the universal market of the world" (86).

28. For the conflation of economic and theological issues in England's troubles with Spain, cf. Hakluyt on the need for "Western Planting": "All other english Trades are grown beggarly or dangerous, especially in all the king of Spain his Dominions, where our men are driven to fling their Bibles and prayer Books into the sea, and to forswear and renounce their

religion and conscience and consequently their obedience to her Majesty" ("Discourse," 211).

29. *Revelation* G1v; *Araygnement* 5.1.139–41. Cf. the entertainment at Elvetham (1591), in which six virgins welcome Elizabeth with this song:

> Now birds record new harmony,
> And trees do whistle melody:
> Now every thing that nature breeds,
> Doth clad it self in pleasant weeds,
>   O beauteous Queen of second Troy,
>   Accept of our unfained joy.
>   (Nichols, *Progresses* 3:109)

Greene ends his *Masquerado* hoping only that God will continue to "shroud us against Spain, the Pope, and all other enemies of the Gospel" (*Works*, 5:288).

30. As if to resolve the problem of the foreign altogether, Hakluyt's "Discourse" imagines North America becoming a kind of English Old World: "This western voyage will yield unto us all the commodities of Europe, Africa, and Asia" (222).

31. Quinn, *Gilbert* 1:161. Cf. Peckham, *True Reporte*, 462; Hakluyt, "Discourse," 235, 270; and two pamphlets by the elder Hakluyt (1585) in Taylor, *Original Writings* 2:332 and 343.

32. Eight years later, this time in the West Indies, Frobisher is back to his old tricks (Keeler, *Voyage*, 192). For another extreme version of an extremely commonplace practice—the use of trifles to allure Indians—see James Rosier in 1605, beguiling two natives and hoping to catch a third: "I opened the box, and showed them trifles to exchange, thinking thereby to have banished fear from the other, and drawn him to return: but when we could not, we used little delay, but suddenly laid hands upon them" (Quinn, *English*, 284). Shakespeare derives the name of Sycorax's god Setebos from a similar story (Eden, *Decades*, 252).

33. Best marvels at his vision of the savages sneaking behind rocks "as though we had no eyes to see them" (*True Discourse*, 74). Incidentally, he considers Frobisher's joke better made by having the savage malingerer shot elsewhere than in his face, so that he can go "away a true and no fained cripple" (75).

34. I am indebted to Frederick Goldin's excellent *Mirror* for these thoughts on Narcissus, though, as my account of Ovid shows, I differ with Goldin about the nature of the Ovidian outcome. Goldin thinks that what happens to Narcissus can best be described as "the mind's discovery that no sensible image can reflect it" (211), but in fact Narcissus's image reflects the mind quite well:

> Thou dost pretend some kind of hope of friendship by thy cheer.
> For when I stretch mine arms to thee, thou stretchest thine likewise.
> And if I smile thou smilest too: And when that from mine eyes
> The tears do drop, I well perceive the water stands in thine.
>   (*Metamorphoses* 3.575–78)

35. Cf. this famous instance of Catholic "juggling" reported by Geoffrey Chamber: "Upon the defacing of the late Monastery of Boxley, and plucking down of the Images of the same, I found in the Image of the Rood called the Rood of Grace, the which heretofore hath been had in great veneration of people, certain engines and old wire, with old rotten sticks in the back of the same, that did cause the eyes of the same to move and stare in the head thereof like unto a lively thing; and also the nether lip in like wise to move as though it should speak; which, so famed, was not a little strange to me and other that was present" (Ellis, *Original Letters* 3:168). Cf. "A Declaration of the Faith," 38; and Foxe, who along with other denunciations of the Rood reprints a ballad on the subject, "The Fantasie of Idolatrie" (*Acts* 5:179, 397, 403–9, 824).

36. The man was in fact embalmed, "preserved to have been sent back again into his own country," presumably to impress the natives with English kindness—the doctor who examined the native declares, for instance, that the man had died from "too liberal" a diet, a situation "brought about by the utmost solicitousness on the part of that great man, the Captain, and by boundless generosity from those with whom he lodged" (Stefannson, *Three Voyages*, 2:135–37, translation in Cheshire et al., "Frobisher's Eskimos," 24, 40). But even if the corpse would prove to the Eskimos that the English had not eaten it, how happy could the dead body make them? Like the paintings, the embalming derives from the desire at once to educate the Eskimos in their own finitude and mortality and to exhibit the uncanny preservative powers of the English.

37. P. H. Hulton seconds Best's testimony by noting that "there are records of payment to the Netherlandish artist Cornelis Ketel, for various portraits of the man—in large and in miniature, in his own costume, in English dress, and naked" ("Drawings," 18). Hulton's article conveniently reproduces the surviving illustrations resulting from the Frobisher voyages.

38. Cf. the elder Hakluyt, who in 1580 advises Pet and Jackman to take "the book of the attire of all nations" (Taylor, *Original Writings* 1:155) as a gift for the Great Khan.

39. As Captain John Smith (1624) reports, however, savage one-worldliness can as easily lead to battle as to flight: "We demanded why they came in that manner to betray us, that came to them in peace, and to seek their loves; he answered, they heard we were a people come from under the world, to take their world from them. We asked him how many worlds he did know, he replied, he knew no more but that which was under the sky that covered him, which were the Powhatans, with the Monacans, and the Massawomeks, that were higher up in the mountains" (*Works* 2:175–76).

40. Spenser's most explicit association of one-worldliness with pastoral appears in *Colin Clouts Come Home Again* (1595), when a fellow Irish shepherd is amazed by Colin's talk of England: "What land is that thou meanst (then *Cuddy* sayd) / And is there other, then whereon we stand?"

(290–91). I will take up the question of Colin's new relation to a plurality of worlds in chapter 5.

41. 200 tons on the second voyage and 1350 on the third (Stefannson, *Three Voyages* 2:131, 69–70).

42. "Discourse," 316–17; my emphasis. A commentator on the 1592 Hayes plan to colonize the New England area is exceptionally skeptical:

> Although at the first & upon the uttermost skirt of a land we find but a naked people, & such as while we stay not to give them law but flatter them with toys, & exchange to their advantage, & so depart, appear well inclined & apt to receive us; yet . . . it may be conceived that they have more with-in-Land towns peopled, & will when they shall see that we attempt upon them, . . . put them selves into resistance. (Quoted in Quinn, *New American World* 3:173)

43. The Virginia Company was repeatedly forced to make laws requiring that corn be planted along with tobacco: see Kingsbury, *Records* 3:147, 263, 278–79, 473, 598, 628, and 633; Rolfe, *True Relation*, 8; and Smith, *Works* 2:284.

44. For the Virginia Company's decision in 1620 to send their colony some trifles instead of food, see my pp. 76–77. Edmund Morgan notes the Virginia Company's almost inexplicable optimism: "In spite of the experience at Roanoke and in spite of the repeated starving times at Jamestown, the company simply did not envisage the provision of food as a serious problem" (*American Slavery*, 87). After reviewing and then convincingly rejecting the standard explanations for Virginia's food problem, Morgan reaches a conclusion similar to my own, that the English could not reconcile the fact of their starvation with the theory of their cultural superiority to the Indians (71–90). In his next two chapters, Morgan demonstrates how the tobacco boom in the 1620s gave the settlers, especially those rich enough to secure food anyway, added reason to ignore food production. Finally, Morgan argues that few bothered to make Virginia livable because few planned to stay: in 1626 the governor and council in Virginia complain that Virginia's colonists "for the most heretofore . . . Have only endeavored a present Crop [of tobacco], and their hasty return" (Kingsbury, *Records* 4:572). The colony's advocates would like to think that various unlucky "distractions & discouragements" were the cause of such recidivism, but, as I have been arguing, the particularly virulent form of homesickness endemic to the English was itself a primary distraction.

45. Even some Englishmen realized, however, that they themselves were the more dangerous Error. After the massacre, an investor in the Virginia Company discovered that, from a total of 700 old colonists and 3,570 new ones sent to the colony in the three previous years, "only 1,240 were alive at the time of the massacre. . . . The Indians had killed 347, but something else had killed 3,000, the great majority of the persons sent" (Morgan, *American Slavery*, 101). James decided that that "something else" was the Virginia Company, which he soon dissolved.

While these observations on English relations to the Indians stem directly from Stephen Greenblatt's account of the "psychic mobility" that helped Europe conquer America, they somewhat qualify Greenblatt's emphasis on "the Europeans' ability again and again to insinuate themselves into the preexisting political, religious, even psychic structures of the natives and to turn those structures to their advantage" (*Renaissance Self-Fashioning*, 224, 227). First, although Greenblatt generalizes the Spanish duping of an entire people, the Lucayans, into a European pattern (226–29), the English were lucky to *encounter* so many Indians, let alone dupe them: Captain John Smith (1612), for instance, says that in the vicinity of Jamestown "6 or 700 [Indians] have been the most hath been seen together" (*Works* 1:160). Second, as I have tried to show, the English were at first interested less in "insinuating" themselves into the savage world than in standing outside that world and witnessing its collapse; the fate of early English colonial efforts demonstrates that English attachment to the negative ideal of a trifle world severely limited their "psychic mobility."

Steven Mullaney extends Greenblatt's argument in the direction I have also taken it, toward English interest in a savage world staged and consumed by this staging, but, like Greenblatt, Mullaney has exaggerated the degree to which "alien or residual cultures" were "consummately rehearsed and thus consummately foreclosed" ("Strange Things," 62). However, in a more recent essay that opens with Frobisher's picture-viewing Eskimo, "Brothers and Others, or the Art of Alienation," Mullaney seems less confident about the total supremacy of the colonizer. He argues that the "art of alienation" ostensibly practiced on the Eskimo can readily turn against its user.

46. Cf. Thomas, who argues that "by *Hobgoblin*, [Harvey] meant barbaric and irrational legend" ("Hobgoblin," 419–20).

47. "Spenser *Ludens*," 94–95. Cf. Nelson on Saint George: "No Renaissance humanist could have thought the legendary life of St. George a respectable literary model. By the sixteenth century accretions of impossible adventure and the buffoonery of village St. George plays must have rendered the story ridiculous; in fact, it had been denounced as apocryphal as early as the fifth" (*Poetry*, 150). Nelson's own explanation for Spenser's burlesque turns Spenser into Disney: the poem's reader can be delighted by Fairyland "only if he does not really believe in those awful monsters, witches, and bloody combats," only if he is removed "just so far from the fiction that he is at once seduced by it and amused by his own seduction" ("Spenser *Ludens*," 99).

The locus classicus for critical recognition of this problem is Richard Hurd (1762): "The age would no longer bear the naked letter of these amusing stories; and the poet was so sensible of the misfortune, that we find him apologizing for it on a hundred occasions" (*Chivalry and Romance*, 150). But Hurd thinks the romance elements of the poem are Spenser's true interest, with their allegorization only a "recourse" (154): Spenser "had no better way to take in his distress, than to hide his fairy fancies under the mystic cover of moral allegory" (152). Bennett, incidentally, assumes that Spenser's peculiar use of Arthur reveals Spenser's untidy "conversion to the Arthurian theme" long after he had begun *The Faerie Queene* (*Evolution*, 61–79).

48. *V* 9:82; see Kendrick, *British Antiquity*, 128–29, and E. K.'s previously cited note to "Aprill."

49. Cf. Frederic Carpenter's claim that the namesake of Spenser's eclogues, *The Kalendar of Shepherdes*, "prompted him to help counteract the influence of this popular manual 'by a member of the Church of Rome in the interest of his church' (Sommer), by the insertion of Protestant doctrine and polemics in his poem. Also not without influence of the same reverse sort on passages of the F.Q., such as the pictures of the Seven Deadly Sins, the House of Holiness, the allegory of the human body, etc." (quoted in *V* 7:240–41).

50. Strong is expanding Yates's brief comments in "Elizabethan Chivalry," 108–9.

51. The phrase is, of course, Yates's, in "Elizabethan Chivalry," 108.

52. Duessa laments to Redcross that after Christ's death his body was "I know not how, convaid / And fro me hid" (*FQ* 1.2.24). According to the Reformers, this sort of error is what makes Catholics worship the pope. As Tyndale has it, "The bishops would have a god upon the earth whom they might see" (*Practice*, 404); or as a cardinal in George North's *Stage of Popish Toyes* says, "I will rather worship him that is visible, than he that is invisible" (91). Duessa as Double-being negatively defines a positive not-oneness: golden on the outside (cf. her "ritch weedes," *FQ* 1.2.21), on the inside rotten ("A loathly, wrinckled hag," 8.46).

53. Isabel Rathborne notes that Gower in the *Confessio Amantis* assimilates Fairyland to a *contemptus* view of earth as illusion: upon Constance's death, Gower concludes, "The god hath made of hire an ende, / And fro this worldes faierie / Hath take hire into compaignie" (2.1593; quoted in *Spenser's Fairyland*, 2). Cf. Oberon the fairy king in Greene's *James IV* (c. 1590), who says he loves the malcontent Bohan "because thou hatest the world" (Ind. 76–77). For the standard Protestant association of fairies with papist imposture and morbidity, see my previous chapter. Rathborne herself connects Spenser's Fairyland to lands of the dead or of unborn heroes such as Elysium in the *Aeneid* book 6 and Lucian's *True History*, or closer to home, Arthur's Avalon; see especially *Spenser's Fairyland* chapters 2 and 3. Yet in the classical and Arthurian sources, the Otherworld constitutes the setting of only an episode or an unseen terminus, not of the entire poem (cf. *Spenser's Fairyland*, 153). In an attempt to explain this peculiar difference, Rathborne resorts to that Elysium of the perplexed Spenser critic, the Poem That Would Have Been Written: "Arthur was to exhibit the private virtues in Fairyland before he was king, in the twelve books of the *Faerie Queene*, and the public virtues in Britain after he was king, in Spenser's projected sequel" (152). At an earlier point in her argument, however, and more in line with her epigraph from Gower, she seems to

consider the absorption of the poem by Fairyland a natural consequence of Spenser's Prospero-like melancholy, his "feeling, which he shared with some of his greatest contemporaries, that the glory of this world, so glittering, so desirable, so praiseworthy, was after all an insubstantial pageant, a mirage whose fragile beauty owed its being to the wand of the enchanter, to the airy dreams of the poets, and was doomed at last to vanish into air, into thin air" (60).

Josephine Bennett disagrees, and argues instead that Spenser's Fairyland recaptures the ancient sense of Britain as the locus of "a higher reality" ("Britain," 140). As evidence for Fairyland considered a Platonic "pattern world," Bennett cites John Grange's *Golden Aphroditis* (1577), in which a lover says to his disdainful beloved:

> And sith you think your beautie such as none enjoys the like:
> To *Plato's* City, fairies' land, or to Utopia wenne [Bennett has "wonne"].
>
> (E1v)

Bennett comments: "In other words, 'you belong in an ideal world' " (138). But the next lines of Grange's poem shows how invidious, and therefore traditional, his reference to Fairyland must be:

> Yea sith you think your wisdom such, as no man hath the like:
> In deserts shrink (as *Timon* did) go seek some cave or den,
> There to enjoy your gifts alone, imparted not to men.

My own conception of Fairyland most closely resembles Harry Berger's elaboration of Nelson's argument about the peculiarity of Spenser's choosing Saint George for his hero. In his often dazzling essay, "Spenser's Faerie Queene, Book I: Prelude to Interpretation," Berger argues as I do that Fairyland represents a kind of illusion, but he exaggerates Spenser's psychological allegory by reducing Redcross's quest to a narcissistic error: "Thinking himself an Elfin justicer, the hero isolates himself from the common world, ventures into a fairyland largely of his own making and undergoes experiences which expose the narcissism and insufficiency of the romance idiom in its literal character" (45). Yet Redcross was stolen from England as a baby; "all" consider him "a Faeries sonne"; he was chosen for his mission by Gloriana, Una, and ultimately God (*FQ* 1.9.53); and, as I will shortly note, he remains in Fairyland.

Anthea Hume explains such British sojourns in Fairyland by commonsensically assuming that the Britishness of a character like Arthur represents his historicity, while his fairy travels represent the fabulous legends surrounding him, to which Spenser self-consciously adds (*Spenser*, 148–51). I would maintain, however, that the fabulous is only one aspect of a more general conception of worldliness in which Spenser wants to place his heroes, and in many ways it is the aspect least pertinent to the gentleman Spenser wants to fashion.

54. This is the adjusted truth about Redcross: a fairy stole him when he was a child; the "base Elfin brood" (*FQ* 1.10.65) she left in his place

may, as Hamilton (ed., *Faerie Queene*, 142) notes, account for the papist legend; and Georgos is the name given Redcross by the fairy ploughman who adopts him (66). When readers like Cullen describe book 1 as "a conflict between the new man of the spirit, *sanctus*, and the old man of the earth, *georgos*" (*Infernal*, 23), they overlook the fact that *georgos* represents a fairy worldliness, not worldliness as such.

55. Neither does Redcross remain in Eden, which, as Parker notes, looks very different from its original description once Redcross reaches it: "At first we are told that it is a kingdom which stretches over all the world, 'from East to Westerne shore' (I.i.5.5) and the defeat of the Dragon would seem to promise a return to its original dominion. But in the final, culminating, canto, it shrinks to a much more limited locus. Like the allegorical persons tied to particular places—Phaedria or Malecasta—it seems to be left behind precisely because it does not participate in the poem's essential movement, its shape-shifting process" (*Romance*, 76). Though Parker ascribes this "essential movement" to the romance mode of Spenser's poem, I would argue that Spenser decided to fashion his imperialist epic as a romance in the first place because of literary and extra-literary exigencies specific to Elizabethan England.

On "shadow," a term otherwise interchangeable in Spenser with the "shade" shepherds desire, see E. K.'s explanation that Spenser "secretly shadoweth himself" (*V* 7:18, 10) under the name of Colin, or Spenser's assertion that Gloriana represents Elizabeth, "and yet in some places else, I do otherwise shadow her" (*V* 1:168). For the rise of millenarianism in the seventeenth century, see Bauckham, *Tudor Apocalypse*, Christianson, *Reformers*, and Firth, *Apocalyptic*. None of these historians argues that Elizabethan millenarianism was an impossibility. In the 1590s Thomas Brightman wrote what was to prove a very influential millenarian commentary on Revelation, *Apocalypsis Apocalypseos*, but the tract remained unpublished till 1609, and even then appeared not in London but in Frankfurt; the first English translation of Brightman's Latin (*A Revelation of the Revelation*, 1615) was published in Amsterdam. If Spenser shared Brightman's beliefs, he also shared his discretion.

56. Blenerhasset, *Revelation*, A3v. Though Spenser insists that Fairyland represents either Elizabeth's "realmes" (2.proem.4) or her "kingdom" (*V* 1:168), he never limits the scope of either term to England's island. *Colin Clout* figures Elizabeth as "*Cynthia* the Ladie of the *sea*" (166; my emphasis). For a brief history of the modern criticism that does insist on a distinction between England and Fairyland, see Hume, *Spenser*, 145–46.

57. It would be tiresome to document the near unanimity of recent critics on this point, a consensus that in most cases depends on mistakenly equating Colin's vision with poetry per se: for example, "Spenser finds in a moment of vision at the recreative center of the pastoral landscape the realized ideal which is the object of his poetic quest, but he

learns too that the pursuit of the chivalric quest must finally diverge from the pursuit of poetry" (Shore, *Spenser*, 146). Certainly the most extreme proponent of the view that "we have seen the truth in the Acidalian vision" is Kathleen Williams, who believes this glimpse of poetry at its best enables us to "accept without trouble the death of the good Meliboe and his people" (*World of Glass*, 222). Louis Montrose seems on firmer ground about the later Spenser when he turns to a sonnet where Spenser, now apparently in propria persona, sounds very much like Colin. "In *Amoretti*, LXXX," claims Montrose, "the earthly paradise of personal love is hemmed in by a public world of toil and obligation" ("Perfecte," 55):

> After so long a race as I have run
> > Through Faery land, which those six books compile,
> > give leave to rest me being halfe fordonne,
> > and gather to my selfe new breath awhile.
> Then as a steed refreshed after toyle,
> > Out of my prison I will breake anew:
> > and stoutly will that second worke assoyle,
> > with strong endevour and attention dew.
> Till then give leave to me in pleasant mew,
> > to sport my muse and sing my loves sweet praise:
> > the contemplation of whose heavenly hew,
> > my spirit to an higher pitch will rayse.
> But let her prayses yet be low and meane,
> > fit for the handmayd of the Faery Queene.

But the sonnet actually follows earlier passages in Spenser's career quite closely: as in the Error episode, what first looks like a respite becomes a "prison" and "mew" to which Spenser claims he resigns himself only because such resignation will ultimately renew his epic project.

Again Berger comes closest to my own position, although he too collapses the distinction between pastoral and poetry in general. Berger sees Acidale as a return to Spenser's earlier pastoral that enables Spenser to perfect not only pastoral but poetry itself; Colin's vision shows the mind, or poetry—curiously interchangeable terms for Berger—"having triumphed" in its powers, yet only in order to turn outward again with new strength ("Secret," 74). I would argue that Spenser imagines the return to pastoral benefiting larger ambitions by *differentiating* them from pastoral.

58. Though now detached from mere worldliness, the post-*Calender* Colin has become addicted instead to illusionary pleasures that in the end still lead him, like the old "Januarie" Colin, to break his pipe in frustration (*FQ* 6.10.18). For the conventional fairies, see *FQ* 6.10.7 and 17. In works prior to *The Faerie Queene* as well, Spenser habitually associates such fairies with pastoral, as for example in the "June" eclogue, where Hobbinol tries to win Colin back to innocent pastoral with the promise that Colin will see "frendly Faeries, met with many Graces, / And lightfote Nymphes" (25–26) dance to the music of the Muses and Pan. But Colin declares himself alienated from such "weary wanton toys" (46–48). Cf. "Maye," 32;

Virgils Gnat, 178–79; and, in *The Teares of the Muses*, the once joyous "Nymphes and lightfoote Faeries" (31) who now depart from the Muses' "groves" (19) lamenting.

59. A friary at Enniscorthy; an Augustinian monastery at New Ross; New Abbey; and Buttevant Abbey; see Judson, *Life*, 102–4, 195. For the horsemen, see *V* 9:121.

60. The first quotation, perhaps the most famous piece of Spenser's prose, is Irenius's description of the Irish who found themselves reduced to nothing by the same rebellion from English authority that brought Spenser Irish land (see Judson, *Life*, 102–4). The passage illustrates Irenius's recommendation that in case of rebellion the natives should be "kept from manurance and their Cattle from Coming abroad," so that "by this hard restraint they would quickly Consume themselves and devour one another" (*V* 9:158). Cf. John Derricke's happier conception of what it means for the Irish to come out of the woods:

> Come each wight which now do haunt the wood,
> Submit yourselves unto your sovereign's law
> Come forth, I say, receive my counsel good
> . . . .
> Instead of woods then houses you may use,
> Instead of bogs, the cities at your will.
> (*Image of Irelande*, 90, 212)

The second quotation, from *A Brief Note of Ireland* (*V* 9:236), which is presumed Spenser's, concerns the later rebellion that forced Spenser to flee Ireland and meet his end. Rudolf Gottfried also notes the connection between this quotation and the first (*V* 9:431). If Spenser intends the allusion, he would seem to have in mind something like the point of his *Prothalamion* (1596), which, as I will argue in chapter 5, suggests that Spenser embraces his real failure as, after book 6, a logical next step in getting his imperialist argument across.

CHAPTER 4. DIVINE TOBACCO

1. For Elizabethan and Jacobean references, see Brooks, *Tobacco* 1:327, 334, 368, 378, 392, 448, 449, 455, 464, 479, and 2:21, 22, 77; Brooks's citations are by no means exhaustive. Spenser's second term of praise for tobacco, "sovereign" (*FQ* 3.5.33), appears at *Tobacco* 1:361, 412, 424, 433, and 2:21, 31, 77, 110. Lyly parodied Belphoebe's herb gathering in his *Woman in the Moon* (c. 1591–93) (3.1.65–70; see Dickson, *Panacea*, 177–78).

Brooks's work, an extraordinary sourcebook for the study of tobacco, cites almost all the tobacco references I will examine; see also the *Supplement*. Dickson's *Panacea* is a fine one-volume history.

2. Cited in *CSP* 8:140; the figures actually cover Michaelmas 1603–Michaelmas 1604. Records of smuggled tobacco are, of course, hard to come by.

3. *Irish*, F4r; quoted in Brooks, *Tobacco* 2:48.

4. The oxymoron is more evident in Spenser's reference to tobacco as

"the soveraigne weede" (*FQ* 3.5.33). Cf. Dekker, *Guls*, 231; quoted in Brooks, *Tobacco* 1:464.

5. Cf., e.g., Nashe: "divine Master *Spenser*, the miracle of wit" (1589) and "heavenly *Spenser*" (1592) (*Works* 3:323 and 1:243).

6. Cf. Greenblatt on Guyon's destruction of the Bower of Bliss as in part an allegory of the English colonist's "need for constant vigilance and unrelenting pressure" in resisting a Circean seduction by the land he colonizes (*Renaissance Self-Fashioning*, 179–88). Again, the Elizabethans generally thought that the murderous greed of the Spanish set the "intemperate" precedent to avoid:

> It is about a hundred years since they discovered a new world, under the conduct of *Christopher Columbus*, who in my judgment would never have undertaken this voyage, if he had thought that the men whom he brought thither, as if they were charmed by the cup of *Circe*, should straightways be transformed into Lions, Panthers, Tigers, and other savage beasts. (Ashley, *Comparison*, 23)

For Spenser's surprising turn to American gold at the end of book 4 (*FQ* 4.11.22), see chapter 5.

7. In her "English Commercial Development and American Colonization 1560–1620," Carol Shammas argues that Elizabethan imperialism was gold centered, while its Jacobean counterpart moved toward commodities-centered schemes. Joan Thirsk's *Economic Policy and Projects* sees more Elizabethan interest in commodification than Shammas allows. This essay, however, tries to highlight a strand of Elizabethan expansionism at once uneasy about gold and, in its most radical form, indifferent to commodification.

8. "Great Chronologie [of England]," MS entry for 1573, quoted in Brooks, *Tobacco* 1:298; *PN* 5:242.

9. James's *Counter-blaste* asserts that some of the gentry have been "bestowing three, some four hundred pounds a year upon this precious stink" (C4v).

10. Brooks, *Tobacco* 1:381. The title character in Chapman's *Monsieur D'Olive* (acted 1605, publ. 1606) seems to allude to this unusual time lapse when he describes tobacco as "an ancient subject, and yet newly / Call'd into question" (2.2.151–53).

11. Parker, *Books*, 76, on Monardes (1571), translated by John Frampton as *Joyfull Newes out of the Newe Worlde* (London, 1577). (For the complicated publishing history of Monardes' work, see Brooks, *Tobacco* 1:245–46, 263–64.) Parker, whose *Books* is a valuable starting point for research into Renaissance English travel literature, adds that "two issues in 1577, another in 1580, and still another in 1596 were not in keeping with the tendency of most English travel books of this period to appear in only one edition, even when they were vigorously imperialistic." His explanation of Monardes' exceptional popularity, "its utilitarian value to medical practitioners," sounds plausible enough, but skirts two problems. First, the timing of the various editions matches two small waves of Elizabethan

propaganda about America, the earlier stimulated by Frobisher's northern voyages (1576–78), the later by Raleigh's Guianan expedition (1595). Second, the translator Frampton was, as Parker notes, a former victim of the Spanish Inquisition and an ardent imperialist: he translated five other exploration tracts, including that of Marco Polo, in hopes to spur his countrymen into action. Parker maintains that this first translation is "the only one . . . in which the political motive is not evident," which is to say, perhaps, only that Frampton became increasingly explicit about his motives. Parker's bibliography of travel literature (243–65) makes clear that his own definition of politics, like the definitions of so many other researchers into travel literature, does not include plants—no tobacco books, not even James's, appear there. My own explanation of Monardes' popularity, which I hope this chapter will make more convincing, is that his herbal provided the sort of information about America that most interested the Elizabethans.

12. John Melton (1609) alludes to tobacco's high-class origins, and subsequent degradation, when he says that it "was wont to be taken of great gentlemen, & gallants, now made a frequent & familiar Companion of every Tapster and Horse-keeper (*Sixe-Folde*, 35; quoted in Brooks, *Tobacco* 1:472; cf. Dekker, *Guls*, 208).

Even James, in the proclamation of 17 October 1604, that levied a heavy custom on the weed, distinguished between "the better sort," who "have and will use the same with Moderation to preserve their Health," and "a number of riotous and disordered Persons of mean and base Condition, who, contrary to the use which Persons of good Calling and Quality make thereof, do spend most of their time in that idle Vanity . . . and also do consume that Wages which many of them get by their Labor" (quoted in Brooks, *Tobacco* 1:406–7). Cf. Doctor Clement in Jonson's *Every Man in His Humor* (1598, publ. 1601) pretending to hold a similar position and scaring Cob the tobacco hater: "What? A tankard-bearer, a thread-bare rascal, a beggar, a slave that never drunk out of better than pisspot mettle in his life, and he to deprave, and abuse the virtue of an herb, so generally receiv'd in the courts of princes, the chambers of nobles, the bowers of sweet Ladies, the cabins of soldiers—*Peto*, away with him, by god's passion, I say, go to" (3.3.108–14). Whether or not the playwrights are mocking James in particular, as Brooks assumes (*Tobacco* 1:424), Chapman's D'Olive too claims to believe that tobacco's "lawful use" should be "limited thus: / That none should dare to take it but a gentleman, / Or he that had some gentlemanly humor, / The murr, the headache, the catarrh, the bone-ache, / Or other branches of the sharp salt rheum / Fitting a gentleman" (*Monsieur D'Olive* 2.2.290–95)—so the rheum itself has come to seem a high-class affectation, like spleen.

13. "On the Continent tobacco had been generally accepted as a panacea since 1560, and as such had been woven into daily life there. But in England, about three decades later (after its fairly limited reception as a wonder-working simple) smoking suddenly and triumphantly became a

social force, developing into an almost national recreation" (Brooks, *Tobacco* 1:43).

14. See Brooks, *Tobacco* 1:47–49, Dickson, *Panacea* 170–74. It is Raleigh's authority that Philaretes seems to have particularly in mind when in a prefatory poem he anxiously tries to distinguish his special attack on tobacco from his general endorsement of Raleigh's American projects: "Let none deny but *Indies* soil can yield, / The sov'reign simples, of *Apollos* field. / Let England Spain and the French *Fleur de Lis* / Let Irish Kern and the Cold seated *Freese* / Confess themselves in bounden duty stand / To wholesome simples of *Guiana* land" (*Work*, A4v).

15. Stow's *Annales* (1615) too say that "Sir Walter Raleigh brought first the knowledge of tobacco" (quoted in *Suppl.* 4:177); while Camden's *Annales* (1615, trans. 1630) maintain that Raleigh's colonists "were the first that I know of, which brought into *England* that *Indian* plant. . . . Certainly from that time, it began to be in great request, and to be sold at an high rate" (quoted in Brooks, *Tobacco* 2:156).

16. For Raleigh's silence, see Brooks, *Tobacco* 1:68. Theodor de Bry reprinted Harriot's tract in four languages as the first volume of his *America* (1590), adding to the original text some engravings from the watercolors of Harriot's fellow colonist John White, along with Harriot's commentary on them (Quinn, *Roanoke Voyages* 1:390–464).

17. "Renaissance Influences," 82–83. Quinn is following Beer, *Origins*, 32–77.

18. Cf. William Barclay's "To my Lord the Bishop of Murray," from his *Nepenthes, or the Vertues of Tabacco* (1614): "A stranger plant shipwracked in our coast, / Is come to help this poor phlegmatic soil" (unpaginated). See Brooks, *Tobacco* 1:389 on the identification of Marbecke as the author of the *Defence*.

19. Cf. the *True Declaration* (1610), which imagines overpopulation as itself an "inundation" that "doth overflow this little Island" (61).

20. As "good Merchandize" Ralph Lane mentions only "Sassafras, and many other roots & gums" (Quinn, *Roanoke Voyages* 1:273). For sassafras as the primary New World commodity garnered by Raleigh's man Samuel Mace in 1602, and by Bartholomew Gosnold in a voyage unlicensed by Raleigh the same year, see Quinn, *England*, 408, 414–16; tobacco is not mentioned in the extant records of either venture.

21. See Strachey, *Historie*, 122–23, 38; quoted in Brooks, *Tobacco* 1:525–26; and see 1:86. Hamor says Rolfe "first took the pains to make trial thereof" in 1612 (*True Discourse*, D4b; quoted in Brooks, *Tobacco* 1:524).

22. Of course, England must have acquired a good deal of tobacco in a happily indirect way also, via privateering; see Andrews, *Elizabethan Privateering*. For the interesting history of homegrown tobacco in the English Renaissance, see Thirsk, "New Crops."

23. Cf. Hakluyt, "Discourse," 223–24.

24. The continuation of Harriot's sentence seems to mark a separation from Indian barbarity, as if the superstitious use of tobacco had not been

felt as entirely barbarous before: "but all done with strange gestures, stamping, sometime dancing, clapping of hands, holding up of hands, & staring up into the heavens, uttering therewithal and chattering strange words & noises."

25. These last three quotations, from Harriot's captions to John White's drawings, are Hakluyt's translations of Harriot's Latin.

26. For example, "*Deer Skins* . . . are to be had of the natural inhabitants thousands yearly by way of traffic for trifles" (Harriot, *Report*, 331). Apparently Harriot came to be regarded as England's resident authority on the subject of Indians misvaluing things. When Newport returned to England in January 1609 with one of Powhatan's sons, "Harriot advised that no expensive gift be made to him but that he would be satisfied with copper decorations only, so that there duly appeared in the [Northumberland house] accounts a payment of three shillings 'for 2 Rings and other pieces of Copper given to the Indian prince.' Similarly, we can identify as probably chosen by Harriot, amongst the goods sent to George Percy in July 1608, 'for blue beads' six shillings and 'for Red copper' nineteen shillings and sixpence, objects Harriot had long ago found the Indians anxious to have" (Quinn, "Thomas Harriot," 50). Cf. Harriot's memoranda for Mace's 1602 voyage, in which we witness the odd spectacle of England's premier scientist carefully directing the production of copper trifles for the Indians (Quinn, *England*, 410–13).

27. From Greville's advice to England in "A Treatise of Monarchy," 390–95; Grosart's comment on this theory of toy trade anticipates my argument here: "as in barter with the Indians" (*Works of Fulke Greville* 1:142).

28. The most famous work to celebrate a newly discovered people who contemn gold is of course *Utopia*, but the topos is a very common one. Cf. Gascoigne's *The Stele Glass* (1576):

> How live the Moors, which spurn at glistring pearl,
> And scorn the costs, which we do hold so dear?
> How? how but well? and were the precious pearl
> Of peerless truth, amongst them published,
> (Which we enjoy, and never weigh the worth)
> They would not then, the same (like us) despise,
> Which (though they lack) they live in better wise
> Than we, which hold, the worthless pearl so dear.
> (*Works* 2:153)

29. Shortly before his disastrous second voyage in search of El Dorado, Raleigh reportedly boasted "that he knew a Town in those parts, upon which he could make a saving Voyage in *Tobacco*, though there were no other spoil" (*A Declaration of the Demeanour and Cariage of Sir Walter Raleigh* [1618], quoted in Brooks, *Tobacco* 1:68 n. 8). Cf. Harcourt (1613): "I dare presume to say, and hope to prove, within a few months . . . that only this commodity Tobacco, (so much sought after and desired) will bring as great a benefit and profit to the undertakers, as ever the Spaniards gained

by the best and richest Silver mine in all their Indies, considering the charge of both" (*Voyage*, 105; quoted in Brooks, *Tobacco* 1:502–3).

30. "In Tabaccam" 1–6, in *Epigrammatum libri II* (1619) (*Works*, 238). Trans. *Suppl.* 4:191.

31. Though Englishmen had smoked tobacco before Lane's men returned home (see, e.g., Brooks, *Tobacco* 1:240, 298), Charles de L'Ecluse's Latin abridgment of Monardes (1605, trans. 1659) notes that "the English returning from thence [i.e., Virginia] brought the like [Indian] Pipes with them, to drink the smoke of Tobacco; and since that time, the use of drinking Tobacco hath so much prevailed all *England* over, especially amongst the Courtiers, that they have caused many such like Pipes to be made to drink Tobacco with" (quoted in Brooks, *Tobacco* 1:417–18). Quinn explains that "what the colonists apparently introduced was the smoking pipe used in Roanoke Island as a model for English pipe-makers" (*Roanoke Voyages* 1:345–46 n. 3).

32. C. T., *Advice*, A3v. This most common of tobacco jibes could appear in the mouths of foreigners—"both *Spaniards* & all other Nations say tauntingly to us, when they see all our goods landed (to use their own words) *Que todo esso sepagtaa con humo*; that all will be paid in smoke" (Bennett, *Treatise*, unpaginated)—and of kings: a proclamation of Charles I (6 January 1631) prohibited the importation of foreign tobacco so that "our Subjects may not unthriftily vent the solid Commodities of our own Kingdom, and return the proceed thereof in Smoke" (quoted in Beer, *Origins*, 82).

33. While it has long been recognized that Lucian presents a similar anecdote (1.163), Dickson sensibly observes that this coincidence alone does not prove the story apocryphal; "It is even possible that Ralegh, having read the story in a Greek or Latin edition of Lucian, carefully arranged the matter of the wager to amuse his royal mistress" (*Panacea*, 172). As it is, I am less concerned with the anecdote's authenticity than with the testimony it offers about contemporary opinions of Raleigh and tobacco.

34. See Dickson, *Panacea*, 174. Cf. T. W. on the Gunpowder Plotters: "In the time of their imprisonment, they rather feasted with their sins, than fasted with sorrow for them; were richly appareled, fared deliciously, and took Tobacco out of measure, with a seeming carelessness of their crime" (quoted in *Suppl.* 3:133).

35. I cite Wands's translation throughout.

36. Cf. the braggadocio Bobadillo in Jonson's *Every Man in His Humor*: "I have been in the Indies (where this herb grows) where neither my self, nor a dozen Gentlemen more (of my knowledge) have received the taste of any other nutriment, in the world, for the space of one and twenty weeks, but Tobacco only. Therefore it cannot be but 'tis most divine" (3.2.70–75).

37. Taylor, *Original Writings* 1:367–68; quoted in Seelye, *Prophetic*, 43, who comments: "So Raleigh's constancy to Elizabeth, his loyalty to his

colony, the Queen's barrenness, and Virgina's ill repute are all spun into an ambiguous fabric of allusion, ending by associating the New World with the paradisiac promised land of the Mosaic epic." Seelye also observes that "Hakluyt lifts himself to a level of expression which he seldom attained" (42), though the quality may in fact be Raleigh's: Hakluyt writes to him that "if there be anything else that you would have mentioned in the epistle dedicatory, you shall do well to let me understand of it betimes" (Taylor, *Original Writings* 1:355).

38. The Latin in the original compensates to some degree for this raciness, as Hakluyt's characterization of Martyr's Latin suggests: "He depicts with a distinguished and skillful pen and with lively colors in a most gifted manner the head, neck, breast, arms, in brief the whole body of that tremendous entity America, and clothes it decently in the Latin dress familiar to scholars" (Taylor, *Original Writings* 1:363).

39. As I will explain in chapter 5, Raleigh is free to enter America only when he has been barred from Elizabeth's presence.

40. For James, tobacco is the food of the belly fillers in Numbers 11.4–6 who *reject* manna (*Counter-blaste*, C4r).

41. The wound occurs during a battle reminiscent of Raleigh's well-publicized Irish skirmishes. For the most recent compilation of evidence that Timias represents Raleigh, see Bednarz, "Raleigh," 52–54.

42. For a fine discussion of the relation between Ariosto's Medoro and Angelica on the one hand and Spenser's Timias and Belphoebe on the other, see Alpers, *Poetry*, 185–94.

43. Raleigh at least understood "Belphoebe" as the queen made approachable. He laments of the angry Elizabeth after his disgrace, "A Queen she was to me, no more Belphoebe, / A Lion then, no more a milk-white Dove" (*Ocean to Scinthia*, ll. 327–28).

44. On flowers, herbs, and weeds as conventional terms for poetry, see, e.g., Gascoigne's *Posies* (1575), a book of poems divided into "Flowers to comfort, Herbs to cure, and Weeds to be avoided" (*Works* 1:17). The locus classicus for the identification of pastoral, poetry, herbs, and erotic frustration is the first book of Ovid's *Metamorphoses*, in which Apollo, the god of herbal cures, notes the irony of his love for Daphne:

> inventum medicina meum est, opiferque per orbem
> dicor, et herbarum subiecta potentia nobis.
> ei mihi, quod nullus amor est sanabilis herbis
> nec prosunt domino, quae prosunt omnibus, artes!
> (*Metamorphoses* 1.521–24)

> (Of Physick and of surgery I found the Arts for need
> The power of every herb and plant doth of my gift proceed.
> Now woe is me that ne'er an herb can heal the hurt of love
> And that the Arts that others help their Lord doth helpless prove.)
> (Trans. Golding 1:635–38)

Apollo must learn to exchange his useless skill in herbs for a more satisfactory skill in the reeds Daphne becomes: what heals his desire for

Daphne is, in other words, its sublimation into poetry. Spenser, however, rejects the innocent pastoral version of such conversion (e.g., "Aprill," 50–51) as too worldly, but believes that his epic "flowers" can indeed cure lustful fixation.

45. Cf. the shepherds' commentary on the equally lovesick lover of Paris, Oenone: "Farewell fair Nymph, sith he must heal alone that gave the wound. / There grows no herb of such effect upon Dame Nature's ground" (*Araygnement of Paris*, 601–2).

46. When Peele later comes round to such dissatisfaction with Elizium, he puts himself in Colin's shoes: "Leave foolish lad, it mendeth not with words, / Nor herbs nor time such remedy affords" ("The Honour of the Garter," 69–70).

47. In equating Spenserian virginity as I do with devotion to "a higher ideal" ("Spenser's Accommodation," 423), H. M. English reveals the practical difficulty of this philosophy when he imagines that Elizabeth can readily combine the alternatives of literal virginity and literal marriage, represented by Belphoebe and Amoret respectively.

48. What enables Raleigh to present his return home as even more pathetic and involuntary than Wyatt's, apparently, is that Wyatt's prince and beloved are now one and the same.

49. The Bower is, for instance, said to be

> A place pickt out by choice of best alive,
> That natures worke by art can imitate:
> In which what ever in this worldly state
> Is sweet, and pleasing unto living sense,
> Or that may dayntiest fantasie aggrate,
> Was poured forth with plentifull dispence,
> And made there to abound with lavish affluence.
>
> (*FQ* 2.12.42)

Elsewhere, the Bower's "Art" seems "halfe in scorne / Of niggard Nature" (50), and delivers such delightful sounds "as attonce might not on living ground, / Save in this Paradise, be heard elsewhere" (70).

50. This "writ" is thus distinguished from the writing on the Bower's gate, which in telling "all the famous history / Of *Jason* and *Medea*" gives the impression that "ye might have seene" the events described (*FQ* 2.12.43–46).

Greenblatt pursues something like this argument about Spenser's oxymoronic allegory when he claims that "*The Faerie Queene* announces its status as art object at every turn" so as "to spare ideology" the skepticism absorbed by the overtly fictional poem (*Renaissance Self-Fashioning*, 190–92). I would argue that Spenser is far more skeptical of certain popular Elizabethan political assumptions than Greenblatt allows; Spenser believes in "ward[ing] off idolatry" (192) not only of the artwork but of Elizabeth herself. Cf. Montrose, "Elizabethan Subject," passim.

No doubt Spenser's conception of his writing as antithetical to idolatry derives in part from Protestant scripturalism, enforced by visitation articles such as the following (1551–52):

> *Item,* that when any glass windows within any of the churches shall from henceforth be repaired, or new made, that you do not permit to be painted or portrayed therein the image or picture of any saint; but if they will have anything painted, that it be either branches, flowers, or posies taken out of Holy Scripture. (Frere and Kennedy, *Visitation Articles* 2:289)

Cf. Sidney on poetry's unique power to convey an image such as idolatry used to paint: reading "that heavenly discourse" of the prodigal son (Luke 15.11–32), Sidney exclaims, "me seems I see before my eyes the lost child's disdainful prodigality, turned to envy a swine's dinner" (*Apology,* 30). But, as I have indicated, Spenser's overtly trifling poetry even shuns what Michael O'Connell has called the Protestant "logolatry" of Scripture ("Idolatrous," 287; cf. esp. 293–94, 298).

51. "It was before 1560, in or about Lisbon, that the gospel of tobacco as panacea was evolved" (Brooks, *Tobacco* 1:236); see Dickson, *Panacea,* 57–80. The most influential publicists of tobacco's divinity were Jean Liebault (1570) and Pierre Pena and Matthias de L'Obel (1570–71); see Brooks, *Tobacco* 1:232–42. Frampton's edition of Monardes (1577) includes a translation of Liebault on tobacco's "divine effects" (*Joyfull Newes,* 93; see Brooks, *Tobacco* 1:232).

52. *His Majesties Gracious Letter* (1622) to the Earl of Southampton, treasurer of the Virginia Colony, includes this similar appraisal by the master of the king's silk works, John Bonoeil: "Sure there is some such sorcery in this weed; it was first sown (it seems) by some Indian Enchanter's hand, with spells and Magic verses, or otherwise you could never so much dote on it" (quoted in *Suppl.* 5:206).

53. The most common way to represent fears about tobacco's ill effect on the English character was to personify tobacco as a witch or whore: e.g., "that Witch *Tobacco*" (James I [1618], quoted in Dickson, *Panacea,* 156); "that Indian whore" (William Fennor [1617], quoted in *Suppl.* 4:182); "a swarty *Indian* [who] / Hath played the painted English *Courtesan*" (Philaretes, *Work,* A4v); "the *Indian Devil,* our bawd, witch, whore, man-queller" (Scot, *Philomythie,* 41r; quoted in Brooks, *Tobacco* 2:8). This particular stigmatization of tobacco is due in part to tobacco's associations with fast living—"It is the thing his soul doth most adore," says John Taylor (1614) of the tobacco taker, "To live and love Tobacco, and a whore" (quoted in Brooks, *Tobacco* 1:522)—but more generally to worries that tobacco will block the production of legitimate Englishmen. William Vaughan (1612) wanted smokers to memorize this rhyme: "Tobacco, that outlandish weed, / It spends the brain, and spoils the seed: / It dulls the sprite, it dims the sight, / It robs a woman of her right" (quoted in Brooks, *Tobacco* 2:131). This physiological argument aside, writers often depict wives complaining about the greater affection their husbands feel for tobacco. The most elaborate diatribe occurs in John Deacon's *Tobacco Tortured* (1616): e.g., "Why dost thou so vainly prefer a vanishing filthy *fume*

before my permanent virtues?" (quoted in Brooks, *Tobacco* 2:12; for more references see 5:280 under "Smokers, wives of"). Uncannily enough, the first Englishman to begin growing commercially successful tobacco in Virginia was also the first Englishman to marry an Indian: in the same breath Ralph Hamor praises John Rolfe's importation of tobacco seeds and his marriage to Pocahontas, both done "merely for the good and honor of the Plantation" (*True Discourse*, D4v; quoted in Brooks, *Tobacco* 1:524). Marlowe associates tobacco with a third un-English choice: he reportedly declared "that all they that love not Tobacco & Boys were fools" (quoted in Shirley, *Harriot*, 182).

54. Reprinted in Brooks, *Tobacco* 1:352–58 and Dickson, *Panacea*, 198–99; I cite Brooks's edition of the poem, one of thirteen extant MS versions. Heffner, "Essex," 23, notes that William Browne alludes to the poem in the course of his meditation on Essex's career in *Britannias Pastorals* 1.4.685–760 (Heffner gives 1625 as the date, though book 1 was first published in 1613). What Heffner fails to note, however, is that Browne also alludes to Timias and Belphoebe in the same passage: returning from war, Essex searches for Elizabeth in the hope that "her skill in herbs might help remove" a wound Envy gave him, but she mistakes him for a beast and kills him. To Browne's mind, Spenser's Timias and the narrator of Essex's poem are the same man.

55. *Institution*, 168r. Cf. Psalms 102.3, Isaiah 51.6, Hosea 13.3.

56. Cf. Simion Grahame (1609) (quoted in *Suppl.* 3:145). Thomas Jenner turned this allegorical potential of tobacco smoking into a very popular poem (1626):

> The Indian weed withered quite
> Green at noon, cut down at night
> Shows thy decay, all flesh is hay,
> Thus think, then drink *Tobacco*.
>
> The Pipe that is so lily white
> Shows thee to be a mortal wight,
> And even such, gone with a touch,
> Thus think, then drink *Tobacco*.
>
> And when the smoke ascends on high,
> Think, thou behold'st the vanity
> Of worldly stuff gone with a puff:
> Thus think, then drink *Tobacco*.
>
> And when the Pipe grows foul within,
> Think on thy soul defil'd with sin,
> And then the fire it doth require
> Thus think, then drink *Tobacco*.
>
> The ashes that are left behind,
> May serve to put thee still in mind,
> That unto dust, return thou must,
> Thus think, then drink *Tobacco*.

Quoted in Brooks, *Tobacco* 2:128; see ibid. n. 2 for a bibliography of the poem's popularity. As if to emphasize the ambiguity of Jenner's position here—does he approve or disapprove of smoking?—the poem was published "Answered by *G. W.* [George Wither?] thus, / Thus think, drink no *Tobacco.*" Incidentally, Wither came full circle on tobacco, and published a similar *contemptus* "Meditation Whilst He Was Taking a Pipe of Tobacco" (1661) lauding tobacco's educative powers, which he composed during his third incarceration at Newgate; see Brooks, *Tobacco* 4:421–23.

57. *Old Fortunatus* (1599), quoted in *Suppl.* 3:116.; Fortunatus himself sounds like Essex when he refers to "that lean tawny face Tobacconist death, that turns all into smoke" (1.1.336–37).

58. See 2 Peter 3. Buttes's awkward comparisons of the gluttonous eater to an empty oven and desolate house depend on this apocalyptic resonance for their coherence. Both occur in the Psalms as figures for God's judgment upon David's enemies (21.9, 69.25; cf. Matthew 23.38).

59. From Trevisa's translation of Bartholomaeus, *De Proprietatibus Rerum* (trans. 1398; 1495 ed.), 4.3.evi.b/2; cf. Bateman's 1582 ed., 4.3.fiii.a/1.

60. For a different account of this process of sublimation, see William Vaughan's *Spirit of Detraction* (1611), whose prefatory epistle has certain "Cavaliers and Gentles" simply aping Monardes' Indian priest: after smoking,

> they fain themselves so long ravished as it were in an ecstasy: until after a thorough perambulation of their barren wits . . . they have coined some strange accident worthy the rehearsal among their boon companions. Then as though they started out of an heavenly trance . . . They recount tales of ROBIN-HOOD, of RHODOMONTING rovers, of DONZEL DEL PHOEBO, of a new ANTI-CHRIST born in BABYLON, of lying wonders, blazing out most blasphemous news, how that the DEVIL appeared at such a time with lightning and THUNDRING majesty . . . and if they had not suddenly blessed themselves better, he had carried away with him men, women, houses, and all right into hell. (Quoted in *Suppl.* 4:158)

61. The standard reference on this subject is Fink, "Milton," supplemented by Stroup, "Climatic"; the theory derives from Aristotle's *Politics* 7.7. For other English speculations on New World climate, see Kupperman, "Puzzle."

62. A satiric epigram from *Humors Antique Faces* (1605) by Samuel Rowlands nicely illustrates, by way of mockery, the idea that tobacco as miraculous fare might alone cure the economic wants Virginia was supposed to supply:

> A Poor Slave once with penury afflicted,
> Yet to Tobacco mightily addicted
> Says, they that take Tobacco keeps their health,
> Are worthy fellows in a common wealth.
> For if (sayth he) Tobacco were our cheer,
> Then other victuals never would be dear.
> Fie on excess; it makes men faint and meek,
> A penny loaf might serve a man a week.
> Were we conform'd to the Chamelion's fare,
> To live by smoke as they do live by air.

O how our men oppress and spoil their sense,
 in making havoc of the elements.
He can give reason for what he hath spoke.
My Salamander lives by fire and smoke.
Necessity doth cause him to repeat,
Tobacco's praise for want of other meat.
(Quoted in *Suppl.* 3:131–32)

Cf. the imp in Warner's *Continuance of Albions England* (1606), who celebrates the "*Indian* weed, / That fum'd away more wealth than would a many thousands feed" (quoted in Brooks, *Tobacco* 1:436).

63. Brathwait, *Smoaking Age*, 196; quoted in Brooks, *Tobacco* 2:41. A leaf explaining Brathwait's picture (reproduced at Brooks, *Tobacco* 2:37) appears only in the Arents copy of *The Smoaking Age*. The use of a smoking blackamoor as a trade sign seems to have been introduced around 1615 (Brooks, *Tobacco* 2:37). For Brathwait's other references to the sign, see *Smoaking Age*, 155 and 164; Jonson appears to allude to an actual black boy used as an advertisement in *Bartholomew Faire* 1.4.116–18.

64. Hall refers to "certain Indian chiefs of the Torrid Zone, so renowned for smoking that they had blackened their insides. It is clear that this color pleased them, for it did not seem right that the inner part of their bodies should differ in color from the outer" (*Mundus*, 96; cited in *Suppl.* 3:129). The joke is recalled by Edmund Gardiner (1610) (*Triall*, 18r–v; cited in Brooks, *Tobacco*, 1:480). For accounts of dissections that supposedly showed internal blackening, see Brooks, *Tobacco* 1:404, 2:11–12 and 89; for brains said to be blackened, see 1:381, 411, 516, and 2:89, 91, 234; on internal blackening in general, see 1:355, 411, 445, 535, and 2:22, 52, 234. The most elaborate version of the conceit that tobacco makes smokers black like Indians, who are themselves black like the devil, is in John Taylor (1614) (*Nipping*, C4v–D3r; quoted in Brooks, *Tobacco* 1:519–22).

65. Marbecke's emphasis; cf. 16, 20, and 63–65. Marbecke believes, moreover, that tobacco compensates for any residue it may leave in the body by purging rheum: "It bringeth no more thither, than it carrieth away from thence" (13). James counters that what tobacco smokers take for rheum is really only smoke condensed, "and so are you made free and purged of nothing, but that wherewith you willfully burdened your selves" (*Counter-blaste*, B4v).

66. Beaumont and his friends subscribe to the Spenserian tobacco tradition with a vengeance: five times in the commendatory verses and poem tobacco is called "divine," five times "sacred," three times "celestial"; five times its effects are "blest"; and then it is also "ethereal," "heavenly," "metaphysical," "immortal"—in short, a "god."

A tradition making Spenser the archetype of the impoverished poet arose almost immediately after his death—e.g., in the third of the *Parnassus* plays (c. 1601–2): "And yet for all, this unregarding soil / Unlac't the line of his desired life, / Denying maintenance for his dear relief: / Careless ere to prevent his exequy, / Scarce deigning to shut up his dying eye"

(*Return* part 1, 1.2.220–24). See Heffner, "Did Spenser Die in Poverty?" and Judson, *Life*, 202–3.

67. Martyr paraphrases a treatise on Indian rites by Ramon Pane, a friar who accompanied Columbus on his second voyage. Pane describes the superstitious use of the herb *cohoba*; the ceremony is very similar to the tobaccoan one Monardes reports, and in fact by the end of the sixteenth century commentators accepted *cohoba* as tobacco (Brooks, *Tobacco* 1:196). Martyr comments to the future Charles V: "Now (most noble Prince) what need you hereafter to marvel of the spirit of *Apollo* so shaking his Sibyls with extreme fury? You had thought that superstitious antiquity had perished" (Eden, *Decades*, 102).

68. Cf. Samuel Walsall's praise of tobacco in his commendatory poem to Buttes: "Sovereign Nepenthes, which Tobacco hight, / Tobacco not to Antique Sages known, / Sage wizards that Tobacco knewen not?" (*Dyets*, Aa3v). An epigram by Sir John Davies (1598?), "apparently the first [poem] in English entirely on the subject" of tobacco (Dickson, *Panacea*, 201), indirectly suggests the literary boost provided by classical ignorance about America:

> *Homer* of *Moly* and *Nepenthe* sings,
> *Moly* the Gods' most sovereign Herb divine:
> *Nepenthe* Heaven's drink, most gladness brings,
> Heart's grief expels, and doth the wits refine,
> But this our age another world hath found,
> From whence an Herb of heavenly power is brought,
> *Moly* is not so sovereign for a wound,
> Nor hath *Nepenthe* so great wonders wrought.
> (Epigram 36.1–8, quoted in Dickson,
> *Panacea*, 201)

For Beaumont on tobacco replacing moly, see *Poems*, 313.

69. *Concilium Limense*, ed. Jose de Acosta (Madrid, 1591); trans. in *Suppl.* 2:102. Acosta "appears to have formulated the decrees and defended them against opponents" (ibid.).

70. Cf. W. B.'s commendatory poem: "There didst thou gather on Parnassus clift, / This precious herb, Tobacco most divine, / Than which ne'er Greece, ne'er Italy did lift / A flower more fragrant to the Muses' shrine: / A purer sacrifice did ne'er adorn / Apollo's altar, than this Indian fire" (Beaumont, *Poems*, 268–69). Nothing English figures in this account of the poem except Beaumont's head, which W. B. compares to a tobacco pipe.

71. The clearest explanation of this process, and the terms I've used, are Greenblatt's, in his discussion of an Accession Day celebration that seems to combine both classical allusion and Catholic ceremony: "The Roman mythology, deftly keyed to England's Virgin Queen, helps to fictionalize Catholic ritual sufficiently for it to be displaced and absorbed" (*Renaissance Self-Fashioning*, 230).

72. Cf. *The Masque of Flowers*, produced by Bacon for Somerset's marriage in 1614, which stages a kind of mock Great Instauration celebration

of modern times. The masque begins with a debate about the relative merits of wine, represented by Silenus, and tobacco, represented by an Indian god described by Harriot, "Kiwasa" or "Kawasha." Part of Kawasha's argument is that "nothing but fumigation / Doth chase away ill sprites, / Kawasha and his nation / Found out these holy rites" (*Masque*, 166). The joke on tobacco is first that Kawasha is himself an ill sprite, and second that no one wants to chase him away, not entirely: the scene of the masque is a walled city, before which sit "on either side a temple, the one dedicated to Silenus and the other to Kawasha" (161). The debate soon gives way to a more explicit account of Britain's superiority to either classical or Indian barbarism, when James transforms some painted flowers— metamorphosed gentlemen, we discover—back into men; a song helps explain the allegory:

> Give place, you ancient powers,
> That turned men to flowers,
> For never writer's pen
> Yet told of flowers return'd to Men.
> Chorus.   But miracles of new event
> Follow the great Sun of our firmament.
>
> (168)

The apparent euhemerism of the allegory, in which the enlightening sun of James reverses the classical transformation of men into myths or "flowers"—poesies—does not demand that superstition be discarded; rather, the enlightened song is itself sung by twelve "Garden-gods," also referred to as "Priests." The masque wants Britain to retain superstition so that potentially heretical claims for Britain's superiority, indeed for its millennialness, may be maintained, but negatively: Britain is here simply "fit to be" the millennial "fifth monarchy" of Daniel 7.27.

73. I refer to the title of the last chapter of Greenblatt's *Renaissance Self-Fashioning*.

74. Keymis, *Second Voyage*, 464. When Beaumont referred earlier to Elizabeth being "worshipt" in America, he may have been either misremembering this Guianan anecdote or alluding to the much less dramatic submission of the Virginian *weroance* or chief, Menatonon, who ordered his vassal king Okisko "to yield himself servant, and homager, to the great Weroanza of England." Menatonon seems to have been impressed less by Elizabeth's virtues than by the fact that at the time Lane held his "best beloved son prisoner with me" (Quinn, *Roanoke Voyages* 1:279, 262).

75. See, e.g., Yates, "Queen Elizabeth," 80–81.

76. *Return from Parnassus* part 2, 1.4.403; part 1, 1.1.368; Dekker, *The Wonderfull Year* (quoted in Cawley, *Voyagers*, 298 n. 152). The *Parnassus* plays, when optimistic, also transform the scholar's material poverty into his spiritual purity: on his way to Parnassus, Philomusus recalls Marlowe—"Though I foreknow that dolts possess the gold, / Yet my intended pilgrimage I'll hold"—while Studioso adds the moral—"Within Parnassus dwells all sweet content, / Nor care I for those excrements of earth" (*Pil-*

grimage to Parnassus 5.594–97). In the later plays of the trilogy, however, after the scholars return to the quotidian world, this otherworldliness becomes more difficult to maintain, and tobacco soon surfaces as a correlative to ambivalence about poetical "spirit," sometimes like ale inspiring mere vapors (*Return* part 2, 1.2.160–62), at other times representing a more positive but still jocular alternative to the gold scholars lack: Philomusus, pleased with Luxurio's wit, prays that "long for a reward may your wits be warm'd with the Indian herb" (part 1, 1.1.432–34).

77. Davies, *Epigrams* 36.9.

78. Noted by Grosart (Beaumont, *Poems*, 265).

79. Pory to Edwin Sandys, 16 January 1620 (Powell, *Pory*, microfiche suppl. 81).

80. For tobacco's fortunes in the seventeenth century, see Morgan, *American Slavery*. Such trifling with the home market also figures in the Virginia Company's schemes for encouraging investments—namely, in lotteries that were advertised as doubly alchemical: on the one hand, they would turn "even but small sums of money" into the cache required to fund Virginia's colonization (Virginia Company broadside: "Whereas"); and on the other, they would repay such "small" investments exorbitantly:

> Full many a man that lives full bare,
>   and knows no joys of Gold,
> For one small Crown may get a share,
>   of twice two Thousand told.
>   (Virginia Company broadside:
>   "Londons Lotterie," 20)

For the real financial significance of the lotteries to Virginia, see Craven, *Dissolution*, 149–50. Due to corruption that, as Edwin Sandys reported, "very much disgraced" the lotteries, the royal license for them was withdrawn in 1621; see Craven, *Dissolution*, 183–84.

81. On the tobacco deals between the company and the Crown, see, e.g., Andrews, *Colonial* 1:55–57. Thirsk notes that "in no other country did merchants and planters manage to secure a total prohibition on domestic cultivation for the sake of the colonial trade" ("New Crops," 87).

82. *A True and Sincere Declaration*, 4; quoted in Beer, *Origins* , 67.

83. Such imposts eventually helped reduce Charles to smoke: "almost to a man prominent Virginia traders supported the Parliamentarian cause" (Pagan, "Growth," 262; see n. 93).

CHAPTER 5. THE TRIUMPH OF DISGRACE

1. By "agreeable to our natures," Hakluyt means the climatological congeniality of Virginia. Cf. Edward Hayes (1592?), who speaks of the northern portions of Virginia as that part of the New World "which in Situation & temperature is nearest unto, and seem[eth] to be reserved for

us" ("Discourse," 158). For more on the significance of climate in early English expansionism, see Kupperman, "Fear."

2. For a chronology of Raleigh's fall, see Rowse, *Raleigh*, 158–69.

3. Cf. Bednarz, *Raleigh*, 61.

4. One of Raleigh's poems to Elizabeth Throckmorton or "Serena"— "To His Love When He Had Obtained Her"—represents his now consummatable love as putting an end to "travail":

> Let's then meet
> Often with amorous lips, and greet
> Each other till our wanton Kisses
> In number pass the days Ulysses
> Consum'd in travail. (19–23)

5. See the final stanza of cantos 2, 4–7, and 9–12. Other oft-cited manifestations in the book of Spenser's supposed exhaustion are the limited roles of the primary heroes Cambel and Triamond (Telamond, the hero named in the headnote to the book, never even appears); the multiplication of heroes; the confusing throngs of characters throughout the book; inexplicable loose ends, like Belphoebe and Timias simply abandoning the helpless Amoret and Æmylia or Scudamour not informed about Amoret; the new prominence of feminine rhymes; and finally the assignment of the book's bravura canto, its best candidate for what C. S. Lewis calls an allegorical center (*Allegory*, 336)—the Temple of Venus episode (canto 10)—to a narrator separate from the author who also speaks in a nostalgic past tense.

Paul Alpers notes that the publication of minor poems such as *Colin Clout* between the time of the first and second editions of *The Faerie Queene* seems a sign of trouble: "Whereas the poems of the 1580's, collected in *Complaints*, can be seen as preparatory to *The Faerie Queene*, these later poems show Spenser going outside his epic to treat subjects and employ modes of expression that formerly would have found a place within it" ("Narration," 35–36). But I take this implied admission by Spenser of *The Faerie Queene*'s inadequacy to be consistent with Spenser's representations of his epic from the start.

6. See Hamilton, ed., *Faerie Queene*, 490 for a discussion of this problem.

7. The characterization is Cecil's: "I find him marvelous greedy to do anything to recover the conceit of his brutish offense" (quoted in Rowse, *Ralegh*, 167); cf. *FQ* 4.7.45.

Oram, "Elizabethan," 43–45 notes the significance of Æmylia's story in relation to Timias, but he considers it a reflection on Timias's lust for Amoret only (whom he identifies with Elizabeth Throckmorton), and so is hard pressed to make sense of the fact that Æmylia's social status is much higher than her lover's.

8. Judith Anderson anticipates my argument here in a number of respects, though she, like O'Connell, believes the moral of the episode to

be the increasing distance between Elizabeth and her possible idealization—"at best a hope or an unrealized promise but no longer, by any
stretch of the epic imagination, a present reality" ("Living," 48). My point
is that Spenser considers Elizabeth's "present reality" complex: he consistently wants his readers to avoid Raleigh's mistake of imagining Elizabeth's ideal significance, her body politic, as wholly contained or realized
within the limits of either her natural body or the English island.

9. This sentiment is not peculiar to book 4 but rather runs throughout
the poem: see, e.g., 1.8.40, 2.2.3, 2.6.46, and 5.1.27.

10. I partly agree with Judith Anderson, then, when she claims that in
book 4 the poet's voice "no longer indicates but *is* the alternative"
(*Growth*, 121), but I disagree that "the more insistently visible presence of
the poet" (114) in the book manifests "a turning inward which results in
an assertion of self made in the face of a more public and intractable
world" (115). In my view, the alternative represented by the poet himself
remains political, indeed imperialist.

11. Nancy Jo Hoffman epitomizes the sentimental critical orthodoxy
on Colin's career when she bemoans the fact that, in *Colin*, "the old relation between queen and poet, their proximity in the charmed circle of
Mount Acidale and in the April eclogue, exists no longer" (*Spenser's Pastorals*, 120). One wonders what Hoffman can mean by "proximity": the
April eclogue, again, presents Colin as already alienated from Eliza; and
on Mount Acidale, from which the queen is absent, Colin begs her pardon
because he is singing of someone else. In fact, the only assertion in Spenser's poetry that he ever literally saw Elizabeth appears in *Colin Clout*.

12. Spenser's self-restraint is an implicit answer to the critics of English
colonialism in Ireland who, like Spenser's Eudoxius, "think it no good
policy to have that Realm reformed or planted with English lest they
should grow as undutiful as the Irish and become much more dangerous"
(*V* 9:210). But it goes somewhat against the thrust of Irenius's own answer
to this criticism in the *View*, when Irenius blames English backsliding on

> the bad minds of the man, who having been brought up at home under a
> strait rule of duty and obedience being always restrained by sharp penalties
> from lewd behavior, so soon as they Come hither where they see laws more
> slackly tended and the hard Constraint which they were used unto now
> slacked, they grow more loose and Careless of their duty and as it is the
> nature of all men to love liberty So they become Libertines and fall to all
> Licentiousness of the Irish, more boldly daring to disobey the law through
> presumption of favor and friendship than any Irish dareth. (211)

Irenius insists, then, on tougher laws more rigorously kept; but for Spenser and the gentlemen he would fashion, such external constraints are
redundant.

13. Oram understates the case when he says of the poem's title that
"it is not immediately clear where 'home' lies" (*Shorter Poems*, 519), as if
the mystery were only a temporary confusion. As many readers have no-
ticed, the problem is matched in the poem by repeatedly contradictory

estimations of Ireland: the shepherds' flocks are "devoyd of dangers feare" (l. 54), and Ireland is a "quiet home" (686) for the shepherds also; but then the country is also a "desart" (91), a "waste" (183), and a "barrein soyle" (656).

14. For a specific echo between Timias and Colin, see, e.g., *FQ* 4.7.39 and *Colin Clout*, 182–83. On the interrelations between book 4 and Raleigh's writing generally, see Goldberg, *Endlesse Worke*, 50–51 n. 4. Commenting on the fact "that Timias's service to Belphoebe is radically incompatible, now, with service to his master," Donald Cheney concludes: "Perhaps by 1596 Spenser has come to see Elizabeth's court, like Belphoebe's, as a place of sterile dalliance not far removed from Phaedria's or Acrasia's bower" ("Spenser's Fortieth Birthday," 24, 25). I disagree only with Cheney's chronology: Spenser's criticism of Elizabeth's court is as old as *The Shepheardes Calender* and *Mother Hubbard's Tale*.

15. The exclusive praise that Colin applies to almost every woman in the Court is quite extraordinary: for example, Theana is "well worthy" of her "honourable place" "next unto" Cynthia herself (*Colin Clout*, 501–2), but then Mansilia is also "worthie next after *Cynthia* to tread" (514). Characteristically, Spenser solves the problem by seeming to ignore it: nine times in his list of the ladies at Elizabeth's court he exclaims that the one he now treats is not less praiseworthy than her predecessor (492, 504, 508, 516, 524, 532, 536, 572, and 574).

16. *Amoretti* 15 is a good instance of the second dilemma. In transferring the praise of Elizabeth to his private beloved, Spenser claims that "my love doth in her selfe containe / All this worlds riches that may farre be found." The "fairest" of those riches is, characteristically, "her mind adorned with vertues manifold," which, like the face and land of *The Faerie Queene*'s second proem, "few behold." But if the beloved alone is supposed to inspire expansiveness as Elizabeth and Fairyland had once done, her reach seems constrained by the original premise of the sonnet: those merchants who "both the Indias of their treasure spoile" do so only because they are ignorant of Spenser's beloved—hence they travel "so farre in vaine."

17. The only reference to Indian knowledge of Elizabeth in the Virginian accounts appears in Ralph Lane's narrative (Quinn, *Roanoke Voyages* 1:279).

18. "The like and a more large discourse I made to the rest of the nations both in my passing to *Guiana*, and to those of the borders" (*Discoverie*, 15). Cf. 51, 53, and 70; Keymis, *Second Voyage*, 444, 456, 464, and 472–73; and "Of the Voyage" (*Discoverie*, 144).

19. Greenblatt, for instance, describes Raleigh's "uneasiness" here as "the tension between his primitivism and his plans for the exploitation of Guiana" (*Ralegh*, 112). Montrose repeats this idea, but recognizes the "peculiar resonance" of Raleigh's ambivalence "in the context of an address to Elizabeth" ("Shaping," 76-77).

20. Quinn, *Roanoke Voyages* 1:84; cf. 122 and 2:575.

21. For Hayes, such indirection in the pursuit of gold is essential to English physiological integrity: trade with "those Countries . . . which possess the fountains of treasure"

> shall purchase unto us gold & silver, dwelling under temperate & whole-some climates: Then how much better shall it be for us there to possess gold & Silver in health of body & delight,: than for greedy desire to possess the Mines, to deprive ourselves of all health & delight by dwelling in Countries within the burning zones. where the heat or Air shall be unto our complex-ions intemperate & contagious. (Quinn, *New American World* 3:163)

For the attribution of the "Discourse" to Hayes and also possibly to Christopher Carleill, see 156.

22. For Gilbert, this pretence of colonization is what will ultimately make colonization a reality: he imagines that, by means of the treasure and ships seized by those privateers who "set forth under such like color of discovery," "there may be easily such a competent company trans-ported to the W. I. [West Indies] as may be able not only to dispossess the S. [Spaniards] thereof, but also to possess forever your Majesty and Realm therewith" (Quinn, *Gilbert* 1:170–75). Cf. Quinn, *England*, 294: "It is clear . . . that the main source of revenue on which a colony could be built was intended to be derived from the plunder of the Spanish merchant fleet and colonies."

23. Cf. Raleigh, *Letters*, 111; Keymis, *Second Voyage*, 444, 481, and 486; and "Of the Voyage" (Raleigh, *Discoverie*, 138–39).

24. In Hakluyt's *Principal Navigations* (1600), Keymis's account and Chapman's poem directly follow Raleigh's account.

Ultimately, of course, Beaumont is as eager for "glorious gold" (*Meta-morphosis*, l. 317) as Chapman is: tobacco in his account is, I have argued, simply a way to defer and therefore strengthen England's golden hopes.

25. The transparency of gold to spirit is a feature of the New Jerusa-lem: "and the city was pure gold, like unto clear glass" (Revelation 21.18).

26. Cf. Keymis, *Second Voyage*, 472–73.

27. Cf. his description of a valley with "as fair ground, and as beautiful fields, as any man hath ever seen, with diverse copses scattered here and there by the river's side, and all as full of deer, as any forest or park in England, and in every lake and river the like abundance of fish and fowl" (*Discoverie*, 64; see also 42).

28. Keymis in fact dubs the Orenoque after the Shepherd of the Ocean, "Raleana" (*Second Voyage*, 476), and declares that "my self, and the remain of my few years, I have bequeathed wholly to Raleana" (481)— not to a land, that is, but to a river. He also lists the discoveries he has made as "a free and open entrance into Raleana," along with "choice of forty several great rivers (the lesser I do not reckon)" (480); while he talks of Guiana's gold and other commodities as actually *"in* the aforesaid riv-ers" (481; my emphasis). His narrative ends with "A Table of the names of the Rivers, Nations, Towns, and Casiques or Captains that in this sec-ond voyage were discovered" (490–95): river names are the most plentiful.

29. For Aeson and Medea, see, e.g., Ovid, *Metamorphoses* 7.162–293.

30. Keymis too recalls Virginian erotics, but with striking alterations that respond to Raleigh's disgrace in a manner quite the opposite of Chapman's: Guiana may possess "whole shires of fruitful rich grounds, lying now waste for want of people," but these shires are said to "*prostitute themselves unto us*," and then only like an anonymous "fair and beautiful woman, in the pride and flower of desired years" (*Second Voyage*, 487; my emphasis).

31. Other servants of Raleigh, like Chapman less directly involved in Raleigh's troubles with Elizabeth, also like Chapman more directly address the issue of plantation than Raleigh does; but their colonial vision is, once again like Chapman, always somehow skewed. Keymis writes, "lucky and prosperous be that right hand, that shall plant and possess a soil"; but the plants that he thinks "may fructify, increase, and grow to good" in Guiana are only England's many unemployed "Gentlemen, soldiers, and younger brothers" (*Second Voyage*, 489). Elsewhere Keymis envisions a Chapmanian "harvest" of "riches" (480). The anonymous author of "Of the Voyage to Guiana," possibly Harriot, speaks in somewhat more Virginian terms of the Guianans "rendering yearly to her Majesty and her successors a great tribute alloting to her use some rich mines and rivers of gold, pearl, silver, rocks of precious stones &c. with some large fruitful countries for the planting of her Colonies" (Raleigh, *Discoverie*, 146). Yet, in an earlier sentence similarly constructed, the incidental nature of plantation to the writer's plans is clear: "Hereby the Queen's dominions may be exceedingly enlarged, and this Realm inestimably enriched,with precious stones, gold, silver, pearl, and other commodities which those countries yield" (138).

32. Spain is, interestingly enough, Raleigh's precedent in proving that the gold of America can make a trifling nation great: "for we find that by the abundant treasure of that country [Peru] the Spanish King vexeth all the Princes of Europe, and is become in a few years from a poor king of *Castille* the greatest monarch of this part of the world, and likely every day to increase" (*Discoverie*, 18–19). Cf. Keymis, *Second Voyage*, 446, 483, and 487. Keymis makes clear, however, that Spain has no other potentiality besides American gold: it is "rich without men, confident without reason, proud and adventurous without means sufficient" (485); "without the Indies [it] is but a purse without money, or a painted sheath without a dagger" (486).

33. Cf. Keymis's more explicitly providentialist final sentence: "It hath pleased God of his infinite goodness, in his will and purpose to appoint and reserve this empire for us" (*Second Voyage*, 501; cf. 487–88).

Berreo tells Raleigh a prophecy found in Peru "that from Inglatierra those Ingas should be again in time to come restored, and delivered from the servitude" of the Spanish (*Discoverie*, 75). "Of the Voyage to Guiana" adds that, even if a delusion, "at least the prophecy will greatly daunt the Spaniards" (*Discoverie*, 139–40).

34. The relation between these two disgraces is underscored by the relation between Raleigh's two prefatory epistles. One of them discusses Raleigh's troubles with Elizabeth; the other discusses his troubles with unbelievers:

> Because there have been diverse opinions conceived of the gold oar brought from *Guiana*, and for that an Alderman of London and an officer of her majesty's mint, hath given out that the same is of no price, I have thought good by the addition of these lines to give answer as well to the said malicious slander, as to other objections. (*Discoverie*, 7)

35. Drake in California (1578) had hung up a plate noting Elizabeth's claim to the country "together with her highness' picture and arms, in a piece of six pence of current English money" (*PN* 9:325–26). This trifling relation to the New World crumbled for Drake the year of Raleigh's voyage, when, according to Thomas Maynard, Drake during his final voyage confessed "that he was as ignorant of the Indies as my self." Implicitly in Maynard's account, America figures to Drake only as the image of the queen from whom he hopes for reward, the virgin mistress as an aging wet-nurse:

> When, good gentleman, (in my conceit) it fared with him as with some care-less-living man who prodigally consumes his time fondly persuading himself that the nurse that fed him in his childhood will likewise nourish him in his old age and finding the dug dried & withered enforced then to behold his folly tormented in mind dieth with a starved body, he had beside his own adventure gaged his own reputation greatly in promising her majesty to do her honorable service and to return her a very profitable adventure and having sufficiently experienced for 7 or 8 years together, how hard it was to regain favor once ill thought of the mistress of his fortune now leaving him to yield to a discontented mind. (Andrews, *Last Voyage*, 101)

36. As he lay dying during his final voyage, the circumnavigator Thomas Cavendish (1592) also composed a narrative of his venture, unpublished till Purchas. It would be hard to imagine another figure in Elizabeth's later years who could have honored the ideal of material weakness so zealously. Confronted with disaster after disaster, and losing crew, food, and equipment to such an extent that "all the men left in the ship were no more than able to weigh our Anchors" ("Thomas Cavendyshe," 120), Cavendish continues to insist that his ship pursue its course rather than return home. Attempting to exhort a mutinous crew who even he admits had "many reasonable occasions to allege against me" (122), Cavendish like Shakespeare's Henry V argues that "the more we attempted being in so weak a case, the more if we performed would be to our honors" (110). His final demonstration of how failure can produce triumph is the narrative itself, written when he has "grown so weak & faint as I am scarce able to hold the pen in my hands" (120).

37. The difficulty in articulating the paradoxical idea of a laboring gentleman, a difficulty especially marked for a narrative attempting to convince its readers that Guiana possesses such treasure as would free one

from labor forever, helps account for the peculiarity of Raleigh's most elaborate prospecting anecdote. At first in that anecdote, gold appears to have been readily available to the English: "Every stone that we stooped to take up, promised either gold or silver by his complexion. Your Lordships shall see of many sorts, and I hope some of them cannot be bettered under the sun." But then Raleigh qualifies the find—"and yet we had no means but with our daggers and fingers to tear them out here and there, the rocks being most hard of that mineral spar aforesaid, and is like a flint, and is altogether as hard or harder, and besides the veins lie a fathom or two deep in the rocks"—until the available "gold" is repudiated altogether: "each of [our companies] brought also several sorts of stones that appeared very fair, but were such as they found loose on the ground, and were for the most part but colored, and had not any gold fixed in them" (55). Of course, this tentativeness reflects Raleigh's worries about his samples—the merely shiny stones kept by some of his more foolish men, Raleigh claims, are the ones that have bred a bad opinion of him in England (55)—but Raleigh's wavering also reflects his desire to represent himself as at once surrounded by gold and yet having to work for it, or as working for it and yet not working too much. The hard rock or "White spar" that covers the "richest" mines is the expedient Raleigh hits upon both to excuse his lack of gold and to distance himself from the labor he must stress his gold requires: "To stay and dig out gold with our nails, had been *Opus laboris*, but not *Ingenii*" (43–44; cf. 8).

It is revealing that, though equally lacking in gold samples, Keymis apparently feels no compulsion to represent prospecting as laborious for the English: at one point, for instance, he intends to hire some Indians "for hatchets and knives to return us gold grains," and, though he can find no Indians at home, his guide "showed me in what sort without digging they gather the gold in the sand of a small river, named Macawini" (*Second Voyage*, 468). Moreover, Keymis twice mentions the fact that the Spanish now have black slaves in Guiana (445, 470), who, he argues, will ultimately benefit England, "since their [the Spanish] preparations of Negroes to work in the mines, their horses, cattle, and other necessaries may (by the favor of God) at our first coming, both store us with quantities of gold ore, and ease us of much trouble, pains, and travail" (445).

38. For other references to the sexual rapacity of the Spanish, see Keymis, *Second Voyage*, 455, 456, 463, 465, 471, and 472.

39. Indians buy women from the cannibals also; see *Discoverie*, 387 and 407.

40. The relation between the prominence of savage women in Raleigh's account and Raleigh's difficulties with the queen is implicit elsewhere in the *Discoverie*, first when Raleigh mentions his propaganda work with "the Canuri, which are governed by a woman (who is inheritrix of that province) who came far off to see our nation, and asked me diverse questions of her Majesty, being much delighted with the discourse of her Majesty's greatness, and wondering at such reports as we truly made of

her highness' many virtues" (70); and second when the beleaguered courtier discusses reports of "those warlike women" the Amazons (26–27), who, when Elizabeth embraces Guiana, "shall hereby hear the name of a virgin, which is not only able to defend her own territories and her neighbors, but also to invade and conquer so great Empires and so far removed" (76). For another reference to the Amazons, see "Of the Voyage," in *Discoverie*, 139.

"Of the Voyage" is, incidentally, the only Elizabethan tract on America that actually raises the prospect of intermarriage: the writer of the tract recommends that the Guianans "give special hostages to be sent into England, which being civiled and converted here, upon their return and receving of others in their rooms they may be matched in marriage with English women" (146). If Raleigh's marriage to Elizabeth Throckmorton is the issue Chapman must skirt, then it is no wonder that Chapman's prophecy of Guianan liberation envisions marriages too, but between Englishmen and Englishwomen who represent a compromise between Raleigh's options—private lovers, but separated as queen and courtier are by disparity of wealth:

> all our Youth take *Hymen's* lights in hand,
> And fill each roof with honor'd progeny.
> There makes *Society* Adamantine chains,
> And joins their hearts with wealth, whom wealth disjoin'd.
> ("De Guiana," 173–76)

41. See Barbour, *Jamestown Voyages* 1:108 n. 1.

42. The title page of the combined *Map of Virginia* and *Proceedings*, innovative as far as New World tracts are concerned, lists Smith as the author of the *Map* and eight other colonists as the authors of the *Proceedings*. All editors of the *Proceedings* see Smith as a determining influence throughout, but in fact the pairing on the title page already implies a synecdochal relation between Smith and the others, especially since Smith is described as "sometimes Governor of the Country." It is significant, then, that not till the title page of the *Generall Historie* (1624) does Smith give himself sole credit—only later in his career does such credit become so important to him. For convenience I will henceforth refer to Smith alone as the author of the *Proceedings*.

43. An Indian in Martyr anticipates this sarcasm: "If your hunger of gold be so insatiable," says the prince of Comogrus to the Spanish,

> that only for the desire you have thereto, you disquiet so many nations, and you yourselves also sustain so many calamities and incommodities, living like banished men out of your own country, I will show you a Region flowing with gold, where you may satisfy your ravening appetites. (Eden, *Decades*, 117)

44. Percy himself notes the invidious Spanish parallel: "BALDIVIA A Spanish General being served somewhat Answerable hereunto in CHILE in

the WEST INDIES who being Surprised by the Indians enforced him to drink up A certain quantity of melted gold using these words unto him now glut they self with gold BALDIVIA having there sought for gold as SICKLE-MORE did here for food" ("Trewe Relacyon," 265).

45. Cf. a later episode in which the only water Smith and his men can find in an Indian village is "such puddle that never till then, we ever knew the want of good water. We digged and searched many places but ere the end of two days we would have refused two barricoes of gold for one of that puddle water" (Smith, *Works* 1:225).

46. Smith's animus toward the company itself comes clearer in the *Generall Historie* (1624), when the company is in the process of being dissolved. See in particular Smith's extraordinary letter of complaint, sent back to England near the end of 1608 (*Works* 2:187–90); cf. Purchas, *Pilgrimes* 19:3. My next chapter will treat the continuing gold love of the company in more depth.

47. For references in the *Map* to the Indians' love of trifles, see, e.g., *Works* 1:160 and 168. Smith reports that the Indians "stuff" the corpses of their kings with "copper beads . . . , hatchets and such trash" (169), and expect "beads, hatchets, copper, and tobacco" (172) as their reward in the afterlife. According to Smith, idleness is by definition a "trifling," as when one of the colonists lets some Indians escape by "trifling away the night" (261; cf. *True Relation*, 31, 61, and 97). When Smith trifles away the time, on the other hand, he does it to deceive (249).

48. Later, when Smith sees gold waning as a colonial prospect, he still maintains that many settlers continue to be addicted to "present gain" and thus neglect "many things [that] might more have prevailed for their good" (*Works* 2:367). Now, however, the colonists hunger not for gold but tobacco, which so degenerates them that the savage comes to seem positively gentlemanly by comparison: at one point, for instance, Smith (1624) describes the Indians "employed in hunting and fowling with our fowling pieces, and our men rooting in the ground about Tobacco like swine" (2:285). For other invidious comments about tobacco, see 2:256, 262, 284, 287, 314, 327, 382, and 3:218, 220, 237, 274. Apparently Smith dislikes tobacco even as a personal habit: one commender declares, "I never knew a Warrior yet, but thee, / From wine, Tobacco, debts, dice, oaths, so free" (Smith, *Works* 1:363). What disgusts him, I would argue, is not so much tobacco's frivolousness as its addictiveness, which too closely proportions trifler to trifle.

49. For other denunciations of riches, see *Works* 1:344 and 360; for commendatory poems that praise Smith's antimaterialism, see 1:316, 2:49, and 3:146.

50. To Smith's mind, Newport neither understands nor cares for the "necessary business" of plantation because he is a sea captain. His sailors even extort money and goods from the landsmen at an exorbitant rate in

exchange for shipboard supplies (*Works* 1:218); while, as the least attached or most mobile representatives of the colony, they manage to misrepresent at home both the hopes and needs of Virginia:

> Those with their great words deluded the world with such strange promises as abused the business much worse than the rest. For the business being builded upon the foundations of their feigned experience, the planters, the money, time, and means have still miscarried: yet they ever returning, and the Planters so far absent, who could contradict their excuses? (1:176)

For other attacks on mariners, see 1:220, 234, 239–40, and also Strachey, "True Reportory," 28, 50–52. It is no wonder that Prospero keeps "the mariners all under hatches stowed" (*Tempest* 1.2.230) while his own georgic-colonial lessons proceed.

51. *Works* 1:217. For other references to the Indians "glutted" with trifles, see, e.g., 211 and 239–40. To Smith, the most egregious instance of his enemies' naïveté is Powhatan's coronation (234, 237), discussed in my introduction.

52. Cf. the earlier version of this anecdote in the *True Relation* (*Works* 1:71).

53. Some Jacobeans seem to have found the very idea of an Indian language amusing: see, e.g., the gibberish "Barbarian tongue" in Tonkis, *Lingua* 4.4 (cited in Brooks, *Tobacco* 2:51); and Taylor, *Nipping*, D3r (quoted in Brooks, *Tobacco* 1:522). A later and more well-known instance of mock-American appears in Massinger's *City Madam* (1632), when some Englishmen disguise themselves as Indians:

> SIR JOHN.   Oh, ha, enewah Chrish bully leika.
> PLENTY.   Enaula.
> SIR MAURICE.   Harrico botikia bonnery.
>
>   (3.3.92–94)

The roughly contemporary *Fatal Marriage*, which also has a fake Indian, makes Indian language sound like pidgin Latin: "Sib, a re, Crib a re, bunck a me tod, lethe, tu: hoc unge, hungarion siped ley" (51).

For a more explicit instance of a word list considered trifling, see Hall's *Mundus* (1605), in which his traveler encounters a nation of foolish triflers called the Troverense (John Healey's translation [1609] renames them the Gew-gawiasters): "He that first devised to blow out bubbles of soap and spittle forth of the walnut shell, is of as great renown amongst them, as ever was the first Printer, or Gun-founder amongst us of *Europe*" (trans. Healey, 87–88). The butt of Hall's humor turns out to be Paracelsian alchemists, who believe, of course, that they can transform *nugas* to gold. But when Hall provides a word list of their "Supermonical" or esoteric language—"Some of the words I will set down in this place, for the good of such as shall travel those countries hereafter" (88–89)—he manages to mock the trifling of both alchemists and voyagers like Smith.

54. Uncharacteristically, Smith says he provides the list only to satisfy

the curiosity of those who "desire to know the *manner* of their language" (*Works* 1:136; my emphasis). Cf. the far more extensive contemporary word list of William Strachey, "by which, such who shall be Employed thither may know the readier how to confer, and how to truck and Trade with the People" (*Historie*, 174–207).

55. The inclusion of dialogue in a vocabulary of foreign words was, of course, nothing new. Cf. a sample of the comic interchange between Torquato and Nolano in John Florio's Italian vocabulary *Second Frutes* (1591) (I quote only the English dialogue):

> NOLANO.   Happy are you, that wish and have.
> TORQUATO. Nay, you have the world at will.
> NOLANO.   You may piss a bed, and say you sweat.
> TORQUATO. I have nothing but you may command.
> (11)

56. For other references to the availability of Indian women, see 1:168, 174, and the famous "maskerado" before Smith of thirty naked young women that ends with the "Nymphs" "crowding, and pressing, and hanging upon him, most tediously crying, love you not me?" (235–36). If a tradition reported by William Stith (1747) is true, love for Pocahontas could have seemed not only a sexual but a status extravagance: Stith says that King James "was highly offended at Mr. *Rolfe*," Pocahontas's future husband, "for marrying a Princess" (*History*, 142).

57. White beads are favored by aristocratic Indian women (Smith, *Works* 1:53, 216).

58. B2v–B3r; Mercator later replies,

> Indeed de Gentlewomans here buy so much vain toys,
> Dat me [we?] strangers laugh a to tink wherein day have their Joys:
> Fait Madonna me will search all da strange countries me can tell,
> But me will have such tings dat please dese Gentlewomans vell.
> (C4r; cf. D4r)

Cf. Francis Meres's proverb in *Wits Treasury* (1598): "As pigeons are taken with beans, and children enticed with balls; so women are won with toys" (quoted in Schoenbaum, *Shakespeare*, 189). A now-lost play (c. 1560s) was entitled *Far Fetched and Dear Bought Is Good for Ladies* (Chambers, *Elizabethan Stage* 4:400).

For other instances of the "far fetcht" proverb in New World literature, see, e.g., Nicholl, *Houre Glasse*, A4v, and John Gerard's *Herball*, which argues that tobacco grown in Europe is better for the English, "notwithstanding it is not so thought nor received of our Tabackians; for according to the English proverb; Far fetcht and dear bought is best for Ladies" (286, quoted in Brooks, *Tobacco* 1:346; repeated in Gardiner, *Triall*, 9r). William Rankins in his *Mirrour of Monsters* (1587) suggests that the trifling desires of women make England savage. He depicts himself as having traveled to "a country named *Terralbon*" (1r)—England, obviously—where he met

Luxuria, who "hanged at her eyes many costly favors of folly far fet from the Indians of *Anglia*" (4v)—once again, England.

59. The colonialist comparison of Elizabeth to Isabella is itself Elizabethan, appearing, for example, in Hakluyt's dedication to Raleigh of his translation of Laudonnière (1587):

> If Elizabeth Queen of Castile and Arragon, after her husband Ferdinando & she had emptied their coffers and exhausted their treasures in subduing the kingdom of Granada & rooting the Moors, a wicked weed, out of Spain, was nevertheless so zealous of God's honor, that (as Fernandus Columbus the Son of Christopher Columbus recordeth in the history of the deeds of his Father) she laid part of her own Jewels, which she had in great accompt, to gage, to furnish his Father forth upon his first voyage, before any foot of land of all the West Indies was discovered, what may we expect of our most magnificent & gracious prince Elizabeth of England, into whose lap the Lord hath most plentifully thrown his treasures, what may we, I say, hope of her forwardness & bounty in advancing of this your most honorable enterprise being far more certain than that of Columbus, at that time especially, and tending no less to the glory of God than that action of the Spaniards. (Taylor, *Original Writings* 2:375)

Cf. 456–57. For the appearance of Queen Isabella in the hortatory conclusions of various works by Smith, see *Works* 1:382, 406, 441, and 2:474; for nostalgia about Elizabeth, see 1:438; 2:63, 91; and 3:159, 301. Cf. Strachey on that "royal spirited Lady *Isabella Princess of Castile*" (*Historie*, 10); and Robert Hayman (1628), who during Charles's reign hopes that Queen Mary will prove "a *Famous Second Isabell*" (*Quodlibets*, 51).

Columbus himself becomes an increasingly important figure in the idealization of the English colonist. Borrowing from Gomara (Eden, *Decades*, 341), Sir George Peckham (1582) makes Columbus the archetype of the disgraceful New World adventurer:

> By how many ways and means was he derided? Some scorned the piledness of his garments, some took occasion to jest at his simple and silly looks, others asked if this were he, that louts so low, which did take upon him to bring men into a Country that aboundeth with Gold, Pearl, and Precious stones? If he were any such man (said they) he would carry another manner of countenance with him, and look somewhat loftier. Thus some judged him by his garments and some others by his look and countenance, but none entered into the consideration of the inward man. (*True Reporte*, 448)

This view of Columbus got a good deal of press in 1609: see Johnson, *Nova Britannia*, 7–8; Gray, *Good Speed*, Bv; and Linton, *Newes*, 29–30. For a similar reference to Columbus earlier than Peckham, see Seall, *Comendation*.

60. The first erotic reference to women as Indian-like triflers appears around the same time as the *Map* and the *True Relation*. Welford in Beaumont and Fletcher's *Scornful Lady* (acted 1613–16) declares that "certainly I am arrived amongst a Nation of new found fools: in a Land where no Navigator has yet planted wit. If I had foreseen it, I would have laded my breeches with bells, knives, copper and glasses to trade with the women for their virginities" (1.1.287–91). Cf. Drayton's "Of His Lady's Not Com-

ing to London" (1627) (*Works* 3:205) and Carew's "To A. D. Unreasonable Distrustful of Her Own Beauty" (1640) (*Poems*, 84). Before that time, Alexander in *Aurora* (1604) likens Aurora to the gold that "sun-parch'd people" "dis-esteem" (song 9.46–54). Constable in "To My Ladie Rich" (MS c. 1592) attempts the same conceit, though in imagining Indians adoring the "treasure" that is Lady Rich, he incompetently implies that Lady Rich is a trifle (*Poems*, 150). (All these references are cited in Cawley, *Voyagers*, 350–51.) Whether or not Smith's references to Pocahontas, the first instance of erotic trifling in English travel literature, directly produced Welford's analogy, the relatively late appearance of the analogy seems indicative of English resistance to the idea of erotic mixture with Indians. I will address this issue more fully in chapter 6.

61. Cf. Thomas Fuller's less generous appraisal of Smith (1662) as "having a *Prince's* mind imprisoned in a *poor man's* purse" (*History*, 180).

For Smith, if there is any nation that can still see the value in immateriality, it is the Dutch, who "have neither matter to build ships, nor merchandize to set them forth; yet by their industry they as much increase, as other Nations decay" (*Works* 1:424; cf. 2:439). At times in Smith's work, Holland even takes England's place as the trifling alternative to golden Spain:

> Who doth not know that the poor Hollanders, chiefly by fishing, at a great charge and labor in all weathers in the open Sea, are made a people so hardy, and industrious? and by the venting this poor commodity to the Easterlings for as mean [commodities], which is Wood, Flax, Pitch, Tar, Resin, Cordage, and such like (which they exchange again, to the French, Spaniards, Portugales, and English, etc. for what they want) are made so mighty, strong and rich, as no State but Venice, [which is] of twice their magnitude, is so well furnished with so many fair Cities, goodly Towns, strong Fortresses, and that abundance of shipping and all sorts of merchandize, as well of Gold, Silver, Pearls, Diamonds, Precious stones, Silks, Velvets, and Cloth of gold: as Fish, Pitch, Wood, or such gross commodities? What Voyages and Discoveries, East and West, North and South, yea about the world, make they? What an Army by Sea and Land, have they long maintained in despite of one of the greatest Princes of the world? And never could the Spaniard with all his Mines of gold and Silver, pay his debts, his friends, and army, half so truly, as the Hollanders still have done by this contemptible trade of fish. (1:330–31; cf. 2:409)

For other instances of Smith's enthusiasm about Holland, see 1:159, 333, 377, 396–97; 2:114, 411, 437–38, 466; and 3:291, 298. For the growing interest of Smith's contemporaries in "contemptible" commodities, see Shammas, "English Commercial Development." At one point Smith raises the possibility that he might work for Holland: he writes to Bacon (1618) that the Dutch, among others, "have made me large offers" (*Works* 1:377).

62. Smith continues, "Yet 30 or 40 of such voluntary Gentlemen would do more in a day than 100 of the rest that must be prest to it by compulsion." Cf. Prince Ferdinand the "patient log-man" in *The Tempest* 3.1; and Smith, *Works* 1:347–48.

63. The version of the proverb that Tilley chooses as archetypical—

"Help, Hands, for I have no lands" (*Proverbs*, H116)—is revealing in its quite different emphasis on hands securing one's fortune rather than simply taking that fortune's place.

64. Cf. *Works* 3:51 and 146–48.

65. Cf. Smith's account of this history in *New Englands Trials* (1620) (*Works* 1:398–99).

66. Writing as a work of the hands already receives implicit recognition in T. A.'s otherwise mysterious dedication "To the Hand," but becomes far more prominent a topos in Smith's dedication of the *Historie* to Frances Howard. "This History," Smith begins, ". . . might and ought to have been clad in better robes than my rude military hand can cut out in Paper Ornaments"; or again, "I confess, my hand, though able to wield a weapon among the Barbarous, yet well may tremble in handling a Pen among so many Judicious" (*Works* 2:41). In what Smith's editor Philip Barbour calls "the first instance in Smith's writings of a definite statement of his authorship," Smith ends the second book of his history with the subscription, "John Smith writ this with his own hand" (129); the gesture is repeated four more times in Smith's works (2:437, 468, and 3:29, 302).

67. Smith calls himself the father of England's colonies (*Works* 1:434, 3:223), while he styles King Charles only their godfather (1:309, 3:278).

68. The *Generall Historie* reprints "a little book" that Smith wrote about Pocahontas, in which he states that "during the time of two or three years, she next under God, was still the instrument to preserve this Colony from death, famine and utter confusion" (*Works* 2:258–59). The book is itself a version of Columbus before Isabella, since it is addressed to Queen Anne, soliciting her favor in order to make good the embarrassingly low "estate" of Pocahontas's husband John Rolfe. John Chamberlain (1617), sending a copy of the famous portrait of Pocahontas to his correspondent Dudley Carleton, expresses the dismissive view of her that Smith presumably wants to combat: "Here is a fine picture of no fair Lady and yet with her tricking up and high style and titles you might think her and her worshipful husband to be somebody, if you do not know that the poor company of Virginia out of their poverty are fain to allow her four pound a week for her maintenance" (*Letters* 2:56–57).

For Pocahontas's expanded role in the *Generall Historie*, see also Smith's *Works* 2:146–52, 182–3, 198–9, 203–4, 243–46, and 260–62.

69. "You did promise Powhatan what was yours should be his, and he the like to you; you called him father being in his land a stranger, and by the same reason so must I do you: which though I [Smith] would have excused, I durst not allow of that title, because she was a King's daughter; with a well set countenance she said, Were you not afraid to come into my father's Country, and caused fear in him and all his people (but me) and fear you here I should call you father; I tell you then I will, and you shall call me child, and so I will be for ever and ever your Countryman" (Smith, *Works* 2:261). Hulme rejects the old, and to his mind "romantic," interpretation of this characteristically self-deprecating, self-aggrandizing

passage in favor of a more modern type of sentimentality: "Nothing is stranger than that Smith should have reported *in direct quotation* what so obviously meant nothing to him at all, almost as if he recognized, even if only fleetingly, the extent of his ignorance of this woman and her culture and, as a final gesture, perhaps a sort of homage, recorded her alien words in his text" (*Colonial Encounters*, 151–52; my emphasis).

70. For the case that the *Legend* does indeed mock Smith in particular, see Vaughan, "John Smith." Jones's restraint regarding women is not the only manifestation of his chastity. Having landed in America, Jones finds only "a dry and desert soil, nor grain nor grass, / Nor drink, but water had they here, nor bread / For thrice twelve months" (5). To get his food, he does battle with the Indians, two thousand of whom he defeats with his twenty-five men, and kills six native kings in the process; Lloyd comments,

> Here some may ask what came of all the wealth,
> (For *Jones* brought nothing home besides himself)
> This conquest gain'd; Sure many precious things
> Must needs attend the death of six such Kings.
> I answer briefly; His heroic desire
> Ascends above earth's excrements as fire:
> Nor can descend to Crowns.
>
> (6)

An expanded version of the *Legend* (1648) more fully develops the anachronistic Elizabethan setting—Jones, for instance, meets one famous Elizabethan adventurer after another (cf. Smith, *Works* 3:301)—and also produces the episode with the Queen of No-land to which the first version merely alludes. She turns out to be "a Maiden Queen" whom neither kings nor princes can move to love, until, of course, she sees Jones. Lloyd is relatively plain about the fact that this "black" queen represents a strange negation of Elizabeth herself: "*Jones* is resolv'd to see and to be seen / Of this great Princess, that our virgin Queen / Might know when he returns what form, what port / This royal virgin carried in her Court" (58). It seems, then, that Lloyd mocks excessively romantic Elizabethan England too: while on his voyages, Jones had "read to him the ancient stories / Of our old English Worthies, and their glories; / How our S. *George* did the fell Dragon gore: / The like achievement of Sir *Eglemore*: / *Topas'* hard quest after th'elf-queen to *Barwick*," etc. (27). For an account of the sources and the effects of such a critical view, see my epilogue.

71. Fuller, *History*, 180, first pagination; for the question of Smith's veracity, see Smith, *Works* 1:lxiii–iv, lxx–lxxi, and the notes passim. On the basis of his own extravagant and materially uncorroborated claims, Raleigh's detractors decided that he had never sailed farther than Cornwall (*Discoverie*, 4), that his golden empire existed nowhere but in his book. El Dorado is, of course, not the only fabulous-sounding feature of Raleigh's

Discoverie, which reports sightings of headless men and Amazons, and critics have long assumed that Raleigh thought he could persuade his readers to believe in El Dorado by making the fabulous seem more credible generally. Yet this line of argument fails to explain why, throughout the *Discoverie*, Raleigh takes pride in lying. He continually boasts that he has successfully deceived not just the Spanish and the Guianans but his own men; in order to keep the crew of his boat rowing, for instance, "we evermore commanded our Pilots to promise an end the next day" (40). No doubt Raleigh hoped that El Dorado truly did exist, and he wanted to persuade his readers, as Spenser wanted to persuade his, "that of the world least part to us is red" (*FQ* 2.proem.2); but it is difficult to escape the implication that Raleigh was willing to grant the fictionality of El Dorado for those readers who needed less material incentives to empire than gold. If this hypothesis is correct, Raleigh can be understood once again to have exaggerated Spenserian logic, by turning the "vele" that "shadowes" Spenser's otherworld from a trifle to a lie.

72. Cf. the *Advertisements*, in which Smith bemoans the colonial work of not just writing but circulating books: "I had divulged to my great labor, cost, and loss, more than seven thousand Books and Maps" (*Works* 3:281). The topos of the travail endured in compiling a book of travels had earlier appeared in Hakluyt, who never traveled to America: see Taylor, *Original Writings* 2:398, 426, and esp. 433–34.

CHAPTER 6. DISTRACTION IN *THE TEMPEST*

1. Cf. Frye, ed., *The Tempest*, 22–23, and Bergeron, *Shakespeare's Romances*, 178. For a bibliography of criticism touching on *The Tempest*'s relation to the New World, see Frey, "*The Tempest*," and also Skura, "Discourse."

2. The oft-remarked analogy in the play between Aeneas's interrupted imperial voyage and the diverted travels of both Alonso and Gates is similarly obtruded and dismissed during the Court party's debate over "widow Dido" (2.1.71–97). Kermode has said that "nowhere in Shakespeare, not even in his less intensive work, is there anything resembling the apparent irrelevance" (Kermode, ed., *The Tempest*, 47) of the passage.

3. In his most recent examination of *The Tempest*, Greenblatt too notes that "the swerve away" from colonial allusions in *The Tempest* "is as apparent as their presence" (*Shakespearean Negotiations*, 154), a paradox he ascribes to the fact that, in Shakespeare, "the aesthetic space—or, more accurately, the commercial space of the theatrical joint-stock company—is constituted by the simultaneous appropriation of and swerving from the discourse of power" (159). Yet even if this view of Shakespearean aesthetics is accurate, it is not clear why a simultaneous appropriation of and swerving from a certain "discourse of power" could not help to establish another such discourse (even, I will eventually argue, almost the same discourse). Greenblatt forestalls this option by abstracting colonialism into "*the* discourse of power" generally.

Other recent critics insist that *The Tempest* is "fully implicated" in "the colonialist project" of its day (Brown, "This Thing," 64, 48), or that "the discourse of colonialism" is "the articulatory *principle* of *The Tempest's* diversity" (Barker and Hulme, "Nymphs," 204); but they too transform Jacobean expansion into a monolithic "discourse" abstract enough to escape the restrictions of practical counterevidence. In response, these historians of discourse might claim that Shakespeare "euphemizes" (Brown) or "represses" (Barker and Hulme) the relation of his play to America—an argument similar to the one I will shortly offer—but their own broad treatment of colonialism itself mystifies the "moment of *historical* crisis" (Brown, "This Thing," 48) they set out to explain.

4. Cf. 5.1.172–73. As I have argued, Spenser continually warns his readers that "wemens faire aspect" has "wondrous powre . . . / To captive men, and make them all the world reject" (*FQ* 5.8.2).

5. Carlton to Chamberlain, 15 January 1604 (quoted in Chambers, *Elizabethan Stage* 3:279).

6. Cf., e.g., the Captain of the Gypsies in Jonson's masque *The Gipsies Metamorphosed* (performed 1621) as he steps back from the heterodoxy of telling James's fortune:

> But why do I presume, though true,
> To tell a fortune, Sir, to you,
>   Who are the maker here of all,
> Where none do stand, or sit in view,
> But owe their fortunes unto you,
>   At least what they good fortune call.
>
>   (334–39)

7. The dress of the "Indian" knights suggests that they are American: "In their hats each of them [had] an Indian bird for a feather with some jewels" (Carleton in Chambers, *Elizabethan Stage* 3:280).

8. Quoted in Strong, *Henry*, 8. For Henry's cult and its heavily Spenserian cast, see Yates, *Majesty*, passim; Strong, *Cult*, 187–91; Strong, *Henry*, passim; and Helgerson, "Land," 69–71.

9. Dugdale, *Time Triumphant*, B3v; quoted in Schmidgall, *Shakespeare*, 252 n. 26.

10. Cf. Schmidgall, *Shakespeare*, 259, and Gilman: "Prospero's undermined masque becomes a delicately subversive maneuver staged in the enemy camp and hinting at the bedazzled, insulated self-regard of such entertainments" ("All Eyes," 220). The classic treatment of the notion that the Stuarts came increasingly to inhabit a theatrical dreamworld is Orgel's *Illusion of Power*.

11. For beating as a description of the pulse, see 5.1.103 and 114; for a mind beating, see 1.2.176, 4.1.163, and 5.1.246; for beating in the sense of literal affliction (*ad fligere*), see 2.1.115, 2.2.156, 3.2.85, 86, 111, and 4.1.173, 175. For the tide as a figure for mentality, see 5.1.79–82.

12. Nashe maintains that if a state cannot "exhale" its potentially rebellious population in foreign wars, "it is very expedient they have some

light toys" like the theater "to busy their heads withal" (*Works* 1:211). Cf. Heywood, *Apology*, 31.

Perhaps the most explicit treatment of the theater and its self-consumption as able to cure expansionist distraction appears in Richard Brome's *Antipodes* (acted 1637). As the play begins, Peregrine has grown "distracted" (1.1.21) by reading Mandeville, and "a fantastic lord" (Dramatis Personae) named Letoy undertakes his cure by staging Peregrine's play-voyage to the antipodes. The moment at which Peregrine fully enters Letoy's illusion—his unscripted attack on and conquest of some "Antipodean" stage props—foreshadows both his ultimate repudiation of such distracting toys and the play's self-repudiating conclusion:

> Wonder he did
> A while it seem'd, but yet undaunted stood;
> When on the sudden, with thrice knightly force,
> And thrice, thrice puissant arm he snatcheth down
> The sword and shield that I play'd Bevis with,
> Rusheth amongst the foresaid properties,
> Kills monster after monster, takes the puppets
> Prisoners, knocks down the Cyclops, tumbles all
> Our jigambobs and trinkets to the wall.
> Spying at last the crown and royal robes
> I'th' upper wardrobe, next to which by chance
> The devil's vizors hung, and their flame-painted
> Skin coats, those he remov'd with greater fury,
> And (having cut the infernal ugly faces
> All into mammocks) with a reverend hand,
> He takes the imperial diadem and crowns
> Himself King of the Antipodes, and believes
> He has justly gain'd the kingdom by his conquest.
> (3.6.14–31)

Ann Haaker notes that Peregrine's violence recalls the "habit" among London apprentices "of attacking and demolishing" whorehouses and playhouses on Shrove Tuesday (Brome, *Antipodes*, 69); *The Antipodes* turns such antitheatricality into the play's self-conquest.

13. Stephano suggests a continuity among these wooden vehicles when he tells Trinculo that he "escap'd upon a butt of sack which the sailors heav'd o'erboard," that he has transferred some of the sack to a bottle "which I made of the bark of a tree," and that to drink from this bottle is to "kiss the book" (2.2.121–30). Part of Prospero's temperate attack on the notion that the body resembles either the rock in which Caliban is stied or the bat's back on which Ariel flies consists of turning rooted trees into uprooted logs and then making the freedom of those logs depend on the pains a body takes in moving them.

14. More precisely, Prospero represents the masque as a failed distraction from distraction. The masque begins with the assurance that the gods who helped plot Proserpine's abduction by Dis (89), Venus and Cupid, have fled the scene; but it ends with Prospero having become Distempered and Dis-made (145, 147).

15. The notion that the theater could physically affect its audience is also a common theme in the antitheatrical literature, though the antitheatricalist would say that the effect is to inspire lust. For a recent celebratory version of the view that Shakespeare "more than any of his contemporaries" exploits the power of the theater to arouse its audience physically, see Greenblatt, *Shakespearean Negotiations*, chap. 3.

16. Sir John Beaumont connects dew to tobacco causally: "from [tobacco's] fumes, ascending to the skies, / Some say the dews and gentle showers arise" (*Poems*, 318; cf. James I, *Counter-blaste*, B4r). The relation between dew and smoke as figures of ephemeralness is established in Hosea 13.3: "Therefore they shall be as the morning cloud, & as the morning dew that passeth away, as the chaff that is driven with a whirlwind out of the floor, & as the smoke that goeth out of the chimney."

17. The earliest caution about North American gold that I have found in the practical expansionist literature is Roger Barlow's in "A Brief Summe of Geographie" (MS c. 1540–41):

> What commodity is within this land as yet it is not known for it hath not been labored, but it is to be presupposed that there is no riches of gold, spices nor precious stones, for it standeth far aparted from the equinoctial whereas the influence of the sun doth nourish and bring forth gold, spices, stones and pearls. (180)

18. The connection between America and Solomon's navigations seemed plausible enough to be authorized by the Bishops' Bible: "Ophir is thought to be the island in the West coast, of late found by Christopher Columbo, from whence at this day is brought much fine gold" (note to Psalm 45; quoted in Opfell, *Translators*, 25).

19. The claim is at least as old as Luce; see Luce's edition of *The Tempest* (1902), 169–70.

20. Cf. Greenblatt, "Learning," 575. Gillies's materialism seems confused in a number of ways, most obviously in the belief that the island as Europeans see it is somehow less physical than the "unimaginable" landscape imagined by Shakespeare, but more generally in the view that a colonial interest in Ovidian topoi of temperance is somehow incompatible with "realism" and "historicity," as if beliefs were an ideally avoidable accident of perception. For Gillies, there is no better sign of the way ideas distort "hard facts" than when contemporaries of the Jamestown settlers interpret their "hard fortune" as a result of "moral failure" ("Shakespeare's Virginian Masque," 702); yet what more fitting explanation does Gillies offer, not only for the settlers' inability to secure food and treat the Indians temperately but also for their very interest in an imperialist venture?

21. According to Strachey, those Bermuda castaways who mutinously want "to settle a foundation of ever inhabiting there" fear that leaving Bermuda and continuing to Virginia will force them "to serve the turns of the Adventurers" for "their whole life" ("True Reportory," 28, 31). For the accuracy of their fears, see Morgan, *American Slavery*.

22. See, e.g., Eden's address to Philip II and Queen Mary (1555) as, among other things, "Regi ac Reginae . . . Neapolis" and "Ducibus Mediolani" (*Decades*, 46). Cf. William Warner's reference (1596) to "the free-*Italian* States, of which the *Spaniards* part have won: / As *Naples, Milan,* royal That, and Duchy This" (*Albions England* 12:75); and Giovanni Botero's assertion (1589; trans. 1606) that "the chiefest parts of *Italy*; that is, the Kingdom of *Naples*, and the Dukedom of *Milan*, are subject to the King of *Spain*" (*Cities*, 79).

23. Hakluyt, "Discourse," 243. Though commonplace in Renaissance England, Hakluyt's sentiments were not universally held: this particular passage is in fact lifted from George Nedham's complaint (c. 1564) about the gold Philip obtained from the Netherlands, which Nedham says are "more profitable" to Philip "than his Indies" ("Letter," 78, 68). Cf. Botero: "The custom of the merchandise of *Milan*, brings more money to the king of Spain's coffers, than the mines of *Zagateca* and of *Salisco*" (*Cities*, 51). English writers did agree, however, that whatever its source, Spain's gold fueled Spanish expansion.

24. Cf. Marnix, *Exhortation*, 14–15; Wernham, *List* 2:416; and Bacon, *Works* 14:478–79. Both Sutcliffe (*Answer*, 169–70) and Lightfote (*Complaint*, G3r–H2r) conjoin descriptions of Spanish crimes in Italy and the Indies. Richard Hakluyt the elder (1585) advises the English to treat the Indians well, so "that we become not hateful unto them, as the Spaniard is in Italy and in the West Indies, and elsewhere, by their manner of usage" (Taylor, *Original Writings* 2:334). The Spanish governor of Milan (1570) himself associates Spain's Old and New World dominions: he writes to Philip that "these Italians, although they are not Indians, have to be treated as such, so that they will understand that we are in charge of them and not they in charge of us" (quoted in Elliott, *Old World*, 82). Raleigh's Spanish alter ego in the pursuit of El Dorado, Antonio de Berrio, nicely embodies this connection between Spain's European and American rapacity: Raleigh explains that Berrio "had long served the Spanish king in *Milan, Naples,* and Low countries and elsewhere" (Raleigh, *Discoverie*, 15).

In a way, Spain had already invaded England by means of an American weapon first wielded against Naples—"the disease which the french call the evil of *Naples*," syphilis. Guicciardini's *Historie* (trans. 1579) explains "that such a disease was transported out of *Spain* to *Naples*, & yet not proper or natural of that nation [Spain], but brought thither from the isles, which in those seasons began to be made familiar to our regions by the navigation of *Christopher Colonnus*" (128). Cf. Thevet, *New Found Worlde*, 70v, and Monardes, *Joyfull Newes* 1:29. For a bibliography of Renaissance Spanish literature on the American origin of syphilis, see Chiappelli, *First Images* 2:851 and 884; for Shakespeare on the relation between Naples and syphilis, see *Troilus and Cressida* 2.3.18–19 and *Othello* 3.1.3–4.

25. "Discourse," 246. Cf. out of many supporting pieces of evidence Sir Roger Williams in a letter to Burleigh, 20 November 1590: "Neither shall we nor our friends give them [the Spanish] the law as we should do,

without ransacking his Indies. For his treasure comes unto him, as our salads to us. When we have eat all, we fetch more out of our gardens. So doth he fetch his treasure out of the ground, after spending all that is coined" (quoted in Wernham, *List* 2:296).

26. This ambivalence figures in Johnson, *Nova Britannia*, who never denies that gold can be found in Virginia; he only wants to suppress discussion of it. The *True Declaration* conventionally warns its readers, "Let no man adore his gold as his God, nor his Mammon as his Maker" (67), and reports the cautionary tale of a colonial ship that while trading for food turns piratical instead, led by "dreams of mountains of gold, and happy robberies" (37); yet the conclusion to its list of Virginian commodities coyly describes Virginia's "five main Rivers . . . promising as rich entrails as any Kingdom of the earth, to whom the sun is no nearer a neighbor" (56). Though he begins his sermon on Virginia by exhorting his listeners "to contemn riches" (*Good Newes*, 1), Alexander Whitaker (1613) similarly goes on to discuss mines in Virginia that provide "argument of much hope"; he adds, tantalizingly, "though I knew all, yet it were not convenient at this time that I should utter all" (38–39). Daniel Price's tangled negations (1609) nicely epitomize the confusion of these writers: "The Country is not unlike to equalize (though not *India* for gold, which is not unpossible yet), *Tyrus* for colors, *Basan* for woods, [etc.]" (*Sauls Prohibition*, F2r). Even Smith, so vehemently opposed to gold hunting, cannot keep himself from ambiguity on the subject: *A True Relation* (1608) mentions rocks "interlaced with many veins of glistering spangles" (*Works* 1:31) and an Indian who brings "a glistering Mineral stone" (95); while the later *Map* (1612) declares of these rocks that "the crust . . . would easily persuade a man to believe there are other mines than iron and steel" (*Works* 1:156; cf. 145). Most telling of all, the oldest hand at double-talk about Virginian gold, Richard Hakluyt, could simultaneously recommend and abjure the quest for gold by dividing his ambivalence between two separate and opposed works: on the one hand, the translation of Lescarbot that Hakluyt promoted (*Nova Francia*, vii); and on the other, a tract published the same year concerning de Soto's Floridan expedition, in which Hakluyt the translator directs the reader to those chapters describing various gold mines "within our limits" (Rye, *Discovery*, 1–4). The fate of this last work helps explain why the Virginia Company could not afford wholly to quash hopes about Virginian gold: of all the company propaganda published before *The Tempest* was produced, only *Virginia Richly Valued*, the one exception to a general restraint about gold talk, saw a second edition.

27. Like tobacco, even the apparently worthless dew of Bermuda can appear to represent imperialist desire: Plutarch (trans. 1579) reports "that the kings of Persia made water to be brought from the rivers of Nilus and Ister (otherwise called Danubie) which they did lock up with their other treasure for a confirmation of the greatness of their Empire, and to show that they were Lords of the world" (*Lives* 4:342).

28. For further evidence of Miranda's physical attraction to Ferdinand, see, e.g., 1.2.458–60 and 3.1.56–57.

29. For the royal commands, see Simpson, *Encomienda*, 10–12, 17–18, 39, 42, and 177 n. 3; for notices of concubinage and intermarriage, see Moerner, *Race Mixture*, 25–27. Moerner believes that the Crown decrees on intermarriage were more experimental and uncertain than Simpson allows: see *Race Mixture* 36–38.

30. In New England, "the problem [of intermarriage] was raised in a formal way in March 1635 when the Massachusetts General Court entertained and then immediately referred a question concerning the propriety of Indian-white marriages, but it never regained the court's attention" (Axtell, "Scholastic," 155). For opposition to intermarriage in Elizabethan Ireland, see Canny, "Permissive," 24.

Michael Zuckerman also notes the singularity of English resistance to intermarriage ("Identity," 145–47).

31. *Encouragement*, 28. Cf. the scruples manifested in the comparatively liberal plan of the anonymous writer of "Of the Voyage": the Guianans "shall give special hostages to be sent into England, which being civiled and converted here, upon their return and receiving of others in their rooms they may be matched in marriage with English women" (Raleigh, *Discoverie*, 146).

32. Kupperman, *Settling*, 118; see Kupperman for another discussion of most of the writers on intermarriage whom I cite.

There is little reason to accept a report on Virginian intermarriage by the Marquess of Flores to Philip II in 1612, though it does seem revealing of the differences between English and Spanish colonialism:

> I have been told by a friend, who tells me the truth, that some of the people who have gone there, think now some of them should marry the women of the savages of that country; and he tells me that there are already 40 or 50 thus married. (Brown, *Genesis* 2:572)

A century later, the governor of Virginia, Alexander Spotswood, claims that the English distaste for intermarriage has not softened:

> And as to beginning a nearer friendship by intermarriage, (as the Custom of the French is,) the inclinations of our people are not the same with those of that Nation, for notwithstanding the long intercourse between the inhabitants of this Country and the Indians, and their living amongst one another for so many Years, I cannot find one Englishman that has an Indian wife, or an Indian married to a white woman. (Quoted in Jacobs, "British-Colonial Attitudes," 92)

33. For Hakluyt's complaints about England's failure to convert the Indians, see his "Discourse of Western Planting" (1584). After noting that the Spanish "more vaunt" of their success in conversions "than of anything else that ever they achieved" there, Hakluyt adds that "I my self have been demanded of them how many Infidels have been by us converted," and a thorough examination of every English venture in America

to that time only defeats him: "In very deed I was not able to name any one Infidel by them converted" (216–17). Fifteen years later, he still complains that "our adversaries daily in many of their books full bitterly lay unto the charge of the professors of the Gospel" the neglecting of conversion (Taylor, *Original Writings* 2:457). Cf. Crashaw, *Sermon*, K2r–v.

34. Cf. Zuckerman: "As the settlers spurned sexual union with the natives, so they scorned spiritual communion" ("Identity," 147).

Meredith Skura gives the most recent positive account of Prospero's final relation to Caliban. She reads Prospero's claim that Caliban is "mine" figuratively and thinks that Prospero, in acknowledging "the child-like Caliban," "moves for the first time towards accepting the child in himself rather than trying to dominate and erase that child (along with random vulnerable human beings outside himself) in order to establish his adult authority." Though Prospero may be "a long way from recognizing the equality of racial 'others,' " Skura admits, "he comes closer than any of Shakespeare's other 'Prosperos' to acknowledging the otherness within, which helps generate all racism—and he comes closer than anyone else in colonialist discourse" ("Discourse," 66). This implausibly comprehensive pronouncement caps Skura's attack on previous critics of *The Tempest* for not "specifying Shakespeare's precise literal and temporal relation to colonialist discourse" (57), but it is difficult to see what Skura herself imagines the practical colonialist upshot of Prospero's "acknowledging the otherness within" to be. She seems right to insist that the play "contains the 'colonial' encounter firmly within the framing story of his [i.e., Prospero's] own family history" (66), but then such containment of Caliban within the larger issue of Prospero's troubles as a brother and child looks a good deal like the attempt "to dominate and erase" that Prospero has supposedly transcended. Over the course of the play, Prospero does move from a Spanish-like colonial policy of enslavement to a more benign and English-like attitude toward Caliban—for example, where in act 4 he labels Caliban a "devil" (4.1.188), in act 5 he can reduce the charge to "demi-devil" (5.1.272)—yet at the same time the question, raised in the play's first act, of Caliban's rights to the island gets dropped entirely.

35. See *Titus Andronicus; Othello* 5.2.347; Fiedler, *The Stranger*, 201; and *Anthony and Cleopatra* 1.1.6 and 1.5.28.

36. See, e.g., the "Argument" to Phaer's translation (1573) of the *Aeneid* (unpaginated).

37. For interesting reflections on the black-white marriage in Shakespeare, see Fiedler, who imagines the intermarriage of Claribel and Tunis as able to "succeed" by its distance "from the world in which Shakespeare had previously demonstrated its inevitable failure" (*The Stranger*, 203). But Sebastian's report of Claribel's "loathness" makes it hard to believe that Shakespeare views relocation so optimistically.

38. Though the first reference to Pocahontas as nonpareil occurs in Smith's *Proceedings*, which was not published till 1612, manuscripts of the work or rumors about Pocahontas could easily have circulated earlier; and

Smith had been back in England since the end of 1609. Hamor (1615) says Pocahontas's "fame hath even been spread in England by the title of *Non-parella* of *Virginia*" (*True Discourse*, 4). Of course, Pocahontas's marriage occurred after *The Tempest* was written.

Miranda's likeness to Pocahontas was first noted by Luce (*The Tempest*, 169–70). Geoffrey Bullough cites the connection and then with no explanation abjures it: "To identify Miranda with Pocahontas is a tempting fancy which must be sternly repressed" (*Sources* 8:241).

39. Caliban is himself only a first-generation native (1.2.282), and a Mediterranean, not American, one at that. Skura rightly notes that he also "lacks almost all of the defining external traits [of the Indian] in the many reports from the New World—no superhuman physique, no nakedness or animal skin (indeed, an English 'gaberdine' instead), no decorative feathers, no arrows, no pipe, no tobacco, no body paint, and—as Shakespeare takes pains to emphasize—no love of trinkets and trash" ("Discourse," 49). Yet, mysteriously, Skura goes on to claim that Shakespeare is "the first writer of fiction to portray New World inhabitants" (58). Even if Caliban were an Indian, and if Skura had said that Shakespeare was the first *English* fiction writer to depict a New World inhabitant, her claim would remain inaccurate: e.g., the cast of characters in Greene's *Orlando Furioso* (c. 1588–91) includes the Kings of Cuba and Mexico. But Greene's Americans, like the inhabitants of Cusco in Thomas Lodge's *Margarite of America* (1596), have names culled from European romance: the King of Cuba is Rodamant; of Mexico, Mandricard. Shakespeare's innovation as an English writer may have been to represent a more savage Indian-like figure—though again, Caliban neither looks nor speaks like the savages in New World travel literature, and he is not American.

40. One character in the play, Roselia, does mention that her island was "inhabited heretofore by warlike women, / That kept men in subjection" (2.2), but these missing Amazons only prove the point that the Europeans have supplanted the natives *as* natives: Roselia even adds that the Amazonian "example" persuaded the Portuguese women to become Amazons themselves.

For a report of an Indian literally cannibalized by the Jamestown settlers during the winter of 1609–10, see McIlwaine, *Journals*, 29.

41. To my knowledge, no Indian character ever appeared on the popular Jacobean stage. If it was acted, the lost *Tragedy of the Plantation of America*, registered the year after the massacre of 1622 (see Bentley, *Jacobean and Caroline Stage* 5:1395–96), must have been an exception that proved the rule: the Indians are subsumed unless they actually murder their European substitutes. Some "Floridans" figure in *The Masque of Flowers* (1614), but again, as in the masque of the magician and Chapman's entertainment, they serve as foils to "the great Sun of our firmament," the king.

Caroline plays began to allow Indians on the stage as disguises. See

Massinger's *City Madam* (1632) and the anonymous *Fatal Marriage* (possibly from the 1620s or 1630s; see xi and Bentley 5:1332–33).

42. Percy, "Trewe Relacyon," 277–78. Smith's *Proceedings* reports a less mysterious transformation of Englishman to Indian: in order to make a rendezvous with his cohorts, one mutineer at Jamestown disguised himself "Savage like" (*Works* 1:259). For the threat to Renaissance English colonies posed by colonists going native, see Canny, "Permissive."

EPILOGUE

1. In a commendatory poem of the same title as Cowley's, Waller also praises Davenant for his American plans. Davenant tells Hobbes in the *Preface to Gondibert* that he will send him the rest of *Gondibert* "from America" (*Preface*, 44). For satire on the praise of Davenant as poet and colonizer, see the poem "Upon the Preface" printed in *Certain Verses Written By Severall of the Authors Friends* (1653) (reprinted in *Gondibert*, 273). On the disastrous outcome of Davenant's American venture, see Harbage, *Davenant*, 110–13.

2. In his dedication of *King Arthur* (1691) to the Marquis of Halifax, Dryden refers to "that fairy way of writing which depends only upon the force of the imagination" (*Works* 8:136).

3. For this scorn of "monsters" in favor of "men," see also the prologue to the 1616 version of *Every Man in His Humor* and the induction to *Bartholomew Fair* (1616), both of which, however, are different from the *Barriers* and more characteristic of Jonson in their scorn for the outlandish.

4. According to Chamberlain, in a letter to Carleton on 19 November 1612 (*Letters* 1:391; quoted in Strong, *Henry*, 84). For a similar attack on Spenser's fairy nationalism, see also Daniel's rejection (1599) of "fained *Paladins*" in favor of "the true designs / Of *Bourchier, Talbot, Nevile, Willoughby*" (*Civill Wars* 5.4).

5. Cf. Hobbes's own thoughts in the *Preface* on the relation between poetry and nature (51).

6. See M. H. Abrams's extraordinary *The Mirror and the Lamp* (e.g., 265–68), upon which much of this epilogue is based.

7. For references to this intellectual world, see *Works* 1:134/4:23, 1:191/4:82, the *Descriptio Globi Intellectualis* ([written c. 1612, published 1653] *Works* 3:727–68), and the frontispiece to *Sylva Sylvarum* (1627)—the work to which *New Atlantis* was appended—which shows the "Mundus Intellectualis" framed by the Pillars of Hercules.

8. Rymer in the preface to his translation of René Rapin, *Reflections on Aristotle's Treatise of Poesie* (1674), 5.

9. Misquoted in Quinn, "First Pilgrims," 345.

10. Quoted in Quinn, "First Pilgrims," 341. Cf. Bullinger (trans. 1577): "For you shall find in these days captious and fantastical men (that is

schismatics) worthy surely to be master builders in Utopia or Cyribiria" (quoted in Sullivan and Padberg, *Supplement*, 15). Anatomizing the character of a "Chameleon"—a creature the Renaissance believed to feed on air—Thomas Scot (1616) later declares that he

> is in *England* a Familist, at *Amsterdam* a Brownist, further on an Anabaptist. He lives by the air, and there builds Castles and Churches; none on the earth will please him: He would be of the triumphant and glorious Church, but not of the terrene militant Church, which is subject to storms, deformities, and many violences and alterations of time: he must find out Sir *Thomas More's Utopia*, or rather *Plato's* Community, and be an *Elder* there. (Philomythie, E5v; cited in Sullivan and Padberg, *Supplement*, 102)

11. For a good introduction to millenarianism during the English Renaissance, see Capp, "The Political Dimension of Apocalyptic Thought."

12. Attacking some Parliamentary opponents, Charles (1642) refers to "that new *Utopia* of Religion and Government into which they endeavor to transform this Kingdom" (Rushworth, *Historical*, 727, cited in Gibson, *Bibliography*, 406).

13. Cited in Gibson, *Bibliography*, 409; cf. Prynne, *Vindication*, 52 and 57–58.

14. For other references, see Gibson, *Bibliography*, nos. 842 (p. 409), 843 (410), and 852 (411).

15. The verses are actually untitled. For English opponents of nonconformity who tried, as Richard Harvey (1590) says, to "banish it into the Novus Orbis," see Quinn, "First Pilgrims" (who cites Harvey at 342).

16. In his poem on the Nine Worthies, Morton says it is a "pity" he

> cannot call them Knights,
> Since they had brawn and brain, and were right able
> To be installed of Prince Arthur's table;
> Yet all of them were Squires of low degree.
> (*Canaan*, 290)

Interestingly, William Bradford derides Morton and his people in fairy terms also: "They also set up a maypole, drinking and dancing about it many days together, inviting the Indian women for their consorts, dancing and frisking together like so many fairies, or furies, rather; and worse practices. As if they had anew revived and celebrated the feasts of the Roman goddess Flora, or the beastly practices of the mad Bacchanalians" (*Plymouth*, 205–6).

17. Wasserman, *Subtler Language*, 142; for the contemporary political significance of William the Conqueror and Lodona, see 113–25 and 133–43.

18. For the comparison between Anne and Elizabeth, see Carrera, "Anne and Elizabeth." The most explicit allusion to Elizabeth in Pope's poem, however, combines her virginal insularity with her international authority: at the new Whitehall "Kings shall sue, and suppliant States be seen / Once more to bend before a *British* QUEEN" (384–85).

19. As the *Twickenham* editors note, the conclusion of the poem is modeled on the conclusion of *Georgics* 4, and, just as the last line of Virgil's poem echoes the first line of his *Eclogues*, so the last line of *Windsor Forest* echoes the first line of Pope's *Pastorals*. For the many other minor allusions to words and phrases from the *Georgics*, and to a lesser degree from the rest of Virgil's poetry, see the editors' notes.

20. The first pastoral, "Spring," begins: "First in these fields I try the Sylvan Strains, / Nor blush to sport on *Windsor's* blissful Plains."

21. The poem does make minor references to actual cultivation, but they always appear in tandem with references to pastoral: for example, the Thames predicts that "safe on my Shore each unmolested Swain / Shall tend the Flocks, or reap the bearded Grain" (369–70; cf. 37–40 and 87–90). The only homely activity to receive extended treatment in the poem is, however, neither Virgilian pastoral nor Virgilian georgic— namely, hunting (93–158). David Morris thinks these problems resolved by conceiving of *Windsor Forest* as figuratively georgic: "Although Virgil in the *Georgics* glorifies agriculture rather than commerce, both he and Pope . . . use commerce and agriculture as symbolic occupations in a profoundly similar way" ("Virgilian Attitudes," 245). Yet it is hard to see how a symbolism lacking interest in both the land and labor, as I will show, can count as georgic. Cf. Addison in his *Essay on Virgil's Georgics* (1697): "A *Georgic* therefore is some part of the science of husbandry put into a pleasing dress" (*Miscellaneous Works* 2:4).

22. Hence at another point "Rich Industry" only "*sits* smiling on the Plains" (41; my emphasis). For more references to Windsor's forest become England's navy, see 222 and 385–86.

23. For Pope's determined investment in *concordia discors* throughout the poem, see the masterful treatment in Wasserman, *Subtler Language*, passim. Spenser's is, of course, not the only way that Elizabethans could relate pastoral to epic. For instance, Drayton's revision of Spenser's "Aprill" eclogue, the third "Eglog" in *Idea The Shepheards Garland* (1593), has Rowland praising Elizabeth as "Beta" the "shepherd's Goddess" (l. 123), but instead of singing to Colin's waterfall, Rowland addresses the more expansive Thames, and ends his pastoral with a prayer that Beta's "large empire stretch her arms from east unto the west" (119). Here pastoral truly has swallowed epic, as if there were no difference between the two; Pope, however, insists on both ease of relation and difference, so as to avoid the unwarranted complacence of such insular imperialism.

24. See also the Spenserian catalogue of English rivers (*Windsor Forest*, 340–48). Pope's resistance to dwelling on England's island explains the only passage in the poem that treats at length a landed England beyond Windsor. The Thames exclaims,

> Behold! th'ascending *Villa's* on my Side
> Project long Shadows o'er the Crystal Tide.
> Behold! *Augusta's* glitt'ring Spires increase,

And Temples rise, the beauteous Works of Peace.
I see, I see where two fair Cities bend
Their ample Bow, a new *White-Hall* ascend!

(375–80)

These two cities, the only English ones besides Windsor that Pope mentions—"Augusta" or London, and Westminster—leave the Thames for
land only so far as to occupy its "banks" (336), and then the only habitations within them that the Thames will describe are those that leave the
land by ascending or rising. Elsewhere, discussing Henry VI and Edward
IV, Pope does invoke the insular limits of England, yet only to imagine
them either exceeded—the two kings were men "whom not th'extended
Albion could contain, / From old *Belerium* to the *Northern* Main" (315–16)—
or else anticipated by the forest: the kings meet in their Windsor "Grave"
(316).

25. The *Twickenham* editors do, however, note the apparent contradiction.

On other occasions too, it is unclear whether Wasserman merely reports or supports Pope's views: for example, "Britain's fleets will bear her
thunder and her Union Jack over the seas, not to create foreign conflict,
but to assure the *concordia discors* of the world" (*Subtler Language*, 167).
This liberal imperialism appears as well in an earlier and, at the time,
more popular celebration of the treaty than Pope's: Thomas Tickell's *On
the Prospect of Peace* (1712). Praising Britannia, "the Ocean's stately queen,"
Tickell demands,

Say, where have e'er her union-crosses sail'd,
But much her arms, her justice more prevail'd!
Her labors are, to plead th'Almighty's cause,
Her pride to teach th'untam'd barbarian laws:
Who conquers wins by brutal strength the prize;
But 'tis a godlike work to civilize.

(25)

But later Tickell more explicitly adopts the language of "command" that
Pope will also employ:

From Albion's cliffs thy wide-extended hand
Shall o'er the main to far Peru command;
So vast a tract whose wide domain shall run,
Its circling skies shall see no setting sun.

(31)

26. The *Twickenham* editors note that "[Joseph] Warton objected to *sable*, saying, 'they are not negroes.' " Cf. Pope's contemporaneous reference (1714) to "*Afrik's* Sable Sons" (*Rape of the Lock* 3.82). Pope does not
seem to envision the Indians growing black due to actual intermarriage—
he expects them, after all, to "reap their own Fruits" (*Windsor Forest*, 410).
For the recurrent conflation of Indians and blackamoors in Elizabethan
literature, see, e.g., Hunter, *Dramatic Identities*, 41 n. 4; for the same in
Restoration pageantry, see Barthelemy, *Black Face*, 47–48 and 52–55.

27. For more explicit evidence of continuing interest in England as an otherworld, see the vigorous attack by Aylett Sammes (1676) on the notion that England had ever been a peninsular "hanger-on" to the Continent (*Britannia*, 25–37).

28. For an introduction to the belief that the westward progress of religion would end in an American millennium, see Lovejoy, *Religious Enthusiasm*, 17–19. Though some English writers were attracted to the idea, it does not seem to have greatly pleased the authorities. For the reports that licensers were troubled by Herbert's lines, see Hutchinson's commentary in his edition of Herbert (*Works*, 547); for Wither's imprisonment as a result of the *Motto*, see the entry for the *Motto* in Pollard and Redgrave, *Short-Title Catalogue* 2:472.

29. E.g., *Paradise Lost* 2.403, 410. For an introduction to seventeenth-century interest in the idea of a plurality of worlds, see McColley, "Seventeenth-Century Doctrine"; for theories about a world in the moon, see Nicolson, *World*; and for the intellectual impact of both these notions, see Lovejoy's *Great Chain of Being*.

30. For *Utopia*'s place in seventeenth-century heterocosmic theory, see, e.g., John Collop's "The Poet" (1656), which declares that when the poet has "o'erview'd" the world, he "can make a new. / A Plato's Commonwealth who can outdo? / A *More*'s Utopia, and *Atlantis* too" (32–34; cited in Sullivan and Padberg, *Supplement*, 24).

31. Addison claims that "among the *English, Shakespeare* has incomparably excelled all others" in that "noble Extravagance of Fancy" by which he comes to create supernatural characters, as "in the Speeches of his Ghosts, Fairies, Witches and the like Imaginary Persons" (*Spectator* 3:572–73). In a similar vein, Nicholas Rowe (1709) cites *The Tempest, A Midsummer Night's Dream, Macbeth,* and *Hamlet* as Shakespeare's most transcendent achievements (see Abrams, *Mirror*, 382 n. 47); while Joseph Warton in *Adventurer* no. 93 (1753) later singles out *The Tempest* as "the most striking instance" of Shakespeare's "boundless imagination" (*Adventurer* 2:134; quoted in Abrams, *Mirror*, 275; cf. 382 n. 48): "The poet is a more powerful magician than *Prospero*: we are transported into fairy-land" (*Adventurer* 2:138). As for Spenser, Addison admits that other poets such as Ovid, Virgil, and Milton may have produced extraordinary instances of "another sort of Imaginary Beings"—personifications—but "we find a whole Creation of the like shadowy Persons in *Spenser*" (*Spectator* 3:573).

32. See Abrams, *Mirror*, for the rising interest in "the psychology of poetic illusion" (270).

33. For the aesthetic, theological, and political ramifications of this ambivalence, see Steven Knapp's *Personification and the Sublime*.

34. Cowley's note to the passage sharpens the contrast between it and the Davenant poem: Cowley explains that "*Poetry* treats not only of all things that are, or can be, but makes *Creatures* of her own, as *Centaurs, Satyrs, Fairies,* &c."

Earlier in his career, Davenant had himself written a "fantastic" imperialist poem, "Madagascar" (1638), in which he envisions an English fleet, which never sailed for Madagascar, as having already conquered the island. The commendations printed along with the poem anticipate the extreme double perspective of later literary theorists. Suckling mocks and praises at once:

> What mighty Princes Poets are! those things
> The great ones stick at, and our very Kings
> Lay down, they venture on; and with great ease,
> Discover, conquer, what, and where they please.
> (In Davenant, *Shorter Poems*, 7)

Davenant may have carried home the laurel, Suckling concludes, "but prithee / In thy next Voyage, bring the Gold too with thee" (ibid.). William Habington is more appreciative of Davenant's immaterial achievement:

> Kings may
> Find proud ambition humbled at the sea,
> Which bounds dominion: But the nobler flight
> Of Poesy hath a supremer right
> To Empire, and extends her large command
> Where ere th'invading Sea assaults the land.
> (Ibid., 9)

But Davenant himself comes closer to Suckling: his poem is a dream vision, and when the dreamer sees Madagascar's gold mines, he exclaims: "I wish'd my Soul had brought my body here, / Not as a Poet, but a Pioneer [i.e., a miner]" ("Madagascar," 425–27. The comparison of this lighter work to *Gondibert* is illuminating: the more serious imperial ambitions expressed in the ancillary material of *Gondibert*, which itself seems to have nothing to do with America, show how even in the context of "natural" poetry, the writer who hopes to combine imperialism and poetry must still resort to a Spenserian reticence.

Bibliography

PRIMARY SOURCES

Unless otherwise noted, all citations from classical authors refer to the
Loeb Classical Library editions.

Addison, Joseph. *The Miscellaneous Works of Joseph Addison*. Ed. A. C.
Guthkelch. 2 vols. London: G. Bell & Sons, 1914.
Addison, Joseph, Sir Richard Steele, et al. *The Spectator*. 1711–14. Ed. Don-
ald F. Bond. 5 vols. Oxford: Clarendon, 1965.
Agrippa, Henry Cornelius. *De Incertitudine & Vanitate Scientiarum & Ar-
tum*. 1530. Trans. James Sandford as *Of the Vanitie and Uncertaintie of
Artes and Sciences*. 1569. Ed. Catherine M. Dunn. Northridge: Calif.
State University Press, 1974.
Alabaster, William. *Elisaeis*. MS, c. 1590. Ed. and trans. Michael O'Con-
nell. *Studies in Philology* 76 (no. 5, 1979).
Alexander, Sir William, Earl of Stirling. *An Encouragement to Colonies*. Lon-
don, 1624.
———. *Poetical Works of Sir William Alexander, Earl of Stirling*. Ed. L. E.
Kastner and H. B. Charlton. 2 vols. Manchester: Manchester Univer-
sity Press, 1921–29.
Andrews, Kenneth R., ed. *The Last Voyage of Drake and Hawkins*. Hakluyt
Soc., 2nd ser., vol. 142. Cambridge: Cambridge University Press, 1972.
Arber, Edward, ed. *The First Three English Books on America*. Birmingham,
1885.
Archdeacon, Daniel, trans. *A True Discourse of the Armie Which the King of
Spain Caused to Bee Assembled in the Haven of Lisbon*. London, 1588.
Ariosto, Ludovico. *Orlando Furioso*. 1516, 1521, 1532. Trans. Sir John Har-
ington. 1591. *Ariosto's Orlando Furioso*, ed. R. McNulty. Oxford: Ox-
ford University Press, 1972.
Armstrong or Urmeston, Clement. "A Treatise Concerning the Staple and
Commodity of this Realm." (C. 1519–35.) In *Tudor Economic Documents*,
ed. R. H. Tawney and E. Power, 3:90–114. 1924. Reprint. New York:
Barnes & Noble, 1962.
Ascham, Roger. *The Scholemaster*. 1570. Ed. Lawrence V. Ryan. Ithaca:
Cornell University Press for the Folger Shakespeare Library, 1967.
A[shley], R[obert], trans. *A Comparison of the English and Spanish Nation*.
London, 1589.

Augustine. *On Christian Doctrine*. Trans. D. W. Robertson, Jr. Indianapolis: Bobbs-Merrill, 1958.

A[verell], W[illiam]. *A Mervailous Combat of Contrarieties*. London, 1588.

Aylmer, John. *An Harborowe for Faith-full and Trewe Subjects*. Strasbourg, 1559.

Bacon, Sir Francis. *The Essayes or Counsels, Civill and Morall*. 1597–1625. Ed. Michael Kiernan. Cambridge, Mass.: Harvard University Press, 1985.

———. *Works*. Ed. James Spedding, Robert Leslie Ellis, and Douglas Denn Heath. 14 vols. London, 1858–74.

Bales, Peter. *The Arte of Brachygraphie*. London, 1597.

———. *The Writing Schoolemaster*. London, 1590.

Barbour, Philip, ed. *The Jamestown Voyages under the First Charter, 1606–1609*. 2 vols. Hakluyt Soc., 2nd ser., vols. 136–37. London, 1969.

Barckley, Sir Richard. *A Discourse of the Felicitie of Man*. London, 1598.

Barclay, Alexander, trans. *The Ship of Folys*. 1509. An enlarged version of Sebastian Brant's *Narrenschiff* (1494). Ed. T. H. Jamieson. 2 vols. Edinburgh, 1874.

Barclay, William. *Nepenthes, or the Vertues of Tabacco*. Edinburgh, 1614.

Barlow, Roger. "A Brief Summe of Geography." MS, 1540–41. Ed. E. G. R. Taylor. Hakluyt Soc., 2nd ser., vol. 69. London, 1931.

Barnfield, Richard. *Poems: 1594–1598*. Ed. Edward Arber. Birmingham, 1882.

Bartholomaeus, Anglicus. *De Proprietatibus Rerum*. [Trans. J. Trevisa (1398).] [London, 1495.]

Bastard, Thomas. *Chrestoleros. Seven Bookes of Epigrames*. 1598. Reprint. Spenser Society, no. 47. Manchester, 1888.

Bateman, Stephen, ed. *Batman uppon Bartholome his book De Proprietatibus Rerum, enlarged a. amended*. London, 1582.

Beaumont, Francis, and John Fletcher. *The Scornful Lady*. 1616. (Acted 1613–1616.) In *Dramatic Works in the Beaumont and Fletcher Canon*, ed. Cyrus Hoy, 2:449–565. Cambridge: Cambridge University Press, 1970.

Beaumont, Sir John. *The Metamorphosis of Tabacco*. 1602. In *The Poems of Sir John Beaumont*, ed. Alexander B. Grosart. Blackburn, Lancs., 1869.

Beaumont, Joseph. *The Minor Poems*. MS, c. 1640s. Ed. Eloise Robinson. London: Constable, 1914.

Bede, the Venerable. *The History of the Church of Englande*. Trans. Thomas Stapleton. Antwerp, 1565. Reprint. English Recusant Literature Series, vol. 162. London: Scolar, 1973.

Bennett, Edward. *A Treatise . . . Touching the Inconveniences that the Importation of Tobacco out of Spaine, hath brought unto this Land*. London [c. 1620].

Best, George. *A True Discourse of the Late Voyages of Discoverie, for the Finding of a Passage to Cathaya, by the Northwest*. 1578. In *The Three Voyages of Martin Frobisher*, ed. Vilhjalmur Stefansson, 1:4–129. London: Argonaut, 1938.

The Bible. [Bishops' Version.] London, 1568; rev. 1572.

————. [Geneva Version.] Geneva, 1560.

Blenerhasset, Thomas. *A Revelation of the True Minerva*. 1582. Ed. Josephine Waters Bennett. New York: Scholars' Facsimiles & Reprints, 1941.

————. *The Second Part of the Mirrour for Magistrates*. 1578. In *Parts Added to* The Mirror for Magistrates, ed. Lily B. Campbell. San Marino, Calif.: Huntington Library Publications, 1946.

Blundeville, Thomas. *The True Order and Methode of Wryting and Reading Hystories*. 1574. Ed. Hugh G. Dick. *Huntington Library Quarterly* 3 (1940): 149–70.

Borde, Andrew. *The Breviary of Helthe*. (Not 1st ed.) London, 1598.

Botero, Giovanni. *A Treatise, Concerning the Causes of the Magnificencie and Greatnes of Cities*. 1589. Trans. Robert Peterson. London, 1606.

Bradford, William. *The Collected Verse*. Ed. Michael G. Runyan. St. Paul, Minn.: John Colet, 1974.

————. *Of Plymouth Plantation 1620–1647*. Ed. Samuel Eliot Morison. 1952. Reprint. New York: Knopf, 1976.

Brathwait, Richard. *A Solemne Joviall Disputation. The Smoaking Age*. London, 1617.

Brightman, Thomas. *Apocalypsis Apocalypseos*. Frankfurt, 1609. Trans. as *A Revelation of the Revelation*. Amsterdam, 1615.

Brome, Richard. *The Antipodes*. (Acted 1637.) Ed. Ann Haaker. Lincoln: University of Nebraska Press, 1966.

Brooks, Jerome E., ed. *Tobacco: Its History Illustrated by the Books, Manuscripts and Engravings in the Library of George Arents, Jr.* New York: Rosenbach Co., 1937–1952.

————. *Supplement* to *Tobacco*. Parts 1–7 ed. Sarah Dickson; parts 8–10 ed. Perry Hugh O'Neil. New York: Rosenbach Co., 1958–62, 1967–69.

Brown, Alexander, ed. *The Genesis of the United States*. 2 vols. Boston, 1890.

Browne, William. *Britannias Pastorals*. 1613. In *Works*, ed. Gordon Goodwin. London, 1894.

Bruno, Giordano. *Le Cena de la Ceneri*. 1584. Trans. Stanley L. Jaki as *The Ash Wednesday Supper*. The Hague: Mouton, 1975.

Bry, Theodor de. *America*. [Latin ed.] Parts 1, 3, and 4. Frankfurt, 1590–94.

Butler, Samuel. *Characters and Passages from Note-Books*. Ed. A. R. Waller. Cambridge: Cambridge University Press, 1908.

Buttes, Henry. *Dyets Dry Dinner*. London, 1599.

Calendar of State Papers, Domestic Series, 1547–1625. 12 vols. London, 1856–72.

Calvin, Jean. *The Commentaries . . . upon the Actes of the Apostles*. Trans. Christopher Fetherstone. London, 1585.

————. *The Institution of Christian Religion*. Trans. T[homas] N[orton]. London, 1561.

————. *Sermons Upon the Epistle to the Galathians*. Trans. Arthur Golding. London, 1574.

Camden, William. *Britannia*. London, 1586; rev. 1587, 1590, 1594. Trans. Philemon Holland. London, 1610.

Camões, Luis Vaz de. *The Lusiads*. 1572. Trans. William C. Atkinson. Harmondsworth: Penguin, 1952.

Campion, Thomas. *Epigrammatum Libri II*. 1619. In *Campion's Works*, ed. Percival Vivian. Oxford: Clarendon, 1909.

Carew, Thomas. *Poems*. Ed. Rhodes Dunlap. Oxford: Clarendon, 1949.

Castiglione, Baldassare. *The Book of the Courtier*. 1528. Trans. Sir Thomas Hoby. 1561. Reprint. New York: Everyman-Dutton, 1928.

Cavendish, Thomas. "T[homas] Cavendyshe [his] [l]ast Voyage." MS, 1592. In *The Last Voyage of Thomas Cavendish*, ed. D. B. Quinn, 50–132. Chicago: University of Chicago Press, 1975.

Caxton, William. *The Prologues and Epilogues of William Caxton*. Ed. W. J. B. Crotch. Early English Text Soc., o.s., vol. 176. London: Oxford University Press, 1928.

Chamberlain, John. *The Letters of John Chamberlain*. Ed. Norman E. McClure. 2 vols. Philadelphia: American Philosophical Soc., 1939.

Chapman, George. *Chapman's Homer*. Ed. Allardyce Nicoll. 2 vols. Princeton: Princeton University Press, 1956; rev. 1967.

———. *The Plays*. Ed. Thomas Marc Parrott. (*The Comedies*, 2 vols.; *The Tragedies*, 2 vols.) 1910–13. Reprint. New York: Russell & Russell, 1961.

———. *The Poems*. Ed. Phyllis Bartlett. 1941. Reprint. New York: Russell & Russell, 1962.

Chaucer, Geoffrey. *The Complete Poetry and Prose of Geoffrey Chaucer*. Ed. John H. Fisher. New York: Holt, Rinehart & Winston, 1977.

Churchyard, Thomas. "A Matter Touching the Journey of Sir Humphrey Gilbarte, Knight." 1578. In *The Progresses and Public Processions of Queen Elizabeth*, ed. John Nichols, 2:226–32. London, 1823.

Collop, John. *The Poems of John Collop*. Ed. Conrad Hilberry. Madison: University of Wisconsin Press, 1962.

["Commentary on the Hayes-Carleill Project." After 1592.] In *New American World: A Documentary History of North America to 1612*, ed. D. B. Quinn, 3:172–75. New York: Arno Press and Hector Bye, 1979.

Constable, Henry. *Poems*. Ed. Joan Grundy. Liverpool: Liverpool University Press, 1960.

Copley, Anthony. *A Fig for Fortune*. 1596. Reprint. Spenser Soc., vol. 35. Manchester, 1883.

Cortés, Hernán. *Letters from Mexico*. Trans. and ed. A. R. Pagden. New York: Grossman, 1971.

[C(ovell), W(illiam).] *Polimanteia . . . whereunto is added, A Letter From England to her Three Daughters*. 1595. Ed. Alexander Grosart. Blackburn, Lancs., 1881.

Cowley, Abraham. *Poems*. Ed. A. R. Waller. Cambridge: Cambridge University Press, 1905.

Crashaw, William. *A Sermon Preached in London Before the Lord LaWarre, Lord Governour of Virginia*. London, 1610.

D., G. *A Briefe Discoverie of Doctor Allens Seditious Drifts*. 1588.

Daniel, Samuel. *The Civill Wars*. 1599. (Not 1st ed.) Reprinted as *The Civil Wars*, ed. Laurence Michel. New Haven: Yale University Press, 1958.

———. *Poems and A Defense of Rhyme*. Ed. Arthur C. Sprague. Chicago: University of Chicago Press, 1930.

———. *Works*. Ed. Alexander Grosart. 5 vols. Blackburn, Lancs., 1885–96.

Davenant, Sir William. *Gondibert*. 1651. Ed. David F. Gladish. Oxford: Clarendon, 1971.

———. *The Shorter Poems, and Songs from the Plays and Masques*. Ed. A. M. Gibbs. Oxford: Clarendon, 1972.

Davenant, Sir William, and Thomas Hobbes. *The Preface to Gondibert Written by Sir William D'Avenant: With an Answer to the Preface by Mr Hobbes*. 1650. In *Gondibert*, ed. David F. Gladish, 3–55. Oxford: Clarendon, 1971.

Davies, Sir John. *The Poems of Sir John Davies*. Ed. Clare Howard. New York: Columbia University Press, 1941.

Davison, Francis, ed. *A Poetical Rhapsody 1602–1621*. Ed. Hyder Rollins. 2 vols. Cambridge, Mass.: Harvard University Press, 1931–32.

"A Declaration of the Faith and Justification of the Proceedings of King Henry the Eighth in Matters of Religion." MS, 1539. In *An Ecclesiastical History of Great Britain*, ed. Jeremy Collier, 2:36–40. London, 1708–14.

Dee, John. *General and Rare Memorials Pertayning to the Perfect Arte of Navigation*. London, 1577.

———. "Great Volume of Famous and Rich Discoveries." MS, 1577. Passages reprinted in *Tudor Geography, 1485–1583*, by Eva G. R. Taylor. London: Methuen, 1930.

Dekker, Thomas. *Dramatic Works*. Ed. Fredson Bowers. 4 vols. Cambridge: Cambridge University Press, 1953–1961.

———. *The Guls Horne-booke*. 1609. In *Non-Dramatic Works of Thomas Dekker*, ed. Alexander Grosart, 2:193–266. Blackburn, Lancs., 1884.

Deloney, Thomas. *The Works of Thomas Deloney*. Ed. Frances O. Mann. Oxford: Clarendon, 1912.

[Dering, Edward.] *A Briefe & Necessary Instruction*. London, 1572.

Derricke, John. *The Image of Irelande With a Discoverie of Woodkarne*. 1581. Ed. D. B. Quinn et al. Belfast: Blackstaff, 1985.

D'Ewes, Sir Simonds, comp. *A Compleat Journal of the Votes, Speeches and Debates, Both of the House of Lords and House of Commons Throughout the Whole Reign of Queen Elizabeth*. 1682. Reprint of 1693 ed. Wilmington, Del.: Scholarly Resources, 1974.

Dixon, John. *The First Commentary on* The Faerie Queene [1597]. Ed. Graham Hough. Privately printed, 1964.

Donne, John. *The Complete English Poems*. Ed. A. J. Smith 1971; 2nd ed. 1976. Reprint. Harmondsworth: Penguin, 1986.

Drayton, Michael. *Works*. 5 vols. Vols. 1–4 ed. J. William Hebel; vol. 5 ed. Kathleen Tillotson and Bernard H. Newgate. Oxford: Blackwell, 1961.

Dryden, John. *King Arthur*. 1691. In *The Works of John Dryden*, ed. Sir Walter Scott, rev. George Saintsbury, 8:123–201. Edinburgh, 1884.

Dugdale, Gilbert. *The Time Triumphant*. London, 1604.

Eden, Richard, trans. *The Decades of the New World or West India*. 1555. Trans. of Peter Martyr [Pietro Martire d'Anghiera], *De Orbe Novo* (1511–30). In *The First Three English Books on America*, ed. Edward Arber. Birmingham, 1885.

———. *A Treatyse of the Newe India*. 1553. Redaction of Sebastian Munster's *Cosmographei* (1544). In *The First Three English Books on America*, ed. Edward Arber. Birmingham, 1885.

Ellis, Sir Henry, ed. *Original Letters, Illustrative of English History*. 4 vols. London, 1846.

Elyot, Sir Thomas. *The Castel of Helth*. London, 1541.

Erasmus, Desiderius. *Collected Works*. Ed. Peter G. Bietenholz et al. Toronto: University of Toronto Press, 1974–.

———. *The Correspondence*. Trans. R. A. B. Mynors and D. F. S. Thomson. In *Collected Works*, ed. Peter G. Bietenholz et al. Toronto: University of Toronto Press, 1974–.

———. *De Contemptu Mundi*. 1521. Trans. Thomas Paynell. London [1532?].

———. *De Contemptu Mundi*. Trans. and ed. Erika Rummel. In *Collected Works*, ed. Peter G. Bietenholz et al., 66:129–75. Toronto: University of Toronto Press, 1974–.

———. *Opus Epistolarium Des. Erasmi Roterodami*. Ed. P. S. Allen et al. 12 vols. Oxford: Clarendon, 1906–58.

———. *Peregrinatio Religionis Ergo*. 1526. Trans. as *A Dialogue . . . Intituled The Pylgremage of Pure Devotyon*. (C. 1536–37.) In *The Earliest English Translations of Erasmus' Colloquia, 1536–1566*, ed. Henry de Vocht. Louvain, 1928.

———. *The Praise of Folie*. 1511. Trans. Sir Thomas Chaloner. London, 1569 [1549].

Ercilla y Zuniga, Alonso de. *La Araucana*. 1569–1590. Ed. Marcos A. Morinigo and Isaias Lerner. 2 vols. Madrid: Clasicos Castalia, 1979.

———. *La Araucana*. Trans. George Carew (?) as *The Historie of Araucana*. Lambeth Palace Library, MS. 688. Ed. Frank Pierce. Manchester: Manchester University Press, 1964.

[Fairfax, Edward?]. "Ida and Opilio." 1600. In *Godfrey of Bulloigne*, ed. Kathleen M. Lea and T. M. Gang. Oxford: Clarendon, 1981.

The Fatal Marriage. (Written c. 1620s?) Ed. S. Brigid Younghughes and Harold Jenkins. Malone Society Reprints. Oxford: Oxford University Press, 1959.

Fitz-Geffrey, Charles. *Sir Francis Drake*. 1596. In *The Poems of the Rev. Charles Fitzgeoffrey (1593–1636)*, ed. Alexander Grosart. Blackburn, Lancs., 1881.

F[leming], A[braham], trans. *The Bucoliks . . . Together with his Georgics*, by Publius Virgilius Maro. London, 1589.

Fletcher, John, and Philip Massinger. *The Sea-Voyage*. (Acted 1622.) In *The Works of Beaumont and Fletcher*, ed. Alexander Dyce, vol. 8. 1843–46. Reprint. Freeport, N.Y.: Books for Libraries, 1970.

Florio, John. *Second Frutes*. 1591. Ed. R. C. Simonini, Jr. Gainesville, Fla.: Scholars' Facsimiles & Reprints, 1953.

[Floyd, John.] *The Overthrow of the Protestants Pulpit-Babels*. By I. R. 1612. Reprint. Menston, Yorks.: Scolar, 1973.

Foxe, John. *The Acts and Monuments*. 1563–1583. Ed. Stephen Cattley and George Townsend. 8 vols. 1837–41, 1843–49. Reprint. New York: AMS, 1965.

Frere, Walter Howard, and William McClure Kennedy, eds. *Visitation Articles and Injunctions of the Period of the Reformation*. Alcuin Club Collections, vols. 14–16. London: Longman, 1910.

Fuller, Thomas. *The History of the Worthies of England*. London, 1662.

Galilei, Galileo. *Discoveries and Opinions of Galileo*. Trans. and ed. Stillman Drake. New York: Doubleday, 1957.

Gambara, Lorenzo. *De Navigatione Christophori Columbi Libri Quattuor*. Rome, 1581.

Gardiner, Edmund. *The Triall of Tabacco*. London, 1610.

Gascoigne, George. *The Complete Works of George Gascoigne*. Ed. John W. Cunliffe. 2 vols. 1907. Reprint. New York: Greenwood, 1969.

Geoffrey of Monmouth. *The History of the Kings of Britain*. Trans. Lewis Thorpe. Harmondsworth: Penguin, 1966.

Gerard, John. *Herball*. London, 1597.

The Golden Coast, or A Description of Guinney. London, 1665.

Gomara, Francisco Lopez de. *The Pleasant Historie of the Conquest of the Weast India . . . by . . . Hernando Cortes*. Trans. T[homas] N[icholas] from the second part of *La Historia de las Indias, y la Conquista de Mexico* (1552). London, 1578.

Gosson, Stephen. *Markets of Bawdrie: The Dramatic Criticism of Stephen Gosson*. (Contains *The Schoole of Abuse* [1579], *An Apologie of the Schoole of Abuse* [1579], and *Plays Confuted in Five Actions* [1582].) Ed. Arthur F. Kinney. Salzburg: Institut für Englische Sprache und Literatur, Universität Salzburg, 1974.

Gower, John. *The Complete Works*. Ed. G. C. Macaulay. Early English Text Soc., 2nd ser., vols. 81–82. 1900–1901. Reprint. London: Oxford University Press, 1957.

Grange, John. *The Golden Aphroditis*. London, 1577.

Gray, Robert. *A Good Speed to Virginia*. 1609. Ed. Wesley F. Craven. New York: Scholars' Facsimiles & Reprints, 1937.

Greene, Robert. *Friar Bacon and Friar Bungay*. (Acted c. 1589.) Ed. Daniel Seltzer. Lincoln: University of Nebraska Press, 1963.

———. *Life and Complete Works in Prose and Verse*. Ed. Alexander Grosart. 15 vols. 1881–86. Reprint. New York: Russell & Russell, 1964.

———. *James the Fourth*. (Acted c. 1590.) Ed. Norman Sanders. London: Methuen, 1970.

Gregory I, Pope and Saint. *S. Gregorii Magni Registrum Epistularum*. Ed. Dag Norberg. 2 vols. Corpus Christianorum, Series Latina, nos. 140–140a. Turnhout: Brepols, 1982.

Greville, Fulke, Lord Brooke. *A Dedication to Sir Philip Sidney.* (Written 1604–14.) In *Prose Works,* ed. John Gouws. Oxford: Clarendon, 1986.

———. "A Treatise of Monarchy." (Written c. 1599–1604, with later revisions.) In *The Remains,* ed. G. A. Wilkes. Oxford: Oxford University Press, 1965.

Guicciardini, Francesco. *The Historie of Guicciardini.* Trans. Geoffrey Fenton from *La Historia di Italia* (1561) and *Dell'historia d'Italia . . . gli ultimi quattro libri* (1564). London, 1579.

Hakewill, George. *An Apology of the Power and Providence of God in the Government of the World.* (Not 1st ed.) London, 1627.

Hakluyt, Richard. "Discourse of Western Planting" ["A Particuler Discourse Concerninge the Greate Necessitie and Manifolde Comodyties That Are Like to Growe to This Realme of Englande by the Westerne Discoveries Lately Attempted"]. MS, 1584. In *The Original Writings and Correspondence of the Two Richard Hakluyts,* ed. Eva G. R. Taylor, 2:211–326. Hakluyt Soc., 2nd ser., vol. 77. London, 1935.

———, ed. *De Orbe Novo Petri Martyris.* Reprint of complete 1530 *Decades.* Paris, 1587.

———, ed. *Divers Voyages Touching the Discovery of America.* 1582. Ed. John W. Jones. Hakluyt Soc., vol. 7. London, 1850.

———, ed. *The Principall Navigations, Voyages and Discoveries of the English Nation.* 1589. Ed. D. B. Quinn. 2 vols. Cambridge: Cambridge University Press for the Hakluyt Society and the Peabody Museum of Salem, 1965.

———, ed. *The Principal Navigations.* 1598–1600. Reprinted in 12 vols. Glasgow: MacLehose, 1903–5.

Hall, Edward. *The Union of the Two Noble and Illustrious Famelies of Lancastre & Yorke.* 1548. Reprinted as *Hall's Chronicles.* London, 1809.

Hall, Joseph. *Mundus Alter et Idem.* 1605. Trans. John Healey as *The Discovery of a New World.* 1609. Ed. Huntington Brown. Cambridge: Harvard University Press, 1937.

———. *Mundus Alter et Idem.* 1605. Trans. John Millar Wands. New Haven: Yale University Press, 1981.

Hamor, Ralph. *A True Discourse of the Present Estate of Virginia.* 1615. Facsimile. Richmond: Virginia State Library, 1957.

Harcourt, Robert. *A Relation of a Voyage to Guiana.* 1613. Reprint. Hakluyt Soc., 2nd ser., vol. 60. London, 1928.

Harleian MS. 530, art. 2, f. 14.

Harpsfield, Nicholas. "A Treatise . . . Concerning the Marriage Occasioned by the Pretended Divorce Between King Henry the Eighth and Queen Katherine." MS, c. 1553–1558. Ed. Nicholas Pocock. Camden Soc., 2nd ser., vol. 21. London, 1878.

Harriot, Thomas. *A Briefe and True Report of the New Found Land of Virginia.* 1588. In *The Roanoke Voyages, 1584–1590,* ed. D. B. Quinn, 1:317–87. Hakluyt Soc., 2nd ser., vol. 104. London, 1955.

Harrison, William. "An Historicall Description of the Iland of Britaine."

1577, rev. 1587. In *Holinshed's Chronicles*, by Raphael Holinshed et al., vol. 1. Reprint. London, 1807.

Harvey, Gabriel. *Gabriel Harvey's Marginalia*. Ed. G. C. Moore Smith. Stratford-upon-Avon: Shakespeare Head, 1913.

H[arvey], I[ohn]. *A Discoursive Probleme Concerning Prophesies*. London, 1588.

[Hayes, Edward, and Christopher Carleill?] "A Discourse Concerning a Voyage Intended for the Planting of Chrystyan Religion and People in the North West Regions of America." MS, 1592? In *New American World: A Documentary History of North America to 1612*, ed. D. B. Quinn, 3:156–72. New York: Arno Press and Hector Bye, 1979.

H[ayman], R[obert]. *Quodlibets, Lately Come Over From New Britaniola, Old Newfoundland*. London, 1628.

Hellwis, Edward. *A Marvell, Deciphered*. London, 1589.

Herbert, George. *The Works of George Herbert*. Ed. F. E. Hutchinson. Oxford: Clarendon, 1941.

Heywood, Thomas. *An Apology for Actors*. 1612. Reprint. London, 1841.

Higden, Ranulph. *Polychronicon. Together with the English Translations of John Trevisa and of an Unknown Writer of the Fifteenth Century*. Ed. Churchill Babington et al. 9 vols. London, 1865–86. [Trevisa here is a collation of two MSS and Caxton's 1482 ed.; Caxton also issued an abridgment of Higden's *Description of England* in 1480.]

Holinshed, Raphael, et al. *Holinshed's Chronicles*. 1577, 1587. 1587 edition reprinted in 6 vols. London, 1807–8.

Hughes, Thomas, et al. *The Misfortunes of Arthur*. 1588. Ed. H. C. Grumbine. Berlin: Verlag von Emil Felber, 1900.

Hycke Scorner. (C. 1515–16.) In *Two Tudor Interludes: The Interlude of Youth and Hick Scorner*, ed. Ian Lancashire. Baltimore: Johns Hopkins University Press, 1980.

James I of England. *A Counter-blaste to Tobacco*. London, 1604.

Johnson, Francis. *An Answer to Maister H. Jacob*. [Middelburg,] 1600.

Johnson, Robert. *Nova Britannia*. London, 1609.

Jonson, Benjamin. *Ben Jonson*. Ed. C. H. Herford and Percy and Evelyn Simpson. 11 vols. Oxford: Oxford University Press, 1925–52.

Jonson, Benjamin, George Chapman, and John Marston. *Eastward Ho!* 1605. Ed. C. G. Petter. London: Ernest Benn, 1973.

The Kalender of Shepherdes. Paris, 1503; London, 1506. Ed. Oskar H. Sommer. London, 1892.

Keeler, Mary Frear, ed. *Sir Francis Drake's West Indian Voyage, 1585–86*. Hakluyt Soc., 2nd ser., vol. 148. London, 1981.

Keymis, Lawrence. *A Relation of the Second Voyage to Guiana*. 1596. In *The Principal Navigations*, ed. Richard Hakluyt, 10:441–501. Reprint. Glasgow: MacLehose, 1905.

Kingsbury, Susan, ed. *The Records of the Virginia Company of London*. 4 vols. Washington: Government Printing Office, 1906–35.

Lane, John. *An Elegie Upon the Death of the High-renowned Princesse, our Late Soveraigne Elizabeth.* London, 1603.

Las Casas, Bartolome de. *The Spanish Colonie, or Briefe Chronicle of the Acts and Gestes of the Spaniards in the West Indies.* From the French version (Antwerp, 1579) of *Brevissima Relacion de la Destruycion de las Indias* (Seville, 1552). London, 1583.

L[ea], I[ames]. *The Birth, Purpose and Mortall Wound of the Romish Holie League.* London, 1589.

————. *A True and Perfecte Description of a Straunge Monstar.* London, 1590.

————, trans. *An Answer to the Untruthes, Published and Printed in Spaine, in Glorie of Their Supposed Victorie Atchieved Against Our English Navie.* London, 1589.

Leland, John. *Assertio Inclytissimi Arturi.* 1544. Trans. Richard Robinson as *A Learned and True Assertion.* 1582. Early English Text Soc., orig. ser., no. 165. London: Oxford University Press, 1925.

Lescarbot, Marc. *Nova Francia: Or the Description of That Part of New France, which is One Continent with Virginia.* 1609. Trans. P. Erondelle from *Histoire de la Nouvelle France.* 1609. Ed. H. P. Biggar. New York: Harper, 1928.

Lightfote, William. *Complaint of England.* London, 1587.

L[inton], A[nthony]. *Newes of the Complement of the Art of Navigation.* London, 1609.

[Lloyd, David.] *The Legend of Captaine Jones.* London, 1631; rev. and enlarged, 1648.

Lobo Lasso de la Vega, Gabriel. *Primera Parte de Cortes Valeroso, y Mexicana.* Madrid, 1588; enlarged, 1594.

Lodge, Thomas. *The Complete Works of Thomas Lodge.* 4 vols. 1883. Reprint. New York: Russell & Russell, 1963.

Lopes de Castanheda, Fernão. *The First Book of the Historie of the Discoverie and Conquest of the East Indias.* Trans. N[icholas] L[ichefield] from *Historia do descobrimento e Conquista de India* (1551). London, 1582.

Lyly, John. *Works.* Ed. R. W. Bond. 3 vols. Oxford: Clarendon, 1902.

McIlwaine, H. R., ed. *Journals of the House of Burgesses of Virginia 1619–1658/59.* Richmond: Virginia State Library, 1915.

Mandeville, Sir John. *Mandeville's Travels.* Ed. M. C. Seymour. Oxford: Clarendon, 1967.

Manley, Lawrence, ed. *London in the Age of Shakespeare: An Anthology.* London: Croom Helm, 1986.

[Marbecke, Roger.] *A Defence of Tabacco: with a Friendly Answer to Worke for Chimny-sweepers.* London, 1602.

Marlowe, Christopher. *The Complete Plays.* Ed. J. B. Steane. Harmondsworth: Penguin, 1969.

————. *The Complete Poems and Translations.* Ed. Stephen Orgel. Harmondsworth: Penguin, 1971.

[Marnix van Sant Aldegonde, Philips van.] *A Pithie, and Most Earnest Exhortation, Concerning the Estate of Christiandome.* Antwerp [London], 1583.

Marston, John. *The Poems of John Marston.* Ed. Arnold Davenport. Liverpool: Liverpool University Press, 1961.

Marten, Anthony. *An Exhortation.* London, 1588.

The Masque of Flowers. 1614. Ed. E. A. J. Honigmann. In *A Book of Masques, In Honour of Allardyce Nicoll,* ed. T. J. B. Spencer et al. Cambridge: Cambridge University Press, 1967.

Massinger, Philip. *The City Madam.* 1632. Ed. Cyrus Hoy. Lincoln: University of Nebraska Press, 1964.

Melton, John. *A Sixe-Folde Politician.* London, 1609.

Milton, John. *Paradise Lost.* 1667; rev. 1674. Ed. Merritt Y. Hughes. Indianapolis: Odyssey, 1962.

Monardes, Nicolas. *Joyfull Newes out of the Newe Worlde.* 1574. Trans. John Frampton. London, 1577. In *The Tudor Translations,* 2nd ser., vols. 9–10. 1925. Reprint. New York: AMS, 1967.

More, Sir Thomas. *The Correspondence of Sir Thomas More.* Ed. Elizabeth Frances Rogers. Princeton: Princeton University Press, 1947.

————. *St. Thomas More: Selected Letters.* Ed. Elizabeth Frances Rogers. New Haven: Yale University Press, 1961.

————. *Utopia.* 1516. Ed. Edward Surtz and J. H. Hexter. Vol. 4 of *The Yale Edition of the Complete Works of St. Thomas More,* ed. Louis Martz et al. New Haven: Yale University Press, 1965.

————. *The Works.* Ed. William Rastell. 1557. Reprinted as *The English Works,* ed. W. E. Campbell. 2 vols. London: Eyre & Spottiswoode, 1931.

————. *The Yale Edition of the Complete Works of St. Thomas More.* Ed. Louis Martz et al. New Haven: Yale University Press, 1963–.

Morton, Thomas. *The New English Canaan.* 1637. Ed. Charles Francis Adams, Jr. 1883. Reprint. New York: Burt Franklin, 1967.

Munday, Anthony. *A Second and Third Blast of Retrait from Plaies and Theaters.* London, 1580.

Nashe, Thomas. *Works.* Ed. R. B. McKerrow. 5 vols. 1903–10. Ed. F. P. Wilson. London: Blackwell, 1958.

[Nedham, George.] "A Letter to the Earls of East Friesland." By W. G. MS, c. 1564. In *The Politics of a Tudor Merchant Adventurer,* ed. G. D. Ramsay. Manchester: Manchester University Press, 1979.

Niccols, Richard. *Expicedium.* London, 1603.

Nicholl, John. *An Houre Glasse of Indian Newes.* London, 1607.

Nichols, John, ed. *The Progresses and Public Processions of Queen Elizabeth.* 3 vols. London, 1823.

Nixon, Anthony. *Elizaes Memoriall.* London, 1603.

N[orth], G[eorge], ed. *The Stage of Popish Toyes.* From Henri Estienne's *Apologie pour Herodote* (1566). London, 1581.

Oakeshott, Walter. *The Queen & the Poet.* New York: Barnes & Noble, 1961.

Of the Newe Landes. [Antwerp, 1511–22?] In *The First Three English Books on America,* ed. Edward Arber. Birmingham, 1885.

Old Christmas or Good Order. 1533. Fragment ed. W. W. Greg in *Collections,* 33–39. Malone Soc., vol. 4. Oxford: Oxford University Press, 1956.

Ovid. *Metamorphoses.* Trans. Arthur Golding. 1567. Reprinted as *Shakespeare's Ovid*, ed. W. H. D. Rouse. London: Centaur, 1961.

Parmenius, Stephen. *De Navigatione.* 1582. In *The New Found Land of Stephen Parmenius*, trans. and ed. D. B. Quinn and Neil Cheshire. Toronto: University of Toronto Press, 1972.

The Parnassus Plays. [*The Pilgrimage to Parnassus* (acted c. 1598–99), *The Return from Parnassus* Part 1 (c. 1599/1600), *The Return from Parnassus* Part 2 (c. 1601–2; publ. 1606)]. Rpt. as *The Three Parnassus Plays (1598–1601)*, ed. J. B. Leishman. London: Ivor Nicholson & Watson, 1949.

[Parsons, Robert]. *A Temperate Ward-word, to the Turbulent and Seditious Wach-word of Sir Francis Hastings Knight.* By N. D. [Antwerp,] 1599.

———. *The Warn-word to Sir Francis Hastings Wast-word.* By N. D. [Antwerp,] 1602.

Patten, William. *The Calender of Scripture.* London, 1575.

Peckham, Sir George. *A True Reporte, Of the Late Discoveries . . . of the New-found Landes.* 1583. In *The Voyages and Colonizing Enterprises of Sir Humphrey Gilbert*, ed. D. B. Quinn, 2:435–82. Hakluyt Soc., 2nd ser., vol. 84. London, 1940.

Peele, George. *Life and Works.* Ed. Charles Tyler Prouty et al. 3 vols. New Haven: Yale University Press, 1952–70.

Percy, George. "A Trewe Relacyon of the Procedeinges . . . in Virginia from . . . 1609 untill . . . 1612." MS. In *Tyler's Quarterly Historical and Genealogical Magazine* 3 (1922): 260–82.

Perez de Oliva, Hernan. *Las Obras.* Cordoba, 1586.

Petowe, Henry. *Elizabetha Quasi Vivens, Elizas Funerall.* London, 1603.

Petrarch [Francesco Petrarca]. Letter to Francesco Dionigi de'Roberti, 26 April 1336 [The Ascent of Mont Ventoux]. Trans. Hans Nachod in *The Renaissance Philosophy of Man*, ed. Ernst Cassirer et al., 36–46. Chicago: University of Chicago Press, 1948.

Phaer, Thomas. *The Whole xii Bookes of the Aeneidos of Virgill.* [Part of 10th book to the end trans. Thomas Twyne.] London, 1573.

Philaretes. *Work for Chimny-Sweepers or A Warning for Tobacconists.* 1602. Reprint. Shakespeare Assoc. Facsimiles, no. 11. London: Humphrey Milford, Oxford University Press, 1936.

Plutarch. *Lives of the Noble Grecians and Romans.* Trans. Sir Thomas North. 1579. Ed. W. E. Heuley. 1895–96. 6 vols. Reprint. New York: AMS, 1967.

Ponet, John. *A Shorte Treatise of Politicke Power.* [Strasbourg?,] 1556.

Pope, Alexander. *The Rape of the Lock.* 1714 version. In *The Twickenham Edition of the Poems of Alexander Pope*, vol. 2. *The Rape of the Lock and Other Poems*, ed. Geoffrey Tillotson, 139–212. London: Methuen, 1940, 3rd ed., 1962. *Windsor Forest.* 1713. In *The Twickenham Edition of the Poems of Alexander Pope*, vol. 1. *Pastoral Poetry and an Essay on Criticism*, ed. E. Audra and Aubrey Williams, 123–94. London: Methuen, 1961.

Price, Daniel. *Sauls Prohibition Staide.* London, 1609.

Prynne, William. *A Brief Necessary Vindication.* London, 1659.

Purchas, Samuel. *Hakluytus Posthumus, or Purchas His Pilgrimes*. 4 vols. 1625. Reprinted in 20 vols. Glasgow: MacLehose, 1905–6.

[Puttenham, George.] *The Arte of English Poesie*. 1589. Ed. Gladys Doidge Willcock and Alice Walker. 1936. Reprint. Cambridge: Cambridge University Press, 1970.

The Queenes Majesties Passage Through the Citie of London to Westminster the Daye Before Her Coronacion. 1559. In *Elizabethan Backgrounds*, ed. Arthur F. Kinney. Hamden, Conn: Archon, 1975.

Quinn, David Beers, ed. *New American World: A Documentary History of North America to 1612*. 5 vols. New York: Arno Press and Hector Bye, 1979.

———, ed. *The Roanoke Voyages, 1584–1590*. 2 vols. Hakluyt Soc., 2nd ser., vols. 104–5. London, 1955.

———, ed. *The Voyages and Colonizing Enterprises of Sir Humphrey Gilbert*. 2 vols. Hakluyt Soc., 2nd ser., vols. 83–84. London, 1940.

Quinn, David Beers, and Alison M. Quinn, eds. *The English New England Voyages 1602–1608*. Hakluyt Soc., 2nd ser., vol. 161. London, 1983.

Raleigh, Sir Walter. *The Discoverie of the Large Rich, and Bewtifull Empyre of Guiana*. 1596. Ed. V. T. Harlow. London: Argonaut, 1928.

———. Letters. In *The Life of Sir Walter Raleigh . . . Together With His Letters*, ed. Edward Edwards, vol. 2. London, 1868.

———. "Observations Concerning the Causes of the Magnificency and Opulency of Cities." In *Sir Walter Raleigh's Sceptick [and Other Works]*, 33–58. London, 1651.

———. *The Poems of Sir Walter Raleigh*. Ed. Agnes Latham. Cambridge: Harvard University Press, 1951.

Rankins, William. *A Mirrour of Monsters*. 1587. Ed. Arthur Freeman. Facsimile. New York: Garland, 1973.

Rastell, John. *A New Interlude and a Mery of the Nature of the Four Elements*. (C. 1519–28.) In *Three Rastell Plays*, ed. Richard Axton. Cambridge: D. S. Brewer, 1979.

———. *The Pastyme of People*. (1530?) Facsimile and transcription ed. Albert J. Geritz. New York: Garland, 1985.

Rich, Barnaby. *The Irish Hubbub*. London, 1617.

Rich, Richard. *Newes From Virginia. The Lost Flocke Triumphant*. 1610. Ed. Wesley F. Craven. New York: Scholars' Facsimiles & Reprints, 1937.

Robinson, Ralph, trans. *Utopia*. 1551. Reprint. New York: Dutton, 1974.

Rolfe, John. "A True Relation of the State of Virginia . . . in May Last 1616." Ed. Henry C. Taylor. 1951. Reprint. Charlottesville: University Press of Virginia, 1971.

Roper, William. *The Life of Sir Thomas More*. 1626 (MS, c. 1555). In *Two Early Tudor Lives*, ed. Richard S. Sylvester and Davis P. Harding. New Haven: Yale University Press, 1962.

[Rowlands, Samuel.] *The Letting of Humors Blood in the Head-Vaine*. London, 1600.

Rushworth, John. *Historical Collections* part 3, vol. 1. London, 1692.

Rye, William Benchley, ed. *The Discovery and Conquest of Terra Florida*. Reprint of *Virginia Richly Valued* (1609). By a Gentleman of Elvas. Trans. Richard Hakluyt. From *Relaçam Verdadeira* (1557). Hakluyt Soc., vol. 2. London, 1851.

Rymer, Thomas. *The Critical Works of Thomas Rymer*. Ed. Curt A. Zimansky. New Haven: Yale University Press, 1956.

Sammes, Aylett. *Britannia Antiqua Illustrata*. London, 1676.

Sanders, Nicholas. *De Origine ac Progressu Schismatis Anglicani*. Cologne, 1585. Trans. David Lewis as *Rise and Growth of the Anglican Schism, with Continuation into Elizabeth's Reign by Edward Rishton*. London, 1877.

———. *The Supper of our Lord*. Louvain, 1566. Reprint. English Recusant Literature Series, vol. 199. London: Scolar, 1974.

Sanford, James, trans. *Houres of Recreation, or Afterdinners*. By Ludovico Guicciardini. 2nd ed. London, 1576.

Sannazaro, Jacopo. *Arcadia*. 1502, 1504. In *Opere Volgari*, ed. Alfredo Mauro. Bari: Laterza, 1961.

Scot, Thomas. *Philomythie or Philomythologie*. London, 1616.

Seall, Robert. *A Comendation of the Adventerus Viage of the Wurthy Captain M. Thomas Stutely*. London [1563].

Segar, William. *Honor Military, and Civill*. London, 1602.

Shakespeare, William. *The Riverside Shakespeare*. Ed. G. Blakemore Evans et al. Boston: Houghton Mifflin, 1974.

Sidney, Sir Philip. *An Apology for Poetry*. 1595. (Written c. 1580–82.) Ed. Forrest G. Robinson. Indianapolis: Bobbs-Merrill, 1970.

———. *The Countess of Pembroke's Arcadia*. 1593. (Written c. 1580–84.) Ed. Maurice Evans. Harmondsworth: Penguin, 1977.

———. *Miscellaneous Prose*. Ed. Katherine Duncan-Jones and Jan Van Dorsten. Oxford: Clarendon, 1973.

———. *The Poetry of Sir Philip Sidney*. Ed. William A. Ringler, Jr. Oxford: Clarendon, 1962.

Skelton, John. *The Complete English Poems*. Ed. John Scattergood. New Haven: Yale University Press, 1983.

Smith, G. Gregory, ed. *Elizabethan Critical Essays*. 2 vols. London: Oxford University Press, 1904.

Smith, John. *Complete Works*. Ed. Philip L. Barbour. 3 vols. Chapel Hill: University of North Carolina Press, 1986.

Smith, Sir Thomas. *A Compendious or Brief Examination*. 1581. (Written 1549.) Reprinted as *A Discourse of the Commonweal of This Realm of England*, ed. Mary Dewar. Charlottesville: University Press of Virginia for the Folger Shakespeare Library, 1969.

———. *De Republica Anglorum*. 1583. (Written c. 1562–65.) Ed. Mary Dewar. Cambridge: Cambridge University Press, 1982.

Sneyd, Charlotte Augusta, ed. and trans. *A Relation, or Rather a True Account, of the Island of England . . . about the Year 1500*. Camden Soc., vol. 37. London, 1847.

Sorrowes Joy. Or, A Lamentation for Our Late Deceased Soveraigne Elizabeth. London, 1603.

Speed, John. *The Theatre of the Empire of Great Britaine.* London, 1611.

Spenser, Edmund. *Works: A Variorum Edition.* Ed. Edwin Greenlaw et al. 9 vols., index, and *A Life of Edmund Spenser* by Alexander Judson. Baltimore: Johns Hopkins University Press, 1932–57.

Stanyhurst, Richard. "Description of Ireland." 1577. In *Holinshed's Chronicles,* by Raphael Holinshed et al., vol. 6. Reprint. London, 1808.

Stefansson, Vilhjalmur, ed. *The Three Voyages of Martin Frobisher.* 2 vols. London: Argonaut, 1938.

Stella, Julius Caesar. *Columbeidos, Libri Priores Duo.* London, 1585.

Stow, John. *The Annales of England.* (Not 1st ed.) London, 1592.

Strachey, William. "The Historie of Travell into Virginia Britania." MS, 1612. Ed. Louis B. Wright and Virginia Freund. Hakluyt Soc., 2nd ser., vol. 103. London, 1953.

———. "A True Reportory of the Wracke, and Redemption of Sir Thomas Gates." MS, 1610. In *Hakluytus Posthumus, or Purchas His Pilgrimes,* ed. Samuel Purchas, 19:5–67. Reprint. Glasgow: MacLehose, 1906.

Strathmann, Ernest A. "Raleigh Plans His Last Voyage." *The Mariner's Mirror* 50 (1964): 261–70.

Strype, John, ed. *Annals of the Reformation and Establishment of Religion . . . in the Church of England.* (Not 1st ed.) 4 vols. Oxford, 1824.

Stubbs, John. *John Stubbs' "Gaping Gulf"* [1579] *with Letters and Other Relevant Documents.* Ed. Lloyd E. Berry. Folger Documents of Tudor and Stuart Civilization. Charlottesville: University Press of Virginia, 1968.

Sutcliffe, Matthew. *A Ful and Round Answer to N. D. Alias R. Parsons, His Warne-word.* London, 1604.

Sylvester, Joshua, trans. *Bartas His Devine Weekes & Workes.* London, 1605.

Symonds, William. *Virgina. A Sermon Preached at White-Chapell.* London, 1609.

T., C. *An Advice How to Plant Tobacco in England.* London, 1615.

Tate, Nahum. "To Mr. J. Ovington, On His Voyage to Suratt." In *A Voyage to Suratt,* by J. Ovington. 1696. Ed. H. G. Rawlinson. London: Oxford University Press, 1929.

Taylor, Eva G. R., ed. *The Original Writings and Correspondence of the Two Richard Hakluyts.* 2 vols. Hakluyt Soc., 2nd ser., vols. 76–77. London, 1935.

Taylor, John. *The Nipping or Snipping of Abuses.* London, 1614.

Thevet, André. *The New Found Worlde, or Antarctike.* Trans. Thomas Hacket from *Les Singularitez de la France Antarctique* (1558). London, 1568.

Thorndyke, Lynn, ed. *The "Sphere" of Sacrobosco and Its Commentators.* Chicago: University of Chicago Press, 1949.

Thorne, Robert. "A Declaration of the Indies." 1527. In *Divers Voyages*

Touching the Discovery of America, ed. Richard Hakluyt, 27–32. Ed. John W. Jones. Hakluyt Soc., vol. 7. London, 1850.

Tickell, Thomas. *A Poem, To His Excellency, The Lord Privy Seal, On the Prospect of Peace.* 1712. In *Poetical Works*, 18–36. Boston, 1865.

Tilley, Morris Palmer. *The Proverbs of England in the Sixteenth and Seventeenth Centuries.* Ann Arbor: University of Michigan Press, 1950.

[Tonkis, Thomas.] *Lingua: or, the Combat of the Tongue.* 1607. (Written c. 1606.) Ed. John S. Farmer. London: Tudor Facsimile Texts, 1913.

Tottel, Richard, comp. *Tottel's Miscellany (1557–1587).* Ed. Hyder Rollins. 2 vols. Cambridge: Harvard University Press, 1928; rev. 1965.

Traherne, Thomas. *Centuries, Poems, and Thanksgivings.* Ed. H. M. Margoliouth. 2 vols. Oxford: Clarendon, 1958.

A True and Sincere Declaration of the Purpose and Ends of the Plantation Begun in Virginia. London, 1610.

A True Declaration of the Estate of the Colonie in Virginia. London, 1610.

Twyne, John. *De Rebus Albionicis, Britannicis atque Anglicis.* (Written c. 1530–50?) London, 1590.

Tyndale, William. *The Practice of Prelates.* 1530. In *The Works of the English Reformers: William Tyndale, and John Frith*, ed. Thomas Russell, 1:381–490. London, 1831.

Vaughan, William. *The Golden-grove.* London, 1600.

Vergil, Polydore. *Polydore Vergil's English History.* An anonymous, roughly contemporary trans. of the first eight books of the *Anglicae Historiae Libri XXVI* (1534). Ed. Sir Henry Ellis. Camden Soc., vol. 36. London, 1846.

Veron, Jean. *A Stronge Battery against the Idolatrous Invocation of the Dead Saintes.* London, 1562.

["Verses on the Puritan Settlement in America, 1631."] In *A Nottinghamshire Miscellany* 21 (1962): 37–39.

V[erstegan, or Rowlands], R[ichard]. *A Restitution of Decayed Intelligence: In Antiquities.* Antwerp, 1605.

Vespucci, Amerigo. *Quatuor Americi Vespucii Navigationes.* 1507. Facsimile in *The Cosmographiae Introductio of Martin Waldseemuller in Facsimile*, ed. C. G. Herbermann. Trans. Mario E. Cosenza. New York: U.S. Catholic Historical Soc., 1907.

Vida, Marco Girolamo. *De Arte Poetica.* 1517. Ed. and trans. Ralph G. Williams. New York: Columbia University Press, 1976.

Virginia Company. Broadside. "Considering there is no publicke action, [etc.]." [London, 1609?]

———. Broadside. "Declaration for the certaine time of drawing the great standing Lottery." London, 1615.

———. Broadside. "Londons Lotterie." 1612. In *An American Garland; Being a Collection of Ballads Relating to America, 1563–1759*, comp. Charles Harding Firth. Oxford: Blackwell, 1915.

———. Broadside. "Whereas sundrie the adventurers to Virginia . . . ." London, 1613.

Warner, William. *Albions England*. London, 1586–1606.

Warton, Joseph, et al. *The Adventurer*. 1752–54. Ed. Donald D. Eddy. 2 vols. New York: Garland, 1978.

Waterhouse, Edward. *A Declaration of the State of the Colony and Affaires in Virginia*. London, 1622.

Webbe, William. *A Discourse of English Poetrie*. 1586. In *Elizabethan Critical Essays*, ed. G. Gregory Smith, 1:226–302. London: Oxford University Press, 1904.

Weever, John. *Epigrammes in the Oldest Cut and Newest Fashion*. 1599. Ed. R. B. McKerrow. London: Sidgwick & Jackson, 1911.

———. *The Whipping of the Satyre*. By W. I. 1601. In *The Whipper Pamphlets*, ed. Arnold Davenport. Liverpool: University Press of Liverpool, 1951.

Wells, William, ed. *Spenser Allusions in the Sixteenth and Seventeenth Centuries*. Chapel Hill: University of North Carolina Press, 1972.

Wernham, R. B., ed. *List and Analysis of State Papers, Foreign Series, Elizabeth I*. 3 vols. London: Her Majesty's Stationery Office, 1964–80.

Wheeler, John. *A Treatise of Commerce*. Middelburg, 1601.

Whitaker, Alexander. *Good Newes From Virginia*. 1613. Reprint. New York: Scholars' Facsimiles & Reprints, 1936.

White, John. *The Planters Plea*. 1630. Ed. Marshall H. Saville. Rockport, Mass.: Sandy Bay Historical Society & Museum, 1930.

Williams, Clare, trans. *Thomas Platter's Travels in England*. London: Jonathan Cape, 1937.

Williamson, James, ed. *The Cabot Voyages and Bristol Discovery Under Henry VII*. Hakluyt Soc., 2nd ser., vol. 120. London, 1962.

W[ilson], R[obert]. *The Three Ladies of London*. (Acted 1581.) Ed. John S. Farmer. London: Tudor Facsimile Texts, 1911.

Wither, George. *Withers Motto*. London, 1621.

Wright, Thomas, ed. *Three Chapters of Letters Relating to the Suppression of Monasteries*. Camden Soc., vol. 26. London, 1843.

Wyatt, Sir Thomas. *Collected Poems*. Ed. Joost Daalder. London: Oxford University Press, 1975.

Young, Edward. *Conjectures on Original Composition*. 1759. Ed. Edith J. Morley. Manchester: Manchester University Press, 1918.

Zarate, Augustin de. *The Strange and Delectable History of the Discoverie and Conquest of the Provinces of Peru*. Trans. Thomas Nicholas from *Historia del Descubrimiento y Conquista del Peru* (1555). London, 1581.

SECONDARY SOURCES

Abrams, M. H. *The Mirror and the Lamp: Romantic Theory and the Critical Tradition*. London: Oxford University Press, 1953.

Adams, R. P. "Bold Bawdry and Open Manslaughter." *Huntington Library Quarterly* 23 (1959–60): 33–48.

Alpers, Paul. "Narration in *The Faerie Queene*." *ELH* 44 (1977): 19–39.

————. *The Poetry of* The Faerie Queene. Princeton: Princeton University Press, 1967.

Anderson, Judith H. *The Growth of a Personal Voice:* Piers Plowman *and the* Faerie Queene. New Haven: Yale University Press, 1976.

————. " 'In living colours and right hew': The Queen of Spenser's Central Books." In *Poetic Traditions of the English Renaissance*, ed. Maynard Mack and George DeForest Lord, 47–66. New Haven: Yale University Press, 1982.

Andrews, Charles M. *The Colonial Period of American History.* 4 vols. New Haven: Yale University Press, 1934.

Andrews, K. R. *Elizabethan Privateering: English Privateering During the Spanish War, 1585–1603.* Cambridge: Cambridge University Press, 1964.

Andrews, K. R., et al., eds. *The Westward Enterprise: English Activities in Ireland, the Atlantic, and America, 1480–1650.* Liverpool: Liverpool University Press, 1979.

Axtell, James. "The Scholastic Philosophy of the Wilderness." 1972. In *The European and the Indian: Essays in the Ethnohistory of Colonial North America*, 131–67. Oxford: Oxford University Press, 1981.

Barker, Francis, and Peter Hulme. "Nymphs and Reapers Heavily Vanish: The Discursive Con-Texts of *The Tempest.*" In *Alternative Shakespeares*, ed. John Drakakis, 191–205. London: Methuen, 1985.

Barthelemy, Antony Gerard. *Black Face, Maligned Race: The Representation of Blacks in English Drama from Shakespeare to Southerne.* Baton Rouge: Louisiana State University Press, 1987.

Bauckham, Richard. *Tudor Apocalypse: Sixteenth Century Apocalypticism, Millennarianism and the English Reformation.* Oxford: Sutton Courtenay, 1978.

Bednarz, James P. "Ralegh in Spenser's Historical Allegory." *Spenser Studies* 4 (1984): 49–70.

Beer, George Louis. *The Origins of the British Colonial System, 1578–1660.* 1908. Reprint. Gloucester, Mass.: Peter Smith, 1959.

Bennett, Josephine Waters. "Britain Among the Fortunate Isles." *Studies in Philology* 53 (1956): 114–40.

————. *The Evolution of "The Faerie Queene."* 1942. Reprint. New York: Burt Franklin, 1960.

Bentley, Gerald Eades. *The Jacobean and Caroline Stage.* 7 vols. Oxford: Clarendon, 1941–68.

Berger, Harry, Jr. *The Allegorical Temper.* New Haven: Yale University Press, 1957.

————. "Mode and Diction in *The Shepheardes Calender.*" *Modern Philology* 67 (1969): 140–49.

————. "Orpheus, Pan, and the Poetics of Misogyny: Spenser's Critique of Pastoral Love and Art." *ELH* 50 (1983): 27–60.

————. "A Secret Discipline: *The Faerie Queene*, Book VI." In *Form and Convention in the Poetry of Edmund Spenser: Selected Papers from the English*

Institute, ed. William Nelson, 35–75. New York: Columbia University Press, 1961.

———. "Spenser's Faerie Queene, Book I: Prelude to Interpretation." *Southern Review* (University of Adelaide) 2 (1966): 18–49.

Bergeron, David M. *Shakespeare's Romances and the Royal Family*. Lawrence: University Press of Kansas, 1985.

Bindoff, S. T. "Clement Armstrong and His Treatises on the Commonweal." *Economic History Review* 14 (1944–45): 64–73.

Bradner, Leicester. "Columbus in Sixteenth-Century Poetry." In *Essays Honoring Lawrence C. Wroth*, ed. Frederick Goff et al., 15–30. Portland, Maine: Anthoensen, 1951.

Brooks, Cleanth, R. W. B. Lewis, and Robert Penn Warren, eds. *American Literature: The Makers and the Making*. 4 vols. New York: St. Martin's Press, 1973–74.

Brown, Paul. " 'This Thing of Darkness I Acknowledge Mine': *The Tempest* and the Discourse of Colonialism." In *Political Shakespeare*, ed. Jonathan Dollimore and Alan Sinfield, 48–71. Ithaca: Cornell University Press, 1985.

Bullough, Geoffrey, ed. *Narrative and Dramatic Sources of Shakespeare*. 8 vols. New York: Columbia University Press, 1957–75.

Cain, Thomas H. *Praise in "The Faerie Queene."* Lincoln: University of Nebraska Press, 1978.

Canny, Nicholas. *The Elizabethan Conquest of Ireland: A Pattern Established, 1565–76*. Hassocks: Harvester Press, 1976.

———. "The Permissive Frontier: The Problem of Social Control in English Settlements in Ireland and Virginia, 1550–1650." In *The Westward Enterprise*, ed. Andrews et al., 17–44. Liverpool: Liverpool University Press, 1979.

Canny, Nicholas, and Anthony Pagden, eds. *Colonial Identity in the Atlantic World, 1500–1800*. Princeton: Princeton University Press, 1987.

Capp, Bernard. "The Political Dimension of Apocalyptic Thought." In *The Apocalypse in English Renaissance Thought and Literature*, ed. C. A. Patrides and Joseph Wittreich, 93–124. Ithaca: Cornell University Press, 1984.

Carrera, Vincent. "Anne and Elizabeth: The Poet as Historian in *Windsor Forest*." *Studies in English Literature, 1500–1900* 21 (1981): 425–37.

Cawley, Robert Ralston. *Unpathed Waters: Studies in the Influence of the Voyagers on Elizabethan Literature*. Princeton: Princeton University Press, 1940.

———. *The Voyagers and Elizabethan Drama*. Boston: D. C. Heath, 1938.

Chambers, A. B. "The Fly in Donne's 'Canonization.' " *Journal of English and Germanic Philology* 65 (1966): 252–59.

Chambers, E. K. *The Elizabethan Stage*. 4 vols. Oxford: Oxford University Press, 1923.

Cheney, Donald. "Spenser's Fortieth Birthday and Related Fictions." *Spenser Studies* 4 (1984): 3–31.

Cheshire, Neil, Tony Waldron, Alison Quinn, and D. B. Quinn. "Frobisher's Eskimos in England." *Archivaria* 10 (1980): 23–50.

Chiappelli, Fredi, ed. *First Images of America: The Impact of the New World on the Old.* 2 vols. Berkeley: University of California Press, 1976.

Christianson, Paul. *Reformers and Babylon: English Apocalyptic Visions from the Reformation to the Eve of the Civil War.* Toronto: University of Toronto Press, 1978.

Connell-Smith, Gordon. *Forerunners of Drake: A Study of English Trade with Spain in the Early Tudor Period.* London: Longman, 1954.

Craven, Wesley. *Dissolution of the Virginia Company: The Failure of a Colonial Experiment.* New York: Oxford University Press, 1932.

Cullen, Patrick. *Infernal Triad: The Flesh, the World, and the Devil in Spenser and Milton.* Princeton: Princeton University Press, 1974.

Dickson, Sarah A. *Panacea or Precious Bane: Tobacco in Sixteenth Century Literature.* Bulletin of the New York Public Library, 1953–54. Reprint. New York: New York Public Library, 1954.

Elliot, John H. *The Old World and the New, 1492–1650.* Cambridge: Cambridge University Press, 1970.

———. "Renaissance Europe and America: A Blunted Impact?" In *First Images of America*, ed. Fredi Chiappelli, 1:11–23. Berkeley: University of California Press, 1976.

Elton, G. R. "Thomas More, Councilor." In *Studies in Tudor and Stuart Politics and Government: Papers and Reviews.* 3 vols. Cambridge: Cambridge University Press, 1974.

English, H. M. "Spenser's Accommodation of Allegory to History in the Story of Timias and Belphoebe." *Journal of English and Germanic Philology* 59 (1960): 417–29.

Fell-Smith, Charlotte. *John Dee (1527–1608).* London: Constable, 1909.

Ferguson, Arthur B. "John Twyne: A Tudor Humanist and the Problem of Legend." *Journal of British Studies* 9 (1969): 24–44.

Fiedler, Leslie. *The Stranger in Shakespeare.* London: Croom Helm, 1972.

Fink, Z. S. "Milton and the Theory of Climatic Influence." *MLQ* 2 (1941): 67–80.

Firth, Katherine R. *The Apocalyptic Tradition in Reformation Britain, 1530–1645.* Oxford: Oxford University Press, 1979.

Fletcher, Angus. *The Prophetic Moment: An Essay on Spenser.* Chicago: University of Chicago Press, 1971.

Franklin, Wayne. *Discoverers, Explorers, Settlers: The Diligent Writers of Early America.* Chicago: University of Chicago Press, 1979.

Frey, Charles. "*The Tempest* and the New World." *Shakespeare Quarterly* 30 (1979): 29–41.

Froude, James Anthony. "England's Forgotten Worthies." 1852. In *Short Studies on Great Subjects*, 1:443–501. 1867. Reprint. London, 1888.

Frye, Northrop, ed. *The Tempest.* Pelican Shakespeare. Harmondsworth: Penguin, 1959.

Fumerton, Patricia. " 'Secret Arts': Elizabethan Miniatures and Sonnets." *Representations* 15 (1986): 57–97.

Garber, Marjorie, ed. *Cannibals, Witches, and Divorce: Estranging the Renaissance*. Baltimore: Johns Hopkins University Press, 1987.

Gibson, R. W. *St. Thomas More: A Preliminary Bibliography of His Works and of Moreana to the Year 1750. With a Bibliography of Utopiana Compiled by R. W. Gibson and J. Max Patrick*. New Haven: Yale University Press, 1961.

Gillies, John. "Shakespeare's Virginian Masque." *ELH* 53 (1986): 673–707.

Gilman, Ernest. " 'All Eyes': Prospero's Inverted Masque." *Renaissance Quarterly* 33 (1980): 214–30.

Goldberg, Jonathan. *Endlesse Worke: Spenser and the Structures of Discourse*. Baltimore: Johns Hopkins University Press, 1981.

Goldin, Frederick. *The Mirror of Narcissus in the Courtly Love Lyric*. Ithaca: Cornell University Press, 1967.

Greenblatt, Stephen. "Learning to Curse: Aspects of Linguistic Colonialism in the Sixteenth Century." In *First Images of America*, ed. Fredi Chiappelli, 2:561–80. Berkeley: University of California Press, 1976.

———. *Renaissance Self-Fashioning: From More to Shakespeare*. Chicago: University of Chicago Press, 1980.

———. *Shakespearean Negotiations: The Circulation of Social Energy in Renaissance England*. Berkeley: University of California Press, 1988.

———. *Sir Walter Ralegh: The Renaissance Man and His Roles*. New Haven: Yale University Press, 1973.

Greenlaw, Edwin. "Spenser and British Imperialism." *Modern Philology* 9 (1911–12): 347–70.

Grosart, A. B., ed. *The Works of Fulke Greville*. 4 vols. Private printing, 1870.

Gury, Jacques. "The Abolition of the Rural World in Utopia." *Moreana* 11 (Nov. 1974): 67–69.

Haller, William. *Foxe's 'Book of Martyrs' and the Elect Nation*. London: Jonathan Cape, 1963.

Hamilton, A. C. "The Argument of Spenser's *Shepheardes Calender*." *ELH* 23 (1956): 171–83.

———, ed. *The Faerie Queene*, by Edmund Spenser. London: Longman, 1977.

Harbage, Alfred. *Sir William Davenant: Poet Venturer, 1606–1668*. 1935. Reprint. New York: Octagon, 1971.

Hartman, Geoffrey H. " 'The Nymph Complaining for the Death of Her Faun': A Brief Allegory." 1968. In *Beyond Formalism: Literary Essays, 1958–1970*, 173–92. New Haven: Yale University Press, 1970.

Heffner, Ray. "Did Spenser Die in Poverty?" *Modern Language Notes* 48 (1933): 221–26.

———. "Essex, the Ideal Courtier." *ELH* 1 (1934): 7–36.

Helgerson, Richard. "The Land Speaks: Cartography, Chorography, and Subversion in Renaissance England." *Representations* 16 (1986): 50–85.

———. *Self-Crowned Laureates: Spenser, Jonson, Milton, and the Literary System*. Berkeley: University of California Press, 1983.

Hoffman, Nancy Jo. *Spenser's Pastorals*: The Shepheardes Calender *and* Colin Clout. Baltimore: Johns Hopkins University Press, 1977.

Hollander, John. "Footing of His Feet: On a Line of Milton's." In *On Poetry and Poetics*, ed. Richard Waswo, 11–30. Tübingen: Gunter Nan Verlag, 1985.

———. "Spenser's Undersong." In *Cannibals, Witches, and Divorce*, ed. Marjorie Garber, 1–20. Baltimore: Johns Hopkins University Press, 1987.

Hotson, Leslie. *Shakespeare's Sonnets Dated and Other Essays*. London: Rupert Hart-Davis, 1949.

Hulme, Peter. *Colonial Encounters: Europe and the Native Caribbean, 1492–1797*. New York: Methuen, 1986.

Hulton, P. H. "John White's Drawings of Eskimos." *The Beaver* (Summer 1961): 16–20.

Hume, Anthea. *Edmund Spenser: Protestant Poet*. Cambridge: Cambridge University Press, 1984.

Hunter, G. K. *Dramatic Identities and Cultural Traditions: Studies in Shakespeare and His Contemporaries*. Liverpool: Liverpool University Press, 1978.

———. *John Lyly: The Humanist as Courtier*. Cambridge, Mass.: Harvard University Press, 1962.

Hurd, Richard. *Letters on Chivalry and Romance*. 1762. In *Hurd's Letters on Chivalry and Romance*, ed. Edith J. Morley. London: Henry Frowde, 1911.

Jacobs, Wilbur R. "British-Colonial Attitudes and Policies Toward the Indian in the American Colonies." In *Attitudes of Colonial Powers Toward the American Indian*, ed. Howard Peckham and Charles Gibson, 81–106. Salt Lake City: University of Utah Press, 1969.

Jones, Howard Mumford. *O Strange New World. American Culture: The Formative Years*. 1952. Reprint. New York: Viking, 1964.

Judson, Alexander. *The Life of Edmund Spenser*. Baltimore: Johns Hopkins University Press, 1945.

Kendrick, T. D. *British Antiquity*. London: Methuen, 1950.

Kennedy, Richard F. "Additional References to More in Renaissance England." *Moreana* 21 (June 1984): 19–23.

Kermode, Frank, ed. *The Tempest*. Arden Shakespeare. London: Methuen, 1954.

Klein, Joan Larson. "From Errour to Acrasia." *Huntington Library Quarterly* 41 (1978): 173–99.

Knapp, Steven. *Personification and the Sublime: Milton to Coleridge*. Cambridge: Harvard University Press, 1985.

Kupperman, Karen Ordahl. "Fear of Hot Climates in the Anglo-American Colonial Experience." *William & Mary Quarterly* 41 (1984): 213–40.

———. "The Puzzle of the American Climate." *American Historical Review* 87 (1982): 1262–89.

———. *Settling with the Indians: The Meeting of English and Indian Cultures in America, 1580–1640*. Totowa, N.J.: Rowman & Littlefield, 1980.

Lee, Sir Sidney. *Elizabethan and Other Essays*. Ed. Frederick S. Boas. Oxford: Clarendon, 1929.

———. *Great Englishmen of the Sixteenth Century*. New York: Scribner's, 1904.

Lewis, C. S. *The Allegory of Love*. Oxford: Clarendon, 1936.

———. *English Literature in the Sixteenth Century, Excluding Drama*. Oxford: Clarendon, 1954.

Lovejoy, Arthur O. *The Great Chain of Being: A Study of the History of an Idea*. Cambridge: Harvard University Press, 1936.

Lovejoy, David S. *Religious Enthusiasm in the New World: Heresy to Revolution*. Cambridge: Harvard University Press, 1985.

Luce, Morton, ed. *The Tempest*. Arden Shakespeare. Ed. W. J. Craig. London: Methuen, 1902.

MacCaffrey, Isabel. "Allegory and Pastoral in *The Shepheardes Calender*." *ELH* 36 (1969): 88–109.

McCann, Franklin T. *English Discovery of America to 1585*. 1951. Reprint. New York: Octagon, 1969.

McColley, Grant. "The Seventeenth-Century Doctrine of a Plurality of Worlds." *Annals of Science* 1 (1936): 385–430.

McCutcheon, Elizabeth. "Denying the Contrary: More's Use of Litotes in the *Utopia*." 1971. In *Essential Articles for the Study of Sir Thomas More*, ed. Richard S. Sylvester and G. P. Marc'hadour, 263–74. Hamden, Conn.: Archon, 1977.

Mack, Maynard. *Alexander Pope: A Life*. New York: Norton; in association with New Haven: Yale University Press, 1985.

McLane, Paul E. *Spenser's "Shepheardes Calender": A Study in Elizabethan Allegory*. Notre Dame: University of Notre Dame Press, 1961.

Maltby, William S. *The Black Legend in England*. Durham: Duke University Press, 1971.

Marius, Richard. *Thomas More: A Biography*. New York: Knopf, 1984.

Mason, H. A. *Sir Thomas Wyatt: A Literary Portrait*. Bristol: Bristol Classical Press, 1986.

Masson, David. *Drummond of Hawthornden: The Story of His Life and Writings*. London, 1873.

Meyer, Arnold Oskar. *England and the Catholic Church under Queen Elizabeth*. 1911. Trans. Rev. J. R. McKee. 1914. Reprint. New York: Barnes & Noble, 1967.

Millican, Charles Bowie. *Spenser and the Table Round*. 1932. Reprint. New York: Octagon, 1967.

Moerner, Magnus. *Race Mixture in the History of Latin America*. Boston: Little, Brown, 1967.

Montrose, Louis Adrian. "The Elizabethan Subject and the Spenserian Text." In *Literary Theory/Renaissance Texts*, ed. Patricia Parker and David Quint, 303–40. Baltimore: Johns Hopkins University Press, 1986.

———. " 'The perfecte paterne of a Poete': The Poetics of Courtship in *The Shepheardes Calender.*" *Texas Studies in Literature and Language* 21 (1979): 34–67.

———. " 'Shaping Fantasies': Figurations of Gender and Power in Elizabethan Culture." *Representations* 2 (1983): 61–94.

Morgan, Edmund S. *American Slavery, American Freedom: The Ordeal of Colonial Virginia*. New York: Norton, 1975.

Morris, David B. "Virgilian Attitudes in Pope's *Windsor Forest.*" *Texas Studies in Literature and Language* 15 (1973): 231–50.

Muir, Kenneth. *Life and Letters of Sir Thomas Wyatt*. Liverpool: Liverpool University Press, 1963.

Mullaney, Steven. "Brothers and Others, or the Art of Alienation." In *Cannibals, Witches, and Divorce*, ed. Marjorie Garber, 67–89. Baltimore: Johns Hopkins University Press, 1987.

———. "Strange Things, Gross Terms, Curious Customs: The Rehearsal of Cultures in the Late Renaissance." *Representations* 3 (1983): 40–67.

Murrin, Michael. *The Allegorical Epic: Essays in Its Rise and Decline*. Chicago: University of Chicago Press, 1980.

Neale, J. E. *Queen Elizabeth I*. 1934. Reprint. New York: Doubleday, 1957.

Nelson, C. E. "A Note on Wyatt and Ovid." *Modern Language Review* 58 (1963): 60–63.

Nelson, William. *The Poetry of Edmund Spenser*. New York: Columbia University Press, 1963.

———. "Spenser *Ludens.*" In *A Theatre for Spenserians*, ed. Judith M. Kennedy and James A. Reither, 83–100. Toronto: University of Toronto Press, 1973.

Nicolson, Marjorie Hope. *A World in the Moon*. Northampton, Mass.: Departments of Modern Languages of Smith College, 1936.

Nohrnberg, James. *The Analogy of* The Faerie Queene. Princeton: Princeton University Press, 1976.

O'Connell, Michael. "The Idolatrous Eye: Iconoclasm, Anti-Theatricalism, and the Image of the Elizabethan Theater." *ELH* 52 (1985): 279–310.

———. *Mirror and Veil: The Historical Dimension of Spenser's* Faerie Queene. Chapel Hill: University of North Carolina Press, 1977.

Olsen, Viggo Norskov. *John Foxe and the Elizabethan Church*. Berkeley: University of California Press, 1973.

Opfell, Olga S. *The King James Bible Translators*. Jefferson, N.C.: McFarland, 1982.

Oram, William. "Elizabethan Fact and Spenserian Fiction." *Spenser Studies* 4 (1984): 33–47.

Oram, William, Bjorvand Einer, Ronald Bond, Thomas H. Cain, Alexander Dunlop, and Richard Schell, eds. *The Yale Edition of the Shorter Poems of Edmund Spenser.* New Haven: Yale University Press, 1989.

Orgel, Stephen. *The Illusion of Power.* Berkeley: University of California Press, 1975.

Pagan, John R. "Growth of the Tobacco Trade between London and Virginia, 1610–40." *Guildhall Studies in London History* 3 (1979): 248–62.

Pagden, Anthony. *The Fall of Natural Man: The American Indian and the Origins of Comparative Ethnology.* Cambridge: Cambridge University Press, 1982.

———. "Identity Formation in Spanish America." In *Colonial Identity in the Atlantic World, 1500–1800,* ed. Nicholas Canny and Anthony Pagden, 51–93. Princeton: Princeton University Press, 1987.

Parker, John. *Books to Build an Empire: A Bibliographical History of English Overseas Interests to 1620.* Amsterdam: N. Israel, 1965.

———. "Religion and the Virginia Colony 1609–10." In *The Westward Enterprise,* ed. K. R. Andrews et al., 245–70. Liverpool: Liverpool University Press, 1979.

Parker, Patricia. *Inescapable Romance: Studies in the Poetics of a Mode.* Princeton: Princeton University Press, 1979.

Parks, G. B. *Richard Hakluyt and the English Voyages.* New York: American Geographical Society, 1928. 2nd ed. New York: Frederick Ungar, 1961.

Patterson, Annabel. "Re-opening the Green Cabinet: Clement Marot and Edmund Spenser." *English Literary Renaissance* 16 (1986): 44–70.

Pollard, A. W., G. R. Redgrave, et al. *A Short-Title Catalogue of Books Printed in England, Scotland, & Ireland and of English Books Printed Abroad, 1475–1640.* 1926. 2nd ed. rev. W. A. Jackson et al. 2 vols. London: Bibliographical Soc., 1976–86.

Powell, William S. *John Pory, 1572–1636: The Life and Letters of a Man of Many Parts.* Chapel Hill: University of North Carolina Press, 1977.

Quinn, David Beers. *England and the Discovery of America, 1481–1620.* New York: Knopf, 1974.

———. "The First Pilgrims." 1966. In *England and the Discovery of America, 1481–1620,* 337–63. New York: Knopf, 1974.

———. "Renaissance Influences in English Colonization." *Transactions of the Royal Historical Soc.,* 5th ser., no. 26 (1976): 73–92.

———. *Set Fair for Roanoke: Voyages and Colonies, 1584–1606.* Chapel Hill: University of North Carolina Press, 1985.

———. "Thomas Harriot and the New World." In *Thomas Harriot: Renaissance Scientist.* Ed. John Shirley. Oxford: Clarendon, 1974.

Quinn, David Beers, and A. N. Ryan. *England's Sea Empire, 1550–1642.* Boston: Allen & Unwin, 1985.

Raleigh, Sir Walter. *The English Voyages of the Sixteenth Century.* Glasgow: MacLehose, 1906.

Rathborne, Isabel. *The Meaning of Spenser's Fairyland.* New York: Columbia University Press, 1937.

Rebholz, R. A., ed. *Sir Thomas Wyatt: The Complete Poems*. 1978. Reprint. New Haven: Yale University Press, 1981.

Rebhorn, Wayne A. *Courtly Performances: Masking and Festivity in Castiglione's* Book of the Courtier. Detroit: Wayne State University Press, 1978.

Reed, A. W. *Early Tudor Drama: Medwall, the Rastells, Heywood, and the More Circle*. London: Methuen, 1926.

Rowse, A. L. *Ralegh and the Throckmortons*. London: Macmillan, 1962.

Sanz, Carlos. *Bibliotheca americana vetustissima: Comentario critico e indice general cronologico*. Madrid, 1960.

Scammel, G. V. "Hakluyt and the Economic Thought of His Time." In *The Hakluyt Handbook*, ed. D. B. Quinn. 1:15–22. Hakluyt Soc., 2nd ser., vol. 144. London, 1974.

Schmidgall, Gary. *Shakespeare and the Courtly Aesthetic*. Berkeley: University of California Press, 1981.

Schoenbaum, Samuel. *William Shakespeare: A Compact Documentary Life*. New York: Oxford University Press, 1977.

Seelye, John. *Prophetic Waters: The River in Early American Life and Literature*. New York: Oxford University Press, 1977.

Sell, Roger. *The Shorter Poems of Sir John Beaumont*. Åbo, Finland: Åbo Akademi, 1974.

Shammas, Carol. "English Commercial Development and American Colonization, 1560–1620." In *The Westward Enterprise*, ed. K. R. Andrews et al., 151–74. Liverpool: Liverpool University Press, 1979.

Sheavyn, Phoebe. *The Literary Profession in the Elizabethan Age*. Manchester: Manchester University Press, 1909.

Shirley, John. *Thomas Harriot: A Biography*. Oxford: Clarendon, 1983.

Shore, David R. *Spenser and the Poetics of Pastoral: A Study of the World of Colin Clout*. Kingston and Montreal: McGill-Queen's University Press, 1985.

Simpson, Lesley Byrd. *The Encomienda in New Spain: The Beginning of Spanish Mexico*. Rev. and enlarged 1950, 1966. Reprint. Berkeley: University of California Press, 1982.

Skura, Meredith Anne. "Discourse and the Individual: The Case of Colonialism in *The Tempest*." *Shakespeare Quarterly* 40 (1989): 42–69.

Stith, William. *The History of the First Discovery and Settlement of Virginia*. 1747. Reprint. New York, 1865.

Stoll, E. E. "Certain Fallacies and Irrelevancies in the Literary Scholarship of the Day." *Studies in Philology* 24 (1927): 485–508.

Stone, Walter B. "Shakespeare and the Sad Augurs." *Journal of English and Germanic Philology* 52 (1953): 457–79.

Strong, Roy. *The Cult of Elizabeth: Elizabethan Portraiture and Pageantry*. London: Thames & Hudson, 1977.

———. *The English Renaissance Miniature*. New York: Thames & Hudson, 1983.

———. *Henry, Prince of Wales, and England's Lost Renaissance*. New York: Thames & Hudson, 1986.

———. *Portraits of Queen Elizabeth I.* Oxford: Oxford University Press, 1963.

———. *Spendour at Court: Renaissance Spectacle and Illusion.* London: Weidenfield & Nicolson, 1973.

Stroup, Thomas B. "Climatic Influence in Milton." *Modern Language Quarterly* 4 (1943): 185–89.

Sullivan, Frank, and Majie Padberg. *Moreana: Material for the Study of Saint Thomas More.* 4 vols., *Index*, and *Supplement*. Los Angeles: Loyola University, 1964–77.

Surtz, Edward, S.J. "St. Thomas More and His Utopian Embassy of 1515." *Catholic Historical Review* 39 (1953): 272–97.

Sylvester, Richard S. " 'Si Hythlodaeo Credimus': Vision and Revision in Thomas More's *Utopia*." 1968. In *Essential Articles for the Study of Sir Thomas More*, ed. Richard S. Sylvester and G. P. Marc'hadour, 290–301. Hamden, Conn.: Archon, 1977.

Sylvester, Richard S., and G. P. Marc'hadour, eds. *Essential Articles for the Study of Sir Thomas More.* Hamden, Conn.: Archon, 1977.

Tatlock, J. S. P. *The Legendary History of Britain: Geoffrey of Monmouth's Historia Regum Britanniae and Its Early Vernacular Versions.* Berkeley: University of California Press, 1950.

Thirsk, Joan. *Economic Policy and Projects: The Development of a Consumer Society in Early Modern England.* Oxford: Clarendon, 1978.

———. "New Crops and Their Diffusion: Tobacco-growing in Seventeenth Century England." In *Rural Change and Urban Growth, 1500–1800: Essays in Honour of W. G. Hoskins*, ed. C. W. Chalklin and M. A. Havinden. London: Longman, 1974.

Thomas, Sidney. "Hobgoblin Runne Away with the Garland from Apollo." *Modern Language Notes* 55 (1940): 418–22.

Thomson, Patricia, ed. *Wyatt: The Critical Heritage.* London: Routledge & Kegan Paul, 1974.

Todorov, Tzvetan. *The Conquest of America: The Question of the Other.* Trans. Richard Howard from *La Conquête de l'Amérique* (1982). New York: Harper & Row, 1985.

Vaughan, Alden T. "John Smith Satirized: *The Legend of Captain Jones*." *William & Mary Quarterly* 45 (1988): 712–32.

Wasserman, Earl. *The Subtler Language: Critical Readings of Neoclassic and Romantic Poems.* Baltimore: Johns Hopkins University Press, 1959.

Wernham, R. B. *The Making of Elizabethan Foreign Policy, 1558–1603.* Berkeley: University of California Press, 1980.

Williams, Kathleen. *Spenser's World of Glass: A Reading of* The Faerie Queene. Berkeley: University of California Press, 1966.

Wilson, Elkin Calhoun. *England's Eliza.* Cambridge: Harvard University Press, 1939.

Wooden, Warren W. "An Unnoticed Sixteenth Century Reference to More's *Utopia*." *Moreana* 15 (Dec. 1978): 91.

Yates, Frances. *Astraea: The Imperial Theme in the Sixteenth Century.* London: Routledge & Kegan Paul, 1975.

————. "Elizabethan Chivalry: The Romance of the Accession Day Tilts." 1957. In *Astraea*, 88–111. London: Routledge & Kegan Paul, 1975.

————. *Majesty and Magic in Shakespeare's Last Plays*. First published as *Shakespeare's Last Plays: A New Approach*. 1975. Boulder: Shambala, 1978.

————. "Queen Elizabeth as Astraea." 1947. In *Astraea*, 29–87. London: Routledge & Kegan Paul, 1975.

Zacher, Christian K. *Curiosity and Pilgrimage: The Literature of Discovery in Fourteenth-Century England*. Baltimore: Johns Hopkins University Press, 1976.

Zavala, Silvio. "Sir Thomas More in New Spain: A Utopian Adventure of the Renaissance." 1947, 1965. In *Essential Articles for the Study of Sir Thomas More*, ed. Richard S. Sylvester and G. P. Marc'hadour, 302–11. Hamden, Conn.: Archon, 1977.

Zuckerman, Michael. "Identity in British America: Unease in Eden." In *Colonial Identity in the Atlantic World, 1500–1800*, ed. Nicholas Canny and Anthony Pagden, 115–57. Princeton: Princeton University Press, 1987.

Index

Compositor: Princeton University Press
Text: 10/13 Palatino
Display: Palatino
Printer and Binder: Princeton University Press